AN AMAZING BOOK!

"This book may do for ESP what Sputnik did for space travel . . . This book was born to cause controversy. Some chapters make science-fiction seem dull and unimaginative by comparison . . . Fact, fancies and fantasies are all there, woven in a vivid style that will stimulate and intrigue every imagination. This is not only a fascinating book but a potential bombshell."

—**Psychic Magazine**

"One of the most exciting books on psychical research which has come to my attention in a great many years."

—Hugh Lynn Cayce

"An eye-opening, fascinating, sometimes frightening and occasionally hard-to-believe book . . . The Russians are actually investigating ESP and its use. The authors are utterly serious, so are the Russians."

—**Publishers' Weekly**

"This book's sheer dynamite! May become the most widely discussed book of the year."

—**Rocky Mountain News**

"A bold, stupendous job of lively reporting, complete to the most fantastic fringes."

—Dr. J. B. Rhine, Foundation for Research on the Nature of Man

Psychic Discoveries Behind the Iron Curtain

Sheila Ostrander and Lynn Schroeder
Introduction by Ivan T. Sanderson

PSYCHIC DISCOVERIES BEHIND THE IRON CURTAIN

A Bantam Book / published by arrangement with Prentice-Hall, Inc.

PRINTING HISTORY

Prentice-Hall edition published May 1970

2nd printing .... May 1970
3rd printing .... June 1970
4th printing ... September 1970
5th printing ... December 1970

Universe Book Club edition published 1970

Excerpts appeared in PARAPSYCHOLOGY REVIEW, NATIONAL ENQUIRER *and* OMEN PRESS

Bantam edition published May 1971

2nd printing ...... August 1971
3rd printing ..... October 1971
4th printing ..... January 1972
5th printing .... May 1972
6th printing ... September 1972
7th printing .... February 1973
8th printing .... June 1973
9th printing ...... August 1973

10th printing

Published simultaneously in the United States and Canada

Bantam Books are published by Bantam Books, Inc., a National General company. Its trade-mark, consisting of the words "Bantam Books" and the portrayal of a bantam, is registered in the United States Patent Office and in other countries. Marca Registrada. Bantam Books, Inc., 666 Fifth Avenue, New York, N.Y. 10019.

PRINTED IN THE UNITED STATES OF AMERICA

AN INTRODUCTION

Probably the most aggravating thing—to both authors and readers—in any published work, is that an introduction should turn out to be a review. A preface is where the authors can sound off on any rankling questions brought on by their editors; and an epilogue is where they can take a final pot-shot at their readers. Reviewers should keep out of the whole mess and go publish some place else. An introduction, especially if written by some person other than the author or authors should, at least in my opinion, offer only some attempt at augmentation of the book's general theme; perhaps bringing to it some corollary and pertinent observations, since a lot of things can be said in an introduction that the authors have not been able to say—or have not been allowed to say—in the body of their text. So, I shall now proceed to offer some such complementary and perhaps impertinent observations for your possible edification.

First, let it be most clearly understood that this book has nothing whatsoever to do with any 'psychic' *anything*. The employment of this word in the title should, rather, be read to mean 'Matters that we have been taught to *call* psychic.' The choice of this title is, nonetheless, quite legitimate, on two counts. First, it will attract a great number of people who would otherwise not even so much as glance at the opus; and second, because it may render a very real service in clearing up this whole preposterous semantic confusion.

Let us start out by taking a look in the dictionaries, always the best place to begin when there is anything involved about which there might be semantic doubts; and, as this is an American book, we will tackle good old Webster first. Herein we find the word *psychic* defined as:—

> "1. Of or relating to the psyche." [Referring back a few lines, we find this in turn defined as "(a) A beautiful princess of classical mythology loved by Cupid. (b) Soul, Self; also Mind."] Webster then goes on about *psychic* as follows:—

"2. *Lying outside the sphere of physical science or knowledge;* immaterial, moral, or spiritual in origin or force. 3. Sensitive to nonphysical or supernatural forces and influences." (*Italics mine.*) The Oxford dictionary gets to the point more simply and directly, and is much more succinct. It states simply:—"Non-physical force assumed to explain spiritualistic phenomena."

Let us first try to unravel the semantics. You will notice that the mind, morals, the supernatural, the spiritual and even the spiritualistic (which is something quite else as most dictionaries make clear) get dragged into the business. However, nary a mention of the two headings under which such matters are most commonly and popularly classed in our language—namely, Mysticism or the Occult.* So, Okay: the 'psychic' concerns itself with the mind, the soul, morals, the supernatural (whatever that may be), matters spiritual and religious, and the spiritualistic—meaning, one must presume, spiritualism. Spiritism and Animism seem to have been overlooked.

Now, if we cannot trust our dictionaries, what *can* we trust in this modern, complex, technological age that is based primarily on communication, and which, in turn is based on semantics? The only means of precise communication that we have is based on speech, the written word, or the computer's binomial interpretation of these. (By this I mean factual communication, not such emotional means as sex, music, the dance, and other arts.) So, above all, we must get our facts straight, and to do this, we have just got to find out precisely what other people are talking about. It is most interesting to note that not even the biggest dictionary, even unto the vast multi-volume Oxford, so much as mentions a single one of the items in this book under any of their headings of psychic. And what are these items?

To list some of them, we find the following:—Mental Telepathy; Hypnotism; Faith Healing; Precognition, Psychokinesis; Auras around plants and animals; Brain Control; Mind Patrol; Astrology; Levitation; Sightless—i.e. eye-

* Occult in point of semantic fact means simply and only 'hidden.'

less—Vision; Dowsing; Acupuncture; Witchcraft; Prophecy; Alchemy; Psychotronics; and what we naïvely call 'ESP.'

Now please note something well. These are just the items that the average Westerner will positively avow constitute the hard core of what he calls 'the psychic.' Moreover, while he may permit the inclusion of other items in this category, such as spiritualism, and possibly even mysticism—if he knows the difference between the two, or has ever learned what these words actually denote—if you try to run religion down his throat within this bailiwick he will probably become insulted, insulting, and somewhat out-of-control mentally. The reason? He has been taught for centuries that existence is clearly divided into three parts:—the Spiritual: namely, religion and such, plus, perhaps the arts, if he has ever given them a thought. The Scientific: which to the average Westerner means primarily technology, or button-pushing and bottle-washing; and third, everything that is left over. This last used to be called metaphysics but is today called simply 'psychic.' The result of this indoctrination is that we of the 'West'—from scientists to imbeciles—seem not to have used our dictionaries and so have failed to realize that we are using this word to cover two quite different and almost diametrically opposed concepts.

By the same token, we are in a similarly confused state with regard to both the words 'science' and 'scientist.' We use the first to cover both basic science, which the dictionaries define as the *search* for knowledge, and applied science or technology which concerns itself with *research*. Likewise we use the word 'scientist' to cover the practitioners of both of these expertises. However, those involved in basic science are really philosophers, and it is very cheering to note that the term 'Philosophical Scientists' is creeping into common usage. It is equally refreshing to encounter the heading 'Science and Technology.'

'Applied Science' is a good term and says clearly what it means, but to speak of an 'applied scientist' sounds as if the poor guy was some kind of screwdriver. As a matter of fact, this is just about what he is, so it is much more polite to dignify him with the somewhat grandiose-sounding title of Technologist. Besides, this links him with technicians, to which brotherhood he frankly belongs.

The average Westerner—and I shall continue to emphasize this qualifying term—lumps everything, other than that which he has been taught is either spiritual or scientific, into one great basket which he then chops up to suit his tastes. He has been told for a couple of centuries now that anything neither science (pragmatic) nor religion (spiritual) can explain must fall into this single encompassing category. And it is because of this that so many misconceptions have arisen. For instance, it would seem to be extremely unlikely that law will ever become wholly scientific, or art purely spiritual, while matters like politics defy any classification. Nonetheless, all these troublesome matters display technological aspects, and they may even be granted some scientific and spiritual qualities, so that the average person takes them in his stride. But when matters that don't seem to be answerable to either pragmatic or spiritual explanation crop up, people simply deny that they exist even as problems. These were once lumped together as metaphysics and are those which today are called psychic.

The old metaphysics—which, incidentally, meant only things left over from Aristotelian so-called physics—is also most clearly divided into two quite separate parts. These are, on the one hand, the Cryptophysical; and, on the other, the Cryptospiritual ('crypto' meaning simply 'hidden'); in other words those items which are not as yet understood or explained to the satisfaction of our current logic. While nobody should deny the existence of the second category, such matters are not as yet the province of what we call science but rather of religion and mysticism. All of those of the first category, on the other hand, most definitely can *not* be denied and *do* fall into that province.

And this is just what the book is about.

Unlike, and diametrically opposed to what the dictionaries classify as 'psychic,' all the items discussed in this book are in every way not only susceptible to truly scientific contemplation but also to technological investigation. What is more, said items have, as this book now relates, been so investigated in the so-called Russian zone. But we of the West still just do not realize this fact.

Doubtless our government scientists and technologists have been aware of this for a long time, but the public is *not* generally aware of it, and the press and other publicists simply will not even believe in it and persist in reporting on it only with snide jocularity. Whether this is under instructions, as so many claim, or due to simple lack of education, who is to say; but, the result has been a crystallization of this stupid attitude and the envelopment of our whole outlook in a sort of tortoise-like shell of protective disbelief. The worse aspect of this mass stupidity (or deliberate mendacity) is, moreover, the bracketing of these matters with what the dictionaries denote as the 'psychic.'

Of course, the major trouble is that, as I said at the outset, we don't have any generally accepted word for these items as a class; though, as a matter of fact, we *do* have a perfectly good one which unfortunately has not yet gotten into any dictionary. The designation is, of course, 'Forteana,' but I won't go any further into this at the moment. Rather, we should try to straighten out another aspect of all this business that is equally pertinent; namely, just where the authors' researches were prosecuted.

This is this new concept of 'The West,' now so beloved of political writers. Despite its now almost universal use, this, too, has not yet gotten into the dictionaries; while even advanced students of international affairs appear not to have the foggiest notion as to how to define the term—geographically, that is. The world of humanity is today divided into eight major blocks. These are basically geographic, but the vast majority of the human inhabitants of each form a compact ethnic majority. These blocks are:— (1) Western Eurasia plus North America, (2) Eastern Eurasia, namely the Slavic domain plus Siberia, (3) The Near East, being the Muhammadan world, from Morocco to West Pakistan, north to the south Slavic border, and south to the Ethiopian block, (4) The Middle East, or the subcontinent of India, (5) The Far East, being all that lies east of the great Mongolian Fold, which runs northeast from the Pamirs to Amuria; together with Indochina, Indonesia, and Micronesia, (6) Australia, with Papua and Polynesia, (7) Latin America, south of the Rio Grande, and (8) Ethiopian Africa. Of course, there are endless human minority groups in each block while the indigenous populations of two—North America and Australia—are now almost completely suppressed. It is interesting to note that the aboriginal Amerinds of Latin America have had a more than profound influence on the Europeans who went to their countries, and that the Australians are beginning to show a very noticeable distinction that would seem to have been in some mysterious way derived from their dying aborigines.

Each of these eight major blocks has an overall approach to life that is now quite distinct, and each appears to look at *its* world, the world generally, and life as a whole, in a noticeably different way. Then, there is another thing. This is that there is really a 'West-West,' a 'Middle-West,' and an 'East-West,' in that North America is, apart from sharing basically the same language with a Middle-West country (i.e. the United Kingdom or Great Britain) just as different in outlook from the Middle-West as that block is from the East-West. Disregarding politics and religion, the three "Wests" (being North America, Western Europe, and Slavonic or Eastern Europe) form a composite cultural block despite their tripartite internal differences. In fact, we three are already in the same bed and we might as well make up our minds to lie in it.

If the authors of this book had visited any block other than the Slavic, they would possibly never have written *any* book for the simple reason that only in that sphere have scientists and technologists approached these matters in the way described in this book. Even the Australians, who are Caucasoids, take an entirely different approach, as do the Latin-Americans. Among the latter there are today many brilliant scholars working in this field, but they have, and perhaps naturally, been greatly influenced in their approach by the racial majority of their populations, which is still Amerindian; a race who, and quite apart from any language barriers left, are mentally almost incomprehensible to any westerner. Ethiopian Africa takes still another approach to these questions and it also has an incredibly ancient culture that is for the most part a mystery to westerners. The Indians and the Far Easterners likewise have for millennia attempted to tackle the same mysterious natural phenomena, each in their own individual ways which are truly incomprehensible to a culture based on technology. Only the Middle-Westerners (i.e. Western Europeans) form a hybrid, mongrel, bastardized intellectual bridge between all of the others—with the possible exception of the Far-Easterners.

The matters that these authors describe and discuss in this book form the hard core of a wide range of investigations that we of the West-West, and to a considerable extent of the Middle-West have always muddled up with some other matters, such as the true (by dictionary definition) psychic and the cryptospiritual, and which have thus been almost wholly ignored by us from a scientific point of view. These matters, as listed on page v, have simply been dubbed 'kooky,' and therefore unworthy of serious investigation or even contemplation. Further, anyone attempting to so investigate them scientifically has had his wings clipped, and as the Spanish say, 'rapidamente.' But, there is still another and sorrier aspect to all this; namely, that those serious scientists who *have* persisted in doing some solid investigation, such as even that real scholar, Dr. J. B. Rhine, have fallen into the old trap by stating that there is a spiritual (i.e. mystical) factor involved in these utterly pragmatic matters, which he first named *para* (like) *psycho* (psychic, see dictionary) *logy* (meaning the study of). Could anything be more mischosen? 'Paranormal' if you like, but why equate these discoveries with psychology which isn't a science and may, in fact, not really exist *per se,* being nothing more than our gropings into ethology, behaviorism, and chemiphysical mental processes. What the inventors of this word actually meant was 'Para*physics,*' and should this have been adopted at the outset, both the stigma of this damned word *psycho* would have been eliminated, and some true scientific investigation possibly initiated.

The same may be said, and even more forcibly, regarding this expression 'Extra Sensory Perception.' These cryptophysical matters are indeed *extra,* or outside the cryptospiritual—i.e. psychic or psycho—but they actually lie solidly within the physical. Even worse, however, is the rest of this silly term. Why only 'perception'? It includes a lot more than perception; and apart from also 'sending' or disseminating. Even SSP, or *super*-sensory perception would be better but this once again implies a necessary biological link, while all these things probably still exist even when there is no living thing—as we define life—around. But 'ESP' has now become a catch-phrase for just about everything that neither religion nor science can explain; and both the cryptospiritual and the cryptophysical.

Separate these two fields and you will find that you have, on the one hand, matters purely of the mind like religious concepts, mathematics, ontology, and the other *intangibles*, and, on the other hand, a seething mass of *tangibles* such as are discussed in this book and which *are* most susceptible to scientific and technological enquiry, if only we would initiate such. The only real mystery lies in that we have not yet pinned them down, and for the most part we do not yet know how they work, or even on what principles, while in the biological field we have not yet found the 'organs' in living bodies through which they do work. We ought by now, however, to have enough to convince even western scientists that there is nothing mystical, spiritual, or above all, 'psychic' about any of them.

Perhaps in the long run, and from the purely historical point of view, it is just as well that Marxist philosophy—as biologically inaccurate as it may originally have been—did arise. Please understand me! I do not equate this with Leninism, Stalinism, Maoism, or any other political or religious matter. Not only 'Western' but Eastern, African, Indian, and every other type of thought was getting bogged down at the end of the last century. It needed a good jolt. One does not wish to be impolite but, speaking as a biologist, increasing knowledge of our environment and of ourselves cried out for a disassembly of a lot of traditions. Right or wrong, necessary or not, 'revolution' in intellect is just as necessary as it is biologically: and it hurts just as much. Without it, maybe we, like so many millions of other species of living creatures, would have already just died away.

Be all this philosophizing as it may, the point I am trying to make is that, as a result of the intellectual climate, in their block, the Slavs of the East-West have tackled 'forteana' in a completely different way from us of the West-West; and the results, as described in this book, will probably be quite shocking to all 'West-Western' readers, while they may shake up some of the Middle-Westerns a bit too! So please read on.

Ivan T. Sanderson
Columbia, New Jersey
January, 1970

ACKNOWLEDGMENTS

We are deeply grateful to the many men and women behind the Iron Curtain who helped us with this book. For various reasons, some of them could not be mentioned by name. To all these people and to the scientists, our heartfelt thanks and our hope that whatever our political differences, the world of psychic research may see increased cooperation and friendship among people of all lands.

In the West our special thanks to: Frances and John Adler; Jim Beal; John Cutten; Nick Daniloff; Douglas Dean; Marjorie and George de la Warr; Joan and Joe Foley; Eileen Garrett; Jaroslav Hosek; R. George Medhurst; Dr. Karlis Osis; Amanda and George Ostrander; Pat and Robert Pfeiffer; Dr. J. G. Pratt; Dr. J. B. Rhine and Dr. Louisa Rhine; Dr. Milan Ryzl; Dr. Ivan T. Sanderson, Grace and Raymond Schroeder.

Grateful acknowledgment is made to Benson Herbert and *The Journal of Paraphysics*, (Paraphysical Laboratory, Downton, Wilts., England) for permission to quote portions of the report by Dr. Z. Rejdak from Vol. 2, No. 3.

Some of the cities in the Communist World where Research on PSI and related phenomena is taking place. Many of the major cities have more than one parapsychology group.

The USSR is made up of 15 Federated Republics, the largest of these being the Russian Soviet Federated Socialist Republic which includes all Siberia as well as a large segment of the western part of the Soviet Union.

Russian Republic
Moscow (capital)
Leningrad
Novosibirsk
Nizhny Tagil
Irkutsk
Khabarovsk
Vladivostok
Tomsk
Omsk
Kazan
Saransk
Saratov
Voronezh
Cheboksary
Ivanovo
Krasnodar
Taganrog
Sverdlovsk

The Ukraine
Kiev (capital)
Odessa
Zaporozhye

Georgia
Tbilisi (capital)

Uzbekistan
Tashkent (capital)

Kazakhstan
Alma-Ata (capital)

Estonia
Tallin (capital)
Tartu

Lithuania
Kaunas

Byelorussia
Minsk (capital)
Grodno

Moldavia
Kishinev (capital)

EAST EUROPE

Czechoslovakia
Prague (capital)
Hradec Kralove
Bratislava
Nitra

Bulgaria
Sofia (capital)
Petrich

Poland
Warsaw (capital)
Poznan

Romania
Bucharest (capital)

East Germany
East Berlin (capital)

CONTENTS

PROLOGUE

In 1967 telepathy pulsed in code from Moscow to Leningrad while sophisticated space-age equipment monitored the brain of the receiver. Soviet scientists say that with the help of the machines they were able to decode the message; they say they were able to transmit words telepathically from mind-to-mind across four hundred miles of space. In other parts of Russia, technical magazines and universities reported something even more startling than computorized telepathy. They published photographs of beautiful colored lights flickering on and around the human body. Was this the "aura" psychics had long talked about? "Electric flames light up, then flares of blue and orange. Great channels of blazing, violet, fiery flashes. It's fantastic, alluring, a mysterious game—a fire world!" said usually circumspect scientists. According to the Soviets, they'd devised a machine that allows anyone to view the fabled, color-filled aura, usually visible only to psychics.

In the Baltic, Soviet geologists walked with dowsing rods; in the Urals they experimented with eyeless sight; by the Black Sea they studied the hands of a psychic healer. Parapsychology, nonexistent just a decade before, was suddenly flourishing all over the USSR.

A rather unlikely chain of events led us over a three year period to become embroiled in this surprising renaissance of psychic research in a Communist country. Aside from the books, articles, plays, and poetry each of us writes in very different fields, we have for several years been writing articles about the Soviet Union. One of us had traveled extensively in Russia in 1961 on a graduate student tour. Our articles covered not Iron Curtain politics, but life behind the lace curtains of everyday Russia. If coexistence with the Soviets is necessary, it seems reasonable to try to know something about them.

In Soviet journals and magazines, we began to come across some very unusual material about life in Russia—

articles on psychic phenomena. Soviet scientists were asking publicly, *"What is man?"* Do we have unused, undreamed of potentials? Can parapsychology melt the barriers and create the supernormal human being? These were heady questions to read in Soviet publications.

In 1966 the influential journal *Science and Religion* put out a special issue, No. 3, on current Russian telepathy research. Outstanding Soviets called for further scientific investigations of telepathy. They included such notables as: Dr. Nikolai Semyonov, a Nobel prize winner in chemistry and Vice President of the Academy of Sciences of the USSR; Academicians Dr. M. Leontovich, Dr. A. Mints,[67]* Dr. P. V. Rebinder, a leading physical chemist;[175] Dr. Gleb Frank, Director of the "Science City" Pushchino, near Moscow.[67] Marxist philosophers spoke out in no uncertain terms. "All critics of telepathy research are only using Marxism-Leninism to support their scientific conservatism. All who throw obstacles in the path of scientific progress should be made to suffer," thundered Dr. V. Tugarinov, head of the Philosophy Department of the University of Leningrad.[393]

It was a very Slavic and more gutsy remark than those we'd heard from most American psychic investigators. Both of us were actively interested in the psychic side of human experience. We'd written of it occasionally, we'd tried to keep up with new developments in psychology and parapsychology, we were members of the American Society for Psychical Research. With the idea of writing an article on the sudden Soviet interest in the paranormal, we started corresponding with Communist scientists. Soon we had enough information to write several articles—enough to write a book.

More important, it became apparent that something unusual actually was happening in Russia—something little known and, from the Western viewpoint, wildly ironic. While people in the West refused to believe that such a strange beast as Soviet ESP existed, we were reading how top-caliber Soviet scientists had already made significant breakthroughs in psychic research, a field usually ignored by Western science.

---

* Ascending numbers are references to be found at the back of the book.

What did this Communist move into the psychic dimension mean? What did it mean scientifically, politically, culturally, philosophically? There were no handy sources with answers. Western Soviet watchers don't seem very interested in ESP, and most American parapsychologists are not amateur Kremlinologists in their spare hours. That's why, when in 1967 we were invited to a forthcoming conference on ESP in Moscow, we decided to accept. We decided to try to get the feeling and the story firsthand of this Communist probing into the psychic, the paranormal side of being. By the time our trip through Russia, Bulgaria and Czechoslovakia was over, our originally slender baggage had grown to three hundred overweight pounds of research material. We hope that some of the scientific and technical data we brought back, which cannot be included in a general book, will eventually be published for specialists in various fields. (Further details will be found in the appendix and bibliography).

There are some facets of the story and of the documentation of ESP in Communist lands which we cannot reveal at the moment. Perhaps one day, as political conditions change, we can round the story out. In the case of private individuals who gave us material, we have occasionally disguised sources to protect them. In no case have we disguised any scientists mentioned nor have we in any way changed or distorted reports of the work being done.

This is the story of what we saw, heard, and read about ESP behind the Iron Curtain. We would have to be megalomaniacs to think that scores of highly reputable scientists from centers across the Soviet Union and the satellite countries all conspired to publish data for a decade and to bluff through interviews to impress us when we happened to meet them. We have recorded what the Communist scientists report they have discovered about ESP. Whether communist observations and theories about psychic happenings are right or not, can only be determined by further investigations East and West.

But, as Vladimir Mutshall wrote of current Soviet telepathy research in the American *Foreign Science Bulletin,* Vol. 4, No. 8.[336] "If the Russian reports are even partly true, and if mind-to-mind thought transference can be used for such things as interplanetary communications or the guiding of interplanetary spacecraft, the reports will obviously have overwhelming significance."

I

RUSSIA

1

"A RIDDLE WRAPPED IN AN ENIGMA"

It was a brilliant, cloudless June day as we stood near the rapidly revolving door of our Moscow hotel waiting to finally meet our first Communist psychic researcher. Muscovites, we noticed, walk like New Yorkers, fast, even in the heat as they jostled along Gorky Street and past the new Minsk Hotel, six scorching blocks from the Kremlin. Around us in the lobby, languages fizzed like bubbles in warm soda. Tourists knotted together; Russians stepped patiently around them. Middle-echelon Soviet bureaucrats on business trips were off to afternoon appointments in their standard summer wear: sandals, slacks, and nylon sport shirts. A tall, lean Russian cut through this crowd straight toward us. Minutely pressed dark suit, French cuffs, he conjured wrinkle-free memories of air conditioning.

"I'm so glad you're here. I'm so very glad," Edward Naumov repeated warmly as he shook various Western hands with both of his. Biologist Edward Naumov is one of the guiding energies of Soviet parapsychology—the study of the supernormal. He has traveled throughout the USSR giving over 460 lectures on ESP and showing scientific ESP films at scores of institutes. Yet just a decade ago Naumov's profession, parapsychologist, didn't exist in the Soviet Union. Then in the early sixties, the Stalinist taboo against all things psychic vanished with a bang.

Top-level physiologists, geologists, engineers, physicists, and biologists abruptly plunged into work on ESP. A free-wheeling, little-known psychic renaissance hit Russia. Bankrolled by their governments, not just Russians, but Bulgarians, Czechs, and Poles are pursuing clues to telepathy, prophecy, and PK—psychokinesis, the ability to move matter with mind alone. These thriving Communist groups hope to prove that supernormal happenings spring from laws of mind. They hope to prove we can harness and use psychic abilities right now.

When we first landed in Moscow in the summer of 1968, we began to wonder if we might have to summon up something like psychic abilities to contact some of these Communist scientists. It wasn't that they'd never heard of us. When we learned of ESP's sudden appearance in Russia, we'd written, without great expectations, to some of the scientists supposedly involved. Many of them surprised us with registered letters and cables telling of their work. And the letters kept coming. From Kiev, Leningrad, Moscow, Novosibirsk, for three years, every few months an envelope plastered with Soviet stamps would appear filled with clippings about ESP tests, about controversy and grandiose plans for psychic investigations. Finally Edward Naumov wrote, "Why not come and see for yourselves what we're doing?" He invited us to an international conference on ESP in Moscow.

Why not? Why not see if we could separate the rhetoric from the results, enthusiasm from facts. We had suitcases packed with questions. Yet when we finally made it to Moscow across five thousand miles of space and, it seemed, about as much red tape, all we really wanted to get over as an opener was, "Here we are." But this was Moscow, a city of phones, but no phonebooks, of streets lined with official institutes, but no detailed street maps. It didn't seem sensible to assume our hosts would know where we were, because no one is told what hotel you'll be staying at until you arrive, body and baggage on the spot.

We shouldn't have worried. We were still thinking in Western terms of reasonable ways of getting in touch with people. Instead, two Americans we'd met in Leningrad bumped into us again in our Moscow hotel. Then they boarded a bus and happened to sit near a beauty queen, Miss Lebanon. Miss Lebanon struck up a conversation with two Englishmen who were in Moscow—for an ESP conference. The sharp-eared Americans soon got us all together. We discovered the intrepid British had already found their man, Naumov, and we were connected.

The intense, thirty-six-year-old Naumov plunged right in. "Look, this will give you some idea of what you're going to be hearing about, some idea of our approach." He dug into his voluminous satchel. "Here's the program for the conference." He held out copies for us and two British delegates, John Cutten and R. George Medhurst (from the Society for Psychical Research in London, the oldest such group in the world).

A program may not sound like much, but this one made us forget about the heat. It was a cornucopia of psychic delights—psychic *and* scientific, the combination we'd come to Russia to find out about. At the conference we'd hear about dowsing, finger tip vision, PK. We'd learn about photographing the human aura and machines that register telepathy. We'd be hearing about these and an afternoon of other subjects from physicists and biophysicists, chemists and mathematicians.

Apart from the top brass roster of scientists, we noticed that Karl Nikolaiev was also scheduled to talk. In 1966 Nikolaiev, the Soviet Union's first "tested" telepathist, had starred in a famous telepathy experiment from Moscow to Siberia. After this success, the Russian people began to hear about "Psi." "Psi—the twenty-third letter of the Greek alphabet Ψ (pronounced sī,) is a general term for the whole field of the paranormal.

Within a year, psychic Nikolaiev took part in some very strange sounding, super modern telepathy tests. At Leningrad University he sat in the wiry clutches of a roomful of machinery which registered his bodily reactions as Moscow scientists attempted to send him Morse code messages via telepathy. They claim they succeeded. They claim that with nothing but mind power from Moscow, they influenced Nikolaiev's brain waves in Leningrad. These shifts in brain waves could eventually be decoded, they said, into a word. A psychic SOS system was in the making.

As the translator coalesced the pages of the program into instant English, Naumov seemed to vibrate with words to come, like a radio paused for a station break. "Of course we want to get together specialists working in ESP in our country. That's one reason for the conference. But there's another reason. We'd like more contacts with foreigners. After all, parapsychology is an international question. And I believe it's more than just a question of an exchange of research. *Parapsychology must develop in the name of good.* It must," he repeated.

We thought of the words the famous Russian poet Evgeny Evtushenko wrote to the American writer, Olga Carlisle. "I think there are only two nationalities—good people and bad people. . . . You are Americans. We are Russians. But good Americans will always be closer to me than bad Russians, and to you I am sure, good Russians are preferable to bad Americans." [282*]

Evtushenko and Naumov are of the same generation.

"I'm so very, very glad you've come," Naumov said once more, and he seemed to mean it right down to his bones. "Particularly from England and America. This meeting will be so helpful. You'll be able to talk to scientists from all over our country at the conference on Monday," he added, shepherding the four of us into the Minsk dining room with its long, white tables. Russians traditionally offer the newly arrived guest bread and salt as symbols of hospitality. The ongoing symbols of hospitality among psychic circles turned out to be more inviting: champagne and ice cream.

Someone at the table brought up the subject of submarines. Submarines have played a big part in the Russian psychic renaissance. Soviet parapsychology actually surfaced atop the U.S. atomic sub *Nautilus*. In 1959 French journalists splashed the now rather infamous *Nautilus* story in headlines.[332] "U.S. Navy Uses ESP on Atomic Sub!" Ship to shore telepathy, according to the French, blipped along nicely even when the *Nautilus* was far under water. "Is telepathy a new secret weapon? Will ESP be a deciding factor in future warfare?" The speculating French sensationalized "Has the American military learned the secret of mind power?"

In Leningrad the *Nautilus* reports went off like a depth charge in the mind of sixty-eight-year-old Dr. Leonid L. Vasiliev, an internationally recognized physiologist. In April 1960 Vasiliev rose to speak to a gathering of top Soviet scientists. They'd met to commemorate the discovery of radio. No one expected to hear revelations about that bourgeois fiction "mental radio." [402]

"We carried out extensive and, until now, completely unreported investigations on ESP under the Stalin regime!" Vasiliev told his startled colleagues. "Today the American

* Ascending numbers are references to be found at the back of the book.

Navy is testing telepathy on their atomic submarines. Soviet science conducted a great many successful telepathy tests over a quarter of a century ago! It's urgent that we throw off our prejudices. We must again plunge into the exploration of this vital field."

Dr. Vasiliev, a corresponding member of the Soviet Academy of Medicine, Chairman of Physiology at the University of Leningrad, holder of the Lenin Prize, was highly respected in the Soviet Union.[41] The Soviet hierarchy apparently bought Vasiliev's advice—perhaps because he stated uncompromisingly, "The discovery of the energy underlying ESP will be equivalent to the discovery of atomic energy."[237]

Within the year Vasiliev headed a special laboratory for parapsychology at the University of Leningrad. (Westerners often call this the world's first government-backed ESP lab; actually, Holland has boasted a government-funded psi institute for years.) However, the Parapsychology Laboratory at the prestigious University of Leningrad was a first, vibrating with implications for the Soviet Union.

A 1963 Kremlin edict gave top priority to the biological sciences, which in the USSR include parapsychology.[405] Major impetus behind the Soviet drive to harness ESP was said to come from the Soviet Military and the Soviet Secret Police. Today the Soviet Union has some twenty or more centers for the study of the paranormal with an annual budget estimated in 1967 at 12 to 20 million rubles ($13 million to $21 million).[283]

As Russia reversed gears and began speeding in pursuit of the supernormal, the United States Navy denied the *Nautilus* story in tones of demi-horror. No one in the Navy has anything to do with telepathy, they said, and have kept saying since 1959.

"Is the *Nautilus* story really untrue?" Naumov asked us.

"Who knows?" was our best answer.

Whether the American *Nautilus* tests happened or not, the reports of them were enough to set the Soviets going on some ESP tests with their own submarines. The Soviet tests (see chapter 3) are much more unusual than the supposed *Nautilus* ones.

The conversation shifted away from submarines as a young physicist, a friend of Naumov's, joined us at our table in the Minsk dining room. More cherry ice cream, black coffee, and good, cold Russian champagne appeared. The talk shot from subject to subject. It seemed there was a great deal to tell us.

For the past ten months biologist Naumov had been Chief of Technical Parapsychology at a special laboratory affiliated with the Department of Physics of the State Instrument Engineering College of Moscow. The creation of this laboratory was presided over by many eminent scientists [158]: Dr. Ya. Terletsky, a physics chairman at Moscow University; Dr. E. Sitkovsky of the Academy of Social Sciences; Dr. Pavel Oshchepkov, founder of radar in the USSR and President of the Engineering Institute.

As one might guess from the title of the laboratory, a major thrust of Soviet ESP work is to develop machines capable of monitoring, testing, and studying ESP. But the Soviets are also eager to study the human, people-to-people aspects of ESP. "We believe ESP is enmeshed with all of everyday life," they told us. "We believe ESP affects any group situation." And perhaps with people as warm-hearted and volatile as the Slavs, ESP does flow more easily.

Many Westerners seem to have the idea Soviet citizens are robotlike people, gray automatons in a well-run machine shop. An American student we met in Leningrad confessed, "I thought the sun never shone in Russia and the people never smiled—boy was I wrong!" We found the characteristic Russian warmth and generosity a constant of everyday life. Casual Soviet acquaintances presented us with huge, rambling bouquets of flowers and books of poetry from their own libraries. Whenever we snapped a Polaroid picture, enthusiastic passers-by crowded in to argue the merits of the shot and exclaim over the wonders of American science. Grandmotherly elevator operators kept us suspended between floors while they hugged us roundly and blessed our ancestors because we'd given them a small gift.

"Telepathy is probably always flowing among people," Naumov said. "We may always be telepathically aware of subtle thoughts and feelings of others in a group. It helps explain why some people get along well and others instantly dislike one another. Our scientists are trying to study and measure ESP objectively among groups of people."

Shortly before his death, Bishop James Pike wrote in

Psychic,[311] "This whole psi field has opened up a much bigger view of human potential for me. The potential of interrelationship, the sensitivity of the mystery of all that goes on between persons beyond just their words, or their actions or touches. There are things like AM and FM and everything else going on and we're just beginning to discover some of this. There are more lines of connection in this universe than I ever realized." Soviet dialectical materialists like Edward Naumov and his scientist friends were talking about the same thing as Pike.

"We believe man has vast hidden potential," Naumov said, and you couldn't help feeling his intense sincerity. "It is vital, we must investigate these untapped resources of human beings in every possible way." He seemed to belong to that Russian school of passionate intellectuals who too often skip meals, sleep, and from their point of view, other such diversions.

The conversation turned to the West. We found the Soviets knew a lot about ESP outside their country. They knew all about Edgar Cayce, the "sleeping prophet,"[244] and had even had a lecture on him in Moscow. They knew about Jeane Dixon, the Washington seeress, and about Gerard Croiset, the Dutch psychic famous for helping the police solve crimes.[34, 96] More surprising to us, the Soviets asked repeatedly about the American Ted Serios, who is supposedly able to make a photograph of a distant building appear on a film by staring at the camera. The Russians, we heard, were also researching this "psychic photography" and wanted all the information they could dig up on Serios.

Soviets knew about American parapsychologists, too. They were certainly familiar with the lifetime of research that Dr. J. B. Rhine has dedicated to the field. Dr. Rhine, formerly of Duke University, now with the Foundation for Research on the Nature of Man, is the most eminent American parapsychologist. "Of course," Naumov went on, "we have more than our share of skeptics here. But thanks in part to Dr. Rhine's proof of ESP, researchers here aren't trying to prove again that ESP exists! We are trying to find out *how* and *why* psi works."

While the Russians knew much about ESP in the West, Westerners were only getting the tiniest snatches of information about the world of Communist ESP. One of the strangest and most bizarre stories to reach the West via the international wire services in the spring of 1968 told of Nelya Mikhailova.[267, 298, 315] This plump Leningrad housewife was apparently a PK medium. She supposedly had the power to move matter with mind alone. "When Nelya Mikhailova wants something, she just stares at it and the object begins to creep toward her."

An Associated Press release from Moscow went further. "Nelya has astounded Soviet scientists with her ability to move such things as match sticks or wine glasses without touching them." Nelya Mikhailova and her supposed mind-over-matter power to move anything from aluminum tubes to apples and water pitchers was question mark number one when we landed in Russia.

"Over forty top scientists, including two Nobel prize winners, have tested Nelya Mikhailova," our Soviet hosts told us. "Dr. Vasiliev did research with her right up to his death in 1966."

We'd heard there were movies of the remarkable Nelya in action.

"I produced a film on Mikhailova myself," Naumov said, "but I don't think I should tell you about it." He paused. "Because you're going to see the film on Monday!" Obviously the Nelya film was to be the caviar of the conference. "And it's possible you'll meet Mrs. Mikhailova too," he said with a broad smile.

Naumov had one last surprise for us. We were all invited to give speeches at the conference. He not only invited, he insisted. With that, Naumov and his friends left to welcome other Western delegates.

We'd met our first Communist parapsychologist. He'd come on strong and talked for three hours straight. The biggest impression he left us was of his kinetic curiosity, his kinetic enthusiasm. If nothing else, it looked as if our two weeks in Moscow weren't going to be dull.

Attempting to order supper through the glass-clinking, foot-stamping roar of a Russian wedding party, we talked with our English friends about the First Moscow International Conference on Parapsychology. The original invitation set the conference in December 1967. Then a letter arrived explaining that some four hundred scientific papers had been submitted, "too many to edit in time," and an expanded conference would be held in May 1968. Soon a note came saying because of "difficulties" the conference would be *sometime* in June. The bulletin advising *when* in June flashed out long after we'd sailed from Montreal for Leningrad on the *M.S. Pushkin.* Meanwhile we spent two news-free weeks on the Soviet liner enjoying Russian lessons, Ukrainian movies and a sporting group of Soviet diplomats who donned tutus and ballet shoes to gallumph through *Swan Lake* on amateur night. After a week of Leningrad's famous White Nights, when it's pearly light even at one a.m., we boarded the Red Arrow Express for Moscow, miraculously arriving just in time for the conference.

"Unfortunately," George Medhurst told us, "John and I are going to miss the second day of the conference. Our visas run out. Intourist says there's nothing we can do about it." There wasn't. You have to tell Intourist, the Soviet agency that oversees foreign visitors, exactly how long you're going to be at each place you stop in Russia—and you have to pay in full well before you're allowed into the country.

As we strolled along Moscow's Gorky Street late that evening we speculated on this new Soviet push into research on the paranormal. When we first decided to do this book, we went to Durham, North Carolina, to consult Dr. J. B. Rhine, the dean of American parapsychologists. "The inspiration of the Communist movement centered on a new understanding of the nature of man, but it only got through to a certain level," he told us. "Now the Russians may be ready for a larger science, a new and more spiritual understanding of man. This new Soviet work in parapsychology at a high scientific level could be very hopeful."

On our way back to New York from Durham, we stopped at the Edgar Cayce Foundation in Virginia Beach, Virginia. Among the volumes of predictions made by the American psychic, we discovered that over forty years ago Cayce had prophesied that one day out of Russia would come a great spiritual development. Was this what the unexpected psychic renaissance pointed toward?

Or did the Russians, as some observers believed, have more devious reasons for exploring ESP and ways to control the mind? For all her famous "mystic soul," her fabulously peopled occult history, Russia since the Communist revolution has been inordinately leery of anything that could not be immediately seen in the clear, material light of day. Why the sudden shift? What were the Soviets up to?

In New York, a famous psychic told us in the spring of 1968, "I see dark clouds hanging over Russia. Very dark indeed," she added grimly.

Had we known then what we now know about the currents pressing toward the surface in the Soviet Union, we would have been a lot more nervous about suddenly being plunged into an area of serious political controversy—ESP.

The Czech invasion was just weeks away. Only days after we arrived in Moscow a manifesto by Dr. Andrei Sakharov, father of the Soviet H bomb, reached the West. This "Report Against the System," reflecting the liberal ideas of the Soviet scientific elite, shocked Soviet officials. There were also open demonstrations by Soviet citizens against policies of the regime—something previously unheard of in Russia. At the same time, backlash Neo-Stalinists were rapidly consolidating control. Soon hundreds of scientists would be fired for political reasons. Soon all of the scientists in the country would be required to undergo political examinations. We had arrived in the Communist world while it was half way between renaissance and inquisition.

Fortunately for our peace of mind that first evening in Moscow, we weren't yet fully aware of all that was rumbling behind the scenes. As we walked along Gorky Street, we half-heartedly made the usual jokes about microphones in the lamp and wondered about the odd circumstances surrounding the conference. The lime trees sent big puffs of fuzz into the warm air. They floated like a surreal snowstorm over the heads of the crowds sauntering now at midnight. Since Sheila's 1961 trip to Russia, New York-style steel and glass buildings had sprung up to reflect the ancient, Asian domes of Moscow. There were new consumer goods, new stores, more cars, better dressed people. As we walked toward the Kremlin and past the old Metropol Hotel, once the Moscow headquarters of Rasputin, the mystic monk who'd held the Tsar and all Russia in his sway, we wondered if we'd find out anything solid about the space-age telepathy of Karl Nikolaiev and about the ways or wiles of Nelya Mikhailova.

The Soviets seemed to be plunging into the psychic realm

from perspectives very different from those of the West. Were they slowly making clear a new understanding of what a human being is? Had the Soviets found proof that we all possess super-normal powers?

2

KARL NIKOLAIEV SELF-MADE PSYCHIC

On April 19, 1966, Karl Nikolaiev, a broth of a Soviet, a Moscow journalist as well as a busy dramatic actor, stepped quickly down the ramp from his plane in Novosibirsk. Like almost anyone else who arrives at this airport, Nikolaiev (Niko-*lī*-ev) had come to test a scientific theory. Novosibirsk's Academgorodok or "science city" is a special place twinkling like a mirage on the white flats of Siberia. The Soviets built this far off city-with-amenities for scientists. A kind of total environment think-tank, the average age in Novosibirsk's science city is around thirty, the average IQ well over 130.

Nikolaiev checked into room 601 at the Golden Valley Hotel and met a welcoming contingent of scientists from the Siberian branch of the Soviet Academy of Science. He was a new sort of specimen for the scientists. Karl, supposedly a psychic, was the man who would try to receive telepathic messages in a landmark experiment that might be called the Grand Moscow-Siberia Telepathy Test.[155, 167, 255]

Karl knew all about skepticism. Yet, that evening he found it harder than usual to shrug off. He was at the Golden Valley Hotel facing a golden opportunity—a full-dress scientific experiment with all the trimmings. He had to vindicate his contention that telepathy can bring two harmonious people into communication no matter how far apart they are. He'd been trying to get someone to test this contention for over twenty years. Nikolaiev tried to submerge into total relaxation, even though three very skeptical scientists eyed him intently. It was almost midnight in Siberia.

Hundreds of miles away in Moscow, the Kremlin clocks struck eight. Yuri Kamensky, a biophysicist, was interrupted in his own relaxing efforts by a committee of scientists. They presented Kamensky with a sealed package. Then they closed the door on his isolated, insulated chamber.

"I didn't know what I was supposed to send telepathically to Nikolaiev," Kamensky reported. "I only knew there'd be six objects and that the committee would bring each to me separately. The time for 'transmission' was ten minutes per object.

"The first package they gave me contained a metal spring of seven tight spirals. I picked it up. I moved my fingers over the coils. I let both the feeling and the sight of it sink into me. At the same time, I envisioned the face of Nikolaiev. I imagined he was sitting in front of me. Then I shifted perspective and tried to see the spring as if I were looking over Karl's shoulder. Finally I tried to see it through his eyes." [67]

About 1,860 miles away, Nikolaiev tensed. According to the eye-witnesses, his fingers groped about something visible only to himself. He wrote, "round, metallic . . . gleaming . . . indented . . . looks like a coil."

When Kamensky concentrated on the impression of a screwdriver with a black plastic handle, Nikolaiev recorded, "Long and thin . . . metal . . . plastic . . . black plastic." [78]

Later Kamensky remarked, "It seems to me every person has this ability to send and receive telepathy. But like any ability, it's necessary to train and develop it. Some people, of course, are more talented at it than others."

On four different nights between April 19th and 27th, Nikolaiev attempted to tune in via telepathy to people in Moscow. Another sender, A. G. Arlashin, a student, chose the six images he would transmit from a large group of objects presented by the scientists. One thing Arlashin chose was a barbell. Nikolaiev jotted, "metal, round, long, fat . . . hard . . . not chromed, iron bar . . . gray, like unpolished iron . . . heavy. What is it? Can it be dumbbells?" [67]

In general, Nikolaiev found it easy to pick up Kamensky's thought but difficult to unscramble Arlashin's. Intertwined in Nikolaiev's commentary as he struggled to come up with the object Arlashin had in mind were the mental associations of the young sender who was busy wondering, "Shall I choose this or that to send?" Karl's difficulty seemed to back up a theory of Soviet parapsychology: a trained sender is almost as important in telepathy as a talented receiver. If the sender's thoughts are hazy, the receiver gets equally foggy pictures.

In a test with the well-known ESP cards, Nikolaiev in Siberia guessing cards being turned in Moscow, correctly identified twelve out of twenty—far higher than the five out of twenty-five predicted by statistical theory. The odds against doing this by chance are about a thousand to one, according to Dr. Ippolit Kogan, director of the Moscow psi research center that ran the test. Yet one test is nothing in the way of proof.

Coil, barbells, screwdriver, these were what caused a star of sorts to be born in Siberia. Karl had thousands of choices. No one can calculate the probabilities of "guessing" a single target out of the infinite variety of things in the world.

"Nikolaiev satisfactorily received half of the telepathic images," Dr. Kogan reported in the scientific journal *Radio Technology*.[75] Karl successfully zeroed in on thought from Moscow not once, but six times. It was a thumping personal vindication and more. Newspapers played him up and set Russians talking about the wonders of Nikolaiev and "mental wireless." It wasn't just journalists who keyed Russians into the mysteries of ESP. The scientists, the high priests of Soviet culture, suddenly were telling the public about the extraordinary Nikolaiev too.

Engineer Victor Popovkin wrote in the official youth paper *Komsomolskaya Pravda* that Nikolaiev's success in Siberia "compels me to join with the opinion of those Soviet scientists who calculate that all people possess telepathic ability in various degrees and that this ability can be trained." [155]

In the same paper, Dr. Kogan, who is a mathematician and cyberneticist, stated: "If the results of this and other tests are taken with due reservation, critically and without gullibility or prejudice, there can be no doubt that finally, though it is mysterious, parapsychology will be an accepted science." [74]

Professor Lazar Soukarebsky, doctor of psychiatry, spoke out in *Moscow Pravda:* "The demonstration of telepathy with Nikolaiev is of great interest, expecially for research into new possibilities in man. . . . Can it be we are involved with a new form of sense, unknown as yet to science? . . . Often one hears, 'I believe in telepathy' or 'I don't believe.'

But what does this really have to do with belief? That is not a scientific formulation of the question. We need to research these problems scientifically." [217]

The Moscow-Siberia Telepathy Test, old-fashioned and classic as a model T, brought Soviet psychic research into a new era. The barrier was breached, the prototype accomplished; now refinements could begin. For the first time Soviet scientists had mentioned publicly that the USSR too possesses a "tested" psychic.

We got our first glimpse of the psychic Nikolaiev when we arrived at the conference.

"Look, there's Nikolaiev," said our translator, pointing across the room. "There, the strong looking man," she said insistently. "See, he's red all over!"

Red-haired Karl Nikolaiev did look as if he'd spent a lot of time out in the scorching Moscow sun. Nikolaiev, who makes his money as an actor, also looked as if he'd be type cast as a Cossack leader galloping across the steppes. Instead, he was acting in a new play that "explored the subtle psychological undercurrents among a group of people returning for a college reunion."

His background was impeccable. Nikolaiev's father, a ranking Bolshevik, edited an important revolutionary newspaper. His grandfather was one of the first Marxists in Russia and is written up in history books. Psychic power didn't run in his family, but being in the vanguard of new ideas and fighting for a cause certainly did. The dedicated family named him Karl in honor, of course, of Karl Marx.

"You must meet him," our translator went right on whispering during the opening speech of the conference. "He's proved once and for all that telepathy exists."

The telepathy she referred to has little to do with Karl's ability to tell in Siberia what someone is thinking about in Moscow. Unlike anything so far reported in the West, it involves the small volts of electricity flickering across the hemispheres of Karl's brain, recorded by an EEG (electroencephalograph). Nikolaiev, the individualist, was wholeheartedly in favor of connecting himself to the impersonal machines. He'd fought a long time to become a guinea pig in the scientists' laboratory.

For years Nikolaiev, in his role as psychic, bulled slowly ahead through tides of opposition. The Commissars proclaimed there were no psychics in Russia. The atheists and the scientific establishment complicated Karl's struggle. ESP didn't fit with their view of the world, so they knew it couldn't exist. But the first person Karl had to deal with was himself.

"I chose to be telepathic," Karl states flatly. "I did *not* have any unusual experiences or talents as a child. I worked hard to realize a potential most people don't even think about. I trained myself to be psychic."

Nikolaiev told us, "What I've done, other people can do. I believe everyone has psychic potential. That's one reason I think scientific tests to prove my abilities are vital. They're *proof* that I taught myself to be telepathic. And if I can, maybe you can—certainly a lot of other people can."

Karl's first battles weren't in the field of ESP, but they led him to it. Barely fifteen when the war broke, he was called up to fight in Russia's death struggle with the Nazis. As the Russians slowly beat the enemy back, Karl was rotated from the front for rest in a Hungarian city. He'd grown up planning to be a journalist like his well-known father, Nikolai Gurvich. (*Nikolaiev* is his stage name, taken from his father's first name.) But, really and passionately, the sturdy teen-ager longed to be an actor. His thirst for theater of any shape led him to a Hungarian show starring Orlando, the stage hypnotist and telepathist.

"I hung on the edge of my seat the first night. The second, I was backstage in the wings watching Orlando's every move."

Karl had seen the "light" and knew it. He scrounged for every book he could find on psychology and ESP in Hungary. Returning to Moscow, a nineteen-year-old veteran, Karl went straight to see Wolf Messing, a rare person in Russia, a celebrated theatrical psychic.

If Orlando could do it, if Messing could do it, *Nikolaiev could do it.*

Face to face with Nikolaiev, most people would decide he could achieve what he sets out to do. Animal magnetism is a bad word in books on parapsychology, but he has something like that. His vitality gave us a needed jolt when we met him late one evening with Naumov and two young physicists. After his evening's turn on the stage, Nikolaiev seemed ready for an all-night talk.

"How did you start to train yourself to be psychic?"

"I started out the only way I knew—by trying. I had friends think orders to me," Nikolaiev said. "They'd think 'light a cigarette, change your mind and crush it out.' Or 'march forward, turn left.' Like any good recruit, I'd turn right. It amused everybody, but me." Karl asked people to hide objects in the room, then mentally direct him on a treasure hunt. "One day an acquaintance, Galya—I'll never forget her—thought, 'go, pick up the pitcher.' And I did."

After that Karl's friends stopped laughing. Instead they got busy trying to figure out a wild scheme to use Karl's newfound talents to help them pass their university exams. Just how successful they were is one of the well-kept secrets of Soviet parapsychology.

A few years ago Lev Kolodny, a Soviet journalist, asked the now scientifically embroiled Nikolaiev whether he could still do his old telepathic parlor tricks. Kolodny remembers:

"I concentrated on the task, careful not to look toward the object I wanted him to bring me. Nikolaiev got up turned his back on me and walked to the far end of the room. He stopped at a corner table. In a few seconds he picked up a copy of the magazine *Ogonyok* and ruffled through the pages. Karl handed me the magazine folded open at page 6, which carried a story entitled, 'Oil Under Moscow.' It was the article I'd mentally commanded him to bring me." [81]

Occasionally Karl's psychic radar was put to more serious use. "Telepathy has helped me in my personal life ever since I began developing it," Karl told us. "To give you an example, I raised a son, all alone without a wife. One summer when the boy was in his early teens, he begged to go north to the country with a group of older friends. Finally I relented and said, 'Go, but write and let me know exactly where you are.' Naturally, he never wrote. So one night I simply got on a train and went to the village the boys had headed for.

"It was late and black when I arrived. I had no idea where to find him. I told myself to relax and just started walking. Soon I felt a force leading or guiding me. I just kept walking with it until all of a sudden it stopped in front of a small frame house. I knocked. No answer. I hadn't come that far to stand there. I opened the door and walked in. A parent's nightmare come to life—the floor littered with vodka and beer bottles, old food, a bunch of bums who were playing cards, and there, square in the middle of the mess was my drunken son. I took my young guttersnipe home, thinking I'd certainly need psychic and every other kind of power to raise him decently." Apparently the "powers" didn't fail Karl. His son recently graduated as a biochemist.

In the early 1950s Karl was a Moscow journalist. He couldn't write about the forbidden ESP, but whenever he got a chance he demonstrated it. "Great show," people said of the "experiments" Nikolaiev did for private clubs and closed editorial groups. Only his formidable appearance kept them from laughing in his face when he patiently explained, "Telepathy is much more than a stunt. Telepathy could be important."

The 1956 Soviet Encyclopedia still wrote, "Telepathy is an antisocial, idealistic fiction about man's supernatural power to perceive phenomena which, considering the time and the place, cannot be perceived."

Then came Dr. Vasiliev's revelations. Soviets finally found out their own scientists had run hundreds of successful tests with this "idealistic fiction." As the shock waves receded, Karl, who'd trained like an Olympic athlete, stood ready.

"Telepathy *can't* exist!" wrote a very skeptical scientist in the *Literary Gazette*. Dr. Alexander Kitaigorodsky continued, "To transmit images from brain to brain requires some sort of electromagnetic waves. We've never found any such waves, so there is no such thing as telepathy."

Karl didn't take that lying down. Like Pushkin and many passionate Russians before him, he loved a duel. Karl strode into the offices of a rival magazine, *Knowledge Is Power*, and threw down the gauntlet. "I challenge Kitaigorodsky to a test!" he announced. "I will meet this professor wherever he wishes. We'll test my telepathy. We'll get to the truth of the matter."

The professor took up the challenge. They set the day and time. The psychic duel was not to take place thirty paces apart in a snowy field, but inside a well-heated office. The "seconds" would be magazine editors and university scientists.

During the psychic duel Karl showed what he could do. He even read Kitaigorodsky's thoughts. The scientist's ivory-tower convictions were skewered and dispatched. The shattered Kitaigorodsky declared in print, "We must study telepathy scientifically." [71, 166]

Moscow scientists soon did just that. The "Popov group," the most vocal and best known psychic research center in the USSR, began a crash program on ESP in 1965. The "Popov group," which Soviets will politely explain is really "The Bio-Information Section of the A. S. Popov All-Union Scientific and Technical Society of Radio Technology and Electrical Communications," soon made the sturdy Nikolaiev their "resident psychic."

After completing a whole series of basic telepathy experiments, the director of the Popov group, Dr. Ippolit Kogan, began to think maybe the methods of physicists could work with telepathy. Subatomic particles aren't "visible" but physicists catch their *tracks* in cloud chambers. Telepathy isn't visible to any instrument, but maybe they could catch the *tracks* of telepathy as it arrived in the brain. To do this Kogan had newly refined EEG equipment to record brain waves and a new way to mathematically analyze the graphs. He also had a fairly dependable telepathy source —the two rigorously trained telepathists, Nikolaiev and Yuri Kamensky.

In March 1967 Karl, accompanied by Edward Naumov, then deputy chairman of the Popov group, boarded the Red Arrow Express for Leningrad where Nikolaiev hoped to pick up telepathic messages from Kamensky in Moscow. These two, Kamensky and Nikolaiev, are the Huntley-Brinkley of Soviet telepathy. They have anchored almost all the important tests of the 1960s, sending images, sounds, light flashes, and coded messages along their telepathic hookup.

Aside from the telepathic pair, two other important people in Soviet parapsychology took part in this attempt to explore the mysteries of telepathy as it unfolds in body and brain. They are Dr. Lutsia Pavlova, electrophysiologist at the Physiology of Labor Laboratory at the University of Leningrad, and her better known colleague, the mathematician Dr. Genady Sergeyev of the A. A. Uktomskii Laboratory run by the Soviet military.

Nikolaiev sat in a soundproof, isolated room bound up and wired to a lab full of monitoring machines. Outside in another section of the laboratory, Dr. Pavlova with Sergeyev and Naumov watched the graphs steadily recording Nikolaiev's respiration, heartbeat, eye movements, muscle activity, and, most importantly, his brain waves.

"I'm usually given about half an hour to get myself into the proper state of relaxation," Nikolaiev comments. "I have to be completely relaxed, but attentive." During this period his brain beamed a steady alpha rhythm, the pattern of rest.

Dr. Pavlova had told her robust guinea pig, "If you feel anything unusual, anything not connected with your uncomfortable state and the electrodes pulling on your scalp, signal by squeezing your hand repeatedly." These signals were electronically recorded outside. Later he would explain each signal. Was it telepathy he thought he felt, or not? This was all the information Nikolaiev was given. He had no idea when the telepathic messages from Kamensky would come. He didn't know how many messages to expect. He didn't know how long Kamensky would concentrate on each. He didn't know when the whole test would end.

The graphs hummed, the computors waited, the scientists waited. Isolated in a chamber in Moscow, Kamensky began his telepathic transmission. Abruptly, three seconds later, in a faraway room in Leningrad, Nikolaiev's brain waves changed "drastically"! [82]

The Soviets had caught the moment when telepathy lights up in the brain! [151, 152] *If* the evidence holds, this is no mean feat in the annals of psychic research. It's a genuine breakthrough. The ramifications lead into far more exciting fields than simple proof of telepathy. But first of all, Drs. Pavlova and Sergeyev's tapes are a new kind of proof, graphic and black and white. Here is evidence that something was happening between Nikolaiev and his partner four hundred miles away—call it telepathy or any other name. After all his determined struggling, Karl's brain waves seemed to have won a battle for him. Other successful long-distance tests followed.

The victory of the brain waves was a triumph for Dr. Sergeyev too. He devised important mathematical and statistical methods for analyzing the EEG [224] which allowed the parapsychologists to catch the "tracks" of telepathy in the brain.[199, 201]

Dr. Pavlova commented cautiously in 1967 about their success in charting telepathy in the brain. "We need still more long-distance tests to come to completely definite conclusions. However, the results of our middle-distance tests, of which we've done a great many, are highly hopeful."[152]

Dr. Kogan referring to telepathy tests in which *both* sender and receiver are attached to the EEG reports "the moment of thought transmission was found to be marked by drastic changes on the EEG tapes of each."[129]

What happens in Nikolaiev's brain during telepathy? Summarizing an extended series of EEG sessions (both long-distance tests and many more middle-distance tests with Kamensky and Nikolaiev in shielded chambers, two rooms apart), Dr. Pavlova reported:[152]

"We detected this unusual activation of the brain within one to five seconds after the beginning of telepathic transmission. We always detected it a few seconds before Nikolaiev was consciously aware of receiving a telepathic message. At first, there is a general nonspecific activation in the front and mid (motor-logical) sections of the brain. If Nikolaiev is going to get the telepathic message consciously, the brain activation quickly becomes specific and switches to the rear, afferent regions of the brain. This specific pattern remains clear on the graphs for some time after the transmission ends."

Telepathy in your brain seems to move in specific directions. Just where activity focuses in the brain depends, according to the Soviet researchers, on what kind of message is being sent. In Moscow Kamensky concentrated on an empty Yava cigarette box. Karl in Leningrad noted, "Something that appears like cigarettes. It is the lid, inside it is empty. The surface is not cold . . . it's cardboard."

Before he consciously received the image of the cigarette box, the activity in Nikolaiev's brain apparently localized in the back occipital region—in the area normally involved with sight. Significantly, when Kamensky telepathically conveyed sound, like a series of buzzes and whistles, the activity in Nikolaiev's brain localized in the temporal section—the area normally involved with sound.

Dr. Pavlova has some intriguing observations from her

extensive EEG work. "It is extremely important for the receiver to be in a peaceful state. Man is not normally capable of maintaining this state of 'operative rest' for an extremely long time, free of involuntary motion, distracting thought." But the Soviets insist, "You can be *trained* to develop this meditative state necessary for telepathic success."

Dr. Milan Ryzl, a biochemist from Prague now living in the United States, is one of the few outside scientists to discuss with the Pavlova-Sergeyev-Naumov team their various EEG experiments. "Using the EEG, they have made important discoveries in the field of ESP," Ryzl says.[380] "These Soviet findings could bring us a long way forward in the control of ESP." [382]

Apart from training in the lab, has Karl done anything to refine his telepathic prowess since the days of "turn left, turn right"?

"Have you heard of yoga?" he asked us. If we hadn't, we would have, because the two scientists who showed up that night with Karl had a portfolio of home developed photos, featuring a thin young man in a lovely, tortuous alphabet of yoga position.

"I don't do the exercises," Karl patted his solid self. (He would make a very abundant lotus.) "But I've studied the philosophy, Raja yoga, and in particular the breathing exercises. I've done them for eleven years. They've given me much finer control of my body and myself . . . and taught me a lot of other things too. Did you know that Stanislavsky developed his famous acting methods through a study of yoga? He believed an actor must be able to eliminate all muscular tensions just before going on-stage. Stanislavsky thought that tensions or 'clamps' on the nerves blocked real freedom of motion and expression."

To find out more about different states of consciousness, Soviets arranged with the Indian government in the early sixties to bring yogis to Russia to be studied in the lab.

Moving back to telepathy again, Karl went on, "We need more tests with the machines. And we're going to have them. We've got to prove telepathy subjectively *and* objectively. Some people are never going to believe it when I say I am getting something telepathically. They don't want to believe it. And I'm not always right." He paused to light another cigarette.

Some psychics seem to be many people in one. Like a subliminal flicker, you can almost glimpse other voices, other faces. Nikolaiev always seemed to be Nikolaiev, even though his activities—photographer, actor, car enthusiast, writer—are broad enough for a group of people. Karl's articles still appear in prominent magazines. At that moment, however, his attention was on telepathy.

"There can be so many problems in regular experiments. Once I was even told that I must get five out of ten images right or they'd report I failed, that I had *no* psychic ability. What if I received only two telepathically, or one?" His unremitting blue eyes flashed. "*Why* is that not a success when I'm miles away?"

Nikolaiev came over with conviction. But it was a sociable forcefulness, not the all-stops-out eloquence of his speech at the conference. Our conference had already been affected by political machinations entering psi research; and only a few weeks before. Karl had been enticed by the *Literary Gazette* into what he now believed to be an unfairly rigged test. That's what he was going to talk about. Thick powerful forearms resting on the lectern, Nikolaiev began. He was there, he said, as a private person, representing no one but himself. And for himself, he was tired of all the senseless attacks on ESP. He was tired of the people who'd never spent an hour studying the field being quoted as experts. He was tired, in short, of all the mucking about in what he considered a fragile new field that could be and should be a great benefit to all people.

Nikolaiev's delivery sounded very much like that of the Russian poet Voznesensky hammering home his rich, angry lines. It is a ringing, thumping, Shakespearean-Churchillian kind of rhetoric that doesn't make it anymore in English. But this uncool blend of emotion and intellect still pervades the real Russian speech even among the scientists.

We met a woman in Leningrad who had psychic talents too. She said of Karl Nikolaiev, "I don't know him, but he's fighting battles for me. By getting the scientists to test telepathy, he's helping prove that I'm not unbalanced, that I am not a fairytale witch. That's what people said about me."

The Soviets have moved *inside* the psychic. This move is just beginning to banish the witch hunt aspects of the scholarly study of psychics. Now, with the telltale machines, mediums may not have to be searched, to be trussed like battlefront prisoners, to endure having their mouths stuffed with marbles and penknives pried under their fingernails—all of which has befallen well-known people with Nikolaiev's sort of talent in this century.

For partisans in the old dualistic debate, the EEG work is no help. It doesn't answer the question, "Is ESP a material phenomenon or a spiritual one?" It doesn't tell what telepathy is or anything about the nature of reality that permits ESP. It simply unravels the physiology of the receiver, or as the Russians call him, the *percipient*. It makes the Soviet word for ESP, "bio-information," more understandable.

The meeting of EEG and ESP has opened new vistas. "Why can't science," one Soviet speculated, "learn to artificially stimulate certain patterns in the brain and turn a person into a more reliable telepathic receiver? Perhaps we can make a medium the way we make a properly circuited radio."

Dr. Pavlova suggested, "We could make an automatic tuning device for Nikolaiev. A signal would tell him when telepathy first showed in his brain. He could then try to focus his attention and get the messages which reach his unconscious but which he sometimes misses."

Dr. Pavlova has done more than speculate. The scientists have led Karl into a strange frontier land where he has gone through a batch of bizarre but highly significant experiences. They've used the very much alive Nikolaiev as if he were a component of a machine in their attempts to develop a telepathic code system for use in outer space. Like his college friends, but for much less light-hearted reasons, they've tried to control and guide Karl's movements with mind power alone. They've attempted to affect his body processes, to see if they could make him sick—with telepathy.

The experiences of Nikolaiev run through much of the telepathy exploration in this book. What happened to him sounds like a cross between science fiction and voodoo.

But it isn't. Backed by sophisticated machinery and mathematical theories, the Soviets are trying to lay bare some of the strange powers of man that have often been whispered about, but have never been tracked down under the bright lights of the laboratories. Karl always said, "Telepathy could be important." When he came home from the war to Moscow in 1945, he probably couldn't have guessed just what that "important" would mean in the 1960s.

Nor could he have guessed that in March 1967, he'd be called to a somber government hall.[13] The Ministry of Communication of the USSR had asked the parapsychologists to report on their brand of communication, telepathy. In particular, Sergeyev explained his new method of analyzing the EEG. Then Nikolaiev joined Kamensky onstage for a "command" performance.

Kamensky hoped to send him an object chosen by the ministry deputies. Nikolaiev sat on the far edge of the platform, his back to Kamensky. The officials heard Nikolaiev say, "Small, glazed surface, brownish color . . . pointed ends." They asked him to open a container holding a penholder, chalk, a coat check, a piece of Mishka candy, and a flower. "Choose the object Kamensky sent you." Nikolaiev picked up the tan, pointy-edged piece of candy.

The accurate Nikolaiev came up a crowd pleaser on this and other "demonstrations." His story isn't quite a Horatio Alger tale. If it were, he'd be head of a new ministry of telepathy. Still, he and telepathy had come a long way since the tolerant girl mentally told the teen-age Nikolaiev to "pick up the pitcher."

We asked him the movie magazine question. "Are you happy? Why did you do all this, why did you struggle so hard to become a telepathist?"

"Why! For what!" Nikolaiev leaned forward and one sensed a sort of heraldic thunder rumbling up in him. "Why, to *be* more. What else is life for? To develop all your possibilities. That *is happiness,* to love what you're doing, to keep expanding, to keep turning into something more."

His two friends and Naumov began telling us about it too. "We're on the threshold . . . undreamed-of talents . . . expansion, realization, soul . . . now!" What would have sounded Pollyanna in New York crackled around us like heat lightning in the humid Moscow night. ("Soul" talk is pretty common in Russia. They seem to worry over their souls like so many subway riding Dostoevskys.)

Settling earthward, our Soviet friends reiterated a theme we found common in the Communist countries. Psychic power may have the widest possible use. Probably, they said, psychic powers can one day be integrated into the personality and used like a real sixth sense.

"The psychic sense has helped me in so many ways," Karl said. "It's made me a better actor. I find it easier now to get into the lives of people I play. I tune in better to other actors and am more sensitive to the audiences. Probably all artists use this power but don't realize what it is. But it doesn't have to be just a power for artists," Karl said and reiterated, "Anyone can learn to develop psychic talent." Karl emphasized that his family and friends are proud of his ESP talent and don't think of it as anything strange or weird.

Remembering that the Soviet parapsychologists are interested in everything about a psychic, even the incidence of sunspots at his birth, we asked Karl when he was born.

"May 18, 1926."

Over here he'd be an astrologer's darling. If you've read even the most wobbly astrological pamphlets, you know that Nikolaiev is a fine specimen of the evolved Taurus. As a fortune-telling weight machine might put it, "You have bull-like good looks and dogged determination. You have a fine voice. (Karl's brings visions of deep-toned, highly polished wood instruments.) You are gregarious and love company. You are fond of children (Karl adopted his son from a war orphanage.) You have full appetites and passions."

With his passion "to be more," Karl Nikolaiev is the full-blooded embodiment of the bright side of Soviet parapsychology. His determination to prove telepathy and to keep on proving it has carried him into a strange world of brain waves and space-age tests that we were just beginning to learn more about.

3

MIND-LINK, BODY-LINK

"Have you ever met a stranger and felt an instant liking, a sort of click?" Edward Naumov asked. "Have you ever been introduced to someone and felt an immediate antipathy for no reason?"

In America this sudden click or clunk is called chemistry. In Russia it's called biological compatibility or incompatability. According to the Soviets, this common experience is merely the visible peak of a rather chilling phenomenon that could be dangerous as it broadens in the subconscious.

"These irrational reactions are very real and have a very real basis," Naumov continued. "Emotions, states of mind, are reflected in the electrical activity of the brain. This is because the brain of one person can 'impose' its rhythm on the brain of another. It's no more or less than spontaneous telepathy.

"Here's another small example. At some time you must have been in a public place and noticed two or three people suddenly yawn at the same moment. Suggestion? We've begun to see from our experiments that physical processes going on in one body *can* be transmitted telepathically to another. And emotions too—cheerful and negative ones—can be sent to the mind of another person telepathically."

The Soviets are exploring the possibilities of biological "imposition" via telepathy. A key man, studying and being studied in this quest is biophysicist Yuri Kamensky, Karl Nikolaiev's telepathic partner. Kamensky grew interested in supernormal powers when, as a child, he got a sudden surprise. He discovered his classmates couldn't recite what their friends were thinking. Neither could they come up with each other's phone numbers by simply putting their minds to it. Yuri Kamensky could—a very handy talent in Russia where there are no phone directories. Now in his thirties, Kamensky is a pleasant anomaly: observer and guinea pig; disciplined scientist and passionate partisan.

Two years ago Kamensky showed that the telepathic sender can be a powerhouse radiating thoughts and then some. Intense light flashed on Kamensky's closed eyes. It was evening and he sat in a lab at the University of Leningrad looking into a binocularlike apparatus. A timing device caused strobe lights to flash at a specific rate into each of his eyes, one rhythm for the left eye, another for the right. Flashing lights bring on known brain wave patterns.

"Light/light," Kamensky murmured, and tried against the flashing distraction to visualize the face of his telepathic partner Nikolaiev. Almost instantly Nikolaiev, sitting in another building, started. He pressed the button to signal that he thought telepathy was aimed at him.[152]

Alone this was a good demonstration of telepathic rapport. But a much more subtle kind of rapport excited Naumov and his co-workers. Dr. Sergeyev quickly decoded Nikolaiev's brain waves with the help of an electronic analyzer. No light flicked on Nikolaiev. He sat in a meditative state. Yet, as the light pulsed on Kamensky, pulsations appeared in Nikolaiev's brain activity. The pattern artificially created in Kamensky's brain had, through thin air, started up activity in Nikolaiev's brain. Something going on in Kamensky's body suddenly caused something to happen in his friend's body.[82, 357, 382]

"It would be impossible for Nikolaiev to bring on this pattern by himself even if he wanted to," Naumov emphasized, talking to us about these unusual tests. "In a sense, it was as if telepathy was photographed on his brain."

Worldwide, scientists have noted that a change of brain waves in one identical twin can cause a similar shift in the other. Dr. Thomas Duane, Chief of Ophthalmology at Jefferson Medical College in Philadelphia, and his colleague Dr. Thomas Behrendt documented this physical telepathy in 1965.[308] They showed that alpha rhythm—the brain wave pattern typical of a resting state—in one twin could bring on the same pattern in the other twin at a distance.

Kamensky performed a complicated feat in inducing a complex pattern in Nikolaiev's brain. His thought seems as supercharged as a strobe light does compared to a twenty-five watt bulb. Besides, Kamensky and Nikolaiev would be hard-pressed to pass as second cousins, let alone identical twins. Kamensky with his earnest, boyish face, receding hair, and turned up nose, has no visible affinities with the sturdy, flamboyant Nikolaiev. Yet training, which included everything from the ability to visualize a scene to the supposed harmonizing of magnetic fields, did produce moments of super twinlike affinity in the two.

People aren't directly aware of what their brain waves are up to. Kamensky and another sender, a talented college student, Alex Monin, sent telepathy to Nikolaiev that he *could feel*—all too well. Monin came into telepathy by way of being an amateur Svengali around age fourteen. He took to hypnotizing his sister. Soon the precocious Monin graduated to casting his spell over a young secretary, Luda. One day, while Luda sat entranced before him, the young hypnotist's mind wandered to a personal hang-up that was bothering him. Then he remembered Luda.

"And now, you will wake up!" Luda woke up and immediately began reciting the vagrant thoughts that had filled Monin's mind during her trance. "How did you know that?" the astonished boy asked. "I don't know," Luda told him. "The words just came to me and I said them."

Instantly a budding parapsychologist, Monin went on a hunt for telepathy books. He probably carried one to enliven the dull spots as he sat, an intense looking boy, day after day on a park bench. Monin waited for a likely looking citizen to come down the path. "Ah, your neck itches madly. Scratch it!" Monin thought. "Feel it. A gnat just landed on the back of your neck. It's biting!"

Some passers by did begin scratching their necks, swatting at invisible gnats. Monin, in effect, was training himself to be a telepathic sender, as Nikolaiev trained to receive. A recent scientific find, Monin works as a lab assistant with the Moscow parapsychologists.

Monin didn't try to influence Nikolaiev into an itchy neck. Instead he and Kamensky returned to the light apparatus. Lights flicking at different rates on each eye cause a sensation of rotation and a "very unpleasant feeling in the viewer." Monin took to the binoculars. Isolated two rooms away, Nikolaiev signaled telepathic contact with him. Not knowing what the test was about, he also felt a sudden sour nausea. Monin and Kamensky could use telepathy to make the unwitting Nikolaiev "seasick." Of course they were trying hard. The superbly trained Nikolaiev purposely put himself into an open, receptive mood. Could this happen outside the lab? Can it happen accidentally?

"Yes," said Dr. Pavel Naumov, who bears no relation to Edward Naumov except his interest in telepathy.[137] A psychologist, Pavel Naumov ran his studies in the bustling, noisy atmosphere of a Moscow gynecological clinic.

"The biological ties between mother and child are incontestable. In the clinic, mothers are in a distant section, separate from their babies. They cannot possibly hear them. Yet, when her baby cries, a mother exhibits nervousness. Or when an infant is in pain, for instance as a doctor takes a blood specimen, the mother shows signs of anxiety. She has no way of knowing the doctor is at that moment with her child." [254]

A two-way hookup is apparently the hallmark of this inborn telepathic connection. A mother is in severe pain. The baby senses it and cries. "We found communication in 65 percent of our cases," Pavel Naumov concluded in a paper he gave at an important Soviet conference in February 1968 on the "Scientific Problems of Telepathy." [158]

Most Russians know a much more famous account of the anxiety and physical pain of a parent being telepathically communicated to his child. Mikhail Lomonosov was a Russian *wunderkind* of the 1800's who soared from his peasant birth to become the country's foremost scholar and founder of Moscow University. One night he dreamed about his father, a fisherman. Mikhail saw the older man awash in a snarling gale. Waves crashed over his father's boat, driving it inexorably toward the bleak, jagged coast of an uninhabited arctic island. Shipwreck! Waking up, the distraught scholar was convinced that his father was in mortal peril and had been trying to reach him. Mikhail was not even in Russia. He was slowly traveling home from Germany. Finally, on reaching St. Petersburg, Mikhail went straight to his brother. No, his father's ship had not been heard from for four months. Mikhail, describing his dream, begged the fishermen of his old village to go and search the island. "And see that my father has a proper burial." Rescue, the grieving Mikhail was sure, would come too late now. The fishermen did find Lomonosov's shipwrecked father, and they buried him as the famous scholar asked.

Many years later, Bernard B. Kajinsky, an early Soviet pioneer in psychic research, noted the telepathic transference of bodily symptoms. A woman felt sudden pains in her stomach. Fourteen hundred miles away, her daughter, unknown to the woman, was undergoing abdominal surgery. There are dozens of stories about such spontaneous symptom shifting.

According to Dr. Pavel Naumov, parents aren't the only people you might have a natural telepathic rapport with. He noted that girls dating boys with telepathic aptitudes correctly received up to 40 percent of the images the boys sent. Long ago researchers in the West observed that spontaneous telepathy flashes most often between members of a family, people in love, and childhood friends.

Some Russians, at least, would extend this invisible connection down into the animal world. The first day we met Naumov he brought up an extremely interesting "telepathy" test. We'd been discussing the fact or fiction behind reports of ESP tests on the American atomic submarine *Nautilus*.

"If your Navy didn't do the *Nautilus* experiment, then Soviet scientists were the first in the world to test ESP from a submarine!" Naumov exclaimed. He wasn't boasting, but he did seem to lay special import on the kind of ESP test the Soviets ran with *their* submarine. "We didn't use human subjects. We used a mother rabbit and her newborn litter."

According to Naumov, these tests took place about three years previously. "As you know, there's no known way for a submerged submarine to communicate with anyone on land. Radio doesn't work. Scientists placed the baby rabbits aboard the submarine. They kept the mother rabbit in a laboratory on shore where they implanted electrodes deep in her brain. When the sub was deep below the surface of the ocean, assistants killed the young rabbits one by one.

"The mother rabbit obviously didn't know what was happening. Even if she could have understood the test, she had no way of knowing at what moment her children died. Yet, at each synchronized instant of death, her brain *reacted*. *There was communication*," Naumov emphasized. "And, our instruments clearly registered these moments of ESP."

What exactly did the Soviets find out in their submarine tests?

"The reports were drawn up and submitted to the proper authorities," Naumov told us. "They are, I'm sorry to say, not public."

"There's something about your story that you didn't go into," the British delegate, John Cutten, remarked. "Surely you don't just commandeer a submarine. What you're telling us implies very close cooperation with the government and the military, doesn't it?" [285]

Naumov spread out his hands. "Mr. Cutten's remark speaks for itself."

Not everything spoke for itself. Naumov's was a take-it-or-leave-it account. The idea of a physiological test certainly fits in well with the major interests of Soviet parapsychology. So does the use of a submarine after all the publicity given the *Nautilus* story in the USSR. And the claims of an extrasensory tie between all creatures doesn't sound as unbelievable as it once did, thanks to the unusual and well tested work of Cleve Backster in the United States. Mr. Backster, Director of the Backster School of Lie Detection in New York, has good evidence to show that there is a sort of "primary perception" inherent in all living things.[270, 294, 297] For instance, when tiny shrimp are killed there is a reaction in other living things—such as plants—in the surrounding areas. "Nothing seems to be able to stop this communication," says Backster, "not even lead shields." [269, 324] The Soviets supposedly found that tons of sea water are no barrier to this live communication either.

There's nothing mystical about the work Backster and the Soviets are doing. The reactions are graphed on impartial, carefully controlled equipment, and Backster's tests, at least, are being duplicated in other laboratories. It is highly significant if the Soviet military is deep into the study of "primary perception." All sorts of potential uses come to mind, one of the best being an unbeatable communication system.

Beyond such practical uses, this discovery of mind-link, body-link between all living things has vast implications for our philosophy, for our own view of the world. The alleged Soviet submarine tests make one wonder if the eighteenth-century English poet William Blake was prophetic in more areas than people suppose:

Each outcry of the hunted hare
A fibre from the brain does tear

Everyone knows that mystics and gurus always insist we are all somehow connected. All is one, the paradox goes, and within the one there is individuality. Dr. Gardner Murphy, President of the American Society of Psychical Research, often compares individuals to volcanic islands projecting above the sea. Underneath, they slope to the ground from which they came, in which they all connect.

If the early Soviet results are correct, currents of communication are crisscrossing beneath the wavery surface of things. Are they charged, the Soviets wondered. Can you telepathically transmit feelings of anger, fear, violence from room to room or from Moscow to Leningrad?

The Russians claim a great many tests. In one particularly good series, the versatile Kamensky gave up his role as sender to the student Alex Monin. Kamensky himself received. Short, mean bursts of emotion came from Monin. He concentrated on the anxiety of suffocation. He imagined a racking attack of asthma, then a choking fit. In other tests, he tried for the sensation of a dizzying blow on the head. Monin also visualized "twisting Kamensky's nose." When generating telepathic emotions, Monin sent each feeling blast nine times.[189] In isolation, Kamensky felt and became consciously aware of the particular emotions in 80 percent of the trials. (The Soviet researchers didn't reveal the number of trials; they just say "many.")

Kamensky got a chance to aim his own negative emotions at Nikolaiev all the way from Moscow to Leningrad. At precisely the moments Kamensky let fly at him, Nikolaiev reported the reception of telepathy and began feeling miserable. Imagination? These emotional telepathy tests would have been dismissed completely before the entry to EEG into Soviet parapsychology. The Naumov-Sergeyev-Pavlova team found their EEG records changed dramatically when the telepathic impulse had an emotional fuse on it.[189, 380]

Dr. Pavlova reported, "Transmission of several successive emotions of a negative character called up the appearance of cross-excitation of the brain. It changed the spontaneous EEG character to the tired state of the brain, dominated by slow, hypersynchronized waves of the delta and theta type." Kamensky and Nikolaiev had more to worry about than tired brain waves. Dr. Pavlova noted, "Receivers themselves experienced unpleasant bodily sensations and strong head pains."

Dr. Pavlova added the punch line. "Following telepathic transmission of positive emotions (feelings of calmness, cheerfulness), the EEG normalized again within one to three minutes. The unpleasant bodily symptoms also disappeared, changing to a sensation of calm during the telepathic transmission of emotions of a soothing character." [152]

"There's one kind of test I really hate," Nikolaiev told us, "the tests with negative emotions. They sometimes make me sick for hours."

Such pioneering Soviet tests tentatively point to a few eye-widening or—depending on your point of view—ominous conclusions. Negative emotions have a bleak effect on your physiology as well as your psychology. Cheerful, "positive thinking" helps the body itself recoup. Drs. Pavlova, Sergeyev, and Naumov uncovered impressive data on the power of thought. It seems you don't even have to boil up your own nasty thoughts. Someone else can cook them up and send them to you. Untelepathically, the Soviets already knew that thought could reach right down to your blood cells. In 1956 Drs. S. Serov and A. Troskin of Sverdlovsk demonstrated that the number of white blood cells rose by fifteen hundred after they suggested positive emotion to patients. After impressing negative emotion, the white cells decreased by sixteen hundred. White blood cells, or leucocytes, are one of the body's main defenses against disease.[359]

In 1959, a Czech, Dr. Stepan Figar, found that intense mental anxiety in one man caused, *at a distance*, a slight change in blood volume in a resting person. He measured this with a plethysmograph, a device like those in lie detectors.[36] British parapsychologist Douglas Dean has done hundreds of well-controlled tests showing telepathic influence on blood volume.

Marxists aren't likely to spend money to prove the verities of voodoo. If ongoing tests continue to support the evidence, the official statement will be similar to the one used whenever parapsychology lights in an area some consider religious. Yes, these things do happen. They are caused by normal human functions until recently undiscovered.

More than the doctrines of voodoo and the work of Figar and Dean lend credence to the Soviet findings. Various psychiatrists in the United States think they have noted telepathic transmission of bodily ills. Perhaps chief among them is Dr. Berthold Schwarz, a New Jersey neurologist, psychiatrist, and writer. He has collected over five hundred cases of parent-child telepathy. Many of these showed, in Dr. Schwarz's words, "possible telesomatic and motor-acting-out responses." It seemed as if the thought of parent or child caused physical reactions in the other, Dr. Schwarz reported in the Journal of the Medical Society of New Jersey.[394]

Typical of the files of cases the knowledgeable Dr. Schwarz has traced is this one about a man who awoke with a thumping toothache. He complained to his wife. Then he called the dentist and made an emergency appointment. Later in the morning, the man's mother phoned to say that for the first time in years she was having a tooth extracted that day. By the time her suffering son got to the doctor in the afternoon, his pain was gone. The dentist found nothing amiss with his tooth. The ache never recurred. The son's paining tooth was in the same spot as the one extracted from his mother.

Should "sympathy pains" be carted into the parapsychology lab? Dr. Schwarz documented a different kind of case involving a man gripped with sudden, red-hot stomach pains while driving to work. When the man turned toward home, the pain vanished. He turned around again heading for the office, but the pain hit again. Shaken, the man turned once more and went home, even though the seizure eased as he neared his house. Hearing his tale, his wife seemed rather unsympathetic. That evening the man discovered his wife's packed suitcases. She'd planned to leave him that morning, taking their two young children while he was out of the way at work. This father believes the unspoken distress of his children communicated and caused the pains that brought him home.

Dr. Schwarz has uncovered cases much more complex and dramatic as he tries to chart this telesomatic current caroming through the mirror house of human psychology. It's unlikely the Soviets will plunge after Dr. Schwarz into depth psychology, a subject more suspect in Russia than parapsychology. The irresistible trend of their own research, however, may one day push them into it.

The Soviet inquiry into the effect of telepathy on bodily actions has moved steadily inward. In his book *Experiments in Mental Suggestion,*[237] Dr. Leonid L. Vasiliev reports that in the 1930s he ran hundreds of experiments trying to think people into action. "Cross your legs." "Raise your right hand." "Walk forward." People did walk forward, people did raise their right hands too often to say "coincidence." Vasiliev concentrated his thought commands on normal men and women and on psychiatric patients. Usually he put them into a light trance to ease reception. Sometimes he blindfolded them.

In a typical experience with a responsive patient in the summer of 1937, Vasiliev found, "Out of thirteen tasks telepathically commanded, six were carried out with total accuracy; there are doubts about three; four weren't carried out."

Vasiliev tried to see if he could mentally influence a person's body to make him well rather than sick. Joined by medical friends, in particular Dr. V. N. Finne, a hypnotist, Vasiliev beamed telepathy at Kouzmina, a twenty-nine-year-old patient in a Leningrad hospital. For years the woman had suffered hysterical paralysis of the left side. Given exceedingly strong, repetitious spoken suggestions while under hypnosis, Kouzmina could move her paralyzed arm and leg.

Would mental suggestion also be strong enough, Vasiliev wondered, to make her move? The setting was a small hospital ward, bare except for a bed in the middle of the floor, and a wooden stool for the doctor six feet behind Kouzmina's head as she lay in the bed. Kouzmina, hypnotized, her eyes tightly bandaged, lay still in the silence. Vasiliev and his colleagues avoided even whispering to each other.

A slip of paper with the desired movement on it was passed to the telepathist, sometimes Vasiliev, sometimes Finne.

Dr. Finne ordered her mentally to stretch *both* arms outward. A minute and a half passed as Finne sent his telepathic command. Then he began to observe convulsive movements of Kouzmina's paralyzed left arm. Gradually she stretched it outward. She didn't move her normal right arm, making the test only half successful.

Vasiliev concentrated on his mental command. "Bend your right leg at the knee." Kouzmina bent her leg. The rest of her remained still. Time, three to five minutes.

Asked why she made the various movements, the hypnotized Kouzmina would reply, "Professor Vasiliev made me do it" or "Dr. Finne's order." She almost always realized who commanded her telepathically.

Dr. Finne concentrated on a tougher telepathic assignment. He mentally suggested stimulation of the ulnar nerve in the paralyzed left arm; next the median nerve; then the radial nerve. Kouzmina raised her left arm. She assumed a position characteristic of the mechanical stimulation of the ulnar nerve, then of the median nerve. She dropped her left arm. Her right hand took the position characteristic of a stimulated radial nerve.

It is less than likely Kouzmina would have known what "ulnar, median, radial" meant, or the characteristic position resulting from the stimulation of these nerves, even if Finne had spoken his command loud and clear.

Intrigued, other doctors came. A dozen people crowded into the silent room. Vasiliev invited a newcomer, Professor A. A. Kouliabko, to send. "Scratch your left cheek and the bridge of your nose." Kouzmina raised her right arm to her left cheek and her lips. She scratched her right cheek with the same hand.

Finne asked the entranced Kouzmina what she was doing. "The right side of my face itches."

Finne asked, "Who talked to you?"

"Not you."

"Who?"

"Professor *Koulbashov*. He made the right side of my face itch dreadfully." The name had come through only slightly distorted. The paralyzed woman had met Kouliabko only briefly for the first time before the test. Twelve people, mostly newcomers, filled her room.

The professors set nineteen tests for Kouzmina in fifteen sessions. In all, Vasiliev noted, in the attempts to effect the movement of Kouzmina's body with telepathy, there were ten complete successes, six partial successes, and only three failures.

Vasiliev realized, as any contemporary of Pavlov's would, that the same subject could not be tested by these methods too long. A conditioned response might blur the telepathic effect. Vasiliev moved inward. He tried to command telepathically a body movement no one notices even when wide awake: body sway. Using sensitive recording apparatus, Dr. Vasiliev found he could telepathically influence body sway in some people without their being aware of it at all. The impact of this thought was enough to force them to take a quick step to keep from falling.

It seems almost impious in an account of the mind's ability to influence the body to completely omit the most famed Russian influencer of them all: Rasputin, the "power hungry" or "mad" or "holy" or "satanic" monk. Wild and fanatically conflicting legends flowed as artlessly as brain waves from this "humble servant of God." Under the theatrical razzle, he did possess genuine psychic powers. Rasputin trained as a *shaman*, a Siberian holy man. The *shaman's* ancient discipline supposedly produces a close knowledge of psychic things—if one survives the course. Rasputin, as everyone knows, was very good at surviving. As is also known, he was the only person who could help Russia's most famous patient, the hemophiliac young Tsarevitch.

Rasputin could vanquish the boy's pain and stop his bleeding. He used hypnotism certainly. But he seems also to have been a psychic healer. Reportedly, he could aid the boy when he was not with him. (Rasputin was also extraordinary at influencing bodies in another way. Daintily bred noblewomen would spend one minute with the matted monk and tumble gurgling into bed with him. It must have taken *some* mental projection to have so many ladies later go on record saying, "All was revealed to me. I slept with God.") The imagination fumbles at the thought of the electrifying Rasputin, with his "glinting eye" and "evil smell" submitting meekly to Dr. Pavlova's electrodes. One can't even imagine him willing to discuss the physical mechanisms of his "holy powers." It was Rasputin's brand of psychic power that Dr. Vasiliev and his colleagues were trying to bury when they began their careful studies only seven years after the monk's murder. These early parapsychologists took into the laboratory the magical belief that a person can influence another person's body from afar.

When Vasiliev's findings were finally published in the early 1960's Dr. Kogan, Edward Naumov, Yuri Kamensky, Dr. Sergeyev, and a great many others started down the paths Vasiliev had marked. Vasiliev telepathically directed body movements. He made the paralyzed Kouzmina lift her arm. The new researchers tried to telepathically influence body processes. Kamensky induced an artificial pattern onto the brain of Nikolaiev. Next they moved to trying to project emotions mentally. At last, emerging from the reassurance of the lab, they supposedly found that a mother suffers severe pain and her baby wails. Aside from added evidence that yes, there is telepathy, such cases open up philosophical, ethical, personal, and scientific questions. Across a distance, is mind influencing body? Is body influencing body? Is body influencing mind? As psi moves into the picture, the iron edges of biology and psychology begin to dissolve and mix, pointing to a whole new dynamism underlying both.

On a personal level, do we ever plug in and out of an unconscious communication system? In this huge unknowing, do we ever influence another? Does anyone influence us? What are the special circumstances that let the telesomatic current flow?

Considering telepathic biological rapport, Edward Naumov spoke again and again of its bearing on human relationships at home and in society at large. "We used to just worry about psychological compatibility, now we must think about biological compatibility and incompatibility as well," he said. Telesomatic currents are an X factor of undetermined size. Naumov believes that consciously elaborating this "X" and its dynamics can only lead to greater understanding and harmony in human relations.

4

WOLF MESSING, THE PSYCHIC STALIN TESTED

Right in the middle of a sellout theatrical performance, two green-uniformed Soviet police suddenly stalked on stage. "We're sorry," they told the audience in the Byelorussian city of Gomel', "but the show is over." Then they hustled the star performer, telepathist Wolf Messing, into a waiting car and sped off to an unknown destination. It was 1940, a time when people were often carted off by the police to disappear forever, with no reason given and no questions asked.

"What about my hotel bill and my trunk?" Messing asked.

The trunk wouldn't be needed and the hotel bill was settled, the secret police indicated.

"We arrived somewhere—I didn't know where," says Messing. "I was led into a room. It seemed to be a hotel. After some time I was led to another room. A man with a moustache came in." The psychic Wolf Messing was face to face with Stalin!

What was happening in Poland and what were the plans of Polish leaders, Stalin wanted to know. Stalin wasn't asking for a psychic reading. He was asking for personal information about some of the psychic's influential Polish friends. He would test Messing's psychic gifts later.

Wolf Messing was no ordinary mentalist, but a celebrated psychic who'd traveled the world, had been "tested" by such luminaries as Einstein, Freud, and Gandhi, and had hobnobbed with people in high places. His friends had included the late Marshal Pilsudski and much of the Polish government. Messing had just fled the Nazi invasion of Poland after Hitler had put a 200,000 mark price on his psychic head.

The first meeting with Stalin led to a series of bizarre but, for Messing, triumphantly successful encounters with the dictator. Stalin knew of Messing's supposed ability to telepathically project his thought into another person's mind, to control or cloud their minds, so to speak. Stalin commanded a straightforward, horrendous trial of Messing's talent. He was to pull off a psychic bank robbery and get 100,000 rubles from the Moscow Gosbank where he was unknown.

"I walked up to the cashier and handed him a blank piece of paper torn from a school notebook," says Messing. He opened an attaché case and put it on the counter. Then he mentally willed the cashier to hand over the enormous sum of money.

The elderly cashier looked at the paper. He opened the safe and took out 100,000 rubles. Messing stuffed the banknotes into the case and left. He joined Stalin's two official witnesses in charge of the experiment. After they had attested that the experiment had been satisfactorily performed, Messing returned to the cashier. As he began handing him the packages of banknotes, the cashier looked at him, looked at the blank piece of notepaper on his desk, and fell to the floor with a heart attack.

"Luckily, it wasn't fatal," says Messing.

Stalin next proposed a more intriguing task from a dictator's point of view. Messing was taken to an important government office—perhaps inside the Kremlin. Three different sets of security guards were ordered not to let Messing leave the room or the building. He had no exist pass.

"I fulfilled the assignment without difficulty," says Messing, "but when I stepped outside onto the street I couldn't resist turning and waving at the high government official watching from the top floor window of the room I just left."

We'd thought a lot of things about Stalin, but never that he was a psychic researcher. These extraordinary accounts weren't smuggled out of Russia in a whisper. The Soviets themselves published them in the important journal, *Science and Religion*, as part of Messing's autobiography. *About Myself*.[119] The mere fact that they passed both the political censors and the official atheistic policy of this influential magazine is in itself good evidence for their validity. In *About Myself* Messing remarks he had many encounters with Stalin.

Communist scientists who know the celebrated psychic,

as well as friends of one of Stalin's granddaughters, told us of another experiment designed by Stalin. Without permission, without a pass, Messing had to enter Stalin's dacha at Kuntsevo. This was like asking someone to dress up as Batman and saunter unmolested into the vaults of Fort Knox. Guards almost as thick as the shrubbery surrounded the country house. A platoon of bodyguards hovered near Stalin. All the staff members at his residences were officially members of the secret police.

Several days later, as Stalin worked in his dacha at a large dining table loaded with official documents and papers, a slightly built, dark haired man entered the dacha without attracting any special attention. Stalin's bodyguards stood back respectfully. The domestic staff made way.

The man walked down a hallway past several rooms, all furnished identically with a sofa, rug, and table. He stopped at the doorway of the room where Stalin sat reading. Stalin looked up astonished. Wolf Messing stood in front of him!

How did he do it?

"I mentally suggested to the guards and servants, 'I am Beria. I am Beria,'" Messing explains.

Lavrenti Beria, the deservedly infamous head of the Soviet secret police, was a constant visitor at Stalin's dacha. The curly haired Messing didn't look anything like Beria. He didn't even bother to assume the Beria trademark, glittering pince-nez.

News of Stalin's experiments with Messing spread widely through the upper echelons of Moscow society. Some feared Messing was a "dangerous man" but evidently Stalin didn't think so. The final outcome of the "checkup" was that Messing received permission from the "highest authorities" to tour freely through the entire Soviet Union.

Not just to Stalin, but to a vast number of Soviets, Wolf Grigorevich Messing has been a sparkler, a sort of superstar known to all levels of society, a legendary figure, for more than a quarter of a century. Messing is a household name even to celebrated scientists. Russia's Nobel Prize-winning chemist, Dr. Nikolai Semyonov, Vice President of the Academy of Sciences of the USSR, said in *Science and Religion,* in September, 1966, "It is very important to scientifically study the psychic phenomena of sensitives like Wolf Messing."

There is good reason for the legend beyond the "tested by Stalin" endorsement. Wolf Messing is a remarkable man who got his psychic way during the most repressive years of Soviet rule. As the government proclaimed in all directions that telepathy did not exist and that no psychics (called "rogues") existed in Russia, paradoxically they also employed Wolf Messing through their Ministry of Culture, just as they would employ any other entertainer. When other telepathists were wary of even broaching the topic in public, when scientists had to research ESP secretly, Messing almost nightly gave public performances that included telepathy. He called his act "Psychological Experiments" and toured almost every city in the USSR. During the most vicious Stalin years, when you'd imagine the last thing a Russian wanted was to have someone read his mind, crowds lined up for Messing's telepathic act. Rumor had it that he could even do miracles.

Much about Messing's life seems miraculous. Fleeing the Nazis, he crossed into Russia hidden in a wagonload of hay in November 1939. A Polish immigrant, a Jew, a psychic—any sensible person would have said he had nothing going for him. Three years later, as a private Soviet citizen, he was able to personally buy and present two fighter planes to the Soviet Air Force. Fur-hatted Russian officers were honored to pose for news photos with citizen Wolf at a special ceremony at which they received the planes—each with the name W. G. Messing written in large letters on the fuselage. This would be a success story in the West; in the Soviet Union, it's "miraculous."

If he hadn't been the "extraordinary" Wolf Messing, he wouldn't have lived to take Russia by storm.

On the first of September 1939, Hitler's Army invaded Poland. For Messing to stay in Poland any longer was impossible. In a Warsaw theater in 1937, in the presence of a thousand people, Messing had predicted, "Hitler will die if he turns toward the East."

"The Fascist Führer was sensitive to this prophecy, and in general to mysticism of all kinds," says Messing. The psychic Eric Hanussen had already been killed by the Nazis for knowing too much about their plans. When word of Messing's prophecy reached Hitler, he put a price of 200,000 marks on the telepathist's head.

On the day of the invasion Messing went into hiding in a Warsaw meat locker. However, he was seized when he ventured into the street one evening. The Nazi officer scrutinized his face—then examined a small booklet he had in his pocket containing photos of wanted people. Grabbing him by the hair, the officer growled, "Who are you?"

"I'm an artist . . ."

"You're Wolf Messing! It is you who predicted the death of our Führer!" He took a step back and, still holding Messing's hair, punched him in the jaw.

"It was the blow of a master torturer," says Messing. "I lost along with a great deal of blood, six teeth.

"At the police station I realized either I leave Poland instantly, or I die," says Messing. Using all his phenomenal powers of mind, he says [119] he compelled all the police who were in the station at that moment to assemble in one room. All, including the chief and the sentry guarding the exit, began to feel a strange urge to go to that particular room in the station. "When, responding to my will, the police had all gathered in that room, I lay entirely motionless, as if dead. Then, quickly, I ran into the corridor. Instantly, before they could come to, I slid the iron bolt on the door. Now I had to hurry."

Fortunately, Messing made the Russian border that night. His father, his brothers, and his entire family were slaughtered in the Warsaw Ghetto. At Brest Litovsk in Russia there were thousands of other refugees fleeing the Nazis. The Soviet Union was a country unknown to Messing—he didn't even speak the language.

At the Ministry of Culture he applied for a job. "We don't want fortunetellers or sorcerers in this country," they said. "And telepathy doesn't exist!"

It would be necessary to change their minds Messing decided. Perhaps a demonstration of his abilities would help to show them this was no trick. Whatever this demonstration was, the manager of the Ministry of Culture immediately hired him, and his Soviet saga began. His first job was touring Byelorussia.

Messing's stage show rarely touches on personal affairs or politics. Members of the audience are simply instructed to think of some task they'd like Messing to perform. The sealed instructions are delivered to a jury also selected by the audience.

"Think only of what you want me to do," Messing advised a volunteer at a recent demonstration before a group of medical people.[67] Without touching a concentrating doctor, Messing began to walk slowly up and down the aisles, orienting himself like a human radar system. He paused before Row P, then focused on his target, a man in seat 4. Messing went up to him, reached into the man's pocket, and took out scissors and a sponge. He held them up for the audience to see. "I don't think I'd better cut the sponge," he said. He took a piece of chalk and sketched the outlines of an animal on the sponge. "It's a dog!" he announced.

The jury checked his telepathic assignment. The medical man had wanted Messing to find his friend and cut a dog out of the sponge in his pocket. Messing picked up the thought, but decided to spare the doctor his sponge.

"People's thoughts come to me as pictures," Messing, now in his seventies, explains. "I usually see visual images of a specific action or place." He constantly emphasizes there is nothing supernatural, nothing mysterious about the ability to read thoughts. Telepathy, he insists, is simply a matter of harnessing natural laws. "I first put myself into a certain state of relaxation in which I experience a gathering of feeling and strength. Then it's easy to achieve telepathy. I can pick up just about any thought. If I touch the sender, it helps me sort out the thought being sent from the general 'noise.' But contact isn't a necessity for me." [118]

Some scientists who saw Messing's show-stoppers became convinced he must be getting the message through ideomotor movements—slight, unconscious muscle movements, facial expressions, changes in breathing—that can tip off a trained observer. If Messing holds the wrist of the sender, as he occasionally does, unconscious tightening of the musculature could signal which way to walk or when to stop, the scientists hypothesized.[154]

"When I'm blindfolded," Messing counters, "telepathy is even easier for me. If I don't see the sender, I'm able to concentrate totally on perceiving his thought."

According to Messing's autobiography in *Science and Religion,* the ideomotor theory got associated with him in 1950 when the Philosophy Department of the Soviet Academy of Sciences was pressed to explain him in terms of the materialistic Communist philosophy. It was the most immobilizing era of the old regime's freeze on thought and life. They had to explain him away safely, and so the Academy came up with the "ideomotor theory."

"What a pity that this explanation henceforth was printed on the program accompanying my performances," says Messing. "It was due to the cult of personality" [i.e., Stalinism].

The fact that *Science and Religion* published Messing's refutation shows that times have changed. Ideomotor movements can't explain the feats Messing supposedly did for Stalin, or telepathy when he's rooms away from the sender. "The ideomotor theory doesn't explain how I receive abstract ideas either. I find complex, original thoughts easier to get, perhaps because they're more interesting," says Messing.

How clearly the thought comes through depends, Messing says, on the ability of the sender to concentrate. If a crowd of conflicting thoughts stream through the sender's mind, the thought-reader's impression will blur—just as the picture used to blur when someone moved in an old-fashioned time photograph. "Curiously," says Messing, "the thoughts of the deaf and dumb are the easiest to get, possibly because they think much more visually than the rest of us."

A reporter visiting Messing's hotel room in Norilsk during one of his incessant tours noted some of the gifts showered on the Soviet sensitive by his many fans: bouquets of flowers, a beautiful handpainted box, a tribute from the people of Norilsk; on the couch, the paws of a shaggy bear, presented by the Arctic people of Igarka.

The reporter asked if he could have a private performance. Messing donned a tight-looking blindfold. The reporter suggested telepathically that Messing locate a copy of the magazine *Ogonyok* and find in it a portrait of Lenin. Further, he commanded him mentally to determine whether the picture was a painting of Lenin or a photo of any actor playing Lenin. Still blindfolded, Messing brought him the magazine opened at the correct page. "It's an original portrait," Messing said.

"He was completely right!" the reporter recalls. "He could also distinguish the colors of the pages of the magazine, without looking at them while I observed carefully." The writer sounds a little overwhelmed. He didn't even wonder if Messing could have peeked from under his blindfold. But that doesn't explain how the psychic knew what the mental command was.[253]

The Norilsk reporter probably became a celebrity with his friends, for Wolf Messing is known to almost everyone in Russia. The head of an Intourist Office in Moscow talked about Messing's talent to us as if she were discussing the playing of Oistrakh or the dancing of Pavlova. "I've heard about Wolf Messing since I was a little girl," she told us. Had she gone to see him a number of times? Well no. "It's because I *know* he is so good that I haven't gone. I don't like the idea of someone looking into my thoughts," she finally admitted.

Messing is constantly asked just how he can look into thoughts. "That's like trying to explain sight in a country of the blind. We can register your brain waves on an EEG. But we still don't have an instrument except a human being that can register your thoughts. Perhaps telepathy works on electromagnetic fields or some field we haven't yet discovered. Dr. Nikolai Kozyrev, the celebrated astrophysicist, thinks telepathy might even be linked to the gravitational field," he says.

"Science must take telepathy away from mysticism and find out how it works. Because it *does* work! Some years ago nothing was known about radio waves. Why can't telepathy bring us similar miracles? It surprises me that scientists don't realize, or don't want to realize, that telepathy happens all the time in their own lives. Isn't this like the savants of the middle ages, afraid to waver from the doctrines of Aristotle, refusing to admit that electricity exists although they saw lightning all the time?"

Messing's own psychic lightning flashed early in life. "I was born on September 10, 1899, in Russia," he says, "to be precise, on the territory of the Russian Empire, in the tiny town of Góra Kalwaria, near Warsaw."

In other words, Messing is Polish, coming from a small Jewish village like those fabled by Sholom Aleichem. Messing as a child was presented to the famous writer. "You will have a shining future!" Aleichem supposedly said. "But it was not a prophecy," admits Messing. "Aleichem told that to every second little boy."

Messing's family was bleakly poor but exceedingly religious, and by age six, thanks to his superb memory, Wolf knew the Talmud extremely well. The rabbi decided Wolf must go to a religious school to be educated for the rabbinate. The family was delighted at this opportunity for their son, but Wolf refused point-blank to go.

"It was then that the first miracle in my life occurred," Messing recalls. "My father had sent me to the store for a package of cigarettes. It was already dusk. The porch of our little wooden house was in darkness. Suddenly on the steps there appeared a gigantic, dark figure clad in a white garment.

" 'My son! From above, I am a messenger to you . . . to foretell your future! Go to the school! Your prayers will please heaven! . . .' The vision vanished.

"It is difficult to convey the impression these words made on the nervous, mystical feelings of a young boy," Messing says. "They were like the flash of lightning, the crash of thunder. I fell to the ground and lost consciousness.

"When I came to, my father and mother were reading prayers over me. I remember their troubled faces. But once I recovered, they became calmer. I recounted what had happened. Father, pretending to cough, uttered:

" 'Thus He wishes it. . . .'

"My mother was silent.

"After this amazing incident, I could no longer resist," Messing says. He dutifully went to the religious school in another village.

But the boy was not happy with a life of prayers. At age eleven, with eighteen cents in his pocket, he set out for the unknown world on the first passing train. He crept under a seat in a half-empty coach and fell asleep. "Naturally I had no ticket." Inevitably the conductor arrived to punch tickets.

" 'Young man'—I can still hear his voice in my ears—'your ticket . . .'

"Nervously, tensely I handed him a worthless piece of paper torn from a newspaper. Our glances met. With all my strength I willed that he would take this piece of paper as a ticket.

"The conductor took it and in a strange way turned it over in his hands. I shrank back, . . . willing him. He took the piece of newspaper in the heavy jaws of the ticket punch. Handing the 'ticket' back to me he asked, 'Since you have a ticket, why are you under the seat? Get up! Within two hours we'll be in Berlin.'

"This was the first time my powers of mental suggestion were manifested," Messing reports.

Since then Messing has done many well-witnessed demonstrations of his ability to "cloud men's minds." (Messing had a rapt pupil in Karl Nikolaiev. Karl also attempted to cloud the minds of train conductors in order to ride free. In *Moscow Pravda,*[81] Karl confessed he's often worked the see-Russia-by-ESP plan. He hoped that society would excuse these youthful misdemeanors, for though he rode the trains a number of times, Nikolaiev says he was caught and fined only once.)

In Berlin Wolf Messing got a job as a messenger in the Jewish quarter. Taking a parcel to a Berlin suburb one day, he fainted from hunger on a bridge. Friendless, a long way from home, he was taken to a hospital. No pulse—no respiration. Body cold. Messing was taken to the morgue. He would have been buried in a common grave if it hadn't been for a medical student who chanced to notice a very faint heartbeat in Messing. It was almost undetectable, beat rarely, but there was a beat.

Even as a "corpse" Messing had a theatrical aura. Following the best horror movie scripts, pulse and heartbeat gradually flickered back in the body and three days later he came to. In the hospital Dr. Abel, a psychiatrist and neuropathologist, explained that Messing's condition was a very rare case of lethargy.

"I not only owe my life to Dr. Abel, but also the discovery and development of my psychic abilities," Messing writes in his autobiography.

"You have the ability of self-induced catalepsy as well as paranormal ability," Abel told him. Catalepsy is the kind of suspended animation that highly trained yogis sometimes demonstrate. Dr. Abel inspired Messing with confidence in his psychic powers. With the help of Dr. Schmidt, a psychiatric colleague, and Schmidt's wife, Abel trained Messing in telepathy.

It was a turning point for the boy. Abel found him an impresario, Mr. Tselmeister, who got Wolf a job in the Berlin Panopticon (waxworks). The "Wonder-boy" Wolf

Messing climbed into a crystal coffin, induced in himself the state of catalepsy, and lay there like a corpse every weekend from Friday till Sunday evening.

"I must have spent at least three solid months of my life in a gold coffin," says Messing, "and for this I was paid all of five marks a day."

On his four free days each week he trained his psychic abilities. Wandering in the marketplace, he tried to "hear" the thoughts of German country people—usually about their homes, families, marriages, prices of products. Often as he "listened" to people's thoughts, he heard the answers to their problems and would tell them, "Don't worry about this or that, all will be well." Then he told them what was going to happen.

Astounded, the people supposedly later came back to report he was correct. He studied and trained his psi abilities for two years. Out of his meager earnings he also paid special tutors for lessons in regular academic subjects and he read voraciously.

Messing's next assignment was the famous Berlin Wintergarten, where he played the role of a fakir. Able to anesthetize various parts of his body at will, he showed no pain when enormous needles were stuck through his chest. Then he acted as a "miracle detective" locating jewels and valuables hidden among the audience.

In 1915, despite the war, the impresario arranged a show for Messing in Vienna. He was the "hit of the season." While in Vienna the sixteen-year-old Wolf starred in what is certainly one of the most delicious psychic experiments on record.

Albert Einstein invited young Wolf to his apartment. Messing still recalls with astonishment the number of books —"they were everywhere, starting with the hall." In Einstein's study Wolf was introduced to the founder of psychoanalysis, Sigmund Freud, who once remarked that if he'd his life to live over again, he would have devoted it to psychic research. So intrigued was Freud with Messing's psychic powers he decided to do a number of tests with him. Freud acted as inductor.

"To this day I still remember Freud's mental command," says Messing. "Go to the bathroom cupboard and pick up some tweezers. Return to Albert Einstein, pull out from his luxuriant moustache three hairs."

After locating the tweezers, Messing gingerly went up to the celebrated mathematician and, begging his pardon, explained to him what his scientist friend wanted him to do. Einstein smiled and turned his cheek to Messing. Freud must have smiled too, because young Messing carried out his mental command faultlessly.[119]

During the next ten years Messing toured the world—Japan, Brazil, India, Argentina, Asia, Australia. In Europe he performed in all the major capitals—Paris, London, Rome, Stockholm, Geneva, Warsaw.

In 1927 in India, Messing met Gandhi. They discussed politics and then Gandhi became Messing's sender for a psychic test. The mental command he gave Messing was a simple one. "Take a flute from the table and give it to one of the people in the room." Messing did so. The man put the flute to his lips and began to play. Suddenly a basket in the room trembled and began to move. A motley-colored snake emerged from the basket and swayed in rhythm to the music.

Having taken the opportunity to observe Indian yogis during his trip, Messing says, "The yogis could stay in a self-induced cataleptic state for weeks, whereas I could not stay in this condition more than three days." [120]

For ten years Messing worked in Poland, achieving great success as a clairvoyant, telepathist, and mind reader. Aside from stage performances of telepathy, he was frequently called in as a psychic sleuth. One of these cases involved Count Czartoryski of the wealthy Polish family long active in affairs of state. The count offered Messing 250,000 zlotys if he could locate the missing family jewels. Police and detectives had searched for months without results.

Messing was flown to the count's castle in the count's private plane. Messing's psychic sense led him to suspect a small boy, the son of one of the servants. Inspecting the toys in the child's room, Messing asked the count to have an enormous stuffed toy bear opened up. When the toy beast was cut open, out flashed bits of colored glass, bottles, Christmas tree ornaments, gilded teaspoons, and the count's long-lost family jewels worth 800,000 zlotys! Apparently attracted by anything that glittered, the little boy had taken the jewels and other shining objects and slipped them inside the stuffing of his bear.

The grateful count offered Messing an even larger reward. "I refused," said Messing. The Jewish psychic asked only one thing in return—that the count use his influence in the Polish government to have a law infringing the rights of Jews abolished. The count agreed. Within two weeks he fulfilled his promise and the law was removed.

Messing also looked into spiritualism. "I belonged to a mystic society, although I am of course an atheist myself. At that time spiritualism was very popular all over. The spiritualists thought skeptics gave off 'negative fluids' which blocked contact with the souls of the dead."

At the seances Messing frequented messages came by rappings and table tipping. Some of the mediums he knew called up spirits who wrote in chalk on blackboards; others called up guitar-playing ghosts.

"When the famous Polish medium Jan Gusyk was with us, we called up the 'spirits' of Napoleon and Alexander of Macedonia!" Messing writes. He admits the spiritualists helped him sharpen his psychic power, but today Messing cites Frederick Engels: "Spiritism is the most savage of all superstitions." For himself Messing says, "I'm convinced spiritualism was all charlatanry." [120]

Spiritualism might be mortal heresy to the good Communist, but it materialized not too long ago in the world's most unlikely setting: the Twentieth Congress of the Communist Party in Moscow, 1961. This was the congress at which Nikita Khrushchev exposed and repudiated the political sins of Stalin. Darya Lazurkina, an elderly delicate woman, rose to address the assembly. Long ago, as an idealistic girl, she'd known Lenin and served as one of his most ardent disciples. In 1937, like most other old Bolsheviks, she was sucked up by the purges and deposited in a slave labor camp. Darya Lazurkina survived for nineteen and a half years in the camps, "because," she told the delegates, "Lenin was in my heart. He sustained and advised me. Yesterday," the still passionate old woman went on, "I again consulted Lenin. He came. It was as if he were there in person before me. Lenin said, 'It is unpleasant for me to lie next to Stalin in the Mausoleum, he caused such harm!' "

The Soviet paper *Izvestia* didn't report Lenin's visitation. It did report that Miss Lazurkina's remarks led to "thunderous and stormy applause," while *Time* magazine found that the final days of the congress were "surrounded by a strange air of magic and the supernatural." Although probably not at Lenin's spirit directive, Stalin's body was soon removed from the Mausoleum in Red Square.[295a]

Because of his buffets with fate Messing retains an ongoing sympathy for people getting hard knocks in life. "I am always willing to use my gift to help people who have misfortunes," he says. His ability to powerfully implant thought in others, he says, can be used in an upbeat way to inspire people who are dangerously depressed. "I often succeed with forceful mental suggestion in giving courage, confidence, and strength to people who are ready to commit suicide."

On tour and at home Messing also spends spare time investigating psychics and exposing frauds. In Warsaw Wolf once saw a fakir try to perform his own kind of cataleptic trance. "The man lay like a plank between chairs as doctors listened for the heartbeat. There was none. It seemed to be catalepsy, but I knew it wasn't. I asked my doctor to go over the fakir. It turned out the man wore a steel corset so he could support the weight of another person on top of him. Two steel balls clanked onto the floor. He'd hidden them in his armpits to stop circulation and cut off any pulse in his wrists.

"When scientists come up against charlatans like these they decide all psychics are frauds." Messing complains. He goes after frauds more with the ire of an artist defending his muse than with the dispassionate probe of the scientist.

Soviet parapsychologists would like to probe deeper into the great Messing himself, and many scientists have been willing to observe his experiments, to serve as senders or members of the jury. They drew on the theories of Pavlov to try to explain what they saw. Contemporary psi researchers see the new discoveries about Karl Nikolaiev's psychic power as a partial explanation of Messing's talents.

Like Jeane Dixon in Washington, Messing has never found time to go to the scientists' labs. "He always promises that one day, when he has time, he'll come to our labs, but he never comes." The scientists we met in Russia and Czechoslovakia knew Messing personally and respected his ability. "Of course he has psychic talent. Maybe not all the time, maybe not every number on a program, but he's shown enough of it through the years." [11] They would like to test him, but "Messing's over seventy now, not very well, and he uses up tremendous energy traveling with his show. Besides, he's an artist; he has the artistic temperament—very emotional." Which is often the clinker in parapsychology. The bold, bright-colored, almost prima donna personalities that seem to release the psychic radiant, are the sort of personalities most difficult to attune to the antiseptics of the lab.

Is Wolf Messing genuine? The scientists we met in psi research apparently think so. Ludmila Svinka-Zielinski, a seasoned observer of the Soviet scene and a contributor to *Atlas,* (the foreign correspondents' news magazine,) wrote about Messing referring to his autobiography, including his Stalin tests, stage performances, demonstrations for international celebrities, and psychic details of his own life: "It is important to remember that under the conditions prevailing in the USSR anything done or written by such a controversial personality as Messing had to be scrutinized, criticized, and subjected to constant censorship, so that he could not get away with fraud, attempted fraud, or anything that even approached a vain boast. In fact, we can be convinced that to survive and to exist in the environment on such a level, Wolf Messing must be thoroughly authentic." [407]

There is one talent in particular of Messing's that would be worth studying, an ability that most famous psychics, if they have it, don't mention. It's hard not to be intrigued, as Stalin was, by Messing's seeming ability to confuse and distort another person's thoughts telepathically. Searching for ways to control someone else's bodily reactions and thought has been a preoccupation of Soviet psychology and parapsychology since the 1920s.

Messing has a gift which is not mentioned in his published biography. Messing has long been a practicing prophet, although this is unknown to many of his fans in Russia where, until recently, prophecy was not openly discussed. Despite the ban on foretelling, Messing's prophecies have, at times, caused reverberations in high Soviet circles. In 1940 Soviet-German relations were cloudless. The year before, Stalin had signed the nonaggression pact with Hitler. Nevertheless, in 1940 Messing gave a speech at a private Moscow club. He prophesied, "Soviet tanks will roll into Berlin!"

Word of Messing's declaration leaked out, creating a sensation among the Communist elite. Unfortunately, this was one aspect of Messing's power that Stalin didn't look into. (A year later Stalin still refused to believe Hitler would invade, even when Nazi tanks had been rolling on Russian soil for over a day.) But if Stalin overlooked Messing's prediction, the Germans did not. The German Embassy immediately lodged a protest. After all, Hitler was still furious over Messing's prediction of his death. The Soviet diplomatic corps huddled in confusion. At last, after long consultation, they stated, "We cannot be expected to answer for the prophecies of Wolf Messing."

Again, in 1943, Messing ventured publicly to make another prophecy. The Baltic, Byelorussia, the Ukraine, the Crimea, all were in the hands of the Nazis. The end of the war was not yet in sight. Messing himself had been evacuated to safety in Siberia. In Novosibirsk, the famous science city of Siberia, Messing spoke before a packed audience at the Opera Theater. He predicted that the war would end in May 1945, probably within the first week of the month.

"My ability to see the future may seem to contradict the materialist understanding of the world. But there is not a particle of the unknowable or supernatural about precognition," Messing says reassuringly. "There is not only the logical, scientific way of gaining knowledge, there is also *direct knowledge*—precognition. Only our indistinct ideas about the meaning of time and its relation to space, and the past, present, and future, make it inexplicable at present." Precognition, which many think implies a ready-made destiny, has always been a horror to Communist ideologists who struggle hard to bring the Russian peasantry out of a swamp of superstition and fatalistic defeatism.

"Of course, there's free will," Messing continues. "But there are patterns. The future is shaped from the past and the present. There are regular patterns of connections between them. The 'mechanism' of these connections is far from being known by most people, but I clearly know myself that it exists."

How does the future come to Messing? "After an effort of will, I suddenly see the final result of some event flash before me. The mechanism of 'direct knowledge' by-passes the logical cause and effect chain and reveals to the psychic only the final, concluding link of the chain." [115]

The censors may not have been wholly reassured by Messing's matter of fact "explanation" of precognition. After the appearance of an announcement that Messing's full autobiography would be printed by Sovietskaya Rossiya in 1967, the book was suddenly withdrawn, although it may be circulating in manuscript form. Maybe prophecy and the revelation of too many "wonders" bothered some well-placed people. Maybe Messing told too many stories involving upper echelons of the Party. (One wonders if Stalin ever put Messing to more practical, political use.) Maybe the cancellation was just another beat in the endless Soviet two-step, thaw and freeze. What we do know of Messing's account of himself indicates that the rest of it could be anything but dull.

Messing is a great entertainer. This is perhaps his biggest secret. It explains why, even when prestigious scientists like Vasiliev found open interest in telepathy forbidden to them, the ever-confident Wolf Messing junketed across the country giving gala performances of his psychological experiment—telepathy.

As to the remarkable powers of the human mind that he has shown to so many people, Messing has a prediction: "The time is coming when man will understand all these phenomena. There is nothing strange. Only what is not yet commonplace."

5

POLITICAL SMOKE SCREENS AND PARAPSYCHOLOGY

The story of Nelya Mikhailova, the PK medium is exceptional and bizarre and much more than the story of any other psychic in Russia exemplifies the political turmoil and shadowy machinations that can sweep Soviet parapsychology and Soviet science. We were scheduled to see scientific films of the amazing Nelya in action the first day of the conference in the "House of Peace and Friendship," a miniature castle of studded stone and candy-cane columns near a glassy new Moscow business district.

The conference hall with its gold chandeliers and white paneled ceiling might once have been an elegant ballroom. Well over a hundred Soviets waited. Some had jetted to Moscow from the far-flung edges of the USSR. There was a large official delegation from Bulgaria, a more amorphous Czech group. Aside from the two English delegates and ourselves, there were five other Westerners. Dr. J. G. Pratt of the University of Virginia was the only American scientist to attend. Our small group of nine sat at the head of a long horseshoe table. A roomful of Russians gazed at us with clear-faced, almost ferocious anticipation.

Dr. Vassili Efimov, a biologist now in his eighties, welcomed the guests. A very small, white-haired man, Efimov spoke quickly and without notes. He warmly recalled his old friend, Dr. Vasiliev, who had pioneered ESP in Russia despite the vast difficulties of the war and the Stalin regime. Since 1959 Vasiliev had sparked two ESP labs in Leningrad, and after his death in 1966 his students continued his work. "Now they are researching PK, telepathy, thought photography, dowsing," said Dr. Efimov. He hinted of the recent discovery of a radiation from the human body that might lead to a new understanding of psi events. But Dr. Efimov seemed more concerned about something else.

"We must widen the consciousness of humanity. It is *vital* that the paranormal powers hidden in humans be used for good."

Scarcely had reports by Western delegates begun when we noticed copies of the Soviet newspaper *Pravda* [22] going from hand to hand around the room. Even the unquenchable interest of the Russians in hearing about the inaccessible West seemed to be deflected by whatever was in the paper. Worried glances followed in the wake of *Pravda* as copies wended their way to the front of the hall.

"It's about Nelya Mikhailova!" one of the interpreters whispered, straining to catch a glimpse over someone's shoulder. Recent news reports had said Nelya Mikhailova (Mi-khīl-ova) could "command" bread, matches, cigarettes, or apples to jump off a table. According to Soviet scientists her PK power (ability to move matter at a distance) had moved and stopped the pendulum of a wall clock, moved plastic cases, water pitchers weighing a pound, and an assortment of dishes, cups, and glasses. And all without touching the objects. Along with the scientists, reporters from *Moscow Komsomol* and *Moscow Pravda,* published by the city's Communist Party organization, said they'd watched the forty-one-year-old Nelya in action and found "no hidden threads, magnets, or other gimmicks."

Even more extraordinary, the list of scientists investigating Mikhailova read like a "Who's Who" of Soviet science. Chairman of Theoretical Physics at the prestigious Moscow University and holder of the Laureate of the State Prize, Dr. Ya. Terletsky, publicly proclaimed on March 17, 1968, in *Moscow Pravda,* "Mrs. Mikhailova displays a new and unknown form of energy."

Physicists from the Soviet Union's Joint Nuclear Research Institute at Dubna had tested Mikhailova,[162] as had those from the Institute of Physics of the Academy of Sciences of the USSR. The list included Nobel prize winners. The Mendeleyev Institute of Metrology also studied Nelya and stated in *Moscow Pravda* that she had moved aluminum pipes and matches under the strictest test conditions, including observation on closed-circuit television. They could give no explanation of "the phenomena of the movement of objects." [80]

"Dr. Vasiliev did many experiments with Mrs. Mikhailova. She was one of his major interests and he worked with her until his death in 1966," Edward Naumov told us. Other scientists we talked to confirmed Vasiliev's investigation of Nelya.[184] It was an interesting bit of information because two of the very few Americans who are expert in both ESP and Soviet affairs had said they'd heard of no work done by Vasiliev in the last six years of his life. "If there is anything, it must be secret." A Soviet scientist who had visited American ESP labs in 1965 told anyone willing to listen that Dr. Vasiliev was not involved in any research at all, his lab was closed. "He's simply writing books now."

More Leningrad scientists than Vasiliev were intrigued by Nelya. Dr. Genady Sergeyev, the mathematician, announced that his studies of Mikhailova revealed some startling discoveries about the human organism.

A number of interested scientists in Moscow told us that even Dr. Peter Kapitsa, a developer of the atomic and hydrogen bombs for the Soviet Union, had seen fit to drop in on one test with Mikhailova.

Some of Naumov's comments perhaps reflect the reasoning behind this high-powered interest in a Leningrad housewife. "Personally, I think Mrs. Mikhailova's talent is very exciting. Right now I'm even more interested in PK than telepathy. I believe we're on the way to discovering the psychophysical basis of PK in our study of Mrs. Mikhailova's remarkable powers. If we can find the laws governing this energy it would have *tremendous* practical application."

A very famous Soviet, an Academician and Hero of Socialist Labor, Professor A. Mikhulin might agree with Naumov. "We've witnessed the discovery of a new force which people possess!" he stated after studying Nelya.[193]

There was something about this Russian woman that also interested scientists from other Communist countries, enough to make them fly into Leningrad to examine her feats personally. Like the scientific support, political support also seemed to be from a high level. Dr. E. Sitkovsky, Professor at the Academy of Social Sciences which is attached to the Communist Party's Central Committee, the real ruling elite of Russia, stated publicly, "Mikhailova's PK has nothing to do with mysticism. When a person thinks, he radiates energy and the energy is stronger in some people. PK is a physical-physiological fact." [193, 267]

Evidently it was no amateur occultists' group involved in the Nelya Mikhailova case. Not since the end of the nineteenth century in England and France had so many outstanding scientists looked into a subject as seemingly far out as psychokinesis. Moreover, these were scientists dedicated to the tenets of Communist materialism. Not all of these scientists were doing research with Mikhailova, but they'd been interested and broad-minded enough to take a look at her.

The translator beside us struggled for another look at *Pravda*. "It's a vicious attack on Mikhailova!" she said. "They've attacked some of the scientists who've worked with her too!"

A brief morning break was declared to digest the news. "This is very serious," Naumov said. "We've been forbidden to show the Mikhailova film and Mrs. Mikhailova has been forbidden to attend the conference."

"Word has come down," Russians kept saying, but no one ever specified from whom or from where.

Our translator was fuming. "This article is full of lies. They call Mikhailova a fraud and a swindler. They're saying she cheated the public out of five thousand rubles. The last story that went round had Mikhailova selling imaginary refrigerators door to door. They're just trying to make trouble. It's all nonsense. This always happens when something new appears here."

Finally we got a glimpse of the prominent feature article in *Pravda* ourselves. We read about the "sorceress" Nelya, "who far surpassed Gogol's fairytale character Patsyuk, in hobnobbing with unclean powers. Mikhailova performs her dextrous tricks with the help of magnets, concealed," the writer said coyly, "in 'intimate places' both higher and lower than the waist." How magnets even in intimate places managed to move nonmagnetic things like glass, eggs, apples, and bread was not explained. The author, we learned, had never seen Mikhailova. He'd decided PK was impossible so she *must* be using magnets.

Russian scientists milled about uncertainly. Naumov was in close consultation with various advisors. "We're being thrown out of the House of Friendship," someone told us. "The entire second day of the conference is canceled."

Compared to psychic society mettings we'd been to in the West, which tended to be as calm as chamber music concerts, Soviet ESP meetings were a startling contrast. We recalled the conference invitation sent us by the Soviets. According to a typographical error in the English translation, we were being invited by the "Union of Soviet Societies of *Fiend*ship." Maybe it had been accurate after all, considering the savage "welcome" given the conference by *Pravda.*

The newspaper attack on Nelya Mikhailova, published the opening morning of the conference, was a premeditated "greeting." *Pravda,* the official Communist Party organ, is supposedly controlled by the Brezhnev clique in the government. Articles do not happen in the six-page daily by chance. Less than a week before, another Russian ESP meeting went on in Moscow. Neither *Pravda* nor anyone else attacked it. Only Nelya, the star attraction of this gathering with foreigners, was singled out.

Other storm signals were flying that the attitude toward cooperation with outsiders was changing in one nameless quarter or another. In Leningrad, at the Bekhterev Brain Institute where world-famous Dr. Vasiliev had headed the Physiology Department for years, they told us they knew nothing about the eminent scientist or his work. Vasiliev's disciple and successor at the University of Leningrad, Dr. Pavel Gulyaiev, told us. "I'm not in parapsychology anymore, my institute is closed for repairs, nothing's going on, and besides, I'm sick."

Six months later Dr. Gulyaiev announced that his research team has developed a device that can detect and record the human aura and the auras of animals and even insects. Soviets have found other auras too, but according to the Soviet press release, the "aura" Gulyaiev found is a complex electric field around the body—a sort of ghostly second self. They hope to use the "electrical aura" to diagnose illness.[330] (See Appendix A, 1.) Other Communist scientists report Gulyaiev's laboratory has been hard at work for over four years studying telepathy between twins, telepathic hypnosis, and control of machines by psi.

A Leningrad friend of ours told us a government directive had circulated the university staff in February 1968. "Do not talk to foreigners" was the gist of it.

We had hoped we wouldn't have to mention politics much in this book. After all, why should you have to bring in the machinations of governments, particularly the complex writhings of the Kremlin, when you're talking about psychic research. But as we traveled and talked to Communist scientists in many centers, something we already knew was impressed even more strongly on us—"everything in Russia is political."

Pravda or not, our conference quickly resumed. Formal reading of Soviet scientific reports had evidently been shelved. Instead, with no explanation, a number of Russian scientists gave informal talks, prefaced with, "I am here only as a private person. I do not represent my place of work or any group."

The same political "freezes" and "thaws" that characterize the Soviet literary scene can, at time, penetrate the sciences. Fifteen years ago cybernetics was heresy according to the ideologists. Now they hail it as "the hope of Russia." Was parapsychology undergoing one of these congealing phases? Or was the opposition just a smoke screen for the benefit of us Westerners?

The French magazine *Planète* in July 1968 reported an important ESP conference held in Moscow the previous February. Many of the USSR's most outstanding scientists doing research on the paranormal were there. "Explosive!" was *Planète*'s assessment. "Soviet science seems to have taken the lead in research on parapsychology!" At this meeting leading Russian scientists revealed wide-ranging, up-to-the-minute work going on in many centers on telepathy. (Their findings are detailed later in this book.) The Soviet's own press agency, Novosti, wrote of this conference, "It is clear that in the USSR official science is actively and passionately inclined henceforth toward the enigmas of parapsychology."

The Soviet Novosti looked forward to the conference we were now at. "It will show *all* the important tests done by very eminent physicists such as Dr. Ya. Terletsky and Dr. N. Kobozev, not only in telepathy but also in other areas of parapsychology."[158]

So it seems parapsychology was very much alive and flourishing not long before June.

Apparently, there had been more than one problem

however just in getting the Mikhailova film to our conference. A Russian acquaintance alluded to some strange maneuvering in the weeks before our meeting—"unknown persons" tailing parapsychologists, attempts to steal the Mikhailova film, telephone threats, physical violence.

We began to wonder if the heavy Russian things-go-bump-in-the-night atmosphere wasn't sending imaginations awry. Perhaps it was just coincidence, as the skeptics of ESP always say. Moscow does have robberies and muggings, even if they aren't tallied up in public statistics the way they are in the West. But three other Russians independently came up with the same tales. Who wanted the film? Why? If the Russians knew, they weren't saying. There are, we later learned, forty-six other films on Mikhailova's PK, and Kiev Films was currently producing a movie, *The Secrets of our Brain,* which included Nelya. Scientific papers on PK and ESP had been delivered at well over twenty-six other conferences on parapsychology, all closed to foreigners except one in 1966 when Mikhailova was not discussed.

Had someone decided that Mikhailova was suddenly getting too much publicity at home and in the West? Naumov's film was to give Westerners their first glimpse of the talented Nelya. A Communist from another country, an engineer, told us. "Our grapevine has it that all the trouble was fomented by scientists directed by 'certain' secret Soviet organizations."

What was there about Nelya that caused all the ruckus? To lead to such complications, there had to be something more than the fact that she could supposedly move a sugar bowl across a table.

We found out later that, coinciding with the *Pravda* article attacking her, a campaign of harassing phone calls was launched against Mrs. Mikhailova. This seemed like an organized job. First of all, there are no telephone books in Russia. To obtain a phone number takes a lot of trouble involving lining up at special address booths in the streets. Secondly, the name "Nelya Mikhailova" is a pseudonym. The callers had to know her real name, Ninel Sergeyevna Kulagina, and her address. The crank calls became so numerous and vicious that the scientists finally decided to hide Mrs. Mikhailova in the country outside Leningrad for a while. As a result she could not attend the conference and no foreign visitor could see her.

That first day of the conference, we could only speculate. One Western scientist commented, "There are a great many important Soviet scientists in this field who aren't here. I've read their research reports on ESP in scientific journals." But the Russians who were there decided to make the most of their hours in the House of Peace and Friendship. Fueled only by a few sips of mineral water, the conference rolled straight through from morning until night, with no more stops and no food. Afterward, we were all crowded by fast-talking, eager Russians who wanted to discuss psi, to trade information. Spurred by the crisis, Sheila's knowledge of Russian came back with some degree of fluency. It seemed the Soviets could have easily gone on for another twelve hours.

The Soviets who'd traveled from all over for this meeting were not about to be put off by anybody. As one set of invisible wheels ground the conference to a halt, other wheels began to turn. There was a free hall at the Czech Embassy equipped with a 35mm movie projector. Perhaps there we might be able to see the Mikhailova film as well as a Czech film on the same topic of PK. This plan was decided on for the second day of the conference.

We hadn't expected to hit Czech soil quite so soon on our trip. There was still superficial solidarity between Russia and Czechoslovakia—at least many Czechs seemed to think so. Moving to foreign soil inside the Czech Embassy compound didn't seem quite as peculiar then as it does now, after the Russian invasion of Czechoslovakia.

Even so, it was clear in Russia that all was not well between the two countries. Westerners who asked friendly Soviets on the street for directions on how to get to the Czech Embassy were rewarded with stony glances as their Russian acquaintances turned and stalked off.

As one of the Russian interpreters at the conference said tersely, "This conference will certainly never be reported in Soviet newspapers!" And it wasn't. But Soviet "reporting" didn't stop there.

Vladimir Lvov, a long-time hatchet man in regard to parapsychology, and the journalist who initially envisioned "magnets in intimate places" in Nelya Mikhailova,[113] even tried to unreport the conference in the West. In a letter printed in the British magazine, *New Scientist,* May 25, 1969, Lvov wrote: "There never was any international conference in Moscow at the House of Friendship, presided over by Edward Naumov in June 1968."

It's a funny bit over here. But the group Lvov fronts for is not very funny at all inside Russia. Lvov isn't a fair game opponent who speaks for scientists who think ESP contradicts the laws of their specialties. Lvov represents the ultra-conservative, or to use a plain label, the neo-Stalinist element in Soviet science and politics. They are opposed to any public talk of ESP inside Russia and to any scientific work on the subject being made known. Since we left Russia in the summer of 1968, as everyone knows, the neo-Stalinists have come back hard and heavy.

6

HAVE THE SOVIETS FOUND THE SECRET OF MIND OVER MATTER?

The film projectors churred and at long last we viewed the elusive Mikhailova PK film. Far from the *Pravda* portrait of Mrs. Mikhailova, which placed her somewhere between the Devil's Consort and a Baba Yaga witch (the sorceress famous in Russian fairytales), we saw on the screen a plump, attractive, open-faced young woman with dark, expressive eyes. She could almost have been a relative of cosmonaut Yuri Gagarin, with her typically Slavic features—high cheekbones and turned up nose. Her dark hair was pulled back into a chignon and she wore a sleeveless lace blouse and plain skirt.

The experiments were taking place in Nelya's new apartment in a startling modern, brand-new district on the edge of Leningrad. This district was once part of the front line she had defended during the war.

Nelya, born a decade after the Russian revolution and the turbulent Civil War, was only fourteen when the Nazis invaded and the siege of Leningrad began. Her city itself was the battleground. Nelya, like many Leningrad children, had to become a soldier. With her brother, father, sister, she joined the front lines of the Red Army. Throughout the three-year surrealistic nightmare, when the bread ration per day was about four ounces, the winter temperature sometimes forty degrees below zero, the water and electricity cut off, and the city razed by bombs and artillery fire, Nelya served in Tank T-34 as a radio operator. "She took part bravely in the attack," a Red Army booklet asserts, and still in her teens became senior sergeant of the 226th tank regiment. It was not unusual in Russia during the war for young girls to become sergeants. The hunger in Leningrad lasted for nearly nine hundred days. Later Nelya and almost all her family served in an armored train which helped bring desperately needed provisions to the stricken city. The fighting finally ended for the girl when she was seriously injured by artillery fire. It was bravery like Nelya's on the part of many citizens that earned Leningrad the official title "Hero City."

Now a woman in her forties, Nelya is married to an engineer and has a son currently completing his army training. She recently became a grandmother.

Mrs. Mikhailova was seated at a large, round, white table in front of a lace-curtained window. The Russians said she had already been physically examined by a medical doctor, who had even had her x-rayed to make sure there were no hidden objects or magnets concealed on her person, nor any fragments of shrapnel lodged in her body from her war injury. He found none.

The five man film crew, scientists and reporters moved in closer. Naumov placed on the table in front of Nelya a compass on a wrist-band, a vertical cigarette, a pen top, a small metal cylinder like a saltshaker, and a matchbox picturing a lunar spaceship—a figurative versions of outer space confronting "inner" space. The objects gleamed against the pale table like a still life by Dali, poised on the edge of the supernatural.

Mikhailova's dark eyes concentrated on the compass—the easiest object to warm up on. PK is easier with rotating objects, say Western researchers. With clocks and compasses there's no static friction.

It sometimes takes Mikhailova two to four hours to rev up her supernormal powers, Naumov mentioned in his commentary as we watched the silent film. Nelya held her long fingers parallel to the table about six inches above the compass and began to move her hands in a circular motion. The strain etched the dimples deep in her cheeks. Twenty minutes passed. Her pulse raced to 250 beats a minute. She moved her head from side to side gazing intently at the compass needle. Her hands moved as though she were conducting some unseen orchestra. And then, as if the atoms in the compass needle were tuned in to her, the needle shivered. Slowly it began to spin counterclockwise, turning like the second hand of a clock. Then the entire compass, plastic case, leather strap, and all, began to whirl.

As the entire compass spun like a carousel, the lines under

Mikhailova's eyes darkened and the wrinkles on her forehead deepened with the intense strain. She fell back exhausted.

"How much power she has depends on weather conditions, too," Naumov told us. "Her PK power diminishes in stormy weather."

In the film, Naumov scattered a whole boxful of matches on the table, a foot or so away from Nelya. He placed a small nonmagnetic metal cylinder and a matchbox near them.

"She is selective," said Naumov. "She can move one or two objects from the group." Again Mikhailova circled her hands above the objects. She shook with the strain. Under her gaze the whole group of matches moved like a log-run on a fast-flowing river of energy. Nearby the metal cylinder also moved. Still interlaced like a raft, the matches went to the edge of the table and fell off one by one to the floor. Naumov put another batch of matches and a nonmagnetic metal case inside a larger plexiglass cube. The cube was to rule out drafts of air, threads, or wires. Mikhailova's hands moved a few inches from the plexiglass cover and the objects shuttled from side to side of the plastic container. Whatever this energy was, it could easily penetrate plexiglass.

Again Mikhailova looked drained. She had lost over three pounds during this half hour. It was as if she were converting the substance of her own body into energy. Many Western mediums also had reported this weight loss during PK.

"She was actually much sicker than she looked in the film," Naumov told us later. "The strain on her heart was so great we had to stop the cameras several times. It took us over seven hours to make the film and afterward she temporarily couldn't speak or see. For days after doing these tests, her arms and legs pained, she felt dizzy and couldn't sleep."

Was Mikhailova genuine or a "mystification," as the Soviet skeptics called it? From what we'd seen so far, PK was taking place under good conditions with competent observers present. It was no amateur home movie, but a costly 35mm professionally produced film, photographed by skilled technicians.

We recalled Soviet writer Lev Kolodny's recent visit to

Mikhailova's apartment.[80] He was busily writing down notes during an interview when, glancing up, he suddenly observed the top of his fountain pen creeping over the lace tablecloth toward him. "A lump stuck in my throat," he said. The top seemed almost to glide above the uneven surface of the lace. His hostess Mikhailova smiled as a glass tumbler also crept along behind Kolodny's pen top. "Both objects moved to the edge of the table as if they were in harness. The tablecloth wasn't moving—the other glasses beside mine were still sitting there. Could she somehow be blowing on them to make them move? There was no draft of cold air and Mikhailova wasn't breathing heavily. Why didn't a jar in their path also move? I ran my hands through the space between Mikhailova and the table. No threads or wires. If she was using magnets they wouldn't work on glass."

Kolodny picked up both moving objects, examined them, felt them all over, hoping to find some clue. Absent-mindedly, he put the glass over his pen top to form a dome. Mikhailova seemed to be intrigued with this arrangement. She glanced at the pen top as she sipped tea. The top of the pen sped from side to side underneath the glass.

"What kind of energy could have caused this motion, and what laws does it work on?" Kolodny wondered.

Of all psychic happenings in life, PK or telekinesis, as it is sometimes called, can be one of the eeriest. Spontaneous movements of objects generally happen at moments of crisis in a person's life. The grandfather clock that "stopped short, never to go again, when the old man died" has been recorded in song. Telepathy doesn't arouse the same shock as suddenly observing a table following you across the room.

The famous Soviet writer, Konstantin Paustovsky, reports his horror in *The Story of My Life*, when a costly thermometer he had borrowed and carefully secured on a table began to move. "I glanced at the table and felt as if the hair was standing up on my head. The thermometer suddenly began to slowly creep to the edge of the table. I wanted to cry out but my breath was taken away. The thermometer moved to the edge, fell, and broke."

Yet another incident of PK haunted Paustovsky. During the Civil War in Russia, he recalls, there was a severe water shortage in Odessa. "We had to carry up water in pails and pour it into a large glass container in the corridor of the apartment building. One day I heard my friend Yasha shouting wildly in the hall. I rushed out of my room and saw a fantastic sight. Before the amazed eyes of Yasha and me, the huge bottle was moving all by itself! For several moments it stood at a tilt like the leaning Tower of Pisa. Then it rose in the air, dropped, and crashed to the floor. It broke into thousands of pieces and our precious water poured along the hall and down the stairs. We would have had time, of course, to catch the bottle, but both of us stood there and watched it as though bewitched."

How does Mikhailova manage to live with events like these happening around her all the time? "I didn't know until a few years ago that I could move things at a distance," she says. "I was very upset and angry that day. I was walking toward a cupboard in my apartment when suddenly a pitcher in the cupboard moved to the edge of the shelf, fell, and smashed to bits.

"After that, all kinds of changes began to take place in my apartment," she says. Objects seemed somehow to be "attracted" to her, as if the inanimate had become animate. It was almost like having a poltergeist in her home. Usually, scientists say, poltergeist activities are caused unconsciously by a young person in a household—generally at the age of puberty. Objects seem to move of their own volition—doors open and close, lights go on and off by themselves, the laws of gravity seem to be reversed.

But unlike most people plagued by a poltergeist, Nelya suddenly realized the "force" was coming from her. She discovered she could control this energy. She could make it happen by wanting it to. She could summon and focus this extraordinary energy at will. At home with her family, holding her grandchild in her arms, she made a distant toy move closer. While a friend gave her a manicure, she made a bottle of nail polish move without touching it with her polish-wet hands. The family dog too watched with bewilderment as objects near his mistress began to gyrate. Her fascinated husband made a home movie of her strange powers of PK.

"I think I inherited this telekinetic ability from my mother," says Mikhailova. "I also passed it on to my son."

Often as we sat waiting in Soviet restaurants, we thought

longingly of Mikhailova's purported ability to sit down at a table and have "dinner" jump toward her.

Soviet writer Vadim Marin, who is connected with the Popov research group, described it: "Mrs. Mikhailova was sitting at a dinner table. A piece of bread lay on the table some distance from her. Mikhailova, concentrating, looked at it attentively. A minute passed, then another . . . and the piece of bread began to move. It moved by jerks. Toward the edge of the table, it moved more smoothly and rapidly. Mikhailova bent her head down, opened her mouth, and, just as in the fairytale, the bread itself (excuse me but I have no other words for it) jumped into her mouth!

"I wasn't hypnotized," he added reassuringly. "It's all on film."

Nelya's influence on food was recorded more seriously in a scientist-made film. They placed a raw egg in a saline solution inside a glass aquarium. Nelya stood about six feet away. As the witnesses and the camera focused on her, Nelya accomplished the improbable. With PK, the Soviets report, she managed to move the white of the egg away from the yolk. Then she put it back together again.[114]

PK was affecting organic matter. Could PK also affect chromosomes or DNA or human tissue? One physicist told us Nelya could cause third degree burns on her stomach by PK. In this line, researchers in the West have already found that under strict test conditions, psychics could influence enzyme and bacterial activity.

In the same film, Mrs. Mikhailova also is supposed to have moved simultaneously five vertical cigarettes that the scientists placed under a bell jar. Afterward the cigarettes were shredded to insure nothing was secreted inside.

At the conference various Russians mentioned the egg and the vertical cigarette test as refutation of the magnet and thread skeptics. Did you ever try to thread a raw egg, or pick one up off the floor with a magnet? But there was even better, scientifically recorded refutation to come.

Going from life to lab, from spontaneous PK to lab PK, what is this unusual PK energy? How does it happen? What is the mechanism that allows Nelya to by-pass the laws of gravity, physics, chemistry? Endless numbers of rigorously controlled PK tests in the West show that humans *can* influence the mechanized fall of dice inside a box. Researchers have also charted PK directed at fungi, plants, and radioactive material.

But what about the human being who was doing the influencing? What were his or her reactions during PK? With no instruments to measure PK, researchers could only file eyewitness accounts and occasionally infra-red films of talented PK mediums like Eusapia Palladino or Rudi Schneider. "Fraud squads" of skeptics almost physically dismantled these mediums to search for magic tricks. The scientists, instead of thinking PK might take place under *certain* "human conditions" just as different laws apply in outer space conditions, rejected PK out of hand.

A group of Soviet scientists took up the challenge of studying PK in the human being. If Nelya Mikhailova was not a fraud and was really beaming some unknown energy at those objects on the table, what was happening inside her? What was happening around her?

Dr. Genady Sergeyev of the A. A. Uktomskii Physiological Institute (a Leningrad military lab) mulled over the problem. Psychokinesis implied action of the mind at a distance. Could a detector at a distance from the medium pick up traces of this PK energy, this uncharted human potential?

Dr. Harold Burr, Professor of Neuroanatomy at Yale University, established in 1935 that all living matter, from a seed to a human being, is surrounded and controlled by electrodynamic fields. This energy envelope around the body is a kind of electronic mold. As the body renews itself, this force field ensures that the new tissue takes the proper shape.[280] Later, Dr. Leonard Ravitz, a Yale neuropsychiatrist, found the *mind could influence this force field around the body*. Measuring this electromagnetic field on the skin, Ravitz found he could even determine a person's state of mind and the depth of hypnosis.

In Leningrad Dr. Sergeyev wondered if this force field had anything to do with PK. The mind could directly influence this cocoon of energy around our bodies. Could he find a way to measure these biological fields and the mind's impact on them *at a distance* around Nelya?

Sergeyev came up with a new invention, a detector that picks up "biological fields" (electrostatic and magnetic) about four yards away from the human body without any direct contact. We saw the graphs made by these detectors in a film, but we were told the construction of the detectors was "not public." (See Appendix A, 2A.)

Sergeyev put his new detecting devices to work measuring Mikhailova's force field while she was resting. He found the electromagnetic field constantly around her body is only ten times less than the 0.6 gauss of the magnetic field of the earth itself. The electromagnetic force field around Nelya is much stronger than average, says Sergeyev. The Leningrad Institute of Metrology also found this increased magnetic field around her body.[184]

Dr. Sergeyev, an intense, solidly built man in his forties, was the only Russian to discuss his research that second day of the conference. Sergeyev's own "force field" radiated seriousness as he spoke. A former radio man in the Baltic during the war, the mathematician, also trained in neurophysiology, was obviously held in very high esteem by his colleagues. "He has done brilliant work," a Czech scientist told us. In almost every lab we visited in the satellite countries we found Sergeyev's latest books on brain research being minutely studied. Communist scientists were particularly excited about Sergeyev's new discovery of an unusual aspect of Mikhailova's brain. "Most people generate three or four times more electrical voltage from the back of the brain than the front," said Sergeyev. "Mikhailova's brain generates *fifty times* more voltage from the back of the head than the front." (Of course, even this much electrical discharge in the brain is so faint it has to be amplified 4 million times just to be recorded and observed.) Sergeyev, who has found this brain pattern in about 7 percent of the people he's ever tested, feels it's a good indicator that they have better than average psychic power.

The second film on Mrs. Mikhailova appeared on the movie screen. "All you've seen so far in the first film is the outer expression of telekinesis. It's PK the way anyone could observe it," Sergeyev said. "Now, with new instruments, we can get some idea of what telekinesis is like from the inside. We can discover what happens to a human being when PK occurs."

In this film Mrs. Mikhailova was seated inside the electronically insulated EEG chamber of a Leningrad physiology lab. She was strapped into a leather headpiece that looked like an early aviator's cap, covered with electrodes. Her wrists were braceleted with leather straps and more electrodes. Like an astronaut, she was all trussed up and wired for sound. Instruments measured heartbeat and brain waves. At a distance from her, the new Sergeyev detectors measured the "biological fields" twelve feet away from her body.

As before, Mikhailova began to circle her hands above the objects on the table. Her face creased with strain as she struggled to activate her PK powers. (We've pieced together what happens next from the film, subsequent interviews, and published reports.) [198–200, 180, 184]

During the revving-up phase, the EEG's showed tremendous activity in the region of the brain controlling sight. Was this explosive activity in this part of her brain one of the reasons she sometimes becomes temporarily blind after a PK test? As she concentrated ferociously, the electrocardiograph showed her heartbeat had increased four times its normal rate, to 240 beats a minute.

The object in front of Mikhailova began to move. Would the new detectors be able to catch PK in action? Suddenly, the Sergeyev detectors revealed something that researchers had never been able to see before. The powerful magnetic fields around Mikhailova's body began to *pulse!* It was as if she'd caused a wave of energy to vibrate through the invisible energy-envelope around her. Brain and heart pulsed in rhythm with these vibrations in her force field! Not only was her entire force field pulsing, the detectors showed that this pulsing force field had *focused* in the direction of her gaze.

But how did this pulsing force field she focused on an object make it move?

"I believe these vibrations in the fields around her body act like magnetic waves," Sergeyev theorized. "The moment these magnetic vibrations or waves occur, they cause the object Mrs. Mikhailova focuses on, even if it's something nonmagnetic, to act as if magnetized. It causes the object to be attracted to her or repelled from her."

Dr. Sergeyev's theory [198] of PK is also based on the supposed Soviet discovery of a new form of energy circulating through the human body which is reported in later chapters. (See Appendix A, 3 and 4.)

So "mind over matter" wasn't quite accurate. It was really "mind over force field." This vibrating force field was the mechanism, according to the Soviets, by which the mind could produce at least some kinds of PK. If these tests are right, the Soviets have scored a walloping breakthrough in PK.

It was strange to be closeted inside the Czech Embassy in Moscow listening to the Soviet scientists tell us about the discovery of "vibrations." Perhaps the Russians aren't aware of it, but for decades mediums deep in trance have been asked, "What makes PK, ESP, or trances happen?" And from mediums all over the world, having no contact with one another, came almost identical answers—"vibrations." The entranced psychics would explain that the human body is made up of an "energy body" or "field" that vibrates. If the *frequency of vibration* of this field is stepped up, energy or information from another "dimension" can come through us, the mediums said. But until the Burr-Ravitz discovery of the body's invisible energy fields, no one knew exactly what it was they were to vibrate, or how to do it. An English medium, Grace Rosher, predicted that we would soon have high-frequency instruments to enhance ESP powers by upping the vibrations of our energy fields. The Soviets claim they've already devised machines to create magnetic and other kinds of artificial fields that increase psychic power, particularly telepathy, and PK (See chapter 10.)

According to Dr. Ravitz in the 1951 *Yale Journal of Biology and Medicine*, the action of the sun and moon also affects the body's force field.[361] Dr. Sergeyev agrees, "The most favorable time for PK is during magnetic disturbances of the earth caused by sunspot activity."

The Soviets say that three things affect our force fields and thus our psi power: (1) fields produced by machines; (2) natural fields produced by sun, moon, and probably planets; (3) most importantly, human emotions. Not only is the psychic's emotional effect on her own force field involved, the Soviets told us, but the emotions of the observers play a part, too.

"This has been a very difficult point to get over to some

scientists," Edward Naumov said. "They expect human beings to turn on like machines. They don't seem to realize their *own* force fields might be affecting Mrs. Mikhailova. She's a very excitable and nervous personality. Some of these scientists with no understanding of psychology or bio-information are radiating unpleasantness and suspicion which she picks up. We're usually able to demonstrate PK any time, but with unpleasant people it may take Mrs. Mikhailova as much as seven hours to be able to turn the compass needle. Their negative influence is not helpful. Surrounded by friendly people, the compass may move within five minutes."

The human force field, the story of the dynamic cocoon of energy surrounding us, had only begun. The Soviets not only had Dr. Sergeyev's detectors to chart this "surround" at a distance, they also seem to have a method of photographing it. (See chapters 16, 17, 18.)

What was beginning to emerge is a new picture of the human being, not an alienated creature, but a being enmeshed in an ebb and flow with everyone and everything around him. The pulsing magnetic fields of machines, earth, moon, and sun, the thoughts and emotions of ourselves and other people—*all* affect the force fields of our bodies and in turn, the Russians say, our psychic powers.

Dr. Sergeyev made another baffling discovery. He set up his detectors some distance from the body of a *clinically* dead man. No brain waves, no heartbeat could be recorded. But the detectors leaped into action! Four yards from the man's lifeless body the electromagnetic force fields were pulsing. It seemed energy was being released.[100]

The famous psychic and clairvoyant, Eileen Garrett, President of the Parapsychology Foundation of New York, has reported seeing spirals of energy leaving the bodies of the recently dead up to three days after death.[302] Were Sergeyev's detectors picking up the same phenomenon?

Even stranger, the detector graphs from the clinically dead body were *similar* to the detector records made when Mikhailova caused objects to move at a distance. In both cases, PK and death, energy seemed to be released.

"With Dr. Sergeyev's new research," said Dr. Zdenek Rejdak (Ray-dek), a prominent Czech scientist connected with a Prague Military Institute, "we've left behind the old approach of observing telekinesis from the outside only. Now we can begin to detect and record these extraordinary human powers with instruments. It's a first step toward understanding and harnessing this new energy."

One of the Western observers, Dr. Jurgen Keil of the University of Tasmania, wrote, "Russian and Czech scientists at the meeting viewed [psychic] phenomena as physical events which eventually will be controlled like those in orthodox sciences. The Russian approach is most impressive and deserves serious interest from Western countries." [319]

One thing seems clear about the research on Mikhailova and all those records of startling changes in brain waves, heartbeat, and electromagnetic fields. The debunkers of Nelya really should think of something less archaic than magnets and threads. Changing your brain waves so drastically with threads or magnets would be a "supernormal" feat in itself.

What was behind the story of fraud [300] involving Mikhailova? Was it all fabrication?

Nelya Mikhailova did not spring full-blown as a PK medium on the Soviet science scene. Several years earlier, Nelya had been convalescing from an illness in a Leningrad hospital. To pass the time she took up embroidery. One day when the nurse brought her a bag of multicolored embroidery thread, Nelya without glancing at it, dipped her hand into the bag. She'd wanted claret, yellow, and green thread. When her hand came out, those were the colors she held. Suddenly she realized she'd selected them from many colors in the dark bag without seeing them. Her hand had somehow recognized color.

Back home she noticed a newspaper article about Rosa Kuleshova, who reportedly could "see" colors with her hands. "I can do this too!" Nelya thought excitedly. Going for a checkup, she mentioned the idea to her doctors, S. G. Feinburg and G. S. Belyaev. It is one of the typical ironies of science that Dr. Feinburg, a confirmed skeptic about "eyeless sight" and psychic ability in general, ended up being a pioneer in confirming that such abilities exist.[56]

Nelya's discovery of her new talents soon led her to one of the greatest physiologists in Russia, Dr. Leonid Vasiliev. Dr. Vasiliev carried out painstaking tests of her ability and had her demonstrate her paranormal talents before scores of scientists. In 1964 a special conference of top-level scientists was called to observe Mikhailova's demonstration and, according to the January issue of *Smena*, it was a success.

Dr. Vasiliev speculated about how skin sight could happen. If Mikhailova's hands could "see," perhaps some sort of "X" energy was pouring out of them. If there was an energy, perhaps it could do other things beside eyeless sight. In the midst of a skin sight experiment with Mikhailova, Vasiliev recalled that a famous Greek researcher, Dr. A. Tanagras, had found one of his subjects could make the needle of a compass turn by holding her hands above it. On the spur of the moment Vasiliev dug out a compass, placed it in front of Nelya, and encouraged her to try. She'd never attempted this before and of course she'd had no chance to make any advance preparations. She held her hands above the compass. The needle turned. Dr. Vasiliev had discovered a talented PK subject! He embarked on a whole series of PK tests. Soon he found Mikhailova could also move other objects by PK at a distance.[184] Nelya Mikhailova, the little girl who'd been on the front lines of the battlefield during the siege of Leningrad, now found herself on the front lines of the struggle to uncover new potentials in the human being. She did many PK demonstrations for scientists. On one occasion university researchers asked Mikhailova to change the flow of sand in an hourglass. Instead of changing the flow of sand, according to reports, she moved the hourglass itself at a distance.[331]

Before Nelya's PK was thoroughly tested, the axe fell. Nelya was accused of exchanging money on the black market. Whether she actually did, we don't know. But black marketeering in Russia must be almost as commonplace as speeding in the West. We were often accosted by black marketeers on Gorky Street in Moscow. In Leningrad and Kiev, even inside the hotels, especially in elevators, Soviets tried to make deals for shoes, clothes, or money. Despite its being commonplace, fraudulent conversion of funds is a serious offense in Russia.

Mikhailova wound up with a prison sentence. Only the intervention of a scientist as prestigious as Dr. Vasiliev, a recipient of the Order of Lenin, one of the highest honors of the Soviet Union, managed to save her. He pleaded she must have been mentally unbalanced at the time she made the deal (if she did make it), and apparently the authorities permitted her to be placed in a hospital instead of a prison.

"The accusations of 'fraud' had nothing to do with her telekinetic abilities," Dr. Rejdak advised us. "No magnets have ever been detected on Mrs. Mikhailova's body," he said. "The Metronomy Institute in Russia that studied Nelya detected only an increased magnetic field near her body—but no hidden magnets. However, instead of examining this phenomenon more closely, they simply assumed there *might* be hidden magnets," said Rejdak.

Everyone has a force field around his body, but Nelya's is stronger than most. All the scientists who studied her found this. But the scientists at the Metronomy Institute were stuck in rut-thinking. It never occurred to them that Nelya's ability to change her unusual field might be the basis of her PK.

Certainly an impressive roster of Soviet scientists agreed with Rejdak, Sergeyev, and Naumov that Nelya's PK was not a fraud.

Dr. Rejdak has tested Mikhailova personally and reported the tests in Czech *Pravda.*[180]

"I visited the Mikhailova [Kulagin] family the evening of February 26, 1968. Mr. Blazek, an editor friend was with me. Also a physician, Dr. J. S. Zverev and Dr. Sergeyev. Her husband, an engineer, was also present. Dr. Zverev gave Mrs. Mikhailova a very thorough physical examination. Tests with special instruments failed to show any indication whatever of magnets or any concealed object.

"We checked the table thoroughly and also asked Mrs. Mikhailova frequently to change position at the table. We passed a compass around her body and the chair and table with negative results. I asked her to wash her hands. After concentrating, she turned the compass needle more than ten times, then the entire compass and its case, a matchbox and some twenty matches at once. I placed a cigarette in front of her. She moved that too at a glance. I shredded it afterward and there was nothing inside it. In between each sets of tests, she was again physically examined by the doctor.

"I placed my gold ring on the table. It moved faster than all the other objects. I was told that whatever this energy is, it affects *gold* more than any other metal. The gold ring she made move was taken by me from my finger and put on the table. She passed her hands over it and the ring moved toward her. Threads or other attachments were out of the question.

"The matches and matchbox belonged to us and Mrs. Mikhailova had no chance to prepare them. We asked her to make the matches move not only toward her but also away from her. We also asked her to move only one match specified by us from the whole group of matches." According to Dr. Rejdak, she did so.

"Later we put two compasses before her and asked her to move only one of them." She did. Her PK energy can be directed by her will, Rejdak says.

"I chose some glass and china objects from the buffet and put them on the table. I took cups, small plates, a glass saltcellar from the cupboard myself. They were selected by myself and she had no opportunity to prepare them. They weighed about eight ounces each. Mrs. Mikhailova made them move as well. On request, she would induce motion in the objects while they were on a chair or on the floor. Fraud was impossible as she was sitting in a fully illuminated room controlled by Dr. Zverev, Dr. Sergeyev, Mr. Blazek, and myself."

Dr. Rejdak told us, "We did another curious test. We filled a glass bowl full of cigarette smoke and placed it upside down in front of her. At a distance, she could cut the mass of smoke in half as if it were a solid substance.

"After doing these tests, Mrs. Mikhailova was utterly exhausted. There was almost no pulse. She could scarcely move and her face was pale and drawn. She'd lost close to four pounds in half an hour. According to Dr. Zverev's report, the EEG showed intense emotional excitement. Her heart action was arrhythmic. There was high blood sugar, and the endocrine system was disturbed. Her whole organism was weakened as if from a tremendous stress reaction. She had lost the sensation of taste, had pains in her arms and legs, couldn't coordinate, and felt dizzy. Later she reported her sleep was disturbed." (See Appendix A, 5 and 6.)

We have seen yet another film of Mikhailova showing similar PK phenomena. In this film she is shown both indoors and outdoors in a garden. Objects near her rotate or slide in different directions. It makes one wonder what happens to the equipment in a car when she's a passenger. Recently, some of the films on Mikhailova reached the West.

Scientists from the other satellite countries have also examined Nelya. They include Dr. Georgi Lozanov, head of the Institute of Suggestology and Parapsychology of Bulgaria. He witnessed PK tests in Leningrad and plans further work with Mikhailova in his own labs.

Dr. Milan Ryzl, (Millen Reezal) a former Prague biochemist and parapsychologist who defected to the United States, has mentioned Nelya Mikhailova in his articles in the West, implying that she might be a fraud. Dr. Ryzl was the first Communist scientist ever to receive a Western prize (the 1963 McDougall Award) for his work in parapsychology. Unfortunately, afterwards, like many Communists who receive Western awards and money, he began to be regarded with suspicion by some of his Soviet colleagues. As a result, Ryzl was never invited to test Mrs. Mikhailova's PK, and Ryzl's reports of Nelya appear to be based on the inaccurate newspaper articles by Vladimir Lvov.

After the conference, over the usual champagne and ice cream, a young physicist who looked remarkably like the novelist Pasternak, told us about his own tests with Mikhailova. He'd also given a report on them at the conference. "This is the very pen top she moved," Dr. V. F. Shvetz said, pointing to the pen in his hand as if it might still have some trace of the elusive energy Mikhailova radiated. "As a physicist I know telekinesis just can't exist, but as a human being I know I saw it. All the physicists at the atomic center at Dubna were very interested in telekinesis," he said. "But they seemed to feel that if they admitted it, they ought to leave physics and start studying parapsychology!"

"What did some of the other physicists think of her?" we asked.

"In one important Moscow test, the physicists (some of them very famous) set up the entire experiment themselves. They put several nonmagnetic objects inside a plexiglass cube. She moved the objects telekinetically. They said, 'We must have set the test up wrong! Perhaps some type of known energy crept in through the fraction of a millimeter between the table and the plexiglass!' " Shvetz chuckled.

"There's been so much criticism of their statement that they're going to retest her."

"If Mikhailova can move an object," we asked, "can she also move chemical molecules such as silver nitrate in a photo emulsion? In other words, could she cause a picture to appear on photographic paper?"

"Yes," said Shvetz. "She can make the letters 'A' or 'O' appear on photo paper. Sometimes she can also transfer a silhouette of a picture she's seen to photo paper." Perhaps the discovery of the fluctuating force field around Mikhailova during PK throws some light on the strange ability of Ted Serios in the United States to supposedly create pictures of his thoughts on Polaroid film. The Soviets we met who were working with Nelya were avid for information about Serios.

In March 1968 Dr. Ya. Terletsky of the chair of physics of Moscow University, who holds the Laureate of the State Prize, said in *Moscow Pravda,* "Mikhailova's demonstrations of telekinesis look natural to me. Could there be forces, neither electromagnetic or gravitational, which move objects as Mikhailova does? *Yes, there can be.* I have come to this conviction as a physicist. Why are these forces connected to man and his brain? To answer this we need more scientific research." [193]

A new force, an energy connected with people, an energy known or unknown that can be directed by mind. That's why excitement, why interest is running high in the Soviet Union. If you think of PK as edging matches around a table, or even sending water pitchers sailing through the air, you're overlooking the Soviets' point. They're trying to find the general laws behind the spectacular but essentially unimportant feat, just as flying a kite to catch a spark of lightning is important only because it led to the discovery of the fecund laws of electricity.

Dr. Alexei Gubko of the Ukrainian Institute of Psychology believes "We'll use PK and ESP in education and in mental control of machines." [26] Other Soviets say, "We'll use this bio-energy in physico-chemical processes and in medicine." Soviet research on Mikhailova so far has yielded valuable insights into the baffling phenomenon of biomagnetism, another field of current emphasis in Russia. Mikhailova's mind could cause the electromagnetic fields around her to vibrate. In England, Baker and Delawarr found that even very weak magnetic fields, *if vibrating,* could lower blood cholesterol and white cell count.[293]

Some Communist scientists believe this new form of energy radiating from humans can be collected and stored. (See Chapter 28.) "PK seems to be the easiest psychic phenomena to do basic experiments with. It is through PK that we'll unlock the forces behind much of the paranormal, giving us a wider grasp of the life forces of the universe," they said.

But there's a dark side to PK. After a fierce eruption of poltergeist PK activity that for months plagued the electrical installations and moved furniture in a building in Rosenheim, West Germany, Herr Brunner, a spokesman for the Municipal Works of Rosenheim who'd been called in to investigate, commented in the *Journal of Paraphysics* (Vol. 3, No. 3, 1969) "It is an alarming thought to consider what catastrophic results could happen in the realm of technology if such forces, outside the will power of technicians, could influence [electrical] relays and upset functions of all kinds. For this reason, it is in the interest of the common welfare of mankind that scientists should endeavor to shed light upon this dark corner of our knowledge.

"It became necessary to postulate the existence of a power hitherto unknown to technology, of which neither the nature nor strength nor direction could be defined. It is an energy quite beyond our comprehension."

It would only take a few instants' application of this "X" energy to any sophisticated installation—a missile base, a hydro plant, the electrical installations of a modern city—to wreak total chaos. An American parapsychologist has commented, "PK could be the ultimate weapon."

Soviet PK researchers like Naumov repeated fervently to us, "I only hope that PK will *not* fall into the hands of those who would use it as a weapon."

In the summer of 1969 word reached us from a reliable source that new work on PK and Nelya Mikhailova is still going on in Russia. The work involves intensive investigation of the fields surrounding her body. It is said that the Soviets have come up with new people with PK talent.

PK research of undisclosed nature is going on in Tbilisi, Georgia. Elsewhere Soviet scientists claim to be investigating a French biologist's statement that through PK humans can influence the rate of radioactive decay.[156] This French scientist, who prefers to remain anonymous although he is well known in parapsychology literature, asked teenagers to try to accelerate or slow down decay of radioactive matter. In a series of tests, he says, the geiger counter showed they succeeded. It's interesting he chose children, a group often linked with poltergeist displays. But the Russians are probably more interested in the claim that the enigmatic PK can influence basic matter. Perhaps Nelya can also affect radioactive matter.

Nelya seems to be an all-round psychic, like Eusapia Palladino and other famous PK mediums of old. She's supposedly telepathic, clairvoyant, and psychometric as well as packed with PK. But the Soviets are not looking at her as a performer or as a personality of exotic plumage. They see Nelya as a means to discovering principles. The important questions about Mikhailova's PK obviously should center not on the medium herself but on the scientific discoveries like those of Dr. Sergeyev—that fluctuating biological fields apparently are involved with PK. Fraud squad-type comments about threads and "magnets in intimate places" are utterly irrelevant and have no relation to research in neurophysiology. Nelya has been a means to helping the scientists elucidate these new avenues. And it's not so easy to be a means. There are the scurrilous personal attacks of news writers like Lvov, which lead to a barrage of crank calls and letters. Aside from public harassment, Nelya also suffers great physical stress during PK tests.

But Nelya Mikhailova grew up fighting; she grew up during the siege of Leningrad under some of the worst deprivation and stress the world has known. There's no reason to think she'll throw in the towel while scientists still believe they can uncover more about the unrealized potential and wonder of the human being by rigging her up like an astronaut and attaching her to a lab full of machines.

7

INNER AND OUTER SPACE

When Yuri Gagarin became the first man to spin in space around the earth, people appeared in the streets of Moscow decked in placards reading, "Hurrah! The Cosmos Is Ours!" The all-flags-flying hoopla, the jubilant, singing throngs pressing into Red Square were real. The deep reverberations in the solar plexus were genuine. No bureaucrat could order the emotional resonance that strikes most Soviets at the thought of the cosmos. They have "upward longings."

Parapsychologists are not immune to the mystique of space. They dream of fusing the exploration of inner space with the exploration of outer space. They have good authority to go on. K. E. Tsiolkovsky is the father of Russian rocketry. He is a sort of combined Wright Brothers–Lindbergh figure in the Soviet pantheon. In the 1930s he said, "Especially in the coming era of space flights, telepathic abilities are necessary. And they will aid the whole development of mankind. While the space rocket must bring men toward knowledge of the grand secrets in the universe, the study of psychic phenomena can lead us toward knowledge of the mysteries of the human mind. It is precisely the solution of this secret which promises man the greatest achievements." [373]

Three decades later, in 1967, *Maritime News* in Russia reported,[357] "Cosmonauts, when in orbit, seem to be able to communicate telepathically more easily with each other than with people on earth. A psi-training system has been incorporated into the cosmonauts training program. It is hoped this will help them sense and avoid oncoming dangers."

Parapsychologists are thinking into far stretches of space. Telepathy, the thinking goes, may be the common language when cosmonauts first hail spaceships from other solar systems; ESP may be a channel of communication between earth and other civilizations in the galaxy. Perhaps ESP could be used to contact or to understand UFOs (unidentified flying objects).[51] But first the Soviets have turned working attention to a creature already in their labs: the human being.

They'd like to equip cosmonauts with live powers of their own, to back up their electronic gear in space. One such live backup scheme involves coded messages via ESP. On earth telepathy has flowed from screened chambers that cancel out radio waves. Theoretically telepathy could be used for communication in space when radio blanks out, which is especially important because radio voids and delays will magnify as spaceships glide further off. The code idea began bubbling in telepathic thinking in the late 1950s, about the time Sputnik I took orbit. Coded messages would enable parapsychologists to send and receive specific, often abstract, information. Language, instead of mute images, would move telepathically.

In March 1967 the Soviets flashed a coded telepathic message from Moscow to Leningrad.[82, 357] To do it they pooled much of their new knowledge of the physiology of ESP. The steadfast Karl Nikolaiev received. Yuri Kamensky sent—virulently. Kamensky imagined with all his senses that he was knocking the *shashlik* out of Nikolaiev. He punched him in the face, kicked his legs, wrestled him to the floor. (As the Soviet reporter of these tests wrote, "Oh, happy scientists!") A long round, lasting forty-five seconds, represented a dash in Morse code. Short rounds of fifteen seconds stood for a dot. Kamensky didn't know the word he was bashing through space from Moscow. He only had a list of time durations. In Leningrad, Drs. Pavlova and Sergeyev plugged Nikolaiev into the EEG and other monitoring devices. The sensitive Nikolaiev began receiving the telepathic impulses. The EEG charted the lengths of reception—long and short. Nikolaiev, conscious of the emotion beaming at him, also noted down the duration of each psychic assault. Seven Morse signals made up the word being sent. The first time through, Nikolaiev, calculating length, got the seven Morse signals right. Decoded, he found Kamensky had sent from Moscow to Leningrad, from brain to brain, the word *MIG*. It means "instant," and instant communication, whether from Minsk to Pinsk or spaceship to earth, is what the parapsychologists have in mind.

Intricate telepathic codes also have been successfully used and are currently being tested and improved in Bulgarian [110] and Czech labs.[378] But perhaps the first person to come up with the basic system is a man who has probably never thought of smacking anyone in the nose, Douglas Dean, an electrochemist, computer professor, and past President of the Parapsychology Association in America. In 1960 Dean learned of an accidental discovery made by Dr. Stepan Figar of Prague. Figar found that the plethysmograph, a device that records changes in blood volume, could indicate when you are being influenced by another person's thought.[36] Dean took off from there. With engineers Robert Taetzsch and John Mihalasky of the Newark College of Engineering in New Jersey, he worked the old-fashioned plethysmograph into a telepathic system that could one day be used by astronauts.

First, he found out something extraordinary. When a telepathic sender concentrates on the name of a person you have an emotional tie with, you may register a change in blood volume. Lying down in a relaxed state, you are not conscious of receiving telepathy. Yet something is "picked up." Something causes minute changes in your body. Apparently about a quarter of us can show this unconscious telepathic reception.[286-88]

Ahead of the Soviets, Douglas Dean clearly demonstrated on the impartial graphs of an instrument that telepathy can influence body processes.

In 1964 Dean spoke about his proposed "Psi Communication System" to the Canaveral Council of Technological Societies at the First Space Conference. In Dean's telepathic system the sender concentrates on a name that has an emotional charge for the receiver. The receiver, hooked to the plethysmograph, registers a change in blood volume. This stands for a dot in Morse code. A dash is signified when nothing is sent for a specific time.[322, 356] Using his loaded names, Dean has communicated from room to room, building to building, and from New York to Florida, 1,200 miles away.

"Space communication is certainly something one looks

toward with this," Dean told us. "Probably the Russians are looking in that direction too. For example, when we venture further away, say to Jupiter, radio communications will lag by over an hour. We think we can knock this time down with telepathy. Or, theoretically, using clairvoyance or precognition, perhaps there could be instantaneous communication—almost."

The Russian parapsychologists we met had all heard of Douglas Dean in far away Newark. So had a lot of other Russians. In 1966 *Komsomolskaya Pravda* wrote up Dean's work.

Both the American and the Soviet psi communication systems get their messages across by relying primarily on the unconscious physical processes caused by telepathy. Thought-Nikolaiev-graph-analyzer-decoder: the human being is a *component* in a communication system just like a television picture tube is. The human is the most sensitive part: no machine can duplicate him. Dean's system has one big plus. You don't need a rigorously trained psychic to receive. Infinitely better funded however than the dedicated Dean, the Russians with their expensive hardware and specialized "receivers," may develop a more flexible system.

Is there any reason to think they're going to bother?

Louis Pauwels, editor of the French journal *Planète*, commenting on information sent him by Novosti about the important parapsychology congress in February 1968, noted that many outstanding Soviet scientists apparently believe psi research is important for furthering both knowledge and technology. "Many have affirmed that in the adventure of space, astronauts would perhaps have recourse to telepathy in order to communicate with earth or each other." Pauwels added, "This reaffirms the position taken in 1966 by a Russian scientist at the astronautics congress in Paris." [342]

The Soviets seem to be trying hard. "In one of our tests," Naumov remarked, "Nikolaiev was kept in a darkened chamber for seven hours. Connected to the instruments, he had to be spoon fed."

In their efforts to work out a psi communication system, the Soviets have gotten away from the rut thinking of always attempting to send images telepathically. They tried blasts of emotion. And they also tried to telepathically communicate blasts of sounds—buzzes or whistles.

Kamensky concentrated on long and short barrages of sound to project a word between two labs in Leningrad. This code word also had seven Morse signals and each was again pulsed seven times. According to Dr. Pavlova, the first time through the word Nikolaiev consciously received five out of seven signals. The next time six. Combined, the results permitted the decoding of "Ira," the correct word.[152] Two other names ticked along telepathically, Jenine and, not surprisingly, Lenin.[162] Is the use of names an echo of the Dean system?

"Out of twenty-one letters transmitted telepathically in code, eighteen were picked up clearly in these tests," Naumov remarked. "Our aim naturally is to send much longer messages, which means we're going to have to think up new combinations. At present the brain eventually falls into habit, develops a conditioned response. We have to use one regimen for fifteen minutes, then switch to another."

Using telepathic images the Soviets also managed to send coded words from Moscow to Tomsk, almost 3,000 miles away.[78] These psi communication systems, at least the ones they told us about, aren't perfected enough for cosmonauts to send chess moves to opponents in other spaceships. (Out-of-this-world chess games is one practical use of telepathy some Soviets are convinced of.) But it would be strange if the Soviets don't keep trying to perfect a telepathic space communications system. Even the conservative Dr. Ippolit Kogan, director of the Popov Bio-Information Section, told the Soviet press that telepathy will have application whenever it's impossible to use other means of transmission. "It can be used in space flight," he said. "Imagine the breakdown of a radio on a cosmic flight. It would be enough to telepathically transmit the number 5, for instance. This would inform earth stations that the radio wasn't functioning and that they should take action. Of course this would require a specialized person. He would be recruited from the gifted and properly trained." Kogan also thought lost or endangered expeditions on earth could use a telepathic SOS.[158] And bearing in mind the curious alliance of psi and submarines, telepathic codes could connect a sub to ship or shore. Further in the shadows, the military could use such a system when other communications would be inconveniently loud.

Have any Russian cosmonauts tested telepathy here or in space? We don't know. Perhaps Dr. Eugene B. Konneci, when he was Director of Biotechnology and Human Research and Technology for the National Aeronautics and Space Administration, did know. In 1963 he told delegates at the Fourteenth International Astronautic Federation in Paris, "The nature and essence of certain phenomena of electromagnetic communication between living organisms is reportedly being pursued with top priority under the Soviet manned space program." Konneci added that the bulk of Western science was just beginning to note these phenomena and mentioned the work of Dr. Henry Puharich, an American neurologist-parapsychologist.[405]

In 1967 another reputable American, a professional man, brought back word from Russia of supposed psi in space. He was told by Soviet parapsychologists that cosmonauts did "truly phenomenal" psychic experiments. The Soviet Union is trying to test all possible ways of communication between the cosmos and earth, the Russians explained. For example, a cosmonaut was instructed to concentrate on certain principles and objects. At the appointed time, telepathists on earth recorded his thought. Like everything military, they told him, data and results are classified.[283]

On the lighter side, two Czech scientists told us that Khrushchev, who was famous for boasting about everything under the sun, didn't overlook psi. Supposedly Chairman Khrushchev said, "We've already used ESP in space."

Kay Sterner, President of the California Parapsychology Foundation in San Diego, was the lone American at the Moscow conference in 1966. She reports that discussions indicated considerable Soviet work was being done on psychic faculties under the weightless conditions of outer space. Soviets were also training cosmonauts in yoga and hypnosis for tests in space, according to Mrs. Sterner. "Of course," she remarked, "they asked a great deal more than they told." [358]

Perhaps because we arrived during a government freeze, whenever we asked about space we got this answer: "Yes, why don't you tell us about the American astronauts? Are they doing anything with psi?" This led to small conversation. There are no officially substantiated reports of ESP training in our program. We didn't want to sell the Russians another *Nautilus* story. If they hadn't already scored a first, such a tale would surely equip the next cosmonaut up with ESP exercises.

The single public announcement of ESP training for cosmonauts that appeared in the *Maritime News* probably relates, in part, to a scheme devised by the late Professor I. Gellerstein, doctor of biology and Popov parapsychologist. In 1966 Dr. Gellerstein gave a speech about precognition, a subject just off the proscribed list. Cosmonauts will travel at such extreme speeds, he said, that they must be able literally to foresee the future. In order to be able to react to emergencies in time, they must learn to see what will happen before it occurs in the present. Some rare human beings apparently have the gift to foretell. Therefore, Gellerstein reported, a program had been designed to try to train cosmonauts to develop at least some amount of precognition.[96]

Here again, the Soviets put their faith in training, in the idea that if one person can do it, then perhaps many can develop some degree of facility. Apart from the Marxist belief in training, Gellerstein could also fall back on the quotable moral authority of space pioneer Tsiolkovsky, whose ideas, like those of most Soviet heroes, are repeated vigorously. Tsiolkovsky was convinced "man will have to develop latent psychic abilities to function well in the strange environment of space."

As it moves into new investigations of biological fields and of man himself, our own space program, which is already credited with some 2,500 new scientific advances, may bring us new and startling breakthroughs in ESP as well.

8

UFOs AND PSI, SEEKING THE COSMIC MESSIAH

Space expert K. E. Tsiolkovsky, who believed in an abundantly populated universe, was the refuge of some Soviet scientists who began to see strange, officially nonexistent things.

Around 9:30 in the evening of July 26, 1965, three Soviet astronomers, Robert Vitolniek, Esmeralda Vitolniek, and Yan Melderes, studied luminous clouds in Ogre, Latvia. Gazing northwest, they suddenly noticed a very bright star moving slowly westward. After checking with binoculars, the astronomers hastily trained their telescope on the "star."

"We saw a lenslike disc about 325 feet in diameter with a small sphere visible in the center. Three other small spheres slowly rotated around the large disc. All four spheres were lusterless pearly green. The entire system diminished in size as if moving away from the earth. After about twenty minutes the outside spheres began to move away from the disc. The sphere in the heart of it also seemed to fly off. By ten o'clock they were all out of sight."

The astronomers estimated these strange green objects hung about 165 miles above the earth. "Judging by the speed of its movement in the field of view, the system stood motionless in space and its seeming movement was nothing but the rotation of the earth," they reported.[232]

A few years earlier, rumors told of large glowing objects darting in the skies of Kazakhstan frightening the peasants back into church. "In truth, Soviet radar has picked up unidentified flying objects for twenty years," announced Dr. Felix U. Ziegel of the Moscow Institute of Aviation, in a dazzling article in the magazine *Smena*, April 1967. Other surprising accounts followed in magazines like *Baikal*, *Youth Technics*, *Soviet Life*, *Knowledge & Work*. Dr. Ziegel, connected with the Popov parapsychologists, was allowed to break the UFO story and let off some of the steamed-up reports that had pressured the authorities for years. Ziegel chose well documented sightings by accredited scientists. A review of just a few of the observers Ziegel quotes shows they aren't likely to mistake the moon, a six inch bit of ball lightning, or Venus rising for a saucer. It also shows why parapsychologists had already begun to theorize about ways to communicate with intelligences from space.

An eight-man geophysical expedition from Leningrad was camped in the mountains of Kazakhstan. It was 11:00 P.M., August 16, 1960. Suddenly they saw a bright orange lenslike object speeding over the mountain tops. The group leader, Dr. Nikolai Sochevanov, a Master of Geology and Mineralogy, reported that the diameter of the strange object was 50 percent larger than the moon from his vantage point. Keeping a constant speed, the orange disc flew north to south, zigged southeast, made an arc, and disappeared behind the mountains. The edges of the object were less luminous than the center.[262]

Another team of scientists bivouacked in the northern Caucasus also saw a reddish disc cavort in the sky. Their leader, geophysicist Dr. V. G. Krylov, reported the trajectory of the object was "somewhat devious, finally spiral." This disc changed from red to a brilliant blue-white.

In 1964 a planeload of Soviets on a TU-104A making the regular run from Leningrad to Moscow watched as a large, bright, metal-looking disc slid under their plane. Dr. Vyacheslav Zaitsev, a student of UFOs in ancient history, was, happily, aboard the plane. He reported that the disc, which flew parallel to the aircraft for some time, had a bulge at the center, resembling a cabin. Dr. Ludmila Tsekhanovich, a geodetic astronomer in the Caucasus, also sighted and tracked a similar bright disc during the daytime in 1965. It too had the cabinlike bulge.[262]

Apparently a number of Soviet planes have been tailed by unknown, seemingly intelligently steered objects. A famous Soviet pilot, Valentin Akkuratov, chief navigator of Soviet polar aviation, reported one of his encounters with UFOs in 1956.

"We were engaged in strategic ice reconnaissance around Greenland. We dropped out of the clouds into clear weather, and suddenly noticed an unknown craft flying parallel to us on our left. It looked like a large pearly lens with pulsating edges. Thinking it might be an unknown American aircraft, we ducked back into the clouds to avoid encounter. After forty minutes' flying, the clouds ended. There on our portside was the same strange object. We didn't see any wings, portholes, aerials, or any exhaust gases. We decided to take a closer look and abruptly changed course to approach it. But as we altered course, the unknown flying machine also changed, always remaining parallel. After about fifteen minutes the mysterious craft sped ahead and up in the sky until it disappeared. It flew at what seemed an impossible speed to us." [263]

What were these bright, colorful things zooming over Russia, flying tandem with her planes? "The hypothesis with the least objections is that UFOs are vehicles from extraterrestrial civilizations," Dr. Ziegel remarked. Other top scientists were willing to speculate. "Who knows," said Dr. Vasily Kuprevich, President of the Academy of Sciences of Byelorussia, "perhaps beings from outer space are still visiting earth without contacting people. Their intellectual development may have attained such a level that they hold us no higher in their opinions than we do our forebears, the cavemen." [262]

On the subject of developed life existing elsewhere in the galaxy, there was a 1967 conference "On Space Civilizations" led by the great Armenian astronomer Victor Ambartsumyam. It came to this conclusion: the existence of extraterrestrial civilizations in the galaxy can practically be taken for granted; therefore, a preliminary study of the scientific and technical problems of our future connections with them should already begin.[32]

"We have well documented sightings from every corner of the USSR," Ziegel revealed. "It's hard to believe all are optical illusions. Illusions don't register clearly on photographic plates and radar." He mentioned a double tracking that involved Air Force Major Baidukov flying at night over Odessa in April 1966. The major spotted an unidentified object on his radar. Various ground radar units also picked up the same high flying blip and watched it drop in forty-five minutes from thirty-one to eleven miles above the earth. (There are even rumors that some Soviet cosmonauts in outer space have seen a saucer near their capsule.)

"I don't think it becomes a real scientist to approach problems like the man who said of the giraffe, 'there ain't no such animal,'" Ziegel said. "Without rejecting the visitors from space hypothesis or any other theory, we must begin a systematic study of the UFO enigma. We must use our astronomical, meteorological, and geophysical observatories, our space rocket and satellite tracking units, our airport and hydrometeorological radar."

Ziegel's first public airing of UFOs in the USSR stirred up Dr. J. Allen Hynek, Chairman of the Astronomy Department at Northwestern University and America's leading scientific expert on UFOs. Writing in *Playboy*, Dr. Hynek confessed his greatest fear: one morning he would unfold his paper to read, "Russians Solve UFO Mystery." Hynek daydreamed the Soviets would come up with some mundane, previously unconsidered explanation of UFOs. Or, much more traumatic, the Soviets would report the first contact with members of an extraterrestrial civilization reconnoitering us. "Either story would shake America so hard that the launching of Sputnik in 1957 would appear in retrospect as important as a Russian announcement of a particularly large wheat crop," Hynek said.[309]

Wise to the ways of the Soviets, Dr. Hynek pointed out how unlikely it was that Ziegel would call for a full-fledged scientific study of UFOs unless one was already in progress.

A month before any public announcement of UFOs, the parapsychologists, anyway, thought there was some reason for discussing them. The parapsychologists combined with two groups of physicists for a seminar on "Possible Ways of Communicating with Extra-terrestrial Civilizations."[132] Engineer Yu. Dolgin spoke of the current scientific search for civilizations in outer space. Then the discussion turned to UFOs. Dr. Ziegel believes parapsychology can be of great service to man. He might have been speaking of psychic research when he said, "What we seem to be dealing with here is a kind of reality still unexplored." He was talking of UFOs. Ziegel mentioned new cameras being developed to photograph UFOs. He spoke of developing communication systems to probe into space seeking intelligent response. "Is it sheer coincidence that sightings increase whenever Mars is closest to Earth?" Ziegel asked. "No one knows."

A proper communication system might rouse a response from the so far unsociable UFO. Telepathy could be one answer. No one at the seminar had, of course, met a space being. But the Soviets were preparing their "speeches" in case they got nominated.

Dr. Vyacheslav Zaitsev, another participant at the parapsychology meetings, is not convinced that no one has ever seen a cosmic visitor. He believes, and has spent years documenting his theories, that spacemen landed on earth bringing with them the dawn of human civilization. "Gods from the sky," he calls them. Zaitsev, a philologist at the Byelorussian Academy of Sciences, scoured old documents, particularly sacred ones, to arrive at his ideas. "The Biblical account of the destruction of Sodom and Gomorrah resembles a nuclear explosion," Zaitsev points out not unreasonably, "as it would be described by an uneducated witness."

According to Dr. Zaitsev, the holy Indian sagas, the *Ramayana* for one, tell of "two-storied celestial chariots with many windows. They roar like lions, blaze with red flames, and race off into the sky until they appear like comets." The *Mahabharata* and various Sanskrit books describe at length these chariots, "powered by winged lightning . . . it was a ship that soared into the air flying to both the solar and stellar regions."

Some Soviet archeologists think the chariots may have left "records" behind. Recently archeologists found 716 stone discs in caves in the Bayan Kara Ula mountain edging China and Tibet. These "records," which the Soviets found to contain traces of metals, have grooves like a modern phonograph record and a hole in the center. Archeologists estimate they were made around 10,000 B.C. and believe they may be a form of writing. Zaitsev reports that when the discs are scraped free of particles, they vibrate as if carrying an electrical charge. In Dr. Zaitsev's opinion, these discs could give new meaning to the venerable Chinese legends of gaunt, yellow-faced men who descended from the clouds.[256]

Zaitsev bolsters his "Gods from the Sky" thesis with a wide knowledge of architectural history. Early peoples, he thinks, modeled their sacred buildings after the machines of the space visitors, thereby immortalizing them. He has books full of examples. The shape of the American Gemini space capsule can be found in ancient structures. Notably, it appears in a textbook example of Judaic architecture, the tomb in the Valley of Cedron. Correspondingly, the silhouette of a classical example of Phoenician sacred building, the tomb of Amrites, resembles the Soviet Vostok. Halfway around the world, the Vostok shape also appears in the very early "stupas" carved in Indian cave temples. Chinese pagodas, like the famous iron pagoda near K'ai-feng, churches, Muslim minarets, all have "a skyward urge," according to Dr. Zaitsev. He points to the minarets surrounding to St. Sophia in Istanbul. They look like rockets ready to launch.

"Preserved by the Messianic ecstacies of religion, these cosmic symbols inspired by our early visitors and benefactors came through into Christianity, into Russia. Look at the spires of the Churches. Compare the onion-shape cupola of the Ivan the Great Bell Tower in the Kremlin to the bell-shaped prow of the Vostok spaceship." Dr. Zaitsev told the parapsychologists that if further research proved these theories, man would have to change his ideas about the origins of civilization and religions, "and our ideas of Messianic beliefs. If we really were visited centuries ago, we may be on the threshold of a 'second coming' of intelligent beings from outer space." [257]

To Zaitsev, "second coming" isn't just a theological allusion. He thinks Jesus came from outer space, that he was a representative of a higher civilization. This supposedly explains, in part, his supernatural powers, his tremendous abilities. "In other words, the descent of God to earth is really a cosmic occurrence," Zaitsev says. He thinks the Soviets should, in this sense, consider the coming of God a real historic event. Only Zaitsev suggests the term God might be changed to "Cosmonaut Jesus Christ." [314]

Too much? In Russia Zaitsev's ideas have generated lively interest. He's just one of a number of Soviet scientists who think our civilizations were sparked by beings from outer space. Before Zaitsev put forward his theories, Professor Modest Agrest, doctor of physical mathematics, created a sensation in the influential *Literary Gazette* (February 1966) by propounding the thesis that the earth has been visited by spacemen for a million years.

Professor Agrest speaks of "tektites," mysterious rocks found in Lebanon that have baffled science. They were formed under nuclear radiation. Why not missiles from outer space? Like Zaitsev and others, Agrest is intrigued by "Dogu," 25-000-year-old statues found in Japan that supposedly resemble astronauts in spacesuits. Agrest too believes biblical events and personalities show the intervention of cosmic visitors.

Strange as they may sound, these ideas are not fringe writing but have been presented as serious, extensively documented scientific hypotheses. Dr. Iosif Shklovsky, a Corresponding Member of the Soviet Academy of Science, stated: "Agrest boldly considers that many surprising Biblical events are based on a visit of astronauts from other planets to the earth. . . . In the summer of 1962 a similar hypothesis was put forward by Karl Sagan, a noted American astrophysicist. Of course, neither the Agrest hypothesis nor the version of it developed by Sagan has, so far, any serious scientific backing. Nevertheless, they merit consideration and must not be dismissed as unscientific nonsense."

We'd never met anyone who'd seen a saucer—not until we went to Russia and talked to a physics professor. When we chatted with this forty-five-year-old scientist who teaches at a prestigious Soviet University, UFOs were again under an official cloud. "I know it sounds odd," he told us, "but I've seen saucers twice. In the summer of 1960, with a group of people, I was waiting for a passing car on the Samarkand highway about twenty-eight miles from Tashkent. This was between nine and ten at night. The UFO, about the size of a large star, flew across the northeast part of the sky. It reversed and moved toward the earth with wavy light ripples. It looked rather like the motion of a water scorpion. The next day I inquired and found that numerous Tashkenters had seen the same object. The fact that this wasn't a plane, a meteorite, or an artificial sputnik was testified to by its flight along broken lines with tremendous changes in speed.

"About a month later, during the same summer, I was in the Crimea with two well-known art teachers and their students. I saw my second UFO—actually not one, but five of them. We watched them perform some sort of maneuver in the zenith, not unlike the games of fireflies." This professor, like Dr. Ziegel, also brought up the famous Tunguska meteorite which laid low a Siberian forest in 1909. The *Soviet Academies of Sciences Reports* [235] in 1967 published studies to show that whatever crashed into Siberia, it was not a comet or meteorite. The same year, the Joint Nuclear Research Institute at Dubna came out with a report that the Tunguska blast, which left a great deal of radioactivity, had all the characteristics of a nuclear explosion. Finally, Dr. Ziegel demonstrated in 1966 (before the saucer publicity) that the Tunguska object made a huge, 375 mile arc in the air before crashing. "That is," Ziegel says, "it carried out a maneuver." [263]

According to some observers, strange objects were still carrying out maneuvers over Communist lands. The Czech military magazine *Periscope* (1966) reported, "Recently UFOs have been sighted over the Soviet Union, Poland, China, and Czechoslovakia."

In October 1967 Air Force Major General Porfiri Stolyarov was elected chairman of the All-Union Cosmonautics Committee, an unofficial UFO study group heavy with scientists and Heroes of the Soviet Union.[301] The society announced itself on television and then went silent. Ziegel called for a world-wide study of UFOs [316, 406] as through the year more sightings in Russia had come in. The Mountain Astrophysical Station of the USSR Academy of Science in the Caucasus reported two notable ones.

On a clear, starry night, astronomer H. I. Potter saw a dense, milky formation with a rosy red nucleus. This cloud paled and disappeared, but the red center hovered. Potter took two hours' worth of photographs of the changing phenomena. A few weeks later, vacationers at Kislovodsk, a mountain resort, were brought up tight when they saw a bright crescent zinging across the sky. Further up the mountain at the astrophysics station, astronomer Anatoli Sazanov and *ten* scientific workers sighted and tracked the same crescent. Faint luminous ribbons, like some sort of exhaust, followed the horns of the crescent. Eventually the brightness of the crescent faded and the object appeared to be a disc.[263]

Before we arrived in Russia, UFOs became officially extinct. Dr. Ziegel, who apparently had gone on TV and created what authorities considered too much of a spectacular, was on an extended vacation until the public flap died down. Consequently, discussion of UFOs, extraterrestrial civilizations, and ways of communicating with them had to be deleted from the June parapsychology conference. All the accounts of saucer sightings mentioned in this chapter, except the eyewitness account of our friend, were published by the Soviets. A number of them were reprinted in *Sputnik,* a Soviet magazine distributed in twenty-eight noncommunist countries.

Said the Soviet Academy of Sciences in March 1968, "the search for UFOs is antiscientific." If they existed, scientists would know about them. The Academy stated, "None of our astronomers have ever seen a UFO. They've never been sighted by any of our ground scientists. Our defensive units, guarding the land day and night, have never seen a UFO." So, the Academy concluded, there can't be any UFOs.[414] Most Western observers believe the pronouncement was for home consumption only, and was made to soothe the populace, a soothed populace being a good thing in the authoritative eye. "Ah well," was the attitude of various Russians we talked to. "Flying saucers will come again with another thaw." Publicly, that is.

Dr. Carl Jung, the great psychoanalyst, wrote a book on flying saucers. They might or might not exist materially, Jung thought. What interested him was the mythic luminescence of the UFOs. What changes in the deep psyche are signified by their sightings, he wondered. As Zaitsev's fairly popular theories of "Gods from the Sky" show, the mythic and mystical side of the flying saucer casts fertile shadows in Russia.

It isn't coincidental that parapsychologists, astrophysicists, and ufologists blend at Moscow seminars. The same push, the same gnawing urge to discover the deep ineffables of life lies just below the exploration of inner and outer space. This urge is basic in the Russian character. Mystic Russia is not dead. She is simply, slowly changing the trappings of her quest. Moving by necessity from religion, she's turned toward science. She looks to it for a new, larger definition of human self. She looks to it for a new understanding of that self's place in the scheme of things. Parapsychology probes inward into being. Astronautics probes outward into the bright black infinity vaulting over the endless lands of the Soviet. Both have the restless, self-tormented centuries of Russia behind them.

Soviets have come up with telepathic powers on the ground; they've launched men into space. It is not unlikely that they have combined, or will combine, the two. It's less likely the Russians will find that they literally have a star-crossed history, that spacemen descended bearing Promethean gifts. Between this likely and unlikely hangs the UFO enigma. It's anyone's guess what these high-flying, exasperating objects are. If they prove to be alien, and if we believe what science fiction writers and occultists tell us about otherworldly beings homing in on sympathetic vibrations—then a nongovernmental Russian may well have the first intergalactic word. In a talk on space beings with super intelligence, Dr. Ziegel asked, "Isn't there still the possibility of common understanding, since we are born in the same universe and obey the same laws of nature?" The optimism of an educated Russian man, a Zaitsev admirer we met over dinner one night in Moscow, went a lot further. "They are like loving parents in the sky," he said. "Now that we have the nuclear power to extinguish ourselves and harm the solar system, they will come. They will not let us destroy ourselves."

9

THE TELEPATHIC KNOCKOUT

The piano player swung into a waltz. A young woman leaned back in the arms of her partner and began to swirl around the polished dance floor of a Black Sea resort. In an anteroom, Dr. K. I. Platonov, a psychologist, put his hand to his eyes and concentrated. Suddenly, in mid-step, the dancing woman fell into a deep hypnotic trance. Platonov telepathically cut in on the waltzing woman, Miss M.

At the 1924 All-Russian Congress of Psychoneurologists, Platonov again knocked out Miss M. telepathically, before a hall full of scientists. The vivacious young woman sat onstage, chatting, so she thought, with a panel of doctors as they waited for a hypnotic demonstration to get under way. Platonov stood out of sight behind a large blackboard. He put his hand to his brow as a signal to the audience and Miss M. suddenly slumped asleep. Then he woke her up, then he put her under again.[154, 237]

Platonov had found more than an exotic way to cure insomnia with his telepathic whammy. The ability to put people to sleep and wake them up telepathically from a distance of a few yards to over a thousand miles became the most thoroughly tested and perfected contribution of the Soviets to international parapsychology. It is *the* Soviet experiment. The ability to control a person's consciousness with telepathy is being mined today in Leningrad and Moscow labs. The sleep-wake test, however, gained a long and intriguing scientific pedigree before it was finally revealed in the early 1960s.

Shortly after the 1924 convention, something unusual happened to a nineteen-year-old Kharkov coed. "When are the experiments going to begin, Professor Dzelichovsky?" the young university student asked her physics teacher. She was exasperated with curiosity. Over a month ago, he'd asked her to be the subject in some very important tests. It was a flattering request. Yet when she once again asked him about it, he simply said the equipment was delayed and went on talking about the solution he was pouring into a test tube.

Professor A. V. Dzelichovsky often invited her to the laboratory during the long wait. He acted almost like a private tutor, never too busy to see her or to talk—to talk about everything except the experiments she was supposed to star in. Finally, the curious girl found herself dropping in at the lab at any odd hour. "Is there any particular reason you've come?" Dzelichovsky would ask. All she could do was flush and stammer, "No . . . no, I just felt like it."

Unknown to herself, the coed had already starred in some very special experiments. As Professor Dzelichovsky made what he hoped was diverting small talk about the test tube he handed his student, he suddenly saw her eyelids flutter, then close. Her breathing slowed, becoming deep, regular. She'd fallen sound asleep.

Down the hall, K. D. Kotkov, a psychologist, also had his eyes shut. He was far from asleep, although he mentally repeated, "sleep, sleep" over and over. At the same time Kotkov vividly imagined the girl's face. The most important ingredient in this bid for secret telepathic control Kotkov found was *wishing*. He wished the girl asleep until he felt a "sort of ecstasy of triumph. Then I knew she was asleep." He noted the time and got set to waken her.

The young student blinked awake, the test tube still in her hand, and resumed talking with the elated, but somewhat stunned Dzelichovsky. The experiment worked! And the girl did not realize anything had happened.

During the two-month test run Kotkov was able to telepathically knock the girl out from the opposite side of town. Telepathy also lay behind her compulsion to drop in on Professor Dzelichovsky. Home in his apartment, Dr. Kotkov mentally directed her to the laboratory. To avoid the possibility that she might drop in spontaneously or, however unlikely, simply snooze off in the middle of a sentence, the professors timed the tests with military precision.

Kotkov tried to telepathically obliterate the girl's consciousness thirty times. He never failed.[237]

The girl, asleep, frozen upright, clutching a test tube, looked as if she were in trance. The Russians later found one can, to some extent, talk to and question a person in telepathic sleep, just as if he were under hypnosis. Is telepathy actually hypnosis a few paces removed? Not exactly, say the Soviets. The mechanisms that turn off your will and turn on trance are different. Hypnosis, according to the Soviets, springs generally from language, suggestive *words* and commands. The telepathic force that knocks you out is generated by men like Kotkov holding strong visual *images* of you.

Telepathic hypnosis sparkles at the heart of the abundant experiments Dr. Vasiliev painstakingly carried out, but couldn't reveal under Stalin's regime. The reality of telepathic sleep-wake, backed by columns of data, was to many the most astonishing part of Vasiliev's *Experiments in Mental Suggestion,* finally published in 1962.

A very bright physiologist, the young Leonid Vasiliev with his full dark hair, strong featured and good looking, possessed a character to match his leonine appearance. He was tenacious and bold in his research. His mind roamed easily through the realms of many disciplines. And as it turned out, he showed a kind of personal nobility in not skewing the truth at a time when it could have been, and perhaps was, so much to his detriment to hold onto his chunk of it.

Theories about the material waves that piggyback telepathic communication from one brain to another buzzed in Vasiliev's head when, in 1932, he was given a task he relished. Stalin was already in tight fisted control. Word came down to the famous Bekhterev Brain Institute, where Vasiliev worked, to get to the bottom of telepathy. Again, no one has ever clarified where word came from except that it was from the very top. Soviet scientists were to unmask a mystery of the ages. They would show the world that telepathy trundles along on well-known physical waves.

First of all, Vasiliev needed telepathy, telepathy that would click on and off in the lab like a light beam to be probed and pulled apart into wavelengths. Gifted mediums were scarce. Besides, Vasiliev needed an unquestionable demonstration of telepathy, one that could be turned readily into a statistic. Vasiliev's answer was, of course, the exquisitely simple telepathic trance.

Vasiliev and his colleagues, I. F. Tomashevsky, a physiologist, and Dr. A. V. Doubrovsky, a psychiatrist, came up with two good female subjects: Ivanova and Fedorova, both twenty-five-year-old neurotic patients of Doubrovsky's. Unlike the Kharkov girl, when the experiments began, Ivanova knew something was happening. She lay on a cot. Electrodes on her right hand traced electric skin currents not under conscious control. In her left hand she held a balloon-like apparatus. "Keep squeezing it, steadily," they told her. In another room impulses from both devices registered on a graph. If she fell asleep the spiking lines would level out.

The scientists telepathically put the women to sleep countless times in a three-year period, from room to room, from building to building. They even wired the balloon apparatus to Ivanova's radio at home, so they could catch the signals in their labs. While she lay in her own bed they knocked her out telepathically. As consciousness flicked off and on again in Ivanova and Fedorova, Vasiliev set up traps for the telepathic waves. He tried to catch "Cazzamalli waves," named for an Italian neurologist who claimed to have detected radio waves crackling out of people when they imagined themselves in violent scenes, such as charging out of a trench with a bayonet. Vasiliev, tuning up and down the specified wavelengths, heard not a crackle.

Still there were plenty of other waves. Vasiliev shut Ivanova into an iron Faraday cage that barred electromagnetic waves. Telepathy went on as usual. The scientists were beginning to worry. If telepathy didn't prove to have a physical basis, it would have to join other emigrés from the Soviet Union. Vasiliev built a lead capsule, a barrier even to radiation. Tomashevsky, the sender, climbed a stepladder and slid into what looked like an oversized antique refrigerator. He lowered the heavy domed lid. It settled into a gully filled with mercury until the capsule was perfectly sealed. No waves could move in or out. Surely telepathy would not happen. Tomashevsky pictured Fedorova asleep inside the Faraday cage. She lost consciousness. This knockout telepathy actually seemed to work somewhat better inside all the leaden shields.

"We were dumbfounded! Vasiliev wrote. "We were ourselves as if hypnotized by these unexpected results!" [402] And they were worried. With the single-mindedness of men trying to isolate a new element in an unwieldy chunk of ore, the dedicated parapsychologists set out to discredit their own work. They tried to prove that conditioned response knocked subjects out, not telepathy. This attempt failed and they tried their telepathy on new subjects—a teacher, a laborer, a student, an interpreter. Still they found consciousness could be blanked telepathically.

Vasiliev knew electromagnetic waves diminish with mileage. He dispatched Tomashevsky to Sevastopol, a Crimean seaside resort more than a thousand miles due south. For once Ivanova didn't know she was in an experiment. She appeared at the psychotherapeutic clinic for her usual session with Dr. Doubrovsky. They talked through the hour and nothing happened. Not the curve of the earth, but a more common obstacle to travelers blocked telepathy. Tomashevsky felt too sick to keep his date. He recovered by Ivanova's next appointment. Standing alone on the boardwalk, Tomashevsky concentrated. A thousand miles away, Ivanova lost consciousness on schedule as she talked to Dr. Doubrovsky.

Ironically, the tireless Vasiliev had built what is still the world's best proof that (known) electromagnetic waves do not carry telepathy. "We fully appreciate," Vasiliev wrote in 1937, "the responsibility involved in reaching such a conclusion." The news didn't hit the world until 1962 when, toward the end of his life, Vasiliev was able to publish his *Experiments in Mental Suggestion.* "I did the best I could, let those who can do better," read the inscription of Vasiliev's long-delayed, explosive book.

Now parapsychologists in Leningrad and Moscow are once more into the telepathic manipulation of consciousness, this time recording successes with the EEG. In *Radio Techniks,*[73] Dr. Ippolit Kogan told other scientists about a girl, Olya, hypnotized normally, then attached to the EEG. In a separate room the telepathic sender, Dr. Vladimir L. Raikov, was also hooked to an EEG. At random moments he was signaled to awake Olya with ESP. Raikov managed to think Olya awake six out of eleven times. Edward Naumov reported a similar series. Telepathy woke up the subject six out of eight times. Naumov remarked that as soon as the telepathic "wake up" is sent, trance becomes less and less deep, full consciousness returning in twenty to thirty seconds.[134] In the Leningrad laboratory of Dr.

Pavel Gulyaiev, friends of subjects have been trained to put them to sleep telepathically.[410]

Why are the Soviets again hard at work on the telepathic control of consciousness? Dr. Kogan, like Vasiliev, is probably doing it for theoretical reasons. He has demonstrated mathematically that an electromagnetic carrier of telepathy is not impossible in *principle* and would involve wavelengths over a mile long. Why other scientists may be delving into control of consciousness by ESP is another question.

Telepathic sleep—or is it trance? Are you simply out, or do you dream your private dreams? Or does something else hold sway? The current Soviets have skimped on divulging psychological details about their telepathic manipulation of consciousness. But Vasiliev made some revelations worth noting. Fedorova and Ivanova could be questioned while under telepathic trance. They often knew who was psychically blanking them out. For the first time in two years, Vasiliev mentally forced Fedorova to sleep. Asked in trance what happened, she said, "Vasiliev is creeping into my head. . . ." Rooms away, Vasiliev decided to think of a bird, a vulture. "Vasiliev," Fedorova went on, "his eyes bulge like a rooster. He's sitting at a circular table. [Correct.] He did it. He took everything from me." When Vasiliev started to bring her round telepathically, the still entranced Fedorova said, "Stop it, Professor Vasiliev. I'll have to wake up—I don't want to." [237]

Not only does this kind of telepathy throw a person into a trance, but it also seems to open up a good channel of communication. Asked about this weird connection, the woman said it was like a telephone, or like being at the end of a ball of yarn, attached to a string that could ravel them up or play them out.

If telepathy can be beefed up, amplified like a telephone signal, architects will have a new problem, Dr. Stefan Manczarski of Poland predicts. They will have to find a way to screen apartments from unwanted telepathy. Manczarski, who believes there's life left in the electromagnetic theories, is one of the few scientists to write publicly about telepathy as an unusually effective way of spreading propaganda. "A great practical advantage," he called it, though he added that people buffeted by telepathic commercials might not think it a wondrous idea.[278] Manczarski, head of Poland's team for the International Geophysical Year 1957, is the only Pole to publish work on psi since the war. His experiments led him to think that telepathy does work on waves, which could be amped up like radio waves or any of the other waves we use every day. Like radio and television, telepathy would become a subtle new modus for the influencers of the world. Dr. Manczarski's wave ideas are debatable. But what about telepathy someday becoming a tool for influencing people?

Current Russian researchers don't discuss who can be entranced telepathically. According to the older scientists, if you can be lulled into deep hypnosis (about 20 percent of us can) you might be put to sleep from afar telepathically. Nevertheless, Dr. Platonov estimated that only four out of a hundred people can *regularly* be blanked out with telepathy.

Hypnotizing someone telepathically probably comes over as a more eerie, mystifying, almost diabolical act in America than it does in Russia. And it's the hypnotism, more than the telepathy, that seems to jolt people. We're just getting used to hypnotism. Since the turn of the century Russians have honed their hypnotic skills and widely explored its possibilities. In the Soviet Union hypnotism is a common tool like x-rays, used in medicine, psychotherapy, physiology, psychology, and experimental pedagogy.

While our Western mind explorers, starting with Freudian complexes, dramatic as Greek tragedies, uncovered startling things about personality, their Soviet counterparts moved in a different direction. With the help of hypnosis, they searched the abilities of the mind. As a simple example, hypnotists found that if you're put into trance you can tell precisely how many trees and telephone poles you passed on your route from home to the doctor's office. Such observations led to complex studies of memory. It was natural for Russians to try to elucidate the psychic mind with hypnosis. Equally compelling, Europeans since the nineteenth century have felt hypnosis can facilitate psychic talents. An American, Stanley V. Mitchell, while President of the International Guild of Hypnotists, found hypnosis unlocked a very happy kind of ESP on a Russian trip in 1964.

Mitchell reported in *Fate* Magazine (September 1964) that the doctors of a Soviet clinic he toured provided him with a nurse as a subject so he could demonstrate his techniques. The nurse fell quickly into trance; she carried out all of Mitchell's instructions beautifully. Only later did he discover that the nurse understood no English! She automatically used some sort of psychic transformer to convert his English commands into action. Mitchell ran into a similar ESP-across-the-language-gap situation in Poland. An old woman sat in the room watching a young relative be hypnotized. As Mitchell gave his commands, the woman also fell into trance. In this state, Mitchell could communicate with her, although she spoke almost no English. Intrigued, he questioned the old woman. She said she could easily understand him under hypnosis. "But when you don't hypnotize, all you say is cha, cha, cha."

Dr. Vasiliev, justifiably proud of his groundbreaking work with telepathic hypnosis, said that he regretted Westerners had not taken up and used his sleep-wake test. The comparatively finicky feeling about hypnosis in the West is one reason subjects weren't receiving a telepathic sleeping pill in American labs.

The Soviets perfected and certified the reality of telepathic trance, but they never claimed to have discovered it. The French did that. Some of the earliest records of this sort of psychic hanky-panky, featured Léonie B., a fifty-year-old French peasant from Brittany who was a variously talented medium.

One particular experiment with Léonie has all the unhinging allure of a Marx Brothers movie, circa 1886. It happened one night after dinner in Le Havre. Around the table sat much of the cream of European psychical research: Pierre Janet, psychologist and one of the fathers of French parapsychology; his collaborator, Dr. M. Gibert; Julius Ochorovicz, still remembered as Poland's most famous psychic researcher; England's Frederic Myers, co-founder of the British Society for Psychical Research; and two scholars of almost equal repute.

The six decided to see if Gibert could put Léonie into trance at a distance, a feat he'd done on other occasions, and if he could summon the entranced woman to him. They synchronized pocket watches. Then Gibert retired to his study; the others made for Léonie's cottage two-thirds of a mile across town. Keeping to the shadows, they surrounded the house. "At that time," Ochorovicz wrote, "there was no one there but Léonie and a cook who was not expecting any activity on our part." Right on schedule, Léonie stepped outside and walked to the garden gate. Ochorovicz, skulking behind the corner of the cottage, was happy to see her eyes were shut tight. But Léonie turned around and re-entered the house. Ochorovicz noted later that at this moment the sender, Gibert, "as a result of the strain of thinking, fainted—or dozed off."

Soon Léonie reappeared walking fast—so fast she almost tangled with Professor Janet, who'd popped out of his hiding spot. "Fortunately she didn't notice her surroundings, or at least she didn't recognize us."

For ten minutes Léonie, eyes shut, hurried along successfully "avoiding street lamps and traffic." None of the other pedestrians seemed to notice anything unusual about Léonie, according to Myers. Perhaps they were too busy gawking at the gaggle of high-collared note takers trailing behind.

Suddenly, Léonie faltered; she looked confused. (Why? Because Gibert had decided the whole experiment was useless and started to play billiards.) Then Léonie picked up speed again. (He'd changed his mind and resumed sending.)

The pack jotting at her heels, Léonie arrived at her destination just as Gibert, wondering what had become of everybody, rushed out the door. They collided head on.

Léonie climbed over the confused Gibert and pressed on into the house. She ran from room to room saying sorrowfully, "Where is he? Where is he?" She searched upstairs and down, surrounded by six nimble-footed scholars, each trying not to be tagged. Finally Gibert sank into a chair and mentally called her.

"She takes him by the arm," Ochorovicz recorded. "She is seized with great joy!" So was Ochorovicz, who was at last convinced you surely could influence people at a distance.

If any current Soviet scientists have lived through such woolly moments summoning a person across Moscow, they don't talk about it. But they have occasionally mentioned efforts to guide someone's movements with telepathy inside their labs. On a closed-circuit TV, the Popov parapsychologists watch an entranced subject in an isolated room. Can ESP not only knock him out, but also knock him down?

Can they telepathically guide the direction—front, back, this side or that—of his fall?

"In one test series," Edward Naumov recorded, "the subject was made to fall ten out of ten times. And he fell in the direction commanded telepathically eight out of ten times." [133] Naumov mentioned casually that over a thousand people had been tested in the last few years in these knock-out and knock-down experiments.

Guiding a person psychically, the way you guide a missile electronically, was taken a step further with Karl Nikolaiev, according to a report given by the respected Dr. Kogan, in *Radio Technology* and at a conference on "Scientific Problems of Bio-Information" at the Soviet Academy Moscow House of Scientists attended by over seven hundred scientists.[75] Naumov, who apparently has some psi talent of his own, sent. Nikolaiev, fully conscious, attempted to let Naumov guide him around the room containing ten targets. "We had feedback in this test," Kogan said, meaning that Naumov, in another room, listened as Karl reported over a one-way microphone the direction he was walking. This hookup allowed Naumov to try to mentally correct any errors in Karl's aim while he was in motion. In twenty-six different attempts, Naumov guided Karl to the target thirteen times. The probabilities of doing this by chance are, according to Kogan, infinitely small.

In their orderly labs Soviet parapsychologists are manipulating consciousness, but what a tiny flick of the mind it is compared to the ballooning psychedelic trips that blossomed in the West. Reportedly, psi sometimes crosses the psychedelic consciousness. In his book, *The Mysterious Phenomenon of the Human Mind*, Vasiliev mentions that he gave a young girl, with no apparent psychic talent, a good dose of mescarine. When her high was in full color, he brought out ten sealed black plastic boxes. Neither Vasiliev nor his happy student (she thought the world was "beautiful") knew what small objects lay swaddled in cotton inside the boxes. "Tell me what you see in here," Vasiliev said, placing a box before the girl. She giggled. "How did you manage to get that in there? It's a big stone building." Unsealing the box later, Vasiliev found a one-ruble stamp carrying the picture of the large, stone Central Telegraph office in Moscow. The girl didn't bother to say anything about one box.

She scored five partial successes with the eight other boxes. For instance, confronted with a package containing distinctive red twigs, she said, "I see a patch of red." It was 1946, the start of the most immobilizing years of the Stalin regime, but apparently the girl had a good and rare trip with her Professor Vasiliev. She said, "Everything seemed so lovely. It seemed as if you could get away with anything."

As to current psychic-psychedelics, Dr. Milan Ryzl mentions that M. S. Smirnov, of the Laboratory of Vision, Institute of Problems of Information Transmission of the USSR Academy of Science, wrote him privately about tests with psilocybin.[382] Supposedly, Smirnov, following Vasiliev's technique, has had some psychic successes with psilocybin.

Generally in their efforts to alter consciousness, however, the Soviet parapsychologists seem to stick to variations on the traditional telepathic hypnosis. Vasiliev and his colleagues were like prospectors sifting electromagnetic waves. The gold they hunted was the "mechanism" of telepathy. Instead of "gold," they ended up with "copper" in the form of the handy, all-purpose sleep-wake test. Vasiliev used it as a specimen of telepathy to dissect, as he would explore a frog in physiology experiments. But the test he perfected may have the makings of a far more lively, interesting future within it. Manipulating someone else's consciousness with telepathy, guiding him in trance . . . colorful uses are too easy to conjure. Try espionage. You focus a mental whammy on the general's aide-de-camp. You give him posthypnotic suggestions to pull this lever, steal these papers. He wakes up, unaware like the Kharkov coed, that anything has happened. Miss M. fell into a trance while waltzing, but what if Miss M. had been driving a car, piloting a plane, standing sentry duty.

This is the facile fantasy of supersonic thrillers. But wouldn't it be naïve to assume no researcher has ever thought of such potential uses for telepathy? The famous Soviet Wolf Messing, with his widely attested ability to influence the minds of others, commented in his autobiography on the time he managed to walk out of a building, past guards ordered to stop him. "This and similar cases should make us reconsider the often-advanced opinion that nobody would perform under hypnosis an act opposed to his convictions. I am sure the guards would not have let me pass if I had directed at them the suggestion to let me pass as myself, but, using my mental power, I made them see in me the high official whom they would let out without a pass. Similarly, a man under hypnosis can be told to shoot a rabbit when in fact he would be shooting at a man." [119]

In the main, what the Soviets are probably seeking in their exploration of ESP's effect on consciousness is control in a more generalized, everyday, pervasive sense. You hear the word *control* often in the USSR, not as a political concept, but in its comparatively upbeat, scientific meaning. As a Moscow scientist told us, "Science has learned to control outer nature to the great benefit of mankind. Now we are trying to learn the laws governing inner nature. Just as an understanding of outer nature allowed us, for example, to generate electricity to light huge cities, so the ability to control the untapped resources of man should bring equally amazing benefits."

Control of schizophrenia is a good thing. Control of a person's attitudes to another person, race, or nation is not.

Czech biochemist Dr. Milan Ryzl stated in *Psychic*,[383] "The bulk of recent telepathy research in the USSR is concerned with the transmission of behavior impulses—or research to subliminally control an individual's conduct."

Visiting Soviet psi labs in 1967, Dr. Ryzl says he was told by a Russian, "When suitable means of propaganda are cleverly used, it is possible to mold any man's conscience so that in the end he may misuse his abilities while remaining convinced that he is serving an honest purpose." [382] Ryzl went on, "The USSR has the means to keep the results of such research secret from the rest of the world and, as practical applications of these results become possible, there is no doubt that the Soviet Union will do so."

10

WHAT MAKES YOU PSYCHIC?

Soviet parapsychologists never seemed to have heard the "Turn on, tune in, drop out" cliché. But these Russian mind-expanders are trying hard to turn on psi and they talk incessantly of tuning it. What switches on your latent psychic force? In 1965 the Popov group began collecting cases of spontaneous ESP. A study of ESP as it flashed, loaded with emotion and life, through the mesh of everyday routine, might reveal something of its elusive ways. It might provide clues for activating psi at will.

The late Popov biologist, Dr. I. Gellerstein chronicled a recent out-of-the-night ESP experience of a well-known Russian lawyer, Alexander Coney, "a man of critical mind, a sensible and shrewd analyzer, and not at all mystical." [96]

Jolting along on a train to Moscow, Coney dreamed that an old friend, Lajechnikov, stretched his hand out and looked at him entreatingly. Coney woke up. He hadn't seen or even thought much of Lajechnikov in a long time. Lajechnikov was old, he ought to call on him soon, Coney thought, and drifted back to sleep. Lajechnikov again took over his dream. This time he clasped Coney by the hand. He asked him something full of imperatives. Coney couldn't remember quite what, but the feeling was so strong that, on arriving in Moscow, he decided not to put off visiting his old friend any longer.

He headed straight for an address kiosk. The kiosk was shut tight. Chagrined, Coney remembered it was Sunday. There was no way to find Lajechnikov's current address. To throw off the strange feeling of his dream, Coney started to walk.

He went down Nikitsky Street, then Zoologicheskaya Street—and again a vivid memory of Lajechnikov seized him. As if compelled, Coney stopped and looked at the door of the house he was passing. The nameplate read,

"E. E. Lajechnikov." An old woman answered Coney's ring and led him upstairs.

"You're too late, Alexander," she said. There in his coffin lay Lajechnikov. "You see," the old woman went on, "he remembered you before he died. He kept saying, 'I wish Alexander were here—he could help me!' "

"It's indisputable that these things happen," Popov director Ippolit Kogan has remarked. "But why?" In their search to find any and all conditions that could help activate ESP, the Soviets eventually moved from the obvious trauma of being on your deathbed to things that are a lot less obvious, like the motion of the moon, the fluctuations of magnetic fields.

"I have studied spontaneous telepathy for almost forty years," Dr. Leonid Vasiliev remarked shortly before his own death in 1966. "I've gathered hundreds of reliable accounts of such spontaneous communication. A few days ago a teacher reported to me an unusual experience with her son." [238]

The woman wrote, "I'm not a superstitious person, but what happened to me eleven years ago is still a strange mystery to me. My son was a student at the Kiev Polytechnical Institute at the time and became ill with tuberculosis. He was being treated in Kiev. Knowing that his condition was serious, I spent many sleepless nights. In order to worry less, I often would spend the entire night reading books.

"On one such night, when I was in the midst of reading Makarenko's *Pedagogical Poem,* suddenly I felt as if an electrical current had shot through my body, and then, clearly, I saw in front of me the exhausted, suffering face of my son! He looked at me imploringly, as if he were trying to say something. Motionless as a stone, I looked at him —then, instantly—he was gone. Trembling and frightened, I clearly understood then that my son was no longer— that he had died on that very night. Crying, I shakily wrote down the hour, day, and date.

"And it was true. Later I received word that at this very time in Kiev, two hundred miles away, my son died."

Commented Dr. Vasiliev, "This woman never had hallucinations before or after that instance."

A Western researcher would try to pinpoint precisely

when the boy's face appeared—just before, during, or after death. The "after" possibility is not explored by the Soviets.

A similarly ambiguous message crackled about the towering Russian composer-pianist Anton Rubinstein. One miserable, window-creaking night, Rubinstein dined with his student, William Nichia. It was a God awful night, Nichia related, even for Leningrad, the city of terrible weather, Rubinstein asked his pupil what the incessant, howling winds reminded him of. "The moaning of lost souls," Nichia replied. A discussion of the possibility of an afterlife followed. "I'm sure there is one," Nichia exclaimed, "and if I die first, I'll come to you and prove it!" Rubinstein looked at his pupil. Finally he said with great solemnity, "It's a bargain then. If I go first, I will try the same."

Six years later, in 1894, Nichia, living in Paris, was catapulted out of his sleep by a horrendous cry. The face of Rubinstein, grotesquely contorted, loomed toward him. Shaking, Nichia sat up, with all the lights on, trying to convince himself that the nightmare was gone. He didn't remember his pact with Rubinstein until, the next afternoon, he saw the headline RUBINSTEIN DIES SUDDENLY. A mutual friend, who'd been at the musician's deathbed in Leningrad, eventually told Nichia that Rubinstein, who suffocated during a heart seizure, died with the most horrible, enraged, agonized cry she'd ever heard. Nichia concluded, "Even in death, as he always did in life, Rubinstein kept his word."

Radiating a crescendo of horror and agony, Rubinstein energized some sort of supernormal powers and apparently tried to keep his bargain. But whether he was in our state, or another, next state is impossible to determine from Nichia's experience. The investigator sorts through these accounts, dispassionate as a claims adjuster picking through a fire-gutted home. To the people electrified for a few psychic moments, however, these experiences can be a pivotal point in life and philosophy.

Dr. Bernard B. Kajinsky stands with Vasiliev as a pathfinding advocate of psychic research in Russia since the beginning of the Soviet era. A young man during the revolution, Kajinsky lived in Tbilisi. One night he woke with a start. He heard something—an odd, silvery, tinkling noise. It sounded, Kajinsky thought, like someone stirring up a drink, clinking the spoon against the side of the glass. The next morning Kajinsky was too worried about a friend laid low in the typhus epidemic then raging in Tbilisi to mull over his interrupted sleep. He hurried the mile across town to the other boy's house. His friend's mother opened the door, weeping. "Oh, Bernard," she said, "last night I went up to give him his medicine and as I put the spoon to his lips, his eyes grew strange . . . opaque. And he died! Right at that moment, he died!"

Kajinsky, possessed of a more steadily analytical mind than some, asked the distracted mother her exact movements before going to the bedside. "I went into the room, poured his medicine into a glass, stirred it—with what? With a spoon, a spoon—then I carried it to him, and right then . . ."

Kajinsky was a convinced materialist. He was also convinced for the rest of his life that it was the foredooming sound of the spoon stirring his friend's medicine that woke him.[276] Unnerved, upset, that morning Kajinsky vowed to scientifically search out the secrets of such fateful communications.

Crisis, sheer and often mortal, any investigator will tell you is one bright red factor in many, many instances of spontaneous ESP. Aside from the desperate need to communicate by any means, there may be another reason that crisis looms so often in psychic annals. The full-colored sight of a friend in agony vibrates in the memory like flashbulb spots on the retina. You can't forget it; it seems worthy of documentation. Less devastating instances of telepathy and clairvoyance might be forgotten or not checked out. To broaden their files, the Popov Society advertised, asking Russians to send in their unusual experiences. Apparently word has gotten around. We bumped into a nautical engineer in a Leningrad park who insisted on an impromptu walking tour of the city. He paused beside a pastel canal. "Over there's the house where they killed Rasputin. And there is where they finally pushed him through the ice." It seemed like a good moment to tell him why we were in Russia. He didn't know much about parapsychology, except, he said, "You should look for an institute in Moscow. I know people are supposed to send any usual dreams and strange premonitions there."

An American, versed in psychic work, reported that 2 years earlier Soviet scientists had told him they were paying peasants a few kopecks to mail in out of the ordinary dreams and visions. All collected cases, according to this reporter, were to be collated by computor.[283] We couldn't confirm this story one way or the other, but it would be a reasonable plan for the Soviets, enamored with cybernetics and information retrieval.

TELEPATHIC SENDER—THE FORGOTTEN PSYCHIC?

Staging an emergency is not an ideal laboratory technique if, like the Russians, you're trying to coax psychic talents into action. But besides emergency, there's something obvious about cases of spontaneous ESP that the Soviets, if no one else, recognize. The person in trouble, the person going down in the quicksand, certainly has something to do with ESP's sudden assault on his friend sleeping peacefully at home. In the West the sender has been a cypher, a forgotten man for the past four decades. It seems as if anyone standing around the lab could be the sender—usually one of the scientists involved. The Soviets consider the sender—or *inductor,* as they term him—a psychic. They train the sender, they study him with physiological machines almost as extensively as they do the receiver.

What's involved in sending a telepathic message? A well-known Russian psychic, Mikhail Kuni, had a number of suggestions for the scientists. Kuni, a big, sandy-haired man now in his sixties, has a wrinkly forehead that looks as if he's in constant, amiable concentration. Like Wolf Messing, he has performed "Psychological Experiments" before large audiences for many years. "He has really remarkable ESP ability," Edward Naumov, who has tested Kuni, told us.

Like the scientists who studied spontaneous ESP, Kuni knew all too well that high-tide emotion can bring on a psychic experience. Years ago when he was an art student, Kuni woke up one morning with a feeling of dread. "I had a terrible dream," he told the two artist friends who shared his small Moscow apartment. "I saw my mother being bitten by a rat! It was so vivid . . . I felt like I was there. Then I saw mother lying on her bed; she was pale and in pain, literally near death." The young artist stared glumly out the lace curtained window. His friends couldn't jog him out of a feeling of foreboding.

Later that day a telegram arrived from Kuni's home town, Vitebsk, a city a few hundred miles west of Moscow. Dated February 21, it read: "MAMA DANGEROUSLY ILL. COME AT ONCE."

"I got to Vitebsk the next day," Kuni recalls, "and found my mother in a very serious condition. Ten days before, on February 11th, a rat had bitten her in the leg. The bite wasn't deep or dangerous, so they thought. But then gangrene set in. By the 20th she was in a high fever and very ill. Early in the morning on the 21st a committee of doctors consulted and decided they'd have to amputate, even though they worried about the outcome because my mother had diabetes. Overhearing fragments of their talk, mother felt her condition was hopeless. This was about 10 o'clock in the morning while I was still asleep in Moscow. The images, the information my mother overheard, and the painful jolt they caused her came to me telepathically at the peak of her emotional experience."[26, 93]

The vision of his sick mother made such an impact on Kuni that it turned him away from life as a painter and led him to the psychic stage. Working with hundreds of people, Kuni has found that emotion is not the only thing that can turn the psychic switch.

"Deaf mutes make better senders than most people," Kuni says. He checked his observation at a sanatorium for mutes at Gelendzhik. "There were three deaf mutes flying with me in the helicopter from Sochi to Gelendzhik. Two men sat in front and a woman sat in the row with me at the rear of the copter. At the moment one of the men ahead started to turn his head toward us, the woman, reading a book beside me, raised her head to him. The reverse also occurred. Hardly had the woman interrupted her reading with the obvious purpose of communicating something, when the deaf mute ahead turned around to her.

"The work we did at Gelendzhik bore out our hypothesis that the deaf and dumb (and all people in a lesser degree) have the ability to sense an unseen person's glance accurately, that is, to sense another person's 'telepathic' signal. Excluding all possible coincidences, the telepathy tests that we also did with the deaf and dumb were equally successful."

Both Kuni and Wolf Messing maintain that deaf mutes have a wonderful ability to project a thought. Why? Both psychics agree it is because the deaf and dumb, as compensation, have learned to visualize to perfection. The ability to visualize easily, vividly, is key, according to the Soviets, in the successful transmission of telepathy. Dr. K. I. Platonov discovered this when attempting to put people under hypnosis telepathically. It wasn't enough, Platonov found, to concentrate mentally on the words "relax," or "sleep," or other verbal commands he used to entrance subjects *vis-à-vis*. "With telepathy I had to visualize my subject asleep."

Aside from advising them to "hold a strong, living picture in your mind," what else do the Soviets tell their senders? Biophysicist Yuri Kamensky, who has a bagful of trial-and-error knowledge from his many attempts to contact Karl Nikolaiev telepathically, has these tips for anybody who wants to send an ESP message. Get comfortable and let tension drop from the body like a bathrobe. Psychologically, you should set aside any cares and emotions. Saturate yourself with confidence. "As you begin a transmission of a picture, you should not indulge in any interior monologue," Kamensky states. "Start by touching the object. You must have a clear cutaneous representation of it. Next, think of the object. Finally, visualize vividly the receiver's face. Imagine the receiver looking at the object, touching the object."

When these conditions were realized, Kamensky reported,[158] thirty-four different people correctly picked up seven out of ten objects sent to them. If you find it easy to fulfill Kamensky's conditions, you must already have a sort of super control. It is precisely to get such control that the Russians train.

The novel idea of a sensuous element in psi fits with the supposed ESP prowess of deaf mutes, who would naturally refine touch as well as vision. The psychic Kuni worked the feel-and-see combination. "I sat holding in my right hand a glass of hot tea. I tried to strongly project this sensation to a group of seventeen men in another room who'd been hypnotized. The men were asked what they felt. To a greater or lesser degree, they all said their right hands felt warm. Then I pricked myself with a pin. Before the group could even be asked, all the men, almost at one time, cried out with pain. We successfully repeated these tests with groups of fifteen to twenty people." [93]

"If one person can do it, other people can do it," insists Karl Nikolaiev. The Soviets are strong on this theory. They aren't just training would-be telepathists; they also think that some other Russians should be able to move matchboxes, like their PK medium Nelya Mikhailova does.

Dr. Genady Sergeyev claims he found an unusual difference in potential in Nelya's brain. Now the Soviets say they've located others with this same fifty-to-one difference in potential between the front and the back of the brain. Teams of these people, picked because they were also aggressive and competitive, are trying hard in practice sessions to summon up something in themselves that will make an arrow on a thread under a glass cover move when they gaze at it. Edward Naumov reports some early success. The Soviets think the arrow on a thread is the easiest thing to move with PK.

If telepathy is a skill or a talent, doesn't it also figure that you should start with what is easy, just as you learn to read with a primer, not a book by Teilhard de Chardin? The Soviets have a few ideas about what is easy and what is hard to communicate telepathically. Dr. Lutsia Pavlova, who found "patterns" of telepathy in brain waves, made one observation that could disconcert some parapsychologists if it proves true. Apparently, having a person guess ESP cards to demonstrate telepathy—the test on which most Western ESP research is based—is just about the toughest way to try to generate ESP.

"We found it best not to send telepathic signals too quickly. If different telepathic bits come too rapidly, the changes in the brain associated with telepathy begin to blur and finally disappear. The ESP card tests are built on the idea of transmitting a great many telepathic bits of information in a very short time to build up statistical evidence," Dr. Pavlova points out. "This is not to say that we should abandon serious quantitative testing, but we should remember what *are* the best conditions for telepathic transmission." [152]

On the other hand, Dr. Vladimir Fidelman seems to have plugged the statistical test into new life. Engineer Fidelman runs the closest thing to a psychedelic light show in Moscow. His group decided to try to send numbers telepathically. Most experimenters would have asked a sender to sit before a card with, say, the number 6 on it. Hopefully the sender would shape his wavering thought into a solid 6.

Fidelman went electronic. He bombarded the sender with sixes, sixes on bright lights, sixes flashing continuously. "Six, six," the sender also murmured over and over as the light pulsed. Fidelman created a sort of polysensory incantation.

As the bombardment of the telepathic sender continued, the correct number would form and "stabilize" in the thought of the receiver some distance away. Sometimes an original wrong number would be driven out, according to the experimenters.

"Actually, any person can telepathically send the image of a number this way," Dr. Fidelman told a special Russians-only conference on parapsychology in February 1968. "We accepted as sender anyone who wanted to try. But we did observe that the number of repetitions needed to be able to transmit a number varied between senders from less than ten seconds up to a minute-and-a-half of light flashes. In the telepathic transmission of 135 numbers over a mile-and-a-half distance, one hundred were received with perfect clarity." [78]

(Fidelman's success with light bombardment makes one wonder about the multimedia circuses, with their kaleidoscoping, pulsing light and sound, that advertise "the ultimate in legal ways to turn on your mind.")

Long before Fidelman conducted his tests, Mikhail Kuni discovered that some peculiar power could spark between mind and numbers. One day when he was twelve years old, a friend at school dropped a box of matches, spilling them on the ground. Instantly Kuni said, "There are thirty-one." His classmates laughed, but after counting the matches found he was right. To Kuni's own amazement, he discovered that without thinking he could immediately give the total of anything—spilled matches, teeth in a comb, or huge columns of figures. The answers just seemed to light up in his mind like numbers on a tote board. Once on a tour to China, Kuni paused to photograph a pond of fish, then went off and forgot his camera. Afterward he recalled, "I set the camera down just as goldfish number 87 was passing!" Kuni's uncanny mathematical prowess now forms part of his telepathic show.[326] A few years ago it took him to Dubna, a city near Moscow, nicknamed "Atomgrad" because it houses the Joint Nuclear Research Institute of the Academy of Sciences. Kuni confronted dozens of the USSR's most renowned scientists. Among the typical tests devised to display the computorlike aspects of his brain is a circle-drawing experiment. Kuni asked a physicist volunteer from the audience to cover a huge blackboard with circles. "They can intersect. They can be inside one another. Draw them any way you wish."

Kuni left the stage and was blindfolded. Finally, scientists turned the blackboard to face the audience. On signal the ruggedly built psychic, crouched like a leopard ready to pounce, turned around and lowered his blindfold. The blackboard was almost white with circles. "167!" It took the Soviet Union's foremost scientists over five minutes to do the calculations necessary to verify Kuni's instant and correct answer.

After this performance of numerical wizardry and telepathy, Kuni received a letter from the scientists at the Joint Nuclear Research Institute: "If we weren't physicists, then it would be extremely difficult to verify that man's brain is capable of accomplishing such miracles." (Dubna, April 12, 1959.)[252]

Kuni's instant calculations may not be what everyone calls psychic but it certainly shows a superconnection to the underside of the mind, the part the Soviets are so anxious to bring into action. In the more strictly psychic line, Moscow parapsychologists decided to explore Kuni's rapport with numbers. They set two blackboards in widely separated rooms, monitoring Kuni's room with closed-circuit TV, Naumov reported, "I began writing figures all over one blackboard. At the end of the allotted time, we checked Kuni's board. He'd written the identical figures. Aside from having remarkable talent, Kuni has always cooperated sincerely with scientists in helping us understand how telepathy works."

AMPING-UP PSYCHIC ABILITY

In trying to spark telepathy with people other than full-blown psychics like Kuni, the Soviets work to ease sender and receiver into *rapport*[137]—a word that in the Soviet lexicon includes a multitude of harmonies, physical and psychological. The sender and receiver practice telepathy, often in the same room so the sender can try to mentally correct errors the receiver makes.

"We suspect that a psychic naturally, probably unconsciously, *attunes* his brain waves to the rhythm of another person's brain," one of the younger physicists told us. "This rapport helps him get the other man's thought, or, as in the case of psychic healers, to affect the other person in some way. We think that many people can learn to tune to each other in about three months." He didn't say how.

The Soviets seem ecstatic when they find proof of physical harmony between sender and receiver—hearts beating in rhythm, brains in pattern—at the time of telepathic communion. "When Kamensky and Nikolaiev are in telepathic contact, their hearts beat as one!" Naumov told us with a grin. He and Dr. Sergeyev found that when contact was made during the sending of emotion telepathically there was synchronization in the cycle of heart activity in sender and receiver. This showed up clearly on the electrocardiograph attached to each of the distant psychics. There was simultaneous increase in arrhythmia, a quicker heartbeat, and greater cardiac noises. The scientists also spoke of simultaneous changes in the frequency and spectral structure of the tremor registration curve during the moment of "biological contact" in telepathy.[133]

The Soviets think this odd bodily rapport is highly significant and perhaps facilitates telepathy. Attempting to bring on biological harmony is one of their aims. Casting about to get psychic abilities switched on and psychics tuned to one another, the Russians have resorted not to fields of pot, but to artificial fields. "We surround both sender and receiver with artificial magnetic fields both before and during ESP tests," they said. "It gives them extra energy. The fields don't have to be strong. Weak fields work just as well." Telepathy had greatly improved under the impact of these fields, they reported.

"Do you beam negative ions at would-be psychics?" we asked. (Negative ions are particles with a negative electrical charge. As a physiologist, Dr. Vasiliev had won the Lenin Prize and worldwide recognition for work on the effects of ions on the body.)

"Our equipment is enormously complex. We use ionized fields, and much more than that. But we can't tell you anything about it because it's secret," the Russians said.

So we were right back to the problem that has bedeviled the non-initiate for centuries. Is it a put-on, or do the Soviets really have something?

Recently a French physicist, Dr. Jacques Bergier, revealed, "The Pavlov Institute in Moscow clandestinely researched the influence of high-frequency magnetic fields on telepathy all through the Stalin years even though telepathy was ill thought of." A few years ago Dr. V. A. Kozak of the Pavlov Institute stated, "Clairvoyance and ESP are provoked by a field of forces, not necessarily electromagnetic."[276]

In the United States a Washington electronics engineer reported to the Parapsychology Foundation, "working with high-frequency machines, my colleagues and I have suddenly found that we are on occasion telepathic." A company had been set up to investigate.

The Russians do seem to think that natural forces, the kind that affect all of us, can help stir up psi or dampen it. Mikhail Kuni speaks of one dismal night he spent onstage, July 8, 1966. "That one evening I made more mistakes than I would normally make during months of performances. I had to repeat some experiments three or four times to get them right.

"I felt fine, but I simply could not mobilize my powers of will and concentration. And I know why. There was a terrible thunder storm in Moscow that night. When there is thunder and lightning it is always difficult for me to work, but what can I do," he jokes. "The timetable of a tour is made without consulting the weather bureau. I have to try to perform like a football player in any weather."

Weather not only affects telepathy. "Lightning storms diminish Nelya Mikhailova's PK power," Dr. Sergeyev says. Unlike Soviet impresarios, Soviet parapsychologists are now making sure psychics don't have to perform under muddy conditions.

ASTROLOGY—OR COSMIC BIOLOGY?

There is an image slowly taking shape in Soviet parapsychology, a moving picture of the human being showing him as a pulsating field, dynamically interacting with all other fields, like a note resonating with all the other notes swirling in a symphony. This live, interacting view of all things is behind the Russians' seemingly astrological interest in sunspots. "We mean solar activity at the time of a person's birth," Edward Naumov clarified.

But how does this affect a person's ability to use psychic power?

"It's too early for final conclusions, but statistical evidence we're accumulating seems to be indicating that good receivers are often born when the sun is quiet, good senders when there is sunspot activity." Other Communist scientists have found ESP flows more easily at full moon.

Russian newspapers don't carry daily astrology guides, nor are there any popular magazines on the subject, but scientists in various fields are beginning to explore the ancient science. Physicist Dr. Konstantin Kobyizev of Moscow University has lectured and written on this move into astrology. He told us, "The influence of large periodic radiations of energy from the sun onto the earth is an exactly established scientific fact. From reports published in the journal *Party Life* you can see that the Soviet pioneer in cosmic biology, Dr. A. L. Chijevsky, an honorary professor at many Asian and European universities, has reported correlations between cycles of sunspot activity and epidemics on earth, including invasions of locusts and rodents. Perhaps even more significant, there is a correlation between these cycles of sunspot activity and great migrations of people, crusades, wars, and revolutions.

"Compilations of graphs of solar activity concur with

chronological tables of all the mass movements of people from 1917," said Dr. Kobyizev, "This was ascertained by a special committee here headed by Dr. Lunacharsky and Dr. Semashko.

"These solar cycles repeat every seven, eleven, thirty-five, end eighty years. There is a flow of fiery plasma and perhaps other energy. On earth at this time there might exist, for example, unjust social conditions, conditions for revolutions, and so forth. These conditions are aggravated by a torrent of sun radiations that activate events and activate the resolution of leaders.

"In the years of high solar activity magnetic storms spring up, which is why electrocommunications sometimes break down completely, why the number of suicides, psychoses, automobile crashes, and deaths of people with severe heart trouble increases. Years of minimal sun activity correspond with epidemics of other illnesses such as diphtheria and with earthquakes. The establishment of laws for these processes would permit us to prepare in advance for them and to take the necessary measures."

Support for the Soviet observations comes from many scientists in the West, such as Professor Cecil Maby (B.Sc., A.R.C.S., F.R.A.S.), who have found the 11½-year sunspot cycle has a clear effect on meteorology, plant growth, and even human industrial productivity. French researcher Dr. Michel Gauquelin also reports similar findings in his book *The Cosmic Clocks*.

Just how do these emanations from the sun affect you? Dr. Leonard Ravitz reported that phases of the moon, the sun's position, cosmic and gamma rays, sunspot radiation, and other disturbances of the earth's magnetic field have an impact on the force fields around our bodies. His discovery of the cyclic nature of these influences lent impetus to the burgeoning study of biorhythms in the West.

Dr. Robert Becker of the Veterans Administration Hospital in Syracuse, New York, revealed at a space symposium in 1962 that these subtle changes in the earth's magnetic fields (caused by the sun, moon, and planets) actually alter the force field of the human body, which in turn affects the nervous system. Do these outer-space influences also have a bearing on PK and ESP?

"The most favorable time for PK to occur is when there

are magnetic disturbances of the earth caused by sunspot activity," Dr. Sergeyev reported to the conference.

The Russians are investigating the relation of magnetic fields to ESP [161] and get regular readings on magnetic weather and cosmic conditions from Pulkovo Observatory before taking to the telepathic channels. (Like temperatures, magnetic fields vary each day. As with weather, there are magnetic storms of differing severity.) Soviet psi experiments are sometimes even set up in the middle of the night to take advantage of optimum conditions. Maybe one of the reasons repeatability has long been a bugbear in Western ESP tests is because none of these varying conditions are considered.

In their attempt to set ESP flowing, the Soviets consider angles most researchers never thought of before—mainly because some of these factors weren't discovered until the beginning of space explorations and the International Geophysical Year in 1957.

CAN ESP BE BUGGED?

Cosmic static affects ESP, the Soviets think. What about static from other minds? To find out, the Russians have tried to bug their own telepathic communications. They've come up with a third party in telepathy, the "Interceptor."

"Kamensky was again trying to send pictures telepathically from Leningrad to Nikolaiev in Moscow," Naumov told us. "Unknown to both of them, there was an interceptor involved in Moscow, in a different building from Nikolaiev, As you'll see, this man, Victor Milodan—I was the only person who knew about him—successfully cut into the telepathic communication." Naumov unrolled a large test chart. We saw that Nikolaiev picked up three of the five images sent. But interceptor Milodan, whom Kamensky had no thought of, also got good information on two items, a mathematical compass and a silver nail brush. For the brush, he correctly wrote, "Dirty, sulphurous, about 3 inches by 1½ inches. It is silver and rectangular," The mysterious Milodan is, we gathered, one of a group of psychics wrapped away from publicity.

Pointing to the "Hour: Minute: Second" columns of his

chart, Naumov stressed, "The interceptor knew at what minutes telepathy was moving between Kamensky and Nikolaiev. He was right five out of five times, although all we told him was the transmission would be sometime during the evening." (Noting the second you think someone is beaming thought at you and the second he stops is an important element in Russian telepathy tests.)

Dr. Fidelman, talking about his light show telepathic sending of numbers, said, "We were also able to verify the possibility of intercepting telepathy." [78]

Naumov added another tidbit: "If an interceptor is a very powerful psychic, he can skew the transmission." It seemed the receiver might get the ideas sent by the interceptor instead of those the sender is transmitting.

If the Soviets are right, and this is an area they would be likely to investigate fully, it seems that even a modern sophisticated spy armed with ESP might still have his messages bugged. But he might stand a chance of tuning in to any other circulating telepathy. Knowing whether telepathy can be intercepted or distorted is important if you want to use psi practically, which is the Soviet goal. One American who conferred with Soviet psi groups says there is thought about using highly trained psychics governmentally, somewhat as the Egyptians used their seers and the Greeks their priestess oracles—psychics as a sort of secret intelligence adjunct. Any government wants all the intelligence it can get.

One big reason for all this concern in Russia seems to come out—the Chinese. A rumor circulating the West has it that some of the push in parapsychology is engendered by fear of China. As a rumor within a rumor, we heard in Russia that Chairman Mao two years earlier had ordered his scientists to make one of their inimitable full-steam-ahead approaches onto the frontier of parapsychology. Interestingly, there is psi research going on in far eastern Vladivostok and Khabarovsk on the disputed Chinese border.

ESP has always been particularly prevalent in wartime. Biologist Dr. Vasily Efimov, a colleague of Vasiliev's, told us at the conference that the wealth of psychic experiences on the battlefield lead him into ESP research. "At a time of grief, telekinetic and telepathic powers are awakened. I began to think there was something to ESP when wounded soldiers told me about their experiences. All their psychic abilities were aroused by the extreme dangers of the Chinese front during the last war."

One case of spontaneous ESP that intertwined with war and death involved the Soviet writer Nikolai Ostrovsky, famous for his novel *How the Steel Was Tempered*. The First World War left the teen-age Ostrovsky half-blind and semi-paralyzed. But Ostrovsky, laboriously using a device that allowed him to feel letters through paper, wrote two best-sellers of the "man-can-triumph-over-anything" kind.

In 1936 Ostrovsky's mother had a double-barreled premonition. "I am a simple peasant woman," she told investigators from the magazine *Ogonyok*, "so don't be offended if I tell you my dream. I was sleeping at home alone in Sochi. In my dream I saw airplanes flying over the sea, many planes that roared and roared until my ears hurt. I understood that war was beginning. I ran outside my house in the dream. I saw my son Kolya [i.e. Nikolai] standing there, completely healthy again, wearing a greatcoat and helmet and holding a rifle in his hands. All around him were trenches, pits, barbed wire. I wanted to ask him about this war, but understood that it was not possible to ask him anything. Then I wanted to return to my house. But the pits grew wider, barbed wire clung to my feet. . . ."

Mrs. Ostrovsky woke up believing war would come, and worse to her, "surely, surely something has happened to Kolya in Moscow." She decided to buy train tickets and go to him. Then a letter arrived from her son saying he was feeling better than usual. "I read it, but my melancholy did not leave. I talked to myself: 'Where do you think you're going, old one? And why, since he writes all is well?' " She gave up her plan.

Later that evening Mrs. Ostrovsky was again asleep when she was startled by a knock on her door. A friend shouted through the door to her that Kolya was ailing and she should get up at once and start for Moscow. "My heart fell to my knees, but I only said, 'The train has already left for today.' "

Her friend insisted, "We can make other arrangements," then drawing closer to the door began to weep. "Kolya is no more. Kolya is dead!"

Five years later, a month after the Germans invaded Russia, Mrs. Ostrovsky's premonitory dream was widely published in the USSR. A more helpful psychic experience, much like the "Interceptor" kind of ESP came to Kolya Zvantsov during the fight for Kharkov. It also appeared in the Soviet press. On a May evening in the smouldering spring of 1942, outside of beleaguered Kharkov, Kolya Zvantsov, a soldier, slumped asleep. He had stared across the spring fields all day waiting for the dreaded Nazis to appear. Even in his dreams the still fields stretched waiting in front of him. Suddenly, in his sleep, he saw Nazi tanks. They wheeled, smashing through the soft spots in the Soviet lines. Overhead, a surprise attack of bombers zeroed in on the disordered defenders. At dawn Kolya reported his vivid dream to the Russian commander. The hard-pressed commander was willing to listen. He readied his defenses to check the German battle plan outlined in Kolya's dream, just as the first Nazi tanks rumbled into range. The fight went exactly as Kolya had foreseen—except that, thanks to his advance information, the Germans were repulsed.

Wouldn't it be an incalculable bonus to any country if they could nurture and bring in any psychic knowledge their people might have? In this age of routine disaster, wouldn't it be handy if gifted men and women could be trained to use their psychic powers in emergencies? Could it be a good idea to listen to people with this talent, to weigh their impressions along with those from more usual channels? The Russians seem to think it's worth a try.

11

FROM ANIMALS TO CYBERNETICS: THE SEARCH FOR A THEORY OF PSI

"Well, what is psi?" we finally asked a group of Soviets. "What is electricity?" one of them shot back. The Russians like to point out that no one really knows the answer to either question. Yet only the rare person like Wolf Messing can actually use psi, while anybody can learn to use electricity. The difference is a theory: we have a theory of electricity and consequently we can light cities, fry eggs, freeze meat with it. To be able to use psi and not have to wait until it strikes like lightning, researchers everywhere and, especially the practical Communists, are hunting for a theory.

Dr. Vasiliev came up with his strange and potent telepathic knockout when he was looking for a theory of telepathy. Since the Revolution, Soviets have hankered for a scientific theory to demystify psi. Some of the first theory hunters worked with four-legged "psychics," a group of talented dogs. The Russians mentioned their famous dog-experiments to us with a note of longing. These experiments still stand as the most extensive and perhaps the best scientific telepathic communication with animals. But then, the Soviets weren't communing with garden variety dogs to find their theory. They used very illustrious canines.

Mars, a strong, beautifully groomed Alsatian dog, was used to high powered attention as a circus star. Russians, who all seem to be born loving the circus, delighted in Mars, the dog who danced, counted, and, for a curtain closer, stood up and said, "Mama!" Mars traveled the major theatrical routes across Russia with Vladimir Durov, a flamboyant, mustachioed swashbuckler often called the "People's Jester." Durov was almost as well known for the way he cracked a satiric whip at high placed human bumblers as he was for dispensing with the whip in animal training.

One night Mars gave a command performance for the most particular audience of his life, the Academicians Vladimir M. Bekhterev and Alexander Leontovitch. To wow the scientists, Mars would have to do something better than call for his mama. He was supposed to show them that a dog can be psychic too. Everything had been set up. Bekhterev passed Durov a note with the instructions for the task he was to send telepathically to the animal. Durov took Mars' head gently in his palms. He stared motionless, silently into the big dog's eyes, then dropped his hands. Nothing happened. Durov again gazed compellingly into the eyes of his dog. Mars shook free and ran through a door into a smaller room behind the lab, a place he'd never entered before. Three rather messy tables holding papers and books stood around the room. Mars reared up at the first, put his paws on the edge, and, it seemed, looked. He dropped back to the floor, trotted to the second table, and repeated his "search." Finally Mars went to the third table and apparently spotted what he was looking for. He dragged a phonebook off the table and carried it in his teeth to Durov in the lab. Mars got the message—telepathically. Academician Bekhterev had asked for the phone book. Mars, the trouper, helped prove Durov's belief that animals of all kinds often know their owners' thoughts telepathically.

The handsome, rebellious Durov had a lot of revolutionary ideas. By himself, he demolished the traditional Russian methods of training animals by fear and brute punishment. Bears were no longer forced onto a blazing hot griddle to learn how to dance. Bears could waltz and ride bicycles even better, Durov showed, if they were gentled and encouraged to learn with little dollops of honey. Durov trained over fifteen hundred animals including some, like the anteater, never before taught by man. Camels, roosters, foxes, rats, cats, raccoons all performed together as actors in plays specially written for them in Durov's "Animal Theater."

Possessed of a seemingly boundless rapport with animals, Durov probably couldn't help observing there can be a special kind of wordless, signless communication between man and a pet—something animal lovers have always insisted on. Durov began experimenting with animal telepathy. He tried using psi, instead of gestures or ultrasonic whistles, to get his mathematical dogs to bark the correct answer in the circus ring. A student of zoology as well as a performer, Durov wanted to check his theories experimentally. During an evening performance in Leningrad, Durov recognized Vladimir Bekhterev in the audience. Only Pavlov was a more celebrated professor in the natural sciences than the renowned neurologist Bekhterev. But Durov had never been shy. Before the Revolution, he and his seditious pig Chuska-Fintiflushka had been barred from St. Petersburg for satirizing the Tsar's Minister of Finance to his face before a huge convulsed audience. They'd also been tossed out of Odessa and Yalta for satiric attacks on the military governors. In Germany, Durov and Chuska-Fintiflushka were declared *persona* (and pig) *non grata* for insulting Kaiser Wilhelm. With this background behind him, Durov strode up to the great neurologist Bekhterev and told him there was something going on in the brains of animals and people that science had not yet accounted for. "Telepathy can be used for training animals," Durov told him.

Bekhterev invited Durov, Mars, and Pikki, a scotch terrier, home to his apartment to experiment. The neurologist was the first person to design ESP tests for dogs that tried to eliminate any sensory clues that might pass, consciously or unconsciously, between trainer and dog. In later laboratory tests with Pikki and Mars, held in Moscow, Durov was usually not present in the testing room and often was not even the telepathic sender. Bekhterev found that the little terrier Pikki could carry out fairly involved thought commands. Reportedly, Pikki, set off by a thought, would bound across the room, jump up on a chair, hop to a table, and retrieve the target piece of paper. The little dog also jumped up on furniture and correctly pawed at a portrait on the wall, when Bekhterev alone knew the task and held it in his mind. According to Soviet records, the animals, like human telepathists, occasionally even picked up thoughts on the edge of the experimenter's mind. A task the scientist was considering, then rejected, was suddenly, spontaneously carried out by the dog.

In Moscow, Bekhterev blindfolded the sender or had him step quickly behind a screen or out of the room as soon as he sent his telepathic command, to avoid giving any clue to the dog on his psychic hunt. The observer who stayed with the animal was not told the task until afterward.

Mars and Pikki fetched on telepathic command and they also barked. Mars, in particular, was headlined as a counting dog. In a typical experiment, the famous Mars lay at the feet of Academician Leontovitch. In a distant room, Bekhterev handed Durov a note. Durov opened it and frowned. He jotted something on the paper, handed it back, and started to concentrate. Mars got up, cocked his head, and barked seven times. He sprawled back on the floor. Almost instantly, to Leontovitch's surprise, Mars jumped up and barked seven more times.

Durov explained to Bekhterev that his animals were only trained to figure up to nine. Durov had simply divided the scientist's target number, fourteen, into seven and seven. The Soviets found that, just like human psychics, their dogs preferred tasks with an emotional kick. Mars and Pikki liked to do their psychic barking at a titillating stuffed animal.

"Mental suggestion can directly affect the behavior of trained dogs," Academician Bekhterev wrote in 1920, when he published his work with Durov's Mars, Pikki, and a St. Bernard named Lord. Bekhterev, the teacher of parapsychologist Leonid Vasiliev, was not too illustrious to learn from the intrepid canine performers. Telepathy with dogs was interesting in itself, but it also fit the early and continuing Soviet interest in commanding actions by telepathy, kinetic ESP, an area generally skipped over in the West.

Bekhterev became interested in the entire psychic spectrum and set up a special scientific commission to study person-to-person telepathy. (This group reported they successfully transmitted over half of nine hundred pictures they tried to communicate telepathically.)

As Bekhterev's interest moved to telepathic people, Durov continued with animals. Between 1922 and 1924, he tried to turn his dogs into psychic laboratory retrievers ten thousand times. Reportedly, when all the scores were tallied, there were only sixteen chances in ten million that the dogs could have performed their tasks by coincidence.[276]

Another pioneer Soviet parapsychologist, the electrical engineer Dr. Bernard Kajinsky, teamed up with Durov. This was something like Dr. Doolittle meeting Jules Verne's Captain Nemo. Kajinsky, as a psychic researcher, was the thinly disguised hero of a famous Soviet science fiction novel, *The Master of the World,* by Alexander Belyaev, a Russian writer often compared to Jules Verne. The book is a Tolkien kind of cosmic good-versus-evil drama and the heroes, "Dr. Kachinsky" modeled after Kajinsky and "Durov" named after Durov, eventually triumph over the wicked protagonist who, possessing the secret of telepathy, almost manages to master the world. It's curious that as future American aquanauts and astronauts fueled their imaginations on Jules Verne, young Soviets took off on imaginary flights into the inner space of the mind.

In his book *Biological Radio Communication,* Kajinsky recalls his first encounter with Durov:

"I wanted to experience ESP myself when I met Durov in 1919. I told him, 'I want to know what it feels like to get a telepathic message and to feel muscular ESP.'

" 'Oh that's easy,' said Durov. 'Just sit still for a few moments.'

"He turned his back on me and quickly wrote something on a concealed sheet of paper. He put the paper on the table, written side down, and covered it with the palm of his hand.

"I felt nothing unusual, but quite automatically the fingers of my right hand touched the skin behind my ear. I barely had time to lower my arm when Durov showed me the paper. 'Scratch behind your right ear,' he'd written.

" 'How did you do it?' " I asked incredulously.

" 'All I did was imagine that the skin behind my right ear badly wanted scratching and that I had to lift my hand to do the scratching. Now what did you feel?'

"Of course, I didn't feel any thought transfer. I merely wanted to scratch behind my ear.

"Durov looked triumphant. 'The remarkable thing is that you made the movement that had been conceived in my brain as if you had followed your own association of ideas and movements, as if you had acted on orders of a dual nature: you felt the effect of skin irritation behind your ear, and your hand made the movement to the ear, and it was the ear I wanted it to be.'

" 'The image in your brain was picked up unconsciously by my brain,' I observed.

" 'Both of us are live radio stations,' Durov joked."

Kajinsky was determined to find out how the message got from Durov's mind to his own, or from Durov's mind to the mind of a dog.

After years of research he reported that he detected high frequency electromagnetic waves 1.8 millimeters in length coming out of the concentrating Durov's head. Today Soviets say Kajinsky's equipment was too primitive to prove anything definite at all.

As Kajinsky and Durov worked, they talked about the seemingly hypnotic power of the eye, the *force* of the gaze. A lifetime of practical observation convinced Durov that the human gaze packed enough wallop to transfix the most snarly beast. He convinced an arena full of panicked Russians that his own gaze, at least, held extraordinary power. According to the Soviet biography of the great animal trainer, a hulking brown bear, triggered by the machinations of a disgruntled employee, once went berserk during a circus performance. The bear sunk his teeth into Durov's arm, wrenched him to the floor, then climbed the barricade and lumbered toward the hysterical, suddenly scrambling crowd. Durov ran after the bear. The huge beast again turned menacingly toward him; Durov held his ground. The bear stopped. "Looking the beast straight in the eye, scolding him severely, Durov slowly made his way to the exit, leading the bear after him." [28]

Kajinsky wondered if there was more than psychological impact in a piercing gaze. Almost everyone has sometime felt an urge to turn around, done so, and found someone staring at him from behind. Coincidence? The Soviets seem to make a habit of exploring coincidences. Durov tried his visual whammy on the napes of various human necks in the lab. Almost all of his subjects, Durov claimed, could tell when he stared hard. They could even determine the angle the look came from. Powerful, invisible radiation pulsing out of the eye could be, Dr. Kajinsky thought, the unknown force that pulsed telepathy. But first attempts to identify a ray beaming from Durov's eyes failed.

Vladimir Durov, the first circus performer ever granted the title "Artist of the Soviet Union," died in the 1930s. His center for animal studies still flourishes. And his interest in the power of the gaze has lingered on in Soviet scientific circles. Planète, No. 8 (1963), reported that Academician P. P. Lazarov led a team in the 1940s that claimed to have found that the gaze isn't felt if a thin metal mesh is put between the subject and the starer. They tried mescaline and other psychedelic drugs in an attempt to increase the mysterious force from the eyes. By the 1960s, a distinguished French scientist reported that the Soviets believe they have ample proof the eye does send out rays. What picks up these rays? The pineal gland, according to the Soviets. The pineal gland, deep within the brain, is generally identified with the "third eye"—the all-seeing, mystic eye of ancient fame. Dr. Kajinsky pointed out that Indian yogis say the third eye is one of the physical centers involved with ESP. According to the Russians, the pineal gland is known to be larger in children than in adults, more developed in women than in men. Possibly, they say, it retains the undeveloped visual ability of what might be called the third eye, which "sees" and emits outward magnetic waves like the ordinary organ of vision. Again the Soviets, trying to unravel something seemingly inconsequential, like the funny feeling somebody is staring at you, wind up with a broader enigma, wind up edging their scientific perspective into the matter and tenets of the classic occult.

In 1962 Dr. Kajinsky was finally able to publish *Biological Radio Communication*, a book about his life in ESP. In it he speaks of his work with Durov and unfolds in detail his idea that the rodlike cells of the eye could act as mini radio antennae sending out telepathic signals. He admits this does little to explain telepathy when people are far apart, but "any verification of action at a distance will start scientists looking into this vital field." Like space pioneer Tsiolkovsky, Kajinsky believed that psi ability is a right-now, very necessary evolutionary development—not just for use in space. As our world uncovers new torrents of information, adding new facets like a sparkle-happy crystal, Kajinsky felt we'd need psi just to keep up.

Like numerous other Soviets who have probed the possibilities of the paranormal, Kajinsky too was moved to warn that telepathy could be misused to influence people subconsciously and against their wills. Writing during the Stalinist era, he stressed misuse of telepathy could be a great danger to all mankind.

Bernard Kajinsky was one of Edward Naumov's psychic mentors and it was the young, kinetic Naumov who finally got the Academy of Science in Kiev to publish Kajinsky's book after it was turned down in Moscow. (In quasi-controversial areas, what one censor board may consider too risky, another may go along with.) Naumov is actively committed to bringing knowledge of psychic things to the Russian public. He showed us a graph with a curve, sweeping up and off, that charted publications about parapsychology. In 1957 there were three articles against the subject, none for. In 1966, 152 articles reported on psychic research, only fifteen taking a negative stand.

"When I first began work with Kajinsky," Naumov said, "he had me investigate the power of the gaze, too, particularly the gaze of snakes and tigers." Naumov's interest in eyeball-to-eyeball confrontation continues. One afternoon he began reeling off up-to-the-minute facts about American scientific research with liquid crystals. "These liquid crystals are man-made. If you cover the body with them, they begin to radiate various colors. Gauging the radiations at a distance, you can gauge shifting emotions in the person and, more importantly, illnesses. This is just the beginning of their usefulness. The future belongs to these crystals. . . . You know, some people think the brain and the eyes are a form of liquid crystal," Naumov added with a speculative look in his own eye.

Reportedly, both Durov's institute and Moscow's Pavlov Institute have kept up a more or less undercover research interest in parapsychology. We asked Naumov if there was any current research like Durov's. "There is definite interest in exploring the telepathic abilities of animals, but one big problem is trying to find someone with the rapport and brilliance of Durov."

The Soviets are trying to understand the homing ability of various birds, insects, and animals—another unexplained although commonplace phenomenon. Books, even movies, have documented dogs trekking thousands of miles of new territory to rejoin their masters. In one of the few parapsychological investigations of animals in America, Dr. J. B. Rhine and his daughter, Dr. Sara Feather, reported on animals tracking down lost owners, which they called "psi trailing."

Russian psychic researchers today seem to be using animals in the more usual, scientific, guinea-pig way. Allegedly, they used a mother rabbit to see if she could "intuit" physiologically when her babies were killed miles away in a submarine. They were intrigued by first reports of a French scientific experiment to see if rats could foretell the future, if they could predict what, to the rats anyway, was a catastrophe—being killed. First the scientists noted the behavior of the rats. Then a machine selected randomly which of the group would be killed. Supposedly, the rats ultimately selected to die did behave oddly *beforehand*, seeming to have a presentiment, to know something the scientists did not yet know.

There is much basic Soviet research with animals that has caused a stir among the ESP specialists. In a Soviet laboratory a small band of fish wheeled and spun through the clear water of an aquarium. Soviet scientist Dr. Y. A. Holodov watched carefully. He had created a permanent weak magnetic field in the aquarium. The fish reacted. Holodov found fish developed conditioned responses to magnetism. But why? Neither a fish nor anyone else has receptors for magnetism. Perhaps magnetism, an enigma itself, was "received" directly by the brain of the fish.[50, 190, 236] Magnetism seemed to parallel the behavior of telepathy. Is there a connection, an analogy?

Fish flicking in an invisible magnetic field don't seem as remarkable as Durov's Pikki getting the telepathic message to nose a picture. However, this kind of basic work, as well as the more bravura experiments with psychics, makes up the stuff of Soviet parapsychology. It abets the theoretical push to discover how psi works.

Soviet researchers disagree on the best routes to building their theory of psi. Dr. Ippolit Kogan, head of the Bio-Information Section of the Popov Radio-Technology and Electrical Communications Society, believes research should concentrate on telepathy. He says, in effect, we know how to get a handle on telepathy, so why not focus all our energies on this area? Dr. Kogan with charcoaled eyebrows, thick curly gray hair is of a more conservative cast than many scientists we met. He represents a slightly older generation that has experienced a great many horrendous comings and goings in Russia and in official Soviet science. Yet within the limits of telepathy that Kogan has set for himself and the Popov group he has come up with much original and imaginative work. He was ultimately responsible for most of the Russian telepathy tests in this book. He originated the "trace method" of tracking ESP in brain waves.

A mathematician, Kogan has shown that, in principle, telepathy between people close together could ride electromagnetic waves.[73] In this he differs from many colleagues. As Dr. Alexei Gubko of the Ukrainian Institute of Psychology, a seasoned researcher, puts it, "Most scientists are now inclined to believe that the brain radiates a special, hitherto unknown type of energy responsible for telepathy."

But Kogan has done more than join the old hunt for waves. As a cybernetician, he's attempting to explain telepathy with information theory. Kogan feels that during telepathy the sender's "thought" itself doesn't take off from his brain and float through space toward the receiver. Instead, only "information about the thought" is picked up by the receiver. This information about the thought may be projected by means of a "psi field" to reach the receiver's brain, where it is gradually made conscious. This is why almost every telepathy message in Russia is divided into "information bits per second received." (See Appendix B for more of Kogan's work and also the novel theories of mathematical physicist Igor Shishkin, an exponent of the idea that some hitherto unknown force is involved with telepathy.)

The combination of cybernetics and ESP is a new idea. The concept of telepathic people as transmitters and radio receivers has been replaced with a model of them as a cybernetic system. Soviets talk of cybernetic instruments that would imitate telepathy in people, and many parapsychology groups are attached to cybernetics and bionics labs.

"Why not look into all kinds of psychic happenings if you're trying to find answers to some of the big questions behind ESP?" biologist Edward Naumov asks. Rather than going after psi mathematically or with cybernetic models, Naumov feels it should be sought for in the multiplicity of living experience. In his view, parapsychology should be at the center of *all* branches of knowledge, the juncture of all disciplines, a synthesis of learning from philosophy to the arts, science to religion. Just as a diplomatic corps compiles a world view from dispatches of ambassadors in many countries, parapsychology compiles a new view of man from research in biology, medicine, biomagnetism, electronics, physiology, to name a few areas. "Parapsychology is summoned to study the nature of man himself," says Naumov, "and that includes *all* man's activities." [130] The psychic part of ourselves, he feels, is involved in everything we do.

For this reason, Naumov believes, ESP research shouldn't be focused on telepathy alone. It should range through PK, psychic photography (like that done by Ted Serios in the United States), dowsing, eyeless sight, precognition, "bio-rapport" (the influence of one man in a group on the others), and the psychological aspects of psi, which many Soviets tend to neglect.

To encompass this expanded view of psi, Naumov broke with the Popov parapsychology group, which works exclusively on telepathy, and founded his own psi research section attached to the Scientific and Technical Association for Instrument Engineering. Naumov's current work involves such variety as: study of a man who uses PK to move a cigarette vertically in a glass, but only when he's drunk; research in skin sight; creation of films of the telepathist Karl Nikolaiev. The Soviets are also probing psychic photography. "We believe anyone can be trained to do this," said Naumov. "But most people's ability to make photos like Ted Serios is quite weak. We plan to use special instruments and artificial fields to step up traces of talent."

Naumov went on in another vein: "One of the most important things for parapsychology is our recent discovery of currents that flow in the body that are neither blood nor electrical." (Naumov was referring to a new discovery in parapsychology and in physiology known as the Kirlian effect, covered in chapters 16, 17, 18.) "We are studying the hands of mediums as they work, using the Kirlian techniques and we're also studying the effect of telepathy and radiesthesia on plants.

"Just recently we held a seminar to discuss our research of telepathic influence on groups. We can get a total electromagnetic impression of a group. Then we introduce a new person into the group. The total electromagnetic pattern of the group changes. There seems to be an effect of one person on a group telepathically," said Naumov. This dedicated young scientist concluded with his own prediction: "The future will see the key problems of the present-day psychology of man revolving around parapsychology. Psi will be seen to be a central aspect of the subconscious, the personality, and the emotions."

It seems like a long leap from telepathic Mars and Pikki to cybernetics to talking of psi as an element of life itself. But if Naumov and others are right and what we call psi is a dynamic all-pervading force, then it should spring up in animals as well as ourselves. Psi would then be a subtle something that links us to all forms of life.

12

ARTIFICIAL REINCARNATION

Recently, in a large sunlit studio in Moscow, a cluster of art students eyed their model intently. Each deep in his own vision of the girl, they glanced up and down checking the curves of the model against the figure growing on their sketch pads. Not one head turned when their instructor, Dr. Vladimir L. Raikov, entered the room and circled around them talking with a visitor.

"I want you to meet one of my best students," Raikov said. A young girl in her early twenties stood up, rather grudgingly it seemed. But then, as if coming to herself, she turned quickly to the visitor and extended her hand. "I am Raphael of Urbino," she said.

The visitor wasn't as surprised at the name as he was at the nonchalant way this seemingly normal, wide-awake girl tried to pass herself off as the great Renaissance painter.

"Could you tell me, by any chance, what year it is?" he asked.

"Why, 1505, of course."

Needing a moment to order his thoughts, the guest stepped back to focus his camera on the pretty young student. Instructor Raikov asked, "Do you know what he has there?"

"No!"

"Well, have you ever seen anything at all similar to it?"

"Never. I've never seen anything like it in my life."

After clicking a few shots, the visitor began talking again about cameras, jets, sputniks, and—as the girl grew more adamant in her denials—about anything that came into his head concerning 1966, the year they were living in.

"Phantasmagoria! It's all foolishness. You're bothering me with nonsense!" the girl cried angrily.

"All right, thank you for letting us talk to you," her instructor said. "Go back to work now. Draw! Draw to the very best of your ability, Maestro Raphael."

"That is an example," said Dr. Raikov to his guest, a writer from *Komsomolskaya Pravda,* "of what we call reincarnation." [228]

This reincarnation of Raphael in Ira, a young science student, has not sent psychiatrist Raikov on a hunt through cobwebs and crumbling churchyard records to corroborate the girl's tale of a glorious past life. Raikov, who works with the Popov parapsychologists, knows how this Raphael became reincarnated—just as he knows how the other three Raphaels in the class came into the flesh again. Raikov called them into being. He is a master hypnotist.

With his dynamic brand of reincarnation, Raikov is trying to evoke the birth of talent, perhaps even genius, in his students. We're not giving people something from the outside with reincarnation, something they don't have, the Soviets say. But few people, if any, realize the extraordinary powers they do possess.

"I am able to evoke this phenomenon of reincarnation only when the subject is in exceedingly deep trance," Raikov reports. "It is a new form of active trance." Action is the dominant beat in Raikov's reincarnation. Alla is a high-ranking physics student at Moscow University. Art really didn't interest her much. She felt she had no talent in drawing. Alla's sketches, when she volunteered for Raikov's experiments, bore out her opinion, showing only a little more feeling than stick figures.

"You are Ilya Repin," Dr. Raikov insisted to the deeply entranced Alla. Repin, a great Russian painter at the turn of the century, is still vigorously studied in the Soviet Union. "You think like Repin. You *see* like Repin. You have the abilities of Repin. You *are* Repin. Consequently, the talent of Repin is yours to command."

After a few reincarnation sessions, anyone could see that Alla sketched much better. She began, after ten afternoons as Repin, to want to draw on her own time and took to carrying a sketch pad. In three months, when Raikov brought her to the end of her twenty-five lesson course, Alla drew like a professional—not like Repin or Raphael, two of her many reincarnations, but as well as a competent magazine illustrator. Her new talent exploded so vibrantly in Alla that she's seriously considering chucking her physics theorems and letting loose at the easel full time.

"Alla could not learn how to do this in the usual state of deep hypnosis, which is passive," Raikov explains. Raikov one of the new breed of young Soviet mind explorers, is thoroughly experienced in passive trance where his word is will to the subject. Raikov has displayed his powers with the Popov group in most of their telepathic sleep-wake experiments, and he has delivered scientific papers on his work in eliciting psychic phenomena under hypnosis. He can easily put Alla into passive trance. He commanded her to "perform" in this state for one visitor. At Raikov's hypnotic word, Alla, her eyes shut, moved around the room with the underwater motions of a sleepwalker. Raikov handed her an invisible glass of apple juice. She gulped down the "juice." "Thank you," she said, "that makes me feel much better."

In reincarnation, Alla is her own person—even if the person happens to be Maestro Raphael. She is alert, extraordinarily wide awake. She sees her model, her pencil, her sketch pad. She consciously composes her own drawing, pours her own feeling into the lines. Not a Svengali-turned-painter, Raikov is offstage as far as Alla is concerned. He is an observer—simply the man who turns the switch.

"Reincarnation brought the girl to a state in which she submits to new laws that have been very little researched. The elaboration of these unknown laws is the goal of my work," Raikov states. "Reincarnation is important for itself. It opens before us the unexplored side of man's psyche." [171]

Dr. Vasiliev, the pioneer parapsychologist, agreed about the importance of the unexplored psyche. Shortly before his death, Vasiliev, writing his thoughts on the arts and creative inspiration, said, "With progress in parapsychology we come closer to unraveling the mysteries of creativity. We now know that man's psychic and creative faculties have much in common." [241]

Parapsychologists and critics of the arts generally recognize that creativity and inspiration are shot through with the force that latter-day scientists have termed ESP.

But—"You too can learn to draw in twenty easy lessons"? The unveiling of Alla the artist seems a little too easy. And it would be, the Soviets agree, by any of the usual modes of instruction. But, they say, reincarnation lets the mind become supercreative, because it allows the mind to operate on new, almost "magical" laws. These laws bear stable gifts. Alla, it appears, didn't come down from her artistic high after she was cut off from Raikov. Neither did his other subjects.

Dr. Raikov and his collaborators ran initial tests with twenty young (late teens, early twenties) unartistic but intelligent students. Raikov gave each of them five to twenty reincarnation experiences. After their final incarnation as a genius some drew better than others, but everyone improved markedly and Raikov has the pictures to prove it. Everyone wound up, in his own opinion, with a newfound talent.[229]

Your activity as a reincarnated master leaves no snatch of memory. Not surprisingly, in their un-reincarnated state these students at first refused to believe they'd drawn the pictures shown them—and they probably didn't want to believe they'd signed "Repin" or "Raphael" with a nice flourish at the bottom. As the sessions progressed, however, the drawing skill acquired as Repin began to filter through into their own conscious personalities. Contrary to all previous experience, students found that they could draw after all. "By the tenth session," Naumov told us, "the new talent is stabilized and part of the conscious equipment of the student. What they've acquired stays with them."

Raikov explains, "The student is thinking, forming relationships and judgments, acquiring his own experience during reincarnation. Consequently the creative potential he develops, draws out, becomes his own."

Another scientist, Dr. Milan Ryzl, working in Prague early in the 1960s, devised a hypnotic system to evoke psychic rather than artistic talent in people. Some of Ryzl's subjects also found that the ESP talent that bloomed under hypnosis stabilized as a new, consciously controlled ability in everyday life.

Asked if he weren't just transplanting something into students in a receptive state, Raikov remarked, "As a hypnotist, I simply get them to this state of super wakefulness, but after that I'm not imposing anything on them; sometimes it is very much to the contrary."

Raikov remembers one girl he reincarnated not as an artist, but as a famous English queen. "We desire to hold a ball," the sudden queen announced. "You," she said to

Raikov, "be off and take care of the arrangements. It is my command!" she said in the best grand manner when the usually commanding Raikov hesistated.

Raikov reincarnated another student, Volodnya, as a nineteenth-century Russian artist listed simply as "N." Volodnya as "N" considered Raikov his personal model. He dedicated his pictures to "my best model and friend, 1883." While drawing, "N" liked to expound his theories of art. "Would you like to publish them?" model Raikov asked. "Of course," the boy sighed, "but they would never pass the censor."

At this juncture, another psychiatrist came into the room. "Ah," said Raikov, "here's our censor now. I'd like you to meet him, please."

The censor-doctor extended his hand. Volodnya jumped up, putting his own hand behind his back. "Never! Never shall I shake the hand of a tsarist censor!" Pacing around them glowering, he shouted to Raikov. "Friend of mine, drive out of here all censors!"

Raikov couldn't resist trying to introduce the high-passioned Volodnya to another student, Elena, also reincarnated for the moment as the famous "N."

"N is, of course, only one person. And *I* am, of course, that person. Now this lady . . . she is a false face," Volodnya observed to Raikov.[172]

Volodnya, like the others, felt he had acquired artistic talent in compressed time. As one Soviet writer put it, "The students feel as if all the spadework is behind them. They feel they've learned the techniques of drawing while reincarnated as a procession of masters—Repin, Raphael, Matisse and others. Now they're ready to synthesise and develop their own style." Raikov's instruction is similar to traditional art teaching, in which the student would sit with a sketch pad in a museum before the paintings of great artists—except that Raikov's reincarnation encapsulates days into hours, years into months. Alla flipped through her sketch pad, from semi-stick figures to a respectable portrait in three months. Her sudden opening up to art through reincarnation only took her a few hours each week.

Raikov has presented students with wider perspectives than "seeing" through the eyes of famous painters. He hypnotically regressed his student Luba so she could see the world with the eyes of a child. But she didn't see it again as a younger Luba; she was reincarnated as another person called Olga, at ages five, eight, ten, and fourteen. Next Raikov provided her with an even wider storehouse of experience. He reincarnated her as a boy named Ilya with the same age shifts bringing her up to seventeen, Luba's age at the time. Her drawings reflected the various stops on her reincarnation route. The pictures done as a girl showed "more plasticity and softness."

Raikov gave an adult an even stranger dose of widened experience. In this case he departed from his mainline effort to evoke creativity, unless you consider self-healing a possible and creative act. As a psychiatrist, Raikov confronted the problem of Boris, a middle-aged, well-educated chronic alcoholic. The man appeared spasmodically for treatment at the psychiatric clinic. He kept drinking, bouts of d.t.'s followed, and his weary family was about to give up and leave. "O wad some Pow'r the giftie gie us, to see oursels as ithers see us!" Robert Burns wrote. Dr. Raikov thought he knew of one such power. He decided to reincarnate Boris' relatives in him. The psychiatrist started with the man's mother, whom he regarded with "warmth and love."

"Who are you?"

"I'm Tatyana Nikolaevna," said Boris, pronouncing his mother's name. Raikov told the man reincarnated as his own mother that "her" son was lying on the couch in a drunken stupor. "He's turned blue, it's sickening, things are really bad." Raikov laid it on.

The patient with his eyes wide open threw himself on the couch and gave "her" son artificial respiration, splashed imaginary water on him, spooned out invisible medicine, and implored the doctors for first aid. "Oh how could you drink like that," lamented the reincarnated mother. "You're dying of alcohol. Your wife is leaving you, your daughter won't love you."

Raikov made a gurgling sound with a bottle of water. "Tatyana Nikolaevna, your son seems to be drinking again," he called. "Tatyana," her face creased with repugnance, tried to grab the bottle from her invisible "son" and smash it.

Later Raikov reincarnated Boris' daughter in him. "Papa," Boris said in a quiet, soft voice, similar to his daughter's, "Papa, why have you been drinking again? What's the matter with you? It's terrible for me." Tears streamed down the face of Boris reincarnated as his own daughter.

Eventually Raikov evoked the man's wife and other members of his family in him. Boris remembered nothing of these emotion-charged moments as his own family. Then, one day, he told his psychiatrist, Dr. Raikov, that he suddenly had begun thinking how his family felt toward him. He almost physically seemed to feel their anger and disgust, "I began to see all the loathsomeness of my drunkenness through their eyes. It's horrifying."

According to Raikov, this medical reincarnation, playing on Boris' strongest ties with life, gradually helped him form a critical attitude toward his behavior. "A type of reincarnation," Raikov says, "can be an excellent addition to psychotherapeutic treatment." It could also be used for rehabilitation of criminals.

Raikov's medical experiments sound promising, yet his project to force creative talent into bloom in his reincarnation hothouse is even more exciting and fertile. It could be used not only for talents, but also for business and industrial retraining, for headstart programs.

As a Soviet psychiatrist, Raikov is naturally interested in the physiological side of this reincarnation that permits even people like a medical student who said not only that she couldn't draw, but also that she disliked art, to quickly develop facility at sketching. Connecting the usual monitoring devices, Raikov confirmed the supposition that the trance of reincarnation is a new thing, is different in kind from the usual passive trance of deep hypnosis, in which the EEG shows the alpha rest rhythm. In reincarnation the alpha disappears completely and the EEG shows a pattern like that normally recorded in high wakefulness.[171] During a student's whirl as Raphael, physiologically she seems to be super awake. Intense concentration shows in the brain, with distraction leveled out. It's as if the entire being was pulled up into one unwavering floodlight. Reincarnation is, in many ways, the antithesis of sleep. Yet reincarnation has affinities with regular trance. Students fall into a deep sleep before snapping back to themselves. Even though Raikov doesn't suggest amnesia, they never remember a pulse of their lives as another person. According to the Soviets, only a widely adept hypnotist can steer people into the freedom of reincarnation. Not every subject can be lulled into the first step, deep trance. And even Raikov has failed to jog some people from this trance to a burst of reincarnation.

Raikov uses a brand-new and highly unusual instrument invented by a talented twenty-nine-year-old physicist, Victor Adamenko, to check his work. This machine registers energy flow in the body using as check points for its electrodes, interestingly enough, the acupuncture treatment points of traditional Chinese medicine. The ancient Chinese inserted long needles at specific points on the skin to cure disease. Physicist Adamenko attaches his wires to the same spots on the skin and picks up changes in body energy caused by alterations of consciousness and varying emotional states.

In Raikov's laboratory Adamenko carefully attached his machine, called the CCAP (Conductivity of the Channels of Acupuncture Points), to test volunteers and control groups. Then Raikov took over. He put subjects into passive hypnosis. Completely in his sway, they saw rose gardens he conjured for them, they gestured like sleepwalkers. He also put subjects into reincarnation hypnosis. Like the student "Raphaels" and "Repins," they were completely on their own in trance.

At the end of many sessions, Raikov and Adamenko checked the graphs of the CCAP. They found a pronounced difference between the different forms of hypnosis Raikov had tried. "With the CCAP we can chart objectively the psychical activity of the mind in states of somnambulism and various levels of hypnosis," the two reported in the 1968 *Journal of Neuropathology and Psychiatry*, of the Sechenov Medical Institute.[173] They'd come up with a new way to see into the mind, to chart consciousness. "These states are very hard to measure by any other method," they said. Raikov and Adamenko found there was even more activity in the mind during reincarnation than there is when a person is wide awake. This corroborates the EEG findings that reincarnation is a state of "super wakefulness" and that it is a very different animal than regular, passive hypnosis.

The CCAP registers changes in bodily energy as emotion and consciousness vary. It provides a clear, scientific way of showing how thought actually affects us. Parapsychologists eventually tried to see if the CCAP could pick up any bodily effect of thought at a distance. (See Chapter 18.) American science doesn't seem to have made use of the CCAP yet. But Adamenko and Raikov's careful reports published by the prestigious Sechenov Medical Institute certainly imply that the CCAP—a new way of looking inside and catching the subtle interplay between thought and body, psyche and soma—will have much wider use than charting the mental states of reincarnated artists.

Music ability as well as artistic talent has been enhanced by Raikov. He reincarnated the master violinist, Fritz Kreisler, in a student at the Moscow Conservatory of Music. Believing himself to be Kreisler, the boy began to play in the manner of Kreisler. This ability became consolidated in his conscious state.

Raikov states that reincarnation can be used in artistic, musical, and scientific training. His quick leap from discovery to application reflects the Soviet preoccupation with searching out new, radical teaching methods. *The Other Side of the Mind,*[405] by business leader and writer W. Clement Stone and journalist Norma Lee Browning, mentioned the first stirrings of renewed ESP research in Russia in the early 1960s. Sensitive to the global competition of the USSR and the USA and to the greatest, often neglected, resource of nations—mind power—Stone went to Washington, where he arranged an interview with Oliver Caldwell, then Acting Commissioner for International Education with the Department of Health, Education, and Welfare. Caldwell, an expert on Russian matters, told Stone and Browning, "I am amazed at the skepticism and sometimes hostility which I encounter when I try to tell Americans about some of the experimentation which is taking place in the USSR in parapsychology and related fields. I find this strange because there is available documentation in translation which substantiates most of the things I saw in the USSR. I am really disturbed, because if the United States does not make a serious effort to move forward on this new frontier, in another ten years it may be too late."

Caldwell spoke of many bold and exciting avenues the Soviets were exploring in their push to open up man's intellectual capacities. He told of a conversation he'd had with the late Lev Landau, one of the two or three top physicists in Russia, about the coming possibility of tuning one mind to another telepathically. Landau told him, "When this happens, the teacher can teach a student beyond the normal capacity of his mind by broadcasting over the defense mechanism into the normally empty 90 percent of the brain."

As a stimulant to creativity and to the use of the dormant part of the brain in pure science, Raikov and his colleagues reincarnated a European mathematical genius in a college math student. What enhances the super concentration of reincarnation is the student's belief that he too is a genius, Raikov says. The boy is supremely confident, no inhibitions block the creative flow. He uses "reserves" in his work that usually lie for a lifetime untapped. The experience gained by this student in his hours as a reincarnated mathematical genius also reflected in his waking life. His grades rose sharply. But if you think you'd like to try reincarnation as a quick cram course, don't. Raikov is explicit about the very real dangers in it. No one, he states, except a completely experienced psychiatric hypnotist should ever attempt to evoke separate personalities in another person (or in himself). All of Raikov's own students survived reincarnation with gusto. They felt "good," "rested" after their sessions. Reportedly, they automatically mastered the technique of self-hypnosis in the process, helping them to achieve greater strength of will and memory.

The imaginative Raikov tried an ingenious experiment with an aeronautics engineer—reincarnation in the future, which most Westerners would call precognition.

"You are a great inventor of the future," Raikov told the engineer. "With your knowledge you can easily design a method of taking photos of cosmic rockets." The "man of the future" agreed and quickly set to work. "We put the designs away in a safe place to see if they ever prove correct," Raikov says.

Raikov's published research on artificial reincarnation ignited interest in professionals from many different fields.[168] One of the most popular Soviet psychologists, Dr. K. K. Platonov, commented. "Developing drawing ability is only a partial example of more general laws. There is much talk here about studying the latent powers of man's psyche, which science has demonstrated are unusually great."

Said an outstanding neurophysiologist, Dr. F. Bassin, "Using hypnosis, Raikov is influencing personal characteristics of a person, trying to open up secrets of intellectual abilities and the possibility of training them. This is a new approach in teaching. It demands attention."

Dr. E. Shorokova, Vice President of the Society of Psychologists of the USSR, said, "One must hail these attempts to penetrate deeply into so personal and complex a process as creativity."

An exciting new popular film, "Seven Steps Beyond the Horizon," produced by Kiev Films in 1969, probes still further into Raikov's brand of artificial reincarnation.[208]

Creativity, inspiration, that sudden dazzling, that sudden processing of a power that one does not normally have, has been courted immemorially. Raikov moved the courtship into the laboratory by trying to develop at least one pragmatic way of breaking the inspiration barrier. Creativity with its psychic coloring is not essentially a laboratory creature. Charisma, presence—every great performer radiates "it" when he's "on." Raikov remarks that Russian actors and actresses often tell him they have become different people, drawing on different powers than those they usually display.

The triumph of creativity flowing, and the struggle to bring it on happens privately in the other arts. One of Russia's most brilliant composers, Sergei Rachmaninoff, created a precedent of sorts for Raikov's work. Rachmaninoff's First Symphony was performed in St. Petersburg to unanimous catcalls. The composer was devastated. He collapsed and determined to give up composing. Over the next few years any music that might have moved in him was blocked. Rachmaninoff felt as though he were wearing mental earmuffs. His friends, fearing he would never compose again, finally convinced him to go to a hypnotist, Dr. Dahl.

"You have great talent. And you have the ability to express it," Dahl suggested to the composer. "Inspiration flows freely in you, nothing can block it." After some training in autosuggestion, music surged back to Rachmaninoff. He wrote down this magnificent, powerful music that flooded like spring through the frozen Russian land. Today it is counted among the world's greatest. It was the famous Second Piano Concerto in C Minor. Rachmaninoff dedicated the concerto to his hypnotist, Dr. Dahl.

Having overcome his mental block, Rachmaninoff later described how his creative gift would seize him. He would often walk in the country and suddenly, as he looked at rain-soaked foliage or a sunset, the music would swirl to him: "All the voices at once. Not a bit here, a bit there. All. The whole grows. Whence it came, how it began, how can I say? It came up within me, was entertained, written down . . ."

Muses and goddesses, spirits and second selves, genies—ever since writers began ordering words they've talked of that *outside* something that comes bearing gifts. The contemporary Soviet poet Andrei Voznesensky describes this feeling better than most: "The poet is two people. One is an insignificant person, leading the most insignificant of lives. But behind him, like an echo, is the other person who writes poetry. . . . Often the real man has no idea what path or what action the other will take. That other man is the prophet who is in every poet."

There is hardly a writer even half-alive who hasn't said, "It came to me. It was like taking dictation."

Creativity isn't bundled into separate fields, as is shown by the career of American's brightest renaissance man, Buckminster Fuller, engineer, cosmogonist, architect (the geodesic dome), mathematician, poet and *ad infinitum.* Fuller thinks the age of telepathy is just about to begin and that it will have a profound effect on life. Considering inspiration-intuition, Fuller told writer Walter McGraw, "I've had mathematical discoveries . . . really flash ones . . . and I've had a most extraordinary sense of a sort of intellectual mustiness—that this idea was known before." [328] Stories are legion of scientists who see their great discovery whole, in a nutshell, and then spend a decade or so drawing plans, making formulae to get the kernel out of the shell to show other people. Many great Russian scientists—Metchnikov, Butlerov, Mendeleyev—have experienced this sudden full flush. D. I. Mendeleyev, the famous chemist, saw his entire periodic table of elements one night in a well-lit dream.

The great mediums have affinities with artists. They too at times seem to have access to knowledge and powers not in their everyday selves. Like the artists with their second selves and muses, mediums have their larger selves and, sometimes, control personalities. It's almost as if an artist directs the power into the medium of words, notes, paint, and plastics, while in the psychic arts, the medium is the medium.

The way in which gifted people can turn on their inspiration interested parapsychologist Vasiliev. The "magic charm" he found was personal and subjective in the extreme. Some people, like Rachmaninoff, take a walk in the country, others lie down with their heads pointing north. You might put on a special smock, pray, read a book, drink, hold your breath, crystal gaze, swim, sharpen pencils, rub a ring. Vasiliev thought that all the infinite antics people go through serve to click off a highly individualized conditioned response. At some point in the past you experienced a burst of inspiration. The mind casts about for something that "caused" it, Vasiliev theorized. You light on something that was probably not really a cause. But it becomes a "cause" if it is ritually repeated every time inspiration is desired. According to Vasiliev, Schiller always kept rotting apples in his desk. He maintained he couldn't write without smelling them. Vasiliev believed Schiller must have conceived or written a brilliant passage one day in the autumn when apples lay going to seed on the ground. The tangy-musty smell became a spring to Schiller's inspiration.

Raikov explains his reincarnation route to inspiration in the same way. "The word 'Repin' or 'Raphael' is only a symbol which helps the hypnotist penetrate into the mystery of man's abilities to reach to the reserves of the organism which are not utilized in the awakened state." By using the word "Repin," Raikov says, the doctor breaks through the "crust" of those centers of the brain that are awake during hypnosis, thereby creating high excitement in other areas of the brain. All of this is then focused solely to creative work: to draw, draw, draw, like Repin.

Dr. Raikov thinks that reincarnation allows the student to connect with some part of the 90 percent of his brain cells that usually lie dormant. A Westerner familiar with Jungian psychology might say that the symbol "Repin" allows the student to connect with and draw on the collective unconscious. There are a lot of theories on what is happening and a lot of semantics to go with them, but the key point is the circumference of the everyday you, the definition of self. Whatever connects in the moment of inspiration is beyond that circle of "you." One of the aims of Communist parapsychologists is to increase the circumference of you: to plug into that waiting part of being, turn on the lights, set more life in motion. The idea is to increase range and power, like the step-up from ukulele to electric guitar.

What about a more long-term form of increase—reincarnation in the traditional meaning? Western parapsychologists, notably Dr. Ian Stevenson of the University of Virginia, have begun scientific investigations of alleged cases of reincarnation. In Iron Curtain countries, other than Russia, that we visited, we found active interest in the idea. Given the political philosophy of the Soviet Union, it would be too sticky a subject to investigate scientifically yet in the USSR. Perhaps the last Russian word on reincarnation should be spoken by a man they still read and revere, Tolstoy. In the early twentieth century Tolstoy wrote, "Our whole life is a dream. The dreams of our present life are the environment in which we work out the impressions, thoughts, feelings of a former life. As we live through thousands of dreams in our present life, so is our present life only one of thousands of such lives which we enter from the other, more real life—and then return to after death. Our life is but one of the dreams of that more real life.

"I believe in it. I know it. I see it without a doubt." [249]

13

TIME—A NEW FRONTIER OF THE MIND

"How far is it to Pulkovo?" we asked the Soviet travel agency, Intourist, in Leningrad. We were arranging an interview with a famous astronomer at Pulkovo, the principal observatory of the USSR Academy of Sciences and the timekeeping Greenwich of Russia.

"It's about four hours from Leningrad," an Intourist girl said.

"But it doesn't look that far on the map."

"How about an hour?" she corrected herself. We still looked dubious.

"Maybe twenty minutes?" she said.

Well it *was* only twenty minutes away, right past our hotel along the Moskovsky Prospect, to the Pulkovo heights overlooking Leningrad. Ironically, we were going to Pulkovo Observatory to discuss the subject of time itself—not the rather foggy time of the Intourist girl, but an amazing new theory of time developed by one of the Soviet Union's most renowned astrophysicists, Dr. Nikolai Kozyrev. (*Ko*-zir-ev)

The road to the observatory, which is the time meridian for the USSR, leads past gleaming new suburban apartments and shopping centers and then abruptly past rows of saw-toothed jagged stones used to halt the advance of the German tanks during the siege of Leningrad. The world famous observatory, begun in 1839, was on the front line and was barbarously destroyed by the Nazis, its costly instruments reduced to blobs of metal, its buildings to charred ghostly skeletons. Yet there it stands again on the heights overlooking the whole panorama of the city of Leningrad.

Strangely, Nikolai Kozyrev's life in a way parallels that of his great observatory. A brilliant student, he published his first scientific paper when he was only seventeen. The logic and precision of his ideas amazed scientists. At that early age he was interested in stellar and solar atmospheres, solar eclipses, and radiation equilibrium. At twenty he graduated in physics and mathematics from the University of Leningrad. At twenty-eight he'd already won distinction as an astronomer and had taught at several colleges. He was brimming with new ideas and life was as good as he could possibly have wished it to be. Then the ax fell. In 1936 he was arrested in the Stalinist repressions and in 1937 he began eleven crushing years in a prison camp. What did he think of during those grim bone-hard years as he watched the sky without a telescope?

Even without astronomical equipment, his intelligence and intuition were keenly active. When he was at last rehabilitated and could return to astronomy, Kozyrev made a series of brilliant predictions about the Moon, Venus, and Mars. Much later, Soviet space probes proved him right. In 1958 he announced to the world there was volcanic activity on the moon in the crater Alphonsus. For future space flights this bulletin was electrifying. It meant in essence that there are vast natural resources on the moon and enormous sources of power that could be used to plunge off further into space. World astronomers and scientists answered Kozyrev's announcement with all-around skepticism. They classed him as an eccentric hunting for gas on the moon. They "knew" this was not possible. But, Dr. Harold Urey, U.S. Nobel Prize winner, after talking to Kozyrev in Moscow, came away so impressed by the Russian scientist that he urged the National Aeronautics and Space Administration to investigate his theories. They did. The enormous "Moon Blink" project was set up. NASA found gas emissions on the moon, indicating the moon has natural resources and may be a valuable piece of real estate. Kozyrev had been right.

Now when Kozyrev proposed a startling new theory of time, some American scientists were ready to listen. "Time," says Kozyrev, "is a form of *energy*! It is to time's properties that we should look in order to find the source that maintains the phenomenon of life in the world." [177]

Dr. Albert Wilson, Associate Director of the Douglas Advanced Research Laboratories in California, who met Dr. Kozyrev recently at an international conference, told us,

"Kozyrev is a remarkable man and has a keen intuition. He has fathomed some basic concepts that may very well be correct. The implications are revolutionary." [100]

Dr. Kozyrev met us at the entrance of one of the observatory buildings at Pulkovo. Now in his sixties, Kozyrev is a tall, handsome, very distinguished looking man. Despite all that he has gone through, with his silver-white hair, his intense pale blue eyes, somehow he gives an impression of great calm, an almost spiritual quality. Tanned and athletic looking, it wasn't surprising to know he often does the spadework for his own experiments whether on the slopes of the active Kamchatka volcanoes near the Bering Sea or on the frosty tundra.

He led us through a maze of corridors and rooms, each entrance sealed with double doors, and through the Pulkovo Museum—a vaulted, domed room filled with gleaming copper instruments, manuscripts by Galileo, Peter the Great's own telescope. Pictures, on the way to his laboratory and office, detailed the reconstruction of the observatory after the Nazi devastation.

In Kozyrev's large, high-ceilinged office, crowded with lab equipment, the astrophysicist led us to his desk near the window. The sea green gyroscope on his desk, he told us with a smile, had played a leading part in some of his experiments with time.

How does the thought you're thinking go instantly from you telepathically to somebody else, or from you to another part of the world? Some Soviet scientists think ESP may involve an unknown form of energy; after seventeen years of strictly controlled, painstaking experiments, Dr. Kozyrev believes he may have found this energy. His instruments have recorded patterns of an unknown energy joining in with the activity of known mechanical and chemical effects. He calls this energy "Time." [86]

"Time is the most important and most enigmatic property of nature. Time is not propagated like light waves; it appears immediately everywhere. The altered properties of a certain second of time will appear instantly everywhere at once, just as time is everywhere. Time links us all and all things in the universe," Dr. Kozyrev told us at Pulkovo.

Kozyrev's "time" has a number of properties which he says can be studied in the scientist's lab. He has found, for instance, that this "X" energy, or "time," is denser near the receiver of an action and thinner near the sender. He showed us some of the instruments he has devised to chart this unusual effect. The basic equipment includes precision gyroscopes, asymmetrical pendulums, and torsion balances. The instruments, when set up in a complex arrangement, react showing a change in time density near a mechanical action (like stretching elastic) or a chemical action (like burning sugar).

This is the gist of what happens in one of the more simple experiments: a long elastic is stretched by a machine. You can think of this elastic as having two poles. The "pull" or *cause* end and the "stretch" or *effect* end. When the elastic is stretched, the registering equipment, consisting mainly of an asymmetrical pendulum made with a gyroscope, arcs toward the effect pole of the elastic. This deflection is imperceptible to the eye, but easily registered on the sensitive instruments. It is a highly important effect. It shows there has been an increase in the density of time, according to Dr. Kozyrev. "This has nothing to do with force fields. We shielded and calculated out any possible influence of electrostatic or any other force." Considering Kozyrev's rarified caliber as a scientist, he probably knows what he's talking about.

His instruments also show a thinning of time near the "cause" end of the elastic. This registration of time density can be picked up with the instruments even when the "cause-effect" equipment is shielded by a wall one yard thick. "It reacts even through iron tubes." Chemical cause-effect also shows the change in time density. Burning sugar is often used, as organic compounds give a particularly good result. "We postulate," Dr. Kozyrev says, "that time is thin around the cause and dense around the effect."

In a very real sense, what Dr. Kozyrev has found in these tests can be called PK. The chemical events act on the gyroscope pendulum *at a distance*. They move it without the use of any known force. Dr. Kozyrev would say that "time density" brings on this startling action at a distance. We usually think of PK not as matter affecting matter at a distance, but as mind affecting matter. Does thought have any effect on this time density?

"Yes," Dr. Kozyrev replied. "Thought definitely affects

the reaction. When I purposefully think of poetry or something emotional during the test, the equipment registers more of a change than when I think of mathematical calculations. Our thoughts may change the density of time."

Would the density of time, then, have something to do with telepathy?

"Telepathy always depends on the density of time. Time would be thin near the sender of the thought and denser around the receiver. We've already done tests in our lab to try to artificially change the density of time. When we can make time dense at will, we can make telepathy happen when we want it," Dr. Kozyrev feels.

What else affects the density of time?

Just like dowsers or the psychics Mikhail Kuni and Nelya Mikhailova, the test equipment was affected by changes in "time density" caused by thunderstorms, weather, the change of season. "I was all set to show off the effect to scientists one day. Suddenly a thunderstorm came up and that was the end of the reaction. It just didn't work." He laughed.

"We've also set up our tests in the very far north, in Murmansk. It worked extremely well there. Here at Pulkovo the effect is more pronounced in winter than in summer." He pointed out the huge double windows to the sea of brilliant flowers waving in the breeze. It was the time of White Nights in Leningrad and it would remain bright all night. "The activity of growing things in the summer, day and night, interferes with the reactions we've been charting. In the winter when everything's covered with snow, the reactions are very strong." Dr. Wilson at the Douglas Laboratories in California is setting up similar experiments and it will be interesting to see what impact the lush vegetation and warmth of California have on the tests.

Dr. Kozyrev is not a parapsychologist as such. In reputation and in work achieved, he is the most important scientist we met. He is attempting to elucidate a new world view, a new cosmogony. Under Kozyrev's new conception, psychic happenings would fall into place. They would no longer be, as they are in the current view of science, something outside the system, something that must be denied to protect the system.

Dr. Kozyrev has already come up with a few things for

parapsychologists. It seems we might need a geography of telepathy. In latitudes where time is dense, like the far north, telepathy should flow more easily. ESP might also flow more easily where there are fewer living things. Perhaps this is why ESP is reported to flow most freely in outer space.[357, 358]

Dr. Kozyrev's equipment for measuring time density might help in setting up effective ESP transmission. "Gravity also has an effect on time density," Dr. Kozyrev said, "and so does the density of matter." This began to sound like the findings of various dowsers who've always maintained that different substances in the earth give off what they call different "vibrations." That's how they identify what substance is hidden below them. Dr. Kozyrev says he is finding something similar in the laboratory. When an action creates greater time density, this density doesn't evaporate instantly; it lingers longer in some substances than in others. It remains twice as long in aluminum as in lead and five times longer in wood than in lead.[88]

Dr. Kozyrev discovered another characteristic of the energy he calls "time"—it has a *flow* pattern.

Dr. Kozyrev thought about all living organisms—animals, plants, people. Our right and left sides are not mirror images. More of the heart is on the left than the right side. Microbes produce colonies of a spiral structure. Protoplasm, the basic building block of life, is not symmetrical either. Asymmetry is a basic property of life. This can't be a chance thing, Dr. Kozyrev thought. Perhaps asymmetry is a special mechanism designed by nature to intensify vital force in living things. Perhaps the energy of "time" flows in this pattern. If so, Dr. Kozyrev figured, he could see it and measure it in a rotating body like a gyroscope. Altering the time pattern in a rotating system should add or subtract energy.

After years of careful experiments, Dr. Kozyrev and his colleagues found that in a left-hand rotating system the time flow is positive—it adds energy. In a right-hand system the time flow is negative.

The Leningrad scientists found that if an organic substance made of molecules that turn to the left (e.g., turpentine) is placed near the cause-effect equipment, it heightens the "PK." The registering device arcs even more toward the elastic. If an organic substance made of molecules turning to the right (e.g., sugar) is used, it diminishes the "PK." In Dr. Kozyrev's view our world is a left-hand system and it has a positive time flow that adds energy to our universe.

Time not only has a *pattern* of flow, says Dr. Kozyrev, but also a *rate* of flow. He calls the "rate of flow" the difference between cause and effect.

"As the rate of the time flow through a substance changes, weight is lost," Dr. Kozyrev told us. "It means that 'levitation' is a perfectly practical possibility. Science is trying step by step to find out methods of levitation." This kind of levitation would work not only for people, of course, but also for objects, machines.

"Over some seventeen years," Dr. Kozyrev said, "our tests have shown it is possible to demonstrate the influence of one process on another at a distance. We think this influence is accomplished by time." (In his view PK and ESP generally happen via the energy of time.)

"What about the PK medium, Nelya Mikhailova?" we asked. "Would your theory help explain how she is able to influence all kinds of substances at a distance?"

He nodded. "I've seen scientific films of Mrs. Mikhailova and they would lead you to believe she *can* move objects under glass, not just metallic objects, but teacups, cigarettes, matches, and so forth. I would very much like to test her," he said.

"How did you as an astrophysicist become interested in PK and telepathy?"

Handing us a scientific paper [87] he'd presented at a 1966 International Conference on Astronomy in Belgium, Kozyrev explained: "There are pairs of stars we call double stars. At first, the two stars are not the same, but gradually over a period of time the secondary star comes to resemble the primary star. It develops the same brightness, develops the same radius, becomes the same spectral type. At such enormous distances, this mirroring effect couldn't be happening through force fields. It would seem the principal star is affecting the satellite star through the energy of time. It's almost as if the stars communed by telepathy," he said with a grin.

In his scientific paper, Dr. Kozyrev asks, "Why is nothing at a state of equilibrium in the universe?" And he suggests,

"It is possible that all the processes in the material systems of the universe are the sources, feeding the general current of Time, which in its turn can influence the material system.

"We've been accustomed to thinking of the stars as enormous nuclear reactors, but I've reached the conclusion it is not nuclear reactions that play first fiddle. What gives stars their energy?

"Time as it develops into a physical reality invests the world with new properties. It is to time we should look to find the source that maintains the phenomenon of life in the world." In other words, stars get some of their energy from time.

The basic drawback of our exact sciences, in Dr. Kozyrev's view, is that they consider past and future identical. Science makes no distinction between past and future. Yet our psychological sense of time seems to tell us time moves from past to future and that eternity is no strip of film that can easily be run backward. Dr. Kozyrev conjectures that time has a tangible property that makes all the difference between past and future, between cause and effect. This property shows time is directed only one way, from past to future. The velocity can be found, Dr. Kozyrev states, theoretically and experimentally. "Time," he says, "contains the whole world of still unexplored occurrences. Time relates to all the phenomena of nature. Time participates in all the things that happen in our universe."

Dr. Kozyrev thinks that time is a form of energy that accomplishes or allows psychic happenings. (It does not "carry" telepathy in the usual sense of the word, for time does not propagate; it is immediately everywhere.) Would Dr. Kozyrev's idea help explain prophecy? The Greek parapsychologist A. Tanagras theorizes that the fulfillment of prophecies is connected to fields of energies which humans direct subconsciously to living things or objects. Thus precognition and PK are linked. According to Tanagras, unconscious motives draw this unknown "psi" energy toward us into the form of events in the way a magnet attracts iron filings. A psychic can sometimes read these energy patterns and, therefore, the future. The energy Kozyrev calls "time" may be the same force Tanagras believes we form into our destinies.

It's impossible to do justice to Dr. Kozyrev's ideas and

experiments in so short a space. As you can imagine, there are vast quantities of complicated figuring and test data behind Dr. Kozyrev's current conclusions. We have grossly oversimplified, of course, hoping to get across a very general idea of this remarkable man's thought and work. If you would like to know more, one of Dr. Kozyrev's scientific papers is available in translation from the U.S. Department of Commerce, Joint Publication Service, 4th and Adam Drive, S.W., Washington, D.C. 20443 ("Possibility of Experimental Study of the Properties of Time," JPRS 45238, May 2, 1968, $3.00.)

Are Dr. Kozyrev's extraordinary new ideas about the nature of time and of the world plausible? We asked Dr. Albert Wilson of the Douglas Research Laboratories in California.

"I feel that something very much like what Kozyrev has hypothesized will be established in physical theory within the next decade or two. Its implications will be revolutionary. It could take a generation of work before the leap he has taken can be incorporated into the body of scientific knowledge. Whether right or wrong, it is the type of imaginative speculation that points to a new way of viewing the world and this is always highly valuable."

A top Western scientist has also come up with the "time as energy" idea. The outstanding American theoretical physicist Dr. Charles A. Muses (in a Foreword to *Communication, Organization, and Science* by Jerome Rothstein)[369] says that time, though subjective, has quantitatively measurable characteristics. "We shall eventually see that time may be defined as the ultimate causal pattern of all energy release," says Muses. He believes the energy released by time is vibrating or oscillating.

Dr. Gardner Murphy, President of the American Society for Psychical Research, has often remarked, "When we have a new understanding of time, we will understand ESP. All the pieces will fall into place." It's a sparse group of people who are capable of elaborating a new scientific theory of time. Dr. Nikolai Kozyrev is one of them and the force of his talent is now channeled in this direction. Recently he's improved his equipment so that the energy he calls "time" is even more easily demonstrated in the lab.[100]

Before leaving Pulkovo, just out of curiosity, we asked, "Is there extraterrestrial life?"

"Most probably, somewhere," said Dr. Kozyrev. "I've never seen it myself, but there may be living things on Venus."

The astronomer led us outdoors, past the observatory buildings which, like most Leningrad buildings, are painted in pastels, some green and white, others pale orange and white. Great clumps of flowers in full bloom, bushy hedges, flowering vines simmered in the brilliant sun. We walked out to a point on the heights overlooking the entire city of Leningrad. Famous landmarks could be seen glimmering in the haze; the golden dome of St. Isaac's Cathedral, the gold spire on the Admiralty building, and through all the city the many canals and branches of the Neva River leading to the sea, the opening on the sea that Peter the Great had long wanted as his "Window on the West."

As he trains the huge Pulkovo telescope into the blue depths of space, as he watches the rotating sea green gyroscope in his laboratory, Nikolai Kozyrev is also trying to open a "window"—a window of the mind on a bright new view of the universe. His kind of theoretical thinking, vaulting the whole of existence, could illuminate the enigmas that challenge his parapsychological colleagues. Dr. Kozyrev's penetration into time and the world might lead to the understanding we need to claim and use, finally, the psychic dimension in all its variety.

14

EYELESS SIGHT

In the early 1960s, about 300,000 people lived in the Ural mountain city, Nizhniy Tagil. One of the least noticeable women in town was Rosa Kuleshova. Rosa was as plain and unmanicured as a potato, rinsed and sitting on the side of the sink. Living in industrial, mining-oriented Tagil, on the border of Europe and Asia, the twenty-two-year-old Rosa inhabited her own odd dreams. Since she'd been sixteen, this short, pudgy girl in her utilitarian print dresses had led drama groups for the town's visually handicapped. Various members of her own family were blind, and with them Rosa had learned to read Braille proficiently.

One day Rosa noticed something strange. After that, an odd daydream began to outpalpitate all the others in Rosa: she would teach the blind to see—to see light, colors, pictures, and even to read *without* Braille.

In the spring of 1962 Rosa told her very doubting doctor, Iosif M. Goldberg, that she could see with her fingers. Then she showed him. Carefully blindfolded by Goldberg, Rosa moved the third and fourth fingers of her right hand over sheets of paper, naming colors, "Green, red, light blue, orange." Goldberg put newspapers, magazines, books under Rosa's impossible fingers. Her hand read as easily as her eyes. It looked like everybody else's hand, but Rosa was acting as if she'd grown a second set of eyes in her fingertips.

"When I first found I could see print with my fingers," Rosa admitted to Dr. Goldberg, "I thought, wouldn't it be grand if I could read notes in my pocket during tests in school."

Goldberg, a neuropathologist, checked and rechecked. Finally he took his patient to a regional conference of the Society of Psychologists, meeting in Nizhniy Tagil in the fall of 1962. For the first time in her life, a lot of eyes were focused on Rosa, even though she couldn't see them through the bandages the psychologists wrapped around her head. Rosa's remarkable fingers, however, did see the color of the scientists' clothes, the shades of objects taken out of their pockets. Her hand "looked" at a person in a photograph. She described the man's posture and appearance. How did she do it? Practice, Rosa said. "I trained myself several hours a day for the last six years."

With this two-finger exercise, the name Rosa Kuleshova lit up in big letters. Russians read all about it. So did the rest of the world. "The riddle of Tagil," "the miracle of Tagil," purred over by professors and argued about in everything from the Party paper to the *Journal of Philosophy*, Rosa was carted to Moscow, to the laboratories of the Soviet Academy of Science. She emerged a celebrity, certified as genuine. She could "see" with her hand. She possessed what the Soviets at first burst, called "the Rosa Kuleshova Phenomenon," what the French call "paraoptic ability," and what Americans call "eyeless sight" or "dermo-optics."

Like a dowdy Pandora, Rosa let loose a mixed and mixed-up bunch of events. Blindfolded Russians took to moving their fingers across newspapers and colored sheets of paper the way their great-grandfathers had taken Ouija boards before the Revolution. The great eyeless sight fad began. Rosa herself got spun around by fame and eventually wound up needing psychiatric care. But away from the games and the limelight, pragmatic Soviet scientists began to uncover fascinating, potentially invaluable information about eyeless sight and to develop a new way for all of us to sense the world.

Does the unextraordinary looking Kuleshova possess something very extraordinary, a genuine and specific sixth sense? Had a new biological sense fallen like a random particle from the evolutionary heavens and landed on Rosa Kuleshova in Tagil? A team of scientists led by a neurologist, Dr. Shaefer, summoned Rosa on her first scientific trip to a psychiatric clinic in Sverdlovsk for a six week study.[37] The girl probably is supersensitive to the texture of dye, the scientists thought. But Rosa, securely blindfolded and behind a thick cardboard screen, was able to identify red, green, and yellow when tracing paper, cellophane, or glass covered the color sheets. She could also read print and sheet music under glass. If not texture, then she must be reacting to minute differences in heat. Black, white, and the colors of the spectrum absorb and reflect varying amounts of heat. Dr. Shaefer decided to heat plates dyed with "cool" colors—violets and blues—and to chill plates dyed with "warm" reddish tones. The sight of Rosa's hand didn't blow hot and cold; she easily identified the thermally distorted plates.

Home again in Tagil, the increasingly famous Rosa became the star subject of Dr. Abram Novomeisky working in the psychology laboratory of the Nizhniy Tagil Pedagogical Institute. Novomeisky asked Rosa to identify the color and shape of a curve of light on an oscillograph. She did. She was asked to make out an arithmetic problem projected from behind onto a screen like that of a television. After fifteen minutes practice, she could read these arithmetic problems with her fingers.[141] Rosa learned also to discern the color and height of liquids in a glass tube. Novomeisky, like Dr. Shaefer, became convinced Rosa's hand saw, but not through supersensitive touch or heat. Perhaps the secret of seeing hands lay in an unknown factor in the skin that could sense light. With a little supervised practice, Rosa was identifying projected rainbows in her palm. Novomeisky filtered all heat from the ray of light. Rosa still could reel off the colors of the spectrum.

Then came the invitation to the ball in Rosa's cinderella story. The prestigious Biophysics Institute of the Soviet Academy of Sciences in Moscow invited Miss Kuleshova, all expenses paid, to a grand bevy of experiments in their labs.[14, 313] Rosa found new mentors, M. S. Smirnov and M. Bongard. Day after day, Rosa showed the Muscovites her wondrous ability to see with her fingers. Finally, speaking for the Institute, Smirnov stated, "Rosa Kuleshova can read a text by touching it, she can identify colors and light with her hands." By this time both of Rosa's hands had developed eyeless sight and were discriminating the colors of everything from neckties and lights to flower petals and hair. She made out pictures on postage stamps and picked out earrings on a woman in a photograph. By this time, too, as Rosa rose higher and higher on a pile of solid supporting evidence, Soviet scientists were beginning to doubt that they had an evolutionary mutant in their labs. Old, sloughed over reports suddenly were excavated. The *Russian Journal of Neuropsychological Medicine* at the turn of the century had included tests on a woman with eyeless sight in her hands similar to Rosa's.

In the 1950s Soviet psychologist Dr. A. N. Leontyev trained a group of men to sense and differentiate green and red light (with heat filtered out) beamed on their palms.

Parapsychologist Leonid L. Vasiliev in the late 1950s reported that eyeless sight was commanded into being in an alcoholic patient in Polotsk Psychiatric Hospital. Hypnotized, the man was told to read the headlines of *Pravda* with his hands. Eventually he was able to read headlines and the small print through a sheet of tracing paper.

While Rosa was off in the larger laboratories of Moscow, her hometown scientists began to seek out others who could see with their hands, vibrating on the Soviet idea: if one can, others can. First they would try to develop skin sight in volunteers, then they would work out the hows and whys.

Dr. Novomeisky started with eighty graphic arts students of the Nizhniy Tagil Pedagogical Institute. He found that about every sixth person could recognize the difference between two colors after about half an hour of trying. What does it feel like to see with your hands?

With their eyes wrapped in black, lightproof bandages, often with their heads and shoulders behind a screen, Novomeisky's students ran their fingers over sheets of colored paper. Boris M. proved a particularly quick learner. "I feel a clinging, pulling, viscid sensation." "That paper is red," Novomeisky told the blindfolded Boris.

Novomeisky's students and the people trained in other Soviet centers all more or less agreed that colors divide into smooth, sticky, and rough sensations. Light blue is smoothest. You feel yellow as very slippery, but not quite as smooth. Red, green, and dark blue are sticky. You feel green as stickier than red, but not as coarse. Navy blue comes over as the stickiest, but yet harder than red and green. Orange is hard, very rough, and causes a braking feeling. Violet gives a greater braking effect that seems to slow the hand and feels even rougher. (Experimenters noted that the fingers of trained students actually did move with greater difficulty over the braking violet and "sticky" red than over the "slippery" yellow.)[142]

Considering the color spectrum, Novomeisky points out that if you start on each side of the middle color, green, the sticky, rough feeling increases as you finger your way toward either end of the band.

Black, according to the Soviets, feels the most sticky, viscid, and braking of all. White is smooth, though with a coarser feeling than yellow. Rosa, in her self-taught way, developed a different description of what her seeing fingers felt. She sensed various colors as crosses, straight lines, wavy lines, dots. It's almost as if Rosa responded more directly to some sort of color field than did the students.

Of course there isn't any actual coarseness, stickiness, or heat, but these new skin-sight sensings translate out that way in consciousness. Novomeisky placed aluminum foil, brass plates, and red copper plates over color sheets lit from below. Running their fingers over the various metal covers, blindfolded students still said, "It clings to me, it's sticky" when red was underneath, "It's very smooth" when pale blue hid below. "Only after many sessions did the new sensation automatically conjure up green or black in their mind's eye," Novomeisky said.

If you want to teach your hands to see, the Soviets recommend [154] you start by learning to sense the difference between two colors from different groups—like sticky red versus smooth light blue. Once the skin sight has come awake, the Russians suggest, you might try sorting checkers into black and white piles, playing cards into red and black suits. If you're serious about competing with the Soviets, you'll have to keep going until your fingers can do the reading as well as the walking through the yellow pages. Three of Novomeisky's volunteers learned to decipher drawings with their fingers, read numbers and letters even under glass.

Could you learn to know the color of something or even read a sentence by simply waving your hands over it like an old-time wizard? The scientists tried to move the students from *contact* hand sight to *distal* (at a distance) hand sight. At first the Russian students couldn't pull off this sort of magic, but they kept trying. Dr. Novomeisky, who believes eyeless sight has something to do with electromagnetic fields, put his colored paper in an insulated tray. Students suddenly began to react to something above the color. Their hands felt something in the air. It felt as if each color radiated to a certain height, as if it extended a particular distance into space. Different people sensed colors at differing heights, but the "steps" up the spectrum were similar. Boris M. felt the red "barrier" fourteen inches above the page; Ludmila L, at eighteen inches; Arkady A. at twenty-eight inches; and Larissa L. at thirty-one inches. Red extended highest for all of them. Light blue extended the least for all.[11, 91, 143]

In the beginning, the art students could only identify a color by a sort of edge in space. As their skill refined, Novomeisky began to hear, "It burns as if my hand were over a flame," "This feels really freezing, cold seems to exude from it." The Soviet students made up a loose scale of identifying sensations. Very generally: red burns, orange warms, yellow barely warms. Green is neutral. Light blue cools, navy blue freezes, and violet cools while simultaneously pinching.

Aside from hot and cold, students also reported that colors stung, bit, hit, pressed, pinched, and, it seemed, blew on their hands.

Today Soviets are working to see if eyeless sight can be explained by what is already known or if it involves principles as yet unknown to science. Something no one seems to have pointed out is that the color and sensation scales put together by the Russian students are very similar to scales put together over a hundred years ago by dozens of sensitives working with the German chemist Baron von Reichenbach. These sensitives could, allegedly, in pitch dark rooms see a force emanating from crystals and other objects. There is a blue pole which feels cool and pleasant to the hand. And an orange-red pole that has warmth, a loathsome tepidity," they reported. Von Reichenbach christened this unknown emanation Odic Force.

The Soviets wondered: is the skin picking up the field of the object, is the field of the hand reflecting back on itself, or is it some interaction of fields? The mysteries of eyeless sight are reminiscent, at this point, of the enigmas of dowsing. Whatever was happening in the hypothetical realm of rays and particles, the students, waving their hands, were propelled into a new dimension. They experienced the bright varieties of light and color that flashed and glowed around them in a new, more intimate way. If eyeless sight isn't a new sense, it is a new sensing. You can knowingly *feel* color and light.

To the art students it was an addition, but not a major one. Eyeless sight could hardly replace the visual delight of seeing the crisp reds, greens, oranges of a tossed salad, let alone the rest of the world. The really red-letter breakthrough inherent in skin sight lay in its possible use by the blind, the people Rosa dreamed of during her long years of self-teaching.

Dr. Yakov Fishelev, after finding that a number of his students at the Sverdlovsk Pedagogical Instiute could also be trained into eyeless sight, headed for the Pyshma school for the blind.[116] He asked a little girl in the second grade, Nadia Lobanova, to hold out her palm. He beamed light on her hand and said, "This is red." Then, "this is green." In a few days Nadia could always tell correctly which ray colored her hand. In a few weeks she learned for the first time to know the rest of the rainbow. Dr. Fishelev moved the blind girl to colored paper. Again she learned to recognize colors. Fishelev put the paper under glass. Nadia still recognized her newfound world of colors. Dr. Novomeisky came and put the color sheets under a copper plate. When Nadia identified the colors, he told her that was something neither he nor her teacher could see.

Nadia lost her sight when she was less than a year old and had no memory of the thing other people called color. How did she determine it? "Red, that's the warmest," Nadia said. Another blind second grader, Yuri, said, "Red, that's rough. It pulls at my fingers."

Fishelev and five teachers helped eighteen more children learn to sense light and to know yellow, red, green, blue. Fishelev began in May 1963 trying to teach Nadia to distinguish the outlines of letters. Week after week she failed. Nadia and Fishelev kept at it. On October 15th Nadia did it. She recognized with her fingers the letters in a first-grade primer. She read her first word, which the Soviets say was *mir*, a word that means both "peace" and "world" —which is almost too fitting. Like the voyage to a new continent, the discovery of a route through the body to the light and color outside could bring a new world to all the blind. In this decade, most of the explorers have been Soviets.

As the blind children gradually worked toward the feel of color, a horde of sharp-eyed young Russians clambered onto the eyeless sight bandwagon, playing a kind of national blind man's bluff. Parents read of the wondrous Rosa Kuleshova. Supposedly over 40 million Soviets saw her perform on a single television program. The same seductive idea seemed to blip simultaneously in hundreds of Russian homes. Maybe little Vania or Tania could also see with their hands. Why shouldn't they be as talented as that girl from Tagil? Festooned in homemade blindfolds of all shapes and colors, an amazing number of little Vanias, Tanias, Sashas, and Tashas instantly could sense the color of a pencil or a book, could identify an unknown object like a green pot. Hand sight got out of hand. With a few waves of their palms, children could, parents proclaimed, see pictures under the rug, what papa hid for them under the mattress, and even objects secreted in a safe! Surely academies would fling wide their gates to these miraculous beings and forget the plodding Rosa. For a short time the children were borne to Moscow; scientists did swoop in and out of far-off towns examining this epidemic of *wunderkinder*. The Russian writer G. Bashkirova told of one such pilgrimage of a special commission of the Soviet Academy of Sciences to see a highly touted ten-year-old girl in a small industrial town. She was one of the "pictures through the rug" readers.

"The little girl was already used to her fame and bore it with dignity, condescending in conversations with the usual guests." Rather than beginning with the special eye mask and the box with black sleeves used in lab tests, the scientists put motorcycle goggles with opaque lenses on the child. She breezed through the tests identifying colors wrapped in cellophane. Was she somehow peeking? They held their cards above her head, then to the right. The little girl's head tilted up, turned slightly to the right.

"Unobtrusively, we exchanged glances, while nearby, melting with happiness, reveling in his unique child, stood papa." They gave her colored cards sealed in black envelopes. "I'm so tired," the little girl said, "I want to go home." [7]

Miss Bashkirova added that for once in her life she was glad she had a turned up nose like the little girl's. "I put on the goggles and found I could peek, a trick none of the straight-nosed scientists could duplicate."

Rosa Kuleshova was also having trouble getting off a merry-go-round of her own making. The story of her trip to Moscow had been, "I came, I *saw*, I conquered." But when she went back to Tagil with the laurels of the Academy, Rosa found life flat. She wired Moscow: "Coming back to give more performances." In the capital Rosa began showing off for scientists, often in their living rooms. Out of the tightly structured, controlled situation of the laboratory, Rosa, like the children, began wavering into all sorts of fantastic claims. She accepted challenges she knew she couldn't meet, like seeing a color pressed under three large books. She failed. "Never mind, I can do even better things." Rosa claimed she could read through a table, identify a picture by sitting on it. She rambled on about the blind. Surely they could all learn to see now. They just had to learn a few simple rules that she knew already. But Rosa could only talk vaguely when asked to explain. She resorted to the scientific stage.

Writer Bashkirova, crushed in the learned audience of "A night with Rosa," reported Rosa swept onstage like a diva to receive the worship of her fans. It was noisy and hot. People stood on chairs to get a better look at this wonder woman. "Modest within reason, coquettish, addressing the audience, she spouts verses and facetious sayings." People asked Rosa to move this way and that so they could see more. "She identifies a picture card with her hand—a storm of applause. Poor, poor Rosa, how your bosses are spoiling you without realizing it. . . . In the general turmoil, the chance to peek comes ten times—how is one not to peek, to take out added insurance, if hundreds of enthusiastic eyes are gazing at you. A saint wouldn't refrain!" Bashkirova concludes.

Rosa wasn't clever. Soon she was caught so easily that her behavior is more reminiscent of a disintegrating mental state than of charlatanry. Rosa lost weight, felt sick (she's been epileptic since a brain infection at age fourteen); she cried all the time. More depressing to her supporters, like writer Bashkirova, Rosa was losing her actual eyeless sight ability. (Researchers in Russia and America find emotional turmoil and illness often blanks out skin sight.) With Smirnov and Bongard of the Academy of Sciences, Dr. Gellerstein, Rosa's favorite professor, finally cut through the morass and tried to salvage the sodden Rosa. They also wanted to salvage their earlier solid tests with her, which the Academy still vouched for.

Rosa loved to play cards. The scientists coaxed her into reading cards with her fingers. Soon, blindfolded again, behind screens with a large piece of cardboard fitted around her neck and extending like a table, and her hand covered with black cloth as extra control, Rosa again determined the color of light beams, recognized light and dark stripes on paper, and read small printing.[7] Sometimes as her hands read, one of the scientists stood behind her pressing his fingers hard against her closed eyelids, using, the Soviets say, hundreds of ounces of force. No one could peek with fingers pressing their eyeballs. After the prolonged force is released and the eyes are opened, you still can't read for several minutes. Rosa, and not a sadistic scientist, thought up this overly straightforward but effective way of proving her skin did see and read.

When *Life* [368] reporter Bob Brigham visited Rosa at the Moscow clinic in 1964, she pressed his fingers hard into her closed eyes. She identified colors for him—blue and orange—first by rubbing, then by merely waving her hands six inches above them. Brigham decided to try her on his business card, something she could have no knowledge of. Rosa read the small print flawlessly—with her elbow. "Even if she had been able to peek," reported Brigham, "she couldn't have seen the card, because it was entirely blocked by her forearm."

Dr. Gregory Razran, head of the psychology department of Queens College in New York and an expert on Soviet psychology for the National Institutes of Health led *Life* to the amazing Rosa. Razran examined her in Russia and conferred with Drs. Novomeisky and Goldberg.

Speaking in *Life* about the Soviet discovery of eyeless sight, Dr. Razran said, "It is, after all, the kind of thing one automatically disbelieves. But there is no longer any doubt in my mind that this work is valid.

"In all my years, I can't remember when anything has

had me more excited than this prospect of opening up new doors of human perception. I can hardly sleep at night. . . . To see without eyes—imagine what that can mean to a blind man!"

By the mid sixties there were reportedly numerous Russians with full-fledged skin sight; a few, like Tania Bykovskaia, seemed to have come by it naturally. Tania, a seventh grader, was "discovered" by her biology teacher. At first try, Tania told the color of a penholder. The teacher began testing in earnest and Tania shortly could identify a picture in a book by running her fingers over it. A blue ribbon commission from Kuban Medical Institute in Krasnodar examined Tania. They report that while specially blindfolded, she could tell the colors of two balls hidden from sight, but not from her hands, behind a screen. She also clearly made out pictures of an ax, tongs, and an alarm clock. Tania explains how she discovered her eyeless sight. "Once when I was lying in bed, I picked up a book and knew its title without looking at it. I didn't think this was important." [401]

Most of the new possessors of eyeless sight hadn't hatched in the heat of the public craze. They were trained by scientists. At the Scientific Conference of the Ural Division of the Society of Psychologists, in Perm, 1965, Dr. S. N. Dobronravov of Sverdlovsk reported that up to 72 percent of children had skin sight potentials. "It is most noticeable in children from the ages of seven to twelve years." Scientists at this convention agreed that the "supersensational, carnival" atmosphere whirling around eyeless sight was harming the subjects and the investigation. Work would continue quietly with subjects anonymous to the public.

Dr. Novomeisky was quietly trying to get information to help the blind. He found that blind adults didn't take to skin sight as readily as did blind children. The adults probably didn't believe that hands could see. Secondly, their acquired sensitivity of touch, and the habit of trying to "read" textures, blocked feeling of the dermo-optic sensations. But when Novomeisky put colored paper in *insulated* trays, ten blind adults suddenly got all the eyeless sight sensations that seeing students experienced. "With the insulated tray," Novomeisky reported, "we didn't find a single blind person who did not have positive tendencies toward skin sight." [143]

The insulation idea came as Novomeisky tried to understand how eyeless sight happens. Some scientists speculated that gifted skin readers have special cells—rods and cones, like those in the eyes—in their finger skin. Others leaned to a "radiant" hypothesis, thinking the ability might be caused by infrared rays or even radioactive rays from isotopes in the body caroming back objects to the palm. Novomeisky suspected some interaction of electromagnetic fields. He noted that when either the material or the "reading" hands of blind people were grounded, eyeless sight gradually faded away.

Electricity it seems may have something to do with eyeless sight. So does light. Like regular sight, skin sight declines in twilight and usually ceases in the pitch black. (Two of Novomeisky's sighted students were however able to hand read in special lightproof chambers. And Rosa was able to read large letters in a dark room; she could also determine the color of aniline dyes, cotton socks, and pencils.

Novomeisky put his best art student, Boris M., under intense red light. Boris couldn't identify color under red light; neither can anyone with regular sight. But Boris hadn't been able to identify color under daylight either when he first tried. After a few practice sessions he began to notice there was still a difference in sensation between colors even under red light. Once Boris learned the identifying differences, his hand saw what his eyes couldn't—colors under red light.

Novomeisky succeeded in training Vasily B., a metallurgist, totally blinded seven years previously, to know color again with his hand by touching, and at a distance. Presented with silver paper, Vasily said, "Something whitish, like gray—no, it's the color of metal, it's steel blue." Running his fingers over cherry red paper, Vasily said, "Close to red. Cherry color. It's the color of unripe cherries." [154]

When the lights were switched off, Vasily, like the sighted trainees, felt skin sight gradually leave his palm, his fingers, and then "sensations, so to speak, trickled off into space from the fingertips." The light clicked on. "Light! I can feel the light coming back again!" Vasily said shakily. He was deeply moved. For the first time in seven years he could sense the waning and rebirth of light.

"The blind should live in very brightly illuminated rooms," Novomeisky declared. When a three hundred watt bulb was substituted for the usual hundred watts in the lab, the blind Vasily sensed the "color barrier" of an object at a much greater distance, up to three feet away. The color of the light in the room also makes a difference. Like heightens like. Under blue illumination, for example, blue is much easier to identify. One can sense it at a greater distance.[143-44]

These simple Soviet observations, if they continue to check out, could be of much greater help to the world's blind than attempting to replace Braille with eyeless sight. If certain critical objects like doorknobs, faucets, telephones, handles on pots, dishes, particularly movable objects were colored, say, yellow in a room brightly lit with yellow bulbs, the blind might actually be able to see with their skin almost as easily as we locate a coffeepot with our eyes.

The blind Vasily and a visually handicapped man, Genady G., both did learn to determine letters and numbers by waving their hands carefully in the air above them. Genady, though his eyes were far too dim to read even large letters, was carefully blindfolded as extra precaution. Dr. Novomeisky's records state Genady could identify seven numbers, two-and-a-half inches large, at a distance on his first try. In following sessions he easily read a dozen long numbers like 606, 16904, 4906137.

Dr. Iosif Goldberg, Rosa's discoverer, discovered in work with the blind that those whose disability is caused by damage to eye or optic nerve can develop eyeless sight. People with damage in the optic centers of the brain cannot see with their skin.

Novomeisky found too that hands could read letters at a greater height above texts sitting on plates charged with a weak current of positive electricity. Once again, the Soviets plunged after a sloughed over human ability, coaxed it, trained it into being, then tried to thrust it to practical use with artificial boosters. Could some sort of plug-in reading stand be developed for the blind to help them read or at least make out pictures?

Apart from the Ural scientists, other researchers are trying to harness eyeless sight for the blind. In Armenia's ancient capital city, Yerevan, the biophysics laboratory of the Armenian Academy of Sciences has successfully trained students. One blind high school sophomore even learned to "see" with his hands inside rubber gloves.

Something stranger was going on in Odessa at the Filatov Institute's Laboratory of the Physiology of Vision. Dr. Andrei Shevalev taught eyeless sight to eight-year-old Vania Dubrovich, blinded in early childhood. His eyes and optical nerves had been removed. Shevalev's team saw a more interesting possibility in skin sight than finger reading. Shevalev attached a lens to Vania's forehead. The boy learned to feel light through the lens, to discriminate levels of brightness. Shevalev spoke of experiments to develop eyeless sight in the forehead, then further work with optical lenses to try to focus in objects from the environment onto the brow. Ultimately these Soviets hope skin "glasses" will allow the blind to get their bearings and wend more easily through any surroundings.[202]

This conjures an occultish monocle-for-the-third-eye image. But the Soviets report that all of your skin can have seeing potential. In the labs, Rosa learned to see with her left hand, then with two weeks of supervised practice her toes began to know weak color sensations. A nine-year-old music student from Karkov, Lena Bliznova, tested at reputable institutes, reportedly could see with her hands, shoulders, and stomach. There are reports of other trainees sensing light and color with the tongue, elbow, and nose. It seems that with practice you could come to know red, green, yellow, the whole spectrum with your whole body, a sensuous expansion to be added to the bag of the mixed-media artists. Full-bodied skin sight, feeling color, blow, press, pluck, warm, and freeze, is synesthesia, the substitution of senses, the seeing of music, hearing of perfume celebrated by poets like Baudelaire, exclaimed over by LSD sugar cube eaters.

Couldn't picture reading, color identification be accomplished by telepathy or clairvoyance, rather than by skin sight? Probably it is, on occasion. The Soviets say, however, that Rosa Kuleshova proved to have no psychic abilities. In Odessa, Dr. Shevalev, casually skipping over one wonder when another is involved, reported that his colleagues found they could often telepathically influence a child attempting eyeless sight. Consequently, all the institute's tests and those at the center in the city of Magnitogorsk are designed so no one knows what color a child is reading at the moment.

The American scientific bloc generally treated reports of Rosa Kuleshova with the disdain allotted to the new and unorthodox. But a Michigan woman, Patricia Stanley, appeared who could do many things Rosa did. Here and there a few scientists began to look into eyeless sight.

One man at least couldn't help observing the Soviet eyeless sight flurry with something like a Gallic shrug. Jules Romains, the French novelist, now in his eighties, published an original study of dermal vision in 1920. Trained in physiology and histology, he says that he focused on eyeless sight because, "I hoped for the advent of a psychology of discovery, which would be far less concerned with multiplying clever speeches on facts long known and more anxious to discover new material. The identifying of a yet unknown sense headed the list on this program of a psychology of discovery." [367]

Long before the Soviets, Romains found that all the skin has eyeless sight capability, or as he named it, paraoptic ability. Hands and face were the most sensitive. Romains' subjects also learned to know color, read print, and sense at a distance with skin sight. A special committee of ophthalmologists successfully checked out some of his subjects. Others displayed their new sense before such luminaries as Henri Bergson and Anatole France.

Speaking of his long-ago treatise published in France and America and of his theory of what allows eyeless sight, Romains wrote, "I was waiting for it to be explained and discussed by others. Forty years later we are still far from this." He remarks that Russian and American scientists can take their time explaining eyeless sight if they want, "But they should have at least the decency not to announce their modest results as an unprecedented discovery."

One person Jules Romains didn't snipe at for being unoriginal was Rosa Kuleshova. Rosa always has been called unstable, a morbid personality, and now apparently she's schizophrenic. Yet Rosa did get the wild idea that skin can see, on her own. Rosa is less educated than the students who sprang up in her wake, students who learned eyeless sight much more quickly than she did. But they wouldn't have been trying to know red and green with their fingers if it hadn't been for Rosa. She set turning the contemporary research into eyeless sight. From this work the blind may one day move a little more easily through a reflected world of light and color, and some of the rest of us may find our sensuous life a little fuller.

Today in the Soviet Union eyeless sight has a new, spruced up name, "bio-introscopy." The deeper the Soviets go into bio-introscopy, the stranger, the more seemingly fantastic their findings get. According to the latest batch of scientific papers, trained students can determine the color of an object *after* it has been removed.[40] It's as if an object leaves a color trace of itself in the air. Not surprisingly, the main thrust of bio-introscopic research now centers on discovering the way skin sight works. Perhaps it is an electromagnetic phenomenon as Novomeisky suspects. However, other scientists point out that Novomeisky's own extensive tests show a force that does not really behave like any known form of electricity, although it does have some analogies to magnetism. Perhaps, the Russians think, there is also a trace of some other force in the "Kuleshova Phenomenon," something to do with the mysteries of dowsing or PK.

As to what might be behind eyeless sight, the American Dr. Razran told *Life*, "For all we know, this may turn out to be some entirely new kind of force or radiation that has gone undetected—and unsuspected—until now. There is nothing ridiculous about this idea. After all, the history of discovery in this field is that we sense something first, then we go out into the sea of energy that surrounds us and look for whatever it was that caused the sensation."

If any of the promises of Soviet eyeless sight come true, some credit must go to the unfortunate little nobody from Tagil who had a hunch, then a sense of mission, and plugged along, by herself, getting her fingers to see. For this, Rosa Kuleshova deserves to be called a somebody.

15

DOWSING: FROM "WIZARD ROD" TO "B.P.E."

East of the fabled Asian cities of Tashkent and Samarkand in the luxuriant valley of the mountains bordering China there stands the dazzling white city of Alma-Ata, a city almost buried in gardens and the scent of the thousands of flowers that decorate its streets. On the outskirts of this Kazakh capital city where wild apricot and apple trees grow in profusion, something happened on the morning of October 21, 1966, that would have astounded the area's one-time conqueror Genghis Khan.

Beside the Alma-Atinka River, two huge mountains suddenly shot up in the air and crashed into the ravines below. Torrents of stone rocketed down from this man-made explosion. Three million cubic meters of rock cascaded over two miles of obstacles.

A bevy of researchers, many from Alma-Ata's famous Kirov University, observed the detonated mountains from various vantage points. Dr. Valery Matveev, leader of the Alma-Ata Geology Survey Group, recorded in his logbook: "We were ten miles from the explosion site. Our team surveyed up to half an hour before the blast. Our instruments registered two clear geophysical anomalies under the ground where we stood."

The explosion shattered the quiet Alma-Ata morning, houses shivered on their foundations, pictures fell, glasses rattled. Water in the city's canals splashed into the streets. Matveev's geology team hastily recharted the land they'd graphed before. Suddenly their instruments recorded growing changes in the curves of the two anomalies. For sixteen minutes the graphs "shivered," the profiles grew steadily larger. At the twenty-second minute, a third new underground force suddenly appeared. "In the following hours, the picture of the underground zone changed fancifully.

After four hours, all these variations disappeared. The first two curves we'd recorded before the explosion took shape again." [157]

About the only thing about that October morning in Alma-Ata that would not have been strange to Genghis Khan was the principal recording instrument used by Matveev's team. Along with magnetometers and other geological equipment, the Soviet geologists walked across the survey area with dowsing rods! The strange reactions to the explosion recorded by the rods are another mystery for the Soviets to explain in their full-scale investigation of dowsing. In the past few years the Russians have piled up stacks of data on dowsing.

For more than seven thousand years, the art of radiesthesia (meaning sensitivity to radiations) has been practiced—it includes water divining and dowsing for all sorts of things, from ore to buried treasure, with a dowsing rod or pendulum. Tales of the seemingly supernatural powers of dowsers to track murderers and thieves with the rod have been handed down in folklore. Bas reliefs from early Egypt portray water diviners equipped with dowsing rods and even headgear with antennae. Kings of ancient China, like King Yu (2200 B.C.), are pictured carrying dowsing rods.

Today in the lethal jungles of Vietnam, engineers from the First and Third U.S. Marine Divisions are also using dowsing rods—this time for survival purposes—to successfully locate tunnels, booby traps and sunken mortar shells.

What makes a dowsing rod move when a dowser walks over a tunnel or underground stream? Is man sensitive to "radiations" of various objects? Why is it that dowsers from many countries report endless case histories of successes, yet most scientists in the West boldly assert they've never yet seen an acceptable dowsing test?

Without a proper, scientific birth certificate to explain where it came from, dowsing has existed in the West as a foundling, outside the realm of science. In the Soviet Union scientists have taken in this orphan. Dowsing in the USSR is a legitimate field of scientific study. Major geology institutes in Moscow and Leningrad have large groups of geologists, geophysicists, and physiologists all researching dowsing.

Dr. A. A. Ogilvy, Chairman of the Geology Department of Moscow State University, announced [157] that the Soviets "stood on the eve of a new birth in the ancient field of prospecting—discovery of the scientific basis of dowsing. Dowsing will be used to solve problems and may supplant many contemporary geophysical methods." He stressed for his Soviet audience, "There's nothing mystical in the ability of man's body to react to underground mines or water."

Perhaps it's harder for Soviet scientists to be as skeptical about dowsing as their Western counterparts. Many Russian scientists themselves find they can skillfully work the dowsing rod. They aren't restricted to just checking the claims of dowsers; they can study the phenomenon or radiesthesia firsthand. Being expert geologists, they are better able to interpret the actions of the dowsing rod.

A few years ago Professor G. Bogomolov, a foremost Soviet water geologist, picked up the ancient "wizard rod," as the Russians call it. He found to his surprise that he could determine the depth of underground streams and cables, and even the diameter of water pipes. Dr. Bogomolov and two hydrology engineers, Drs. Tareev and Simonov, became convinced dowsing was more than "mystical beliefs" or autosuggestion. Test after test showed man did seem to possess a strange ability to sense substances deep in the earth. This talent is vital to science; it must be understood and used, they thought. In the closed Stalin era, they took the daring step of publishing their findings on the wizard rod in a scientific journal, *The Journal of Electricity*, January 1944.

Could dowsing really work? The article stirred crosscurrents in the scientific community. Commissions gathered. Over one hundred men, some from a geology institute, some from the Red Army, were ordered up to take part in a large-scale dowse-in. "You must find electrical cables, water pipes, and seeping ground water," they were told.

The hundred well-marshaled dowsers, each with a Y-shaped wooden branch cut from a shade tree, moved out slowly along the terrain. Each man held the branch by its forked ends, parallel with the earth. At the moment they crossed an electrical cable or ground water, the free end of the rod dipped or rose. Whether the fork of the branch went up or down depended, the Soviets reported, on which way the current flowed in the cable or stream.

The scientific commissions came out with a "Yes, dowsing works," verdict. "The 'wizard rod,'" they said, "is the simplest of all conceivable electrophysiological instruments." The wooden fork, they found, had supersensitivity to underground objects in the hands of a human being. The force of this mysterious pull on the twig reached one hundred and even one thousand grams per centimeter.

Nothing seemed to shield humans from sensitivity to these radiations that caused the twig to move. No matter how quickly the dowser walked or how carefully he was screened with rubber or steel plates or even lead armor, the dowsing rod still reacted in a man's hands to underground water. Only if the water flowed inside a rubber hose was the dowsing rod stilled.

The forked twig used by the Soviet dowser had to be cut from a shade tree. But after two or three days its sensitivity would drop sharply, and the dowser would have to go to a willow, peach, or witchhazel tree and hack off another twig. The Russians found if the twig accidentally broke and the dowser tried to patch it up, the "wizardry" disappeared from the "wizard" rod.

Are women better dowsers than men? The Russians ran a series of two hundred tests. In 20 percent of the trials with men and 40 percent of those with women, the dowser's rod begun to revolve as soon as the dowser arrived at a spot where a stratum of lead, zinc, or gold lay hidden 240 feet below.[187, 214]

After many tests, painstakingly evaluated by statistical methods, the Russians concluded the wizard rod can be used with striking success for resolving technical problems: locating underground electrical cables, water pipes, damaged points in cable networks; for finding minerals and water. Czech water diviner S. Dokulil reported to the Russians in 1961 that he'd been successfully locating wells with the dowsing rod for agricultural co-ops all over Czechoslovakia for thirty-two years. (In Czechoslovakia, we learned from scientists, "The Czech Army proved out concretely the practical nature of dowsing in war conditions." Czech Army Journal *Periscope*, 1966, ran a special article on the possible use of parapsychology for war, including dowsing.)

Today dowsing is ensconced in Soviet science under a

safe, new demystified name—"The Biophysical Effects Method," or "BPE"—to conceal its magical origins. Of course, a major thrust behind all this work on the BPE is the desire to use dowsing to uncover the enormous natural resources of the Soviet lands. But for all their hurry to put it to use, the Russians aren't overlooking another factor in the dip of the wizard rod—the "why" of it all. What sort of "communication over a distance" is this between body, rod, and ore buried under tons of earth? Understanding the seemingly mysterious energy or forces involved could, in the long run, prove more valuable than the discovery of water on the commune or gold in the mountains. Perhaps it's an energy we already know about, like electromagnetism, or perhaps man has an unknown sense organ that picks up information from minerals. Speculation accelerated as dowsing research expanded in the mid 1960s.

One Soviet leading the dowsing renaissance is a topnotch Leningrad scientist, a specialist in geology and mineralogy and an expert dowser himself, Dr. Nikolai Sochevanov. In the summer of 1967 he directed a geological expedition in the Zabaikal and Northern Kirgiz Region, near Russia's border with China. Sochevanov himself served as one of the "operators"—the updated term for "dowser."

Does a vast and powerful river, a mass of colossal rushing energy, have more of an effect on our body's sensitivity than a small stream? If we're flying over rugged terrain in an airplane, does some part of us react to and measure the strength of river and streams, the depths of mines? Sochevanov's diary for the expedition holds some clues. "We flew over the River Chu. The 'index' (dowsing rod) showed the usual profile of a wet section. But the river, despite the vast amount of water and the speed of the current, did not make the 'index' react especially strongly. Only near the shore on each side was the force strong enough to cause the dowsing rod to make a revolution. Apparently the friction of the water on the shore was one cause of this release of energy. Water seems to influence man most strongly not where a huge quantity of water moves at great speed but where the water saturates a great mass of soil and slowly moves along small capillaries."

Do mineral deposits deep in the earth emit some sort of radiation which we are somehow sensitive to?

"Mines influence the divining rod as strongly as water," says Sochevanov. "Crossing a river, the indicator may make two rotations, and crossing a brook, one. But above a lead deposit deep beneath the surface, the dowsing rod rotated eighteen times. Eighteen revolutions on a path less than ten yards long! Of course, this occurred over a very thick ore body. But our 'operators' also clearly located ore deposits only three inches thick at a depth of more than 150 yards."

The force that moves the rod seems so great, it can, at times, almost pull the rod from the operator's hands. As long as he holds on, the rod swings in circles.

Sochevanov decided to retire the traditional Russian Y-shaped wooden divining rod and create a rod that would rotate easily. The number of rotations, he thought, would make a good indicator of the force he was trying to measure. He made his diviner of steel. Unlike live wood, the metal rod can be used any time of year and in any number of tests.

To make a Soviet style dowsing rod, you need 59 inches of ⅛-inch wide steel wire. Bend an 8-inch loop in the middle of the wire and extend the ends out 6 inches on each side and downward a foot on each side to form a "U." Bend out 3 inches on the sides to form handles. (See pic. sec.) Space between sides is about 2 feet. The rod is held horizontally in the outstretched hands with the handles against the palms like roller bearings. When the dowser walks over an electrical cable or underground water, the rod revolves. (The typical Western amateur rod can be made from two 34-inch strips of coathanger wire. Each strip is bent at right angles 8 inches from the end to form an "L." With one wire in each hand held parallel 3 inches apart, the 26-inch pointers swing apart or together over a dowsing area. Users report great success with the coathanger rods locating everything from buried treasure to pipes, seepage, or tree roots in their own backyards.)

Sochevanov claims the number of turns his revolving rod makes can help estimate depth and size of underground streams and mineral deposits. Sochevanov next engineered an automatic recording device that attaches to the rod and graphs its behavior. This updated extra makes the rod a more reliable and objective means of prospecting, he feels. From the graphs made by the dowsing rod, Soviet scientists constructed profiles of different areas of the earth's surface.

They established maximum "anomalies" (places where the rod revolved with the greatest speed and force). They compared graphs made by various dowsers walking over the same stretch of land. Studies with the electrocardiograph show that almost anybody, dowser or nondowser, registers a physiological change when walking over a dowsing zone, but dowsers are somehow able to make this conscious and objective through the movement of the dowsing rod. Just as people have different reaction times before stepping on the brakes of a car, Soviets found different dowsers react at different speeds to the apparent muscular stimulation of a dowsing zone.

Using dowsers whose sensitivities he knew, Sochevanov pinpointed differences in the dowsing rod's reactions at various times of the day and year, and under shifting weather conditions. His data may indicate a reason why many superficial tests of dowsing in the West have been failures. Whatever this force is that comes up from minerals and water in the earth's crust, it fluctuates. For instance, dowsers find it hard to get a reaction during lightning storms. Apparently changing weather and geophysical conditions cause the force from the minerals to reflect like rays of light at different angles. Australian dowser Evelyn Penrose lends corroboration to the Russian claims of variations throughout the day and year. Gold is particularly hard to find for this reason, she says. At sunrise the dowsing reaction is directly above the gold deposit, but as the sun moves across the sky, the force field from the gold deflects to other spots some distance from the actual vein.[337] Once the degree of deflection is known by geologists, they may be able to make the necessary corrections for it.

Russian dowsing "operators" also took to the fields in trucks, cars, and buses. The recording devices on their dowsing rods were hooked up with the drive shafts of the cars to register the ratio of the speed of the car to the revolutions of the rod.

"The speed the dowser travels doesn't affect the dowsing rod's sensitivity," says Sochevanov. At approximately twelve miles per hour the dowsing rod made about two times less revolutions than on foot. At forty miles per hour the number of revolutions was twenty times less than at twelve miles per hour. The number of revolutions of the rod were always in ratio with the speed.

"The metallic body of the bus or car didn't influence the dowsing reactions either," says Sochevanov. "Inside or out of the car, the dowser still got the identical response. It means that this unknown energy is *not* electrical, because the body of the car would screen out electrical energy and insulate the dowser from the ionized fields of the earth."

Still more riddles showed up in the Soviet scientific investigation of the divining rod. "Operators" tried dowsing in gloves made of cotton, rubber, and leather. Neither cotton nor rubber affect the phenomenon, but when a dowser put on leather gloves, whether they were rough, all-purpose leather gloves or smoothly elegant ones, the leather gloves acted as insulators and immediately "killed" the divining powers of the rod. What kind of force can penetrate steel but not kid gloves?

Could the power of the rod be strengthened in any way? Soviets tried attaching more "antennae" to the dowser, sixty inches of wire to each wrist. The "mysterious signals" were ten times weaker.

Sochevanov began to wonder if magnetism could have anything to do with the "why" of the dowsing rod. Powerful horseshoe magnets were fastened to the backs of the heads of the operators. When the magnets were very close to the head, the number of revolutions of the rod diminished, but at a distance of about eight inches the divining rod in the hands of the operator unexpectedly moved in the direction of the magnet.

Dr. S. Tromp of Holland, also studying the baffling question of how magnetism affects the human body, discovered dowsers could chart an artificial magnetic field as tiny as 0.001 gauss in a room. Dowsers could also tell when there was a disturbance of the earth's magnetic field, later confirmed by measurements with magnetometers.[412]

Would hypnosis improve dowsing? Leningrad hypnotherapist Dr. A. Zakarov tested three operators. They were put into a deep hypnotic trance and ordered to increase the number of revolutions of the rods. The entranced operators, their muscles relaxed, could scarcely keep a firm hold on the divining rod, and instead of increasing, the revolutions decreased. Hypnosis did not appear to enhance sensitivity to these mysterious radiations.

Could a dowser transmit his sensitivity to a nondowser? Sochevanov gathered a group of nonoperators—people who'd never been able to get any response with a dowsing rod. They were to walk across terrain above underground streams. When a seasoned dowser touched the hand of a nonoperator during a test, the divining rod in the non-dowser's hands suddenly came to life. The sensitivity to forces deep in the earth could somehow be transferred from person to person.

Could it work the other way round? Could the non-talented skeptic block a dowser's sensitivity? When several "nonoperators" who were also strong skeptics touched a dowser, it completely extinguished the dowsing effect. The rod ceased to turn in the dowser's hands.

The Russians also wondered if a dowser could up his sensitivity with the help of other dowsers. A group of dowsers formed a chain and tried to transmit their sensing power to a dowser at the head of the line. The force did not increase. It was only as great as the power of the strongest dowser in the group, the geologists reported.

In scientifically assessing the Biophysical Effect Method (dowsing), the Russians amassed, in the words of engineer Victor Popovkin "a tremendous amount of material: workers' journals, diaries, reports of operators, surveys of anomalies, tables, graphs, EEG tapes." [210–215, 157]

Soviet findings coincide with dowsing research in Germany and Holland. When a dowser gets a reaction on the rod, his entire body is actually reacting—there doesn't seem to be a particular sensing "organ" involved. Professor J. Walther of Halle, West Germany, found dowsers showed higher blood pressure and pulse rate above a dowsing zone. Dr. S. Tromp, a Dutch geologist researching dowsing for UNESCO, reported, in the Winter 1968 *International Journal of Parapsychology*, that the body's reaction to water or minerals in the earth can be clearly registered with an electrocardiograph.

The many careful experiments by Russian geologists, biologists, physiologists, and mineralogists, all pointed to a conclusion many Western researchers had also reached: force fields of an unknown nature exist.

"Living organisms [plants, animals, and people] react to this unknown physical field springing up near mines or deposits of underground water," says Dr. Ogilvy. This was a statement of considerable importance, coming as it did from the Chairman of the Geology Department of Moscow State University, one of the most respected universities in the world. What *kind* of reactions do plants, animals, and people have to these unknown fields, and can they, as many dowsers assert, affect our health?

Dr. E. Jenny, Director of the Children's Hospital at Aarau, Switzerland, placed mice in a long hut, half on, half off a dowsing zone. The mice refused to sleep inside the dowsing zone. From 1934 to 1940, 6434 mice slept outside the zone, only 1626 inside.

Dr. Jenny and his colleagues also found that cucumbers, celery, onions, maize, privet hedges, and ash trees would hardly grow if planted in ground above a dowsing zone. Agricultural experts could find nothing wrong with the soil or any reason for the plants not growing. The same type of plants beside them, just outside the zone, grew prolifically.[412]

What effects do dowsing zones have on human health? This is not adequately researched yet, but some scientists have observed that rheumatics, if placed in a dowsing zone, experience muscular contractions or pains in their joints. That living and working in a strong dowsing zone could cause stress to the body was a concept known in ancient China.

Though there seemed to be increasing mysteries behind the wizard rod's behavior, the Soviets pressed on with the pragmatic angle of dowsing. "All the uses of dowsing aren't known yet," Sochevanov noted in *Knowledge Is Power* magazine in 1967, "but so far we've found that on a section of land charted by geological surveys, dowsing anomalies coincide with unknown geophysical anomalies. The places charted by the rod coincide with 'abnormal' electrical poles of the earth, areas we often prospect with the aid of explosives." He reported, "Helicopter dowsing surveys are planned to measure intensive anomalies at different heights from the earth."

Any stockholder in a mining or oil company probably knows the cost of exploration and the cost of the many empty drill cores and useless wells that are sunk before a producing oil well or lucrative mine is discovered. A survey by a dowser to supplement other geological surveys could help eliminate some of these errors and save millions of dollars.

Apparently in the early 1930s, the government of British Columbia, Canada, was astute enough to realize this. The Minister of Finance, the Attorney General, the Minister of Mines, and the Deputy Minister of Agriculture all had high praise for Australian dowser Evelyn Penrose, whom they'd commissioned to dowse for minerals and oil in British Columbia. Her findings, they said, "coincided exactly" with engineering and geological reports. The Deputy Minister of Agriculture stated: "Having personally accompanied Miss Penrose on both water- and oil-finding trips, I am in a position to vouch for her outstanding ability. Solely on her advice many drilling and digging operations were initiated and many satisfactory reports have been received after sinking the wells." [337]

The Soviets, with vast and varied lands to open up, stand to save tremendous amounts of rubles and manpower by using dowsing in coordination with geology to precisely locate ore deposits. Rather than trying to disprove dowsing, the Soviets looked at it, saw something happened, and after wide testing, put it to use.

On October 31, 1966, the All-Union Astro-Geodesic Society of Moscow held a special seminar on dowsing. In April 1968 an important two-day scientific conference was held in Moscow devoted exclusively to the BPE Method (alias dowsing). Dr. Ogilvy, greeted scientists from all parts of the Soviet Union who gave papers and showed films on their research and use of the dowsing rod. Delegates reported, for instance, that the "biophysical effect method" was being used in the Yakut Republic in northern Siberia;[117] in engineering geology in Lithuania;[69] in the search for water in the desert;[8] in prospecting for ore deposits in Central Asian USSR;[16] and was being extensively studied in field and laboratory by Leningrad and Moscow geology institutes.[212]

In contrast with the Soviet explore-anything approach, some Western scientists look like conservationists desperately trying to preserve the last species of outmoded ideas. Outside the scientific preserve, dowsing has long been in use in all countries of the world. Verne L. Cameron, a famous American dowser, reports that the angle-rod divining rod is used by almost every water and pipe line company in the United States. The British have devised a highly sophisticated dowsing rod so sensitive it can apparently be used in archeology. The Soviets, with their mechanized, graphed-up dowsing equipment, have come a long way from the mythical "wizard rod." Just where dowsing will turn up next in the USSR is hard to say, but with Soviet ingenuity, it's bound to be surprising.

Besides locating water and minerals, other uses of radiesthesia have fascinated mankind for centuries; the ability to diagnose illness with a pendulum, and the intriguing Sherlock Holmes aspect of dowsing—the ability to locate criminals, murderers, stolen goods, or the tracks of thieves with a divining rod or pendulum. The Russians evidently are looking into these uses too.

It was from them we first heard the story of the legendary Jean Aymar of France. The Crown procurator of Lyon recorded his exploits, according to the Soviets: "Arriving in the cellar where the murder had taken place, Aymar displayed obvious signs of agitation. He began to shiver, his pulse quickened, and the forked twig in his hands swung to the place where the dead bodies had been found. Having 'tuned' his dowsing rod, he set off in search of the murderers. Along the way, Aymar located all the places where the fugitives had stopped, knowing, to the great astonishment of the onlookers, the beds in which the murderers slept, the tables where they ate, the pitchers and glasses they had touched."

Abbé Mermet, an early pioneer of radiesthesia, insisted it was a science and had nothing to do with the occult. His alleged successes included archeological finds made at the request of the Pope himself, and locating survivors of an expedition to the North Pole. Mermet's ability to trace missing people was known throughout Europe. In 1934, French records show he traced the whereabouts of twenty missing persons. The stories of his radiesthetic sleuthing report that he was able to follow the wanderings of a suicide or murdered man to the point where death occurred. If the victim had been drowned, the corpse was traced to a point on a lake or river where it had come to rest. With the pendulum, the Abbé could even indicate the exact depth at which the body would be found. Invariably, the accounts say, bodies were recovered exactly where the Abbé had indicated.

Russian scientist-dowsers aren't anywhere near the Abbé's supposed whodunit expertise, but they are just beginning to explore the wizard rod's reaction to people as well as ore. The experimental data they've assembled shows that all people can be classified into four different groups, according to the polarities of the force field around their bodies.

The first group includes all women and some men: as the dowser approaches from any side, these people cause the dowsing rod to be attracted toward them. The remaining three groups are comprised of men only. As the dowser approaches the Group 2 type of man from any side, the dowsing rod is "repulsed," causing it to turn away from the Group 2 member. Groups 3 and 4 show a half and half polarity: Group 3 attracts the rod along the side of the back and the stomach and repulses it along the side of the shoulder. Group 4 charts the opposite effect: the shoulder "attracts" the rod; the back and stomach repulse it.

Dutch scientist Dr. S. Tromp also came up with polarity maps of the human body using an electrocardiograph on the dowser to chart the changes.[412]

Why does the dowsing rod divide people into four classes? The Soviets don't know. Just as they don't know what those caroming "anomalies" are that the rod picks up deep in the earth after an explosion, like the big one at Alma-Ata. Soviet scientists don't even know exactly why the rod revolves over hidden caches of gold or water. They do know, as in some other areas of parapsychology, that the human being is a vital component of the system, he is part of the dowsing apparatus. The rod will not dip if tacked up on its own and propelled over the land, according to the Soviets.

It looks to the Soviets as if unknown force fields surround water, minerals, and perhaps many other things and that some of us are able to sense them. How? Perhaps, as they theorize with PK, the body's own force field interacts with the fields of dowsable things. On this premise, one American dowser rechristened his dowsing equipment an "Aurameter."

Electrocardiagrams apparently indicate that whether you can dowse or not, your body is still registering dowsing zones at an unconscious level. It appears from the Soviet tests that the body's sensitivity is truly fantastic. It reflects mines, underground water, the changing magnetic fields of the earth, electrical cables in and out of buildings, the electrostatic and electromagnetic fields of other human bodies.

What is the nature of man? Soviet scientists, open-mindedly exploring ancient knowledge with painstaking modern scientific tests, are beginning to uncover some surprises. It's beginning to look like the human being connected to the rod is more of a wizard than he thought.

16

KIRLIAN PHOTOGRAPHY— PICTURES OF THE AURA?

"A spectacular panorama of colors, whole galaxies of lights, blue, gold, green, violet, all shining and twinkling!"

"An unseen world opened before my eyes. Whole luminescent labyrinths, flashing, twinkling, flaring. Some of the sparks were motionless, some wandered against a dark background. Over these fantastic galaxies of ghostly lights there were bright multi-colored flares and dim clouds."

"It's indescribable! Electric flames light up, then flares or crowns of blue and orange. Great channels of blazing violet, fiery flashes. Some lights glitter constantly, others come and go like wandering stars. It's fantastic, alluring, a mysterious game—a fire world!"

"Like summer lightning . . . 'craters' erupted—not fiery lava, but radiance like the aurora borealis!"

These extraordinary accounts of an amazing new world of pulsating multicolored lights weren't coming from Soviets blowing their minds at a psychedelic electric circus. They weren't visions from an LSD trip. The shining galaxies and brilliantly colored radiant labyrinths and sparkling flares these Soviets saw came from *the human body* itself. These brilliant lights in the body became visible when the body was placed in a field of high frequency electrical currents.

Was it the "aura" they were seeing, that envelope of colors surrounding the body which psychics and clairvoyants have long claimed to see and which they use to diagnose a person's state of health? Was this the astral body —the luminescent body of energy which psychics say we all have?

It wasn't a group of psychics viewing this phenomenon in Russia, however. It was scientists—Russia's foremost learned men from the prestigious Presidium of the Academy of Sciences of the USSR, scientists and researchers from some of the leading institutes and universities across the entire Soviet Union. It was going to take them some twenty years to begin to understand just what it was they'd discovered about the strange powers of the human body.

The concept of a human aura, a radiating luminous cloud surrounding the body, goes back centuries. Pictures from early Egypt, India, Greece, Rome, showed holy figures in a luminous surround long before artists in the Christian era began to paint saints with halos. This convention may actually have been based on the observations of clairvoyants who could reportedly see the radiance surrounding saints. The famous psychic, Mrs. Eileen Garrett, reports in her book *Awareness*,[303] "I've always seen every plant, animal, and person encircled by a misty surround." According to people's mood, the surround changes colors and consistency, she says.

Clairvoyants are quick to point out, however, that the aura is actually a misnomer; they believe the human body is interpenetrated by another body of energy and it is the luminescence from this *second* body radiating outward that they see as the aura. We look, they say, something like an eclipse of the sun by the moon, the luminous astral body being completely concealed by the physical body. Paracelsus, the philosopher, chemist, alchemist, and doctor, also believed a half-corporeal or "star" body lives in the flesh and is its mirror image.

In the early 1900s, Dr. Walter Kilner of St. Thomas' Hospital in London, discovered that by looking through glass screens stained with dicyanin dye, he could actually see the aura around the human body. According to Kilner, it was a cloud of radiation extending out about six to eight inches and showing distinct colors. Fatigue, diseases, or mood could alter the size and color; this radiation was also affected by magnetism, hypnosis and electricity.[321] He developed an entire system for diagnosing illness from the aura, and research on the aura is still continuing in Europe.

You can learn to see the aura yourself, some psychics say. If you stand in front of a blank wall in an almost dark room and squinch your eyes up, you may be able to see slight traces of smoke-like energy coming from the tips of your fingers. For a psychic, this smoke-like surround is full of color, constantly changing according to health and mood.

The first hint that there was more to the human body than had previously been thought by Russian scientists, began back in 1939 in Krasnodar, capital city of the Kuban region in the south of Russia near the Black Sea. "Where can I get technical equipment repaired?" a research scientist asked a colleague. Repairs of any type are a real dilemma in Russia. Soviets at research institutes, labs, businesses all agreed: "Go to Semyon Davidovich Kirlian, if you want a repair done properly. He's the best electrician in Krasnodar."

Kirlian was called. At the research institute to pick up the equipment, Kirlian (pronounced Keer-lee-an) chanced to see a demonstration of a high-frequency instrument for electrotherapy. As the patient received treatment through the electrodes of the machine, Kirlian suddenly noticed there was a tiny flash of light between the electrodes and the patient's skin. "I wonder if I could photograph that," he mused. "What if I put a photographic plate between the patient's skin and the electrode?"

But the electrodes were made of glass and the photo plate would be spoiled by exposure to light before the machine could be switched on. He would have to use a metal electrode which would be dangerous. "Never mind," he said, as he attached the metal electrode to his own hand. "You have to make a few sacrifices for science."

He switched on the machine. Kirlian felt a stabbing pain in his hand under the metallic electrode. It was a severe burn. Three seconds later, the machine was switched off and Kirlian rushed the photo plate into the emulsion. As the picture developed in the dark room he could make out a strange imprint on it, a kind of luminescence in the shape of the contours of his fingers. "I studied the picture with pain, excitement, and hope all combined," says Kirlian. "Did I have a discovery? An invention? It wasn't clear yet."

Scientists, he found, had observed this phenomenon before, but it had just been filed in their research reports and forgotten. For some reason, Kirlian had an intuitive hunch that he was onto something. He persisted. His highly esteemed talent and ingenuity at electronics were soon at work on this new project. Other techniques of photographing without light—x-ray, infrared, radioactivity—were of no help. He would have to devise a whole new process to record on film the luminous energy coming from the human body.

With his wife Valentina, a teacher and journalist, Kirlian invented an entirely new method of photography that comprises some fourteen patents.

Basically, photography with high frequency electrical fields involves a specially constructed high frequency spark generator or oscillator that generates 75,000 to 200,000 electrical oscillations per second. The generator can be connected to various clamps, plates, optical instruments, microscopes or electron microscopes. The object to be investigated (finger, leaf, etc.) is inserted between the clamps along with photo paper. The generator is switched on and a high frequency field is created between the clamps which apparently causes the object to radiate some sort of bioluminescence onto the photo paper. A camera isn't necessary for the photography process.

The very first photographs were a "window on the unknown" say the Kirlians. A leaf torn from a tree, when placed in the field of a high frequency current, revealed a world of myriad dots of energy. Around the edges of the leaf there were turquoise and reddish-yellow patterns of flares coming out of specific channels of the leaf. A human finger placed in the high frequency field and photographed, showed up like a complex topographical map. There were lines, points, craters of light and flares. Some parts of the finger looked like a carved jack-o'-lantern with a glowing light inside.

But the photographs only showed static images. Soon the Kirlians had developed a special optical instrument so they could directly observe the phenomenon in motion. Kirlian held his hand under the lens and switched on the current. And then, a fantastic world of the unseen opened before the husband and wife team.

The hand itself looked like the Milky Way in a starry sky. Against a background of blue and gold, something was taking place in the hand that looked like a fireworks display. Multicolored flares lit up, then sparks, twinkles, flashes. Some lights glowed steadily like Roman candles, others flashed out then dimmed. Still others sparkled at intervals. In parts of his hand there were little dim clouds.

Certain glittering flares meandered along sparkling labyrinths like spaceships traveling to other galaxies.

What did these twinkling flares mean? What were they illuminating? The pulsating sparks weren't playing some game of chance. Their game seemed to have rules, but what were they?

The Kirlians placed a fresh leaf under the lens of a microscope connected to the high frequency generator. They saw a picture similar to that of the human hand. Next they tried a half-withered leaf. It looked like a great metropolis turning out its lights for the night. They tried an almost completely withered leaf. There were almost no flares and sparks and "clouds" scarcely moved. As they watched, the leaf seemed to be dying before their eyes and its death was reflected in the picture of energy impulses. "We appeared to be seeing the very life activities of the leaf itself," the Kirlians said. "Intense, dynamic energy in the healthy leaf, less in the withered leaf, nothing in the dead leaf."

The investigators examined every conceivable substance under their high-frequency microscope—leather, metal, wood, leaves, paper, coins, rubber. The pattern of luminescence was different for every item, but living things had totally different structural details than non-living things. A metal coin, for instance, showed only a completely even glow all around the edges. But a living leaf was made up of millions of sparkling lights that glowed and glittered like jewels. The flares along its edges were individual and different.

"What we saw in the panorama through the microscope and our optical instruments seemed like the control board of a huge computer. Here and there lights brightened and dimmed—signals of processes inside. If something's wrong inside or conditions need adjustment, the engineer at the control board can read the signals in the lights," the Kirlians said.

"In living things, we see the signals of the inner state of the organism reflected in the brightness, dimness and color of the flares. The inner life activities of the human being are written in these 'light' hieroglyphs. We've created an apparatus to write these hieroglyphs. But to read them we're going to need help."

By 1949, the Kirlians had a whole array of instruments through which to examine the play of high-frequency currents on humans, plants, and animals as well as on inanimate matter. They felt by then they had perfected the technique enough to show their results to biologists, physiologists, botanists, and other scientific specialists.

Soon the greats of the Soviet scientific world began to trek to Krasnodar. There were the famous and the curious. There were members of the Academy of Science, Ministers of the Government. Over some thirteen years, there were hundreds of visitors. Biophysicists, doctors, biochemists, electronics experts, criminology specialists, all appeared at the door of the little one-storied, pre-revolutionary wooden house on Kirov Street in Krasnodar.

The bespectacled, slightly bald Semyon, who radiates the quiet concentration of a chess champion, and his dark-haired, attractive wife, Valentina, welcomed the scores of guests to the two frugal rooms where they lived and worked. One room was their living quarters, the other, a diminutive entrance hall, had been converted into a tiny laboratory and crammed with the instruments they'd invented for high frequency photography.

One day the Chairman of a major scientific research institute arrived. He had with him two identical leaves for the Kirlians to photograph with their new process. The two "twin" leaves were from the same species of plant, torn off at exactly the same time.

The Kirlian team was working that evening on the photographs when something strange happened. From testing leaves from various plants they knew that each species of plant has its own unique energy pattern—like individual television test patterns broadcasting from each type of plant.

But the photos of the "twin" leaves the scientist had given them differed sharply from each other. Were the leaves from two different species of plants? Had they made an error?

They did picture after picture. Still the same results. The luminescence from one leaf showed roundish, spherical flares scattered symmetrically over the entire image of the leaf. The second leaf showed tiny geometrical dark figures grouped sparsely here and there on the leaf's image.

Semyon and Valentina worked all through the night until

morning doing picture after picture of the two leaves. No matter how they adjusted their equipment, the results were the same.

In the morning, weary and worried, they showed their troubling results to their celebrated scientist guest. To their surprise, his face lit up with delight: "You've found it!" he said excitedly.

The two exhausted inventors forgot their fatigue as the botanist explained, "Both leaves were torn from the same species of plant all right. But one of these plants had already been contaminated with a serious plant disease. You've found this out immediately! There is absolutely nothing on the plant or this leaf to indicate that it has been infected and will soon die. No tests on the actual plant or the leaf show anything wrong with it. With high-frequency photography you've diagnosed illness in the plant *ahead of time!*"

It was electrifying news to the Kirlians. They studied the diseased leaf carefully. Not even up to the leaf's death a day or so later did it give any outer sign of illness. (The plant it had been taken from died some time later.) The Kirlians began to realize that the galaxies of sparkling lights they saw in their high-frequency photographs were a kind of energy counterpart body of the leaf. Long before illnesses manifested themselves in the physical body of the plant, they existed in this "counterpart body" of energy.

Soon institutes were bringing the Kirlians hundreds of "green patients"—leaves of grapevines, apple trees, tobacco and so on. In every case, the Kirlians could establish whether or not the plant was ill long before there were any physical pathological changes in the leaves or the plants, by studying the leaf's energy counterpart body in high frequency photos.

By diagnosing a plant disease long before it actually struck, it might be possible to counteract the disease conditions and perhaps save precious agricultural crops.

The philosophical implications were even more extraordinary. It seemed living things had two bodies: the physical body everyone can see, and a secondary "energy-body" the Kirlians saw in their high frequency photos. The energy body didn't seem to be merely a radiation of the physical body. The physical body appeared somehow *to mirror* what was happening in the energy body. If an imbalance in this energy-body of the plant occurred, it indicated illness, and gradually the physical body would reflect this change. Would this be true of human beings too, they wondered.

One day the Kirlians were momentarily expecting the visit of two famous scientists from a Moscow Institute. Before a visit, they always got their apparatus in working order so that everything would be ready for a demonstration.

For some unknown reason, the "temperamental" optical device would not work. No matter how Kirlian tried to focus it, the picture would not show clearly through the lens. Hastily the Kirlians dismantled the equipment and reassembled it. Still the same blurry results. They checked some of their other instruments to make sure they were all in working order. Kirlian put his hand into the instruments and ran off test photos on four other devices. They weren't working properly either. Nothing but dark spots and clouds in the pictures. Frantically, Kirlian began to dismantle everything. With parts of the equipment scattered all over the work table, Semyon bent over to reassemble one of the instruments when suddenly he began to feel dizzy and faint. These attacks of dizziness always were a forerunner of an oncoming attack of an illness of the vascular system he had from time to time. The only remedy was immediate rest.

Valentina Kirlian put her husband to bed and quickly reassembled the instruments as the important guests arrived at the door. She demonstrated the photographic process for the two scientists placing the tip of her finger on the photo plates and switching on the high frequency current. Every photograph was clear and well focused. She placed her hand under the special optical instrument for direct observation. The play of light flares in her hand was clear and distinct. The scientists were delighted and the entire demonstration was a success.

After the scientists left that night, Kirlian staggered out of his sickbed. Wasn't it strange that all the instruments should suddenly work properly when Valentina operated them but refuse to work for him? "We took turns on all the instruments. There was absolutely no doubt. My hands showed a confused, chaotic pattern of energy, blurred and cloudy. Valentina's hands showed a clear pattern of the discharging stream of energy, the colored flares bright and sharp." What Semyon had seen earlier and thought might be a flaw in the lens or focussing of the equipment, was actually a forerunner of his own illness showing up in the "energy pattern" of his hand before it actually manifested itself physically as an attack of his illness. Now, the illness itself showed clearly in the high frequency picture as total turmoil in the energy flares.

"There's nothing bad without some good in it," Semyon thought as he lay in bed recuperating. Maybe they could diagnose all kinds of illnesses long before they manifested as physical disorders. Perhaps even cancer could be caught when it was still a confusion in the energy pattern and not yet a tumor in the body. The Kirlians felt they'd made an important discovery in finding that illness could tremendously alter the energy discharge coming from the body. They were soon to find that many other things also affect these sparkling galaxies of light in humans.

"Our special optical apparatus gave us more trouble than anything else we've invented," the Kirlians said. "It would be hard to imagine a more capricious instrument. It had to be tuned in three ways, the optical lenses, the tension and the high-frequency discharge. The success of the demonstration depended entirely on proficiency and practice. It was impossible not to get nervous with it."

The Kirlians were checking out their instruments for a demonstration for another VIP guest when difficulties arose. "I was watching my hand through the eyepiece when suddenly it looked as if all the flares in the picture had declared a strike," said Kirlian. "The violet colored flares would start to spin, then they'd turn yellow-rose; then the whole field would stop swimming and it looked as if everything had gone out of focus."

They replaced the lenses thinking the glass had become overheated. They checked again. Everything was fine.

The scientist arrived and the demonstration began. The still photos turned out, but when Kirlian nervously placed his hand under the lens of the optical device, the machine began to act up again. Through the eyepiece he couldn't see the background of his hand and the channels of the light patterns weren't clear. "Please excuse me," he begged his eminent guest. "I'll have to adjust the machine." Hurriedly he changed the lenses, tuned up the device again, turned on the generator—and there was the same infernal unfocused picture of his hand.

The guest, tired of waiting, asked to look through the eyepiece. Strangely, it seemed to Kirlian, the guest appeared to like what he saw. Kirlian inwardly breathed a sigh of relief and as his guest's interest increased in the phenomenon, Kirlian could feel his nervous tension seeping away. In fact, he even began to feel calm. At that moment, the guest exclaimed with astonishment at what he was seeing through the eyepiece.

Kirlian suddenly remembered the time was up. It wasn't advisable to leave his hand in the high-frequency field for too long. As he ended the demonstration he glanced through the eyepiece himself. The machine was now working perfectly and he hadn't adjusted it!

"What a despotic creation!" the inventors despaired. Just when they wanted to show it off, their invention behaved like a bad child. Demonstration after demonstration they had the same trouble until suddenly they got the clue. It was *themselves* and not the machines that were acting up. It was *their* nervous excitement, *their* worries about the reaction of the important guests that lay printed in the panorama of the lights coming from their skin.

From the very first seconds of the demonstration (and even while preparing for it) their emotions and thoughts blared out instantly in the colored signals of the flares. If the guests had known how to decipher the code, how to interpret the colors and positions of the flares, they would have seen more than a light show in the Kirlians' hands.

"These changes in the energy pattern occur very rapidly," the inventors point out. "In the interest of science," the Kirlians suggest with a smile to observers, "drink a glass of vodka." Observing their own hands in the high frequency discharge, the visitors could see the stimulating influence of the alcohol instantly shoot out in the multicolored energy patterns of the body. Of course, the Kirlians add, the observer's own attitude plays a part and may influence just exactly when these flares of energy may discharge.

Illness, emotion, states of mind, thoughts, fatigue, all

make their distinctive imprint on the pattern of energy which seemed to circulate continuously through the human body. (In the pictures, you can see the fingertip of a normal, healthy person photographed by the Kirlian process. The second picture shows the same fingertip of the same person, but this time he is fatigued and over-strained. More energy appears to pour out of the body when tired.)

For centuries, mediums have been describing a phenomenon they called the aura. They diagnosed illnesses, and states of mind from the cloud of energy they saw around people. Probably the aura seen by a psychic is made up of numerous elements of the human force-field, including perhaps heat radiation, electromagnetic fields, and many other things still unknown to us. The Kirlian pictures appear to show at least some of the elements of the aura, a new part of it that no other device has shown or recorded so far. Mediums often said that the aura had something to do with "frequency," and the Kirlian process makes this form of the aura visible by running high-frequency electrical fields through living things. The Kirlians say that at varying frequencies, different details show up in the photographs of bio-luminescence, depending on the dominant frequency.

One hundred years ago, the famous German chemist, the discoverer of creosote, Baron Von Reichenbach, had also reported extensive research on some sort of energy or luminescence radiating from humans and plants and animals. He'd called it "odic force," naming it after the Norse god Odin to suggest the idea "all-pervasive." Curiously, the Reichenbach accounts are identical with what the Soviets describe and what we saw in the Kirlian color photographs.

Within two basic colors: blue and reddish-yellow, Reichenbach's mediums described, "flares of green, red, orange, violet, appearing and disappearing. Violet red appearing and dying away in a smoke-like vapor; all intermingled with many small, brilliant sparkles or stars." [362]

In the color Kirlian pictures of plant leaves we saw the same basic colors: blue and reddish-yellow. Within these colors there were multi-colored flares. Reichenbach considered the blue and reddish-yellow colors indicated that the "odic energy" was polarized.

Dr. Walter Kilner in London, using special dye-filled

lenses, reported viewing this same phenomenon. This aura of energy around the body was constantly in motion and, just as the Kirlian photos showed, colored flares of energy emerged from it and shot off from the body into space. Ill health, fatigue, depression all affected the aura, according to Kilner, and soon he had learned to diagnose according to the colors and form of the aura. Some people, Kilner found, could change the colors of their aura at will. Various patches of disturbed patterns in the colors indicated diseased areas as he reported in his book *The Human Aura.* These were the same patterns the Kirlians had described.

Now the Soviet world of science was seeing this same phenomenon in the Kirlian photographs. What was this "bioluminescence? Some Soviet scientists maintained, "this energy is neither electric nor electromagnetic." Had the Kirlians stumbled onto a strange new energy? Should they and could they go ahead and explore it?

For thirteen years the fate of Kirlian photography and their fantastic new "window on the unknown" rested in the balance. "This is a big find, a diamond in the rough," said Ministers of the Government.

"This is an entirely new form of photography," said Academician Gleb M. Frank, then Scientific Director of the Institute of Biological Physics of the Academy of Science and now head of the lavish new Science City—"Pushchino" near Moscow. "I've long known about Kirlian photography," he told the Soviet press. "I myself presented the Kirlian method to the lab of applied photography and cinematography of the Soviet Academy of Sciences. This technique must be used for all science and technology," said the outstanding Academician.

Medical professors such as Dr. S. M. Pavlenko, Chairman of the Pathology-Physiology Department of the First Moscow Medical Institute, reported, "Kirlian photography can be used for early diagnosis of disease, especially of cancer."

Medical scientist, Dr. Lev Nikolaevich Fedorov was "carried away" with the Kirlian process. At his urging the Ministry of Public Health of the USSR financed some of Kirlian's research. Unfortunately, Dr. Fedorov died and the grants ended.

The Kuban Agricultural Institute directed by P. F.

Varukoi felt the Kirlian process would be a great boon to agriculture. "We want to study the discovery. We've even found the money to finance the project, but the government has refused us the staff of scientists to do the work."

The Kirlians drew praise from Soviet Academician A. V. Topchiyeva of the Presidium of the Academy of Science of the USSR who reported publicly "further study is a must. High-frequency photography presents undoubted scientific interest."

A. F. Garmashev, President of the Committee for Inventions of the Soviet government told the press he considered the Kirlian discovery a triumph. "We must work on it immediately."

Dr. L. A. Tumerman, leading Soviet biophysicist of the Institute of Radiation and Physico-Chemical Biology of the Academy of Science urged the Academy to supply lab space to the inventors.

Almost every scientist, doctor, researcher, who had seen high-frequency photography and the remarkable phenomenon of "bioluminescence", came away convinced the Kirlian technique would be useful in every area of science and technology.[10] Medicine, dentistry, criminology, geology, agriculture, archeology, forensic medicine, all might benefit from the Kirlian breakthrough. Many researchers began work on their own.

Meanwhile, like Marie and Pierre Curie researching radium, Semyon and Valentina Kirlian patiently struggled on trying to unravel the mysterious "luminous hieroglyphs" they'd found pulsating out of human beings. Gradually the records of their steadily mounting discoveries filled two heavy volumes.

Working day and night in their tiny lab, they perfected, at their own expense, one process after another. They crated new optical instruments, and new techniques enabling Kirlian photography to be hooked up to the powerful electron microscope. The dedicated, patriotic husband and wife team turned the patents on all their inventions over to the State.

The Kirlians had done a quarter century of painstaking experiments on this mysterious human energy. Would the Soviet Union and the rest of the world ever see their remarkable discovery?

In the early 1960s, Soviet journalists published a number of hard-hitting exposés on the plight of the Kirlian invention.[9, 10] "This situation is as bad as before the Revolution," one of them said, "when the evil hand of Tzarist bureaucrats determined there was too much uncertainty in novelty!" The outraged writer continued, "All the scientists who have seen the Kirlian work agree research is urgent and that the Kirlian discovery can bring great benefits to man. *Twenty-five years have passed* since the Kirlians made this discovery. Yet the Ministeries in charge still haven't released any funds either to the Kirlians or any scientific research institute to carry out this work."

At last in the 1960s it happened! Suddenly, the Kirlian invention emerged from a bureaucratic abyss. Suddenly the Kirlians were given a pension, a new apartment in a pleasant new district in Krasnodar and a specially equipped lab. Suddenly, fullscale scientific research began in Kirlian photography in institutes, labs and universities all over the USSR. In 1962 Soviet Union Magazine,[98] reported that entire scientific research establishments had been set working on the Kirlian phenomenon. (See Appendix A, 9.)

Semyon Davidovich Kirlian and Valentina Chrisanfovna Kirlian had created a way for us to see the unseeable. But what did it mean—this maze of colored energy within us? Now they set the world of Soviet science on the track of some truly awesome discoveries about the nature of man. The Kirlians' "window on the Unknown" might revolutionize our entire concept of ourselves and our universe. It seems they had discovered far more than the aura.

17

SCIENCE PROBES THE ENERGY BODY

Is there such a thing as an "astral body", an "energy body" that duplicates the physical body of a human being? For centuries, seers, writers, clairvoyants as well as ancient philosophies and religions spoke of an invisible body we all possess. Through the ages it's been called the "subtle body", the "astral body", the "etheric body", "fluidic body", "Beta body", "counterpart body", "pre-physical body", to name a few.

People who have had a limb amputated often continue to sense the missing arm or leg as if it were still there. Doctors explain this away as a wish fulfilling hallucination; as nerves still registering what is gone; or as a psychological tendency to continue viewing the body as a whole. But psychics and clairvoyants have often claimed to actually "see" phantom limbs. The missing arm or leg is in a fluidic form, they say, and still attached to the body.

According to some psychics, this human double is larger than the physical body and the aura or light they see radiating around the body is simply the outer edge of this human double.

One of the most outstanding and reliable mediums of our time, Eileen Garrett, a highly successful business executive and President of the Parapsychology Foundation in New York, writes in her book *Awareness*, "Throughout my whole life I have been aware of the fact that everyone possesses a second body—a double. The double is a distinct fact in Eastern and theosophical teaching and as such it is said to be an energy body, a magnetic area associated with the physical human corpus, an area in which the immaterial forces of the cosmos, the solar system, the planet and one's more immediate environment are normally transformed in the life and belief of the individual."

The aura or "surround" is a phase of the operation of the human energy body or the double, she says. Most important of all, the double, according to Mrs. Garrett, can be used for the expansion of consciousness. *"The double is the medium of telepathic and clairvoyant projection."*

If Mrs. Garrett is right, the secret of ESP is tied up with the so called "astral body". But what scientific evidence do we have for the existence of this "energy body"?

Dr. Wilder Penfield of McGill University in Montreal has done numerous operations in which he removed massive segments of patients' brains. Still the "mind" seemed to carry on as before without any disturbance of consciousness. "Perhaps we will always be forced to visualize a spiritual element . . . a spiritual essence that is capable of controlling the mechanism. The machine will never fully explain man, nor mechanisms the nature of the spirit," says Dr. Penfield.[400]

A highly reputable English medium, Geraldine Cummins reported [284] something in the 1930's that is startingly relevant to what we were to discover in Russia. "Mind does not work directly on the brain. There is an etheric body which is the link between mind and the cells of the brain. . . . Far more minute corpuscular particles than scientists are yet aware of travel along threads from the etheric body, or double, to certain regions of the body and to the brain. I might call them life units. . . . This invisible body—called by me the double or unifying mechanism—is the only channel through which mind and life may communicate with the physical shape. Should a thread snap between the two, there is immediately a failure in control. . . . Each animal has a unifying invisible body made out of modified ether. It should be possible to devise in time an instrument whereby this body can be perceived."

If this so called double could ever be made visible and accessible to science, the results would be revolutionary. Not only would it vastly revise our concept of ourselves and other living things, it would also enlarge medicine, psychology, religion, biology. Exploration of the "double" would also give us a new handle with which to grasp telepathy and clairvoyance.

Have the Soviets made the breakthrough? Have they made the human double visible? And explorable? The Kirlians discovered high-frequency photography on an intuitive hunch back in 1939. By the 1960s, research on the bio-luminescence phenomena revealed by the Kirlian camera was going forward in universities and research institutes all over the USSR.

In Russia, a young Soviet scientist, a student of Kirlian photography, sat down at a table with us. From a brimming briefcase he pulled out a sheaf of photographs. "Look at this," he said, as he spread out a large photograph of a plant leaf which had been tremendously magnified. The picture had been produced by the Kirlian method in a high-frequency electrical field. It was the kind of leaf picture we'd become familiar with—a mass of sparkling lights all over the leaf; here and there brilliant, vivid flares and around the edges a precise aura of luminescence. He handed us a second picture. It looked like the same leaf except . . . there seemed to be a line down the middle of the right side of the leaf. Beyond that line the sparkling outline and veins seemed airier, the background fluffier.

"This *is* the same leaf as the first picture," the young scientist explained. "The actual leaf itself has been cut. One third of it has been removed. But the energy pattern of the *whole* leaf is still there!"

In other words, we were actually seeing the "ghost" of part of the leaf—a phantom counterpart of pure energy.

"What is this substance?" we asked, pointing to the cut-off part of the leaf that shouldn't have been there.

"It's a form of energy," said the scientist. "This energy may have its origin in electrical activity or electromagnetic fields, but the nature of this energy is entirely different. We consider it to be a kind of plasma." (In physics, plasma is the fourth state of matter—streams of masses of ionized particles.)

"What happens if you cut away more than a third of the leaf?"

"Then the leaf dies and the whole 'energy body' of the leaf vanishes."

If a human being loses a finger or an arm or has a leg amputated, does he still retain this 'counterpart' body—a sort of ghost of the finger or leg?"

"Yes," the scientist nodded.

From what we'd seen, the Soviets appeared to have evidence that there is some sort of energy matrix in all living things, some sort of unifying invisible body or luminiscence penetrating our physical bodies. But just what exactly is this energy body? How does it function? Where does it come from?

The exploration that answered those questions began near Soviet space centers in far off Kazakhstan. At the highly respected Kirov State University of Kazakhstan in Alma-Ata, a group of biologists, biochemists and biophysicists clustered around a huge electron microscope. The Kirlians' equipment had come a long way. Now it was hooked up to this sophisticated, intricate electronic instrument. The scientists, peering through the eyepiece of the electron microscope, saw it the silent high frequency discharge something once reserved only for clairvoyants. They saw the living "double" of a living organism in motion.

Scores of experiments were done on live plants, animals and humans with the Kirlian effect. What was this "double"? "Some sort of elementary plasma-like constellation made of ionized, excited electrons, protons and possibly other particles," they said. "But at the same time, this energy body is not just particles. It is not a chaotic system. *It's a whole unified organism in itself.*" It acts as a unit, they said, and as a unit the energy body gives off its own electromagnetic fields and is the basis of biological fields.

In 1968, Doctors V. Inyushin, V. Grishchenko, N. Vorobev, N. Shouiski, N. Fedorova and F. Gibadulin announced their discovery: All living things—plants, animals and humans—not only have a physical body made of atoms and molecules, *but also a counterpart body of energy:* They called it "The Biological Plasma Body".[57-60, 198]

The implications are awesome.

In a book-long scientific paper published by the State University of Kazakhstan, "The Biological Essence of the Kirlian Effect", (Alma-Ata, 1968), they described their research into the living "energy body". (See Appendix A, 7.)

"The bio-luminescence visible in the Kirlian pictures is caused by the bio-plasma, not the electrical state of the organism," they say. One of the most distinctive features of this vibrating, colorful energy body in all living things, according to the Kazakh scientists, is that "it has a specific spatial organization." It has shape. Inside the energy body, say the scientists, processes have their own labyrinthine motion absolutely unlike the pattern of energy in the physical body. The bio-plasmic body is also polarized.

"The biological plasma of the energy body is specific for every organism, tissue and possibly bio-molecule," they said. "The specificity determines the form of the organism."

Within the last few years, many scientists in many countries have postulated that there is some kind of matrix, some kind of invisible organizing pattern inherent in living things. In the Soviet Union, for instance, Dr. Alexander Studitsky at the Institute of Animal Morphology in Moscow minced up muscle tissue and packed it into a wound in a rat's body. The body grew from this an entirely new muscle, as if there were some sort of organizing pattern.[392]

An American neurologist found he could pick up traces of the electrical field pattern of the missing limb of a salamander.[275] Other scientists have taken a blob of protoplasm that should grow into the arm of a fetal animal and placed it in the leg position. A leg, not an arm grows, again implying an organizing field.

Is the brillant body of light the Kirlians discovered, this organizing mold or pattern? If it is, what is the relationship between the all important energy body and the physical body?

In the photos shown us by Soviet scientists, we saw that if part of the physical body of a living thing is cut away, the bioplasmic body remains, whole and clearly visible in a high frequency field. When this energy body itself disappears, the plant or the animal dies.

"There is a *strict ratio* between the physical and the energy body (between atomic-molecular matter and the plasmic state of living things)," the Kazakh scientists reported. The energy of any living thing is made up of energy from its physical cells and the more mobile energy of bio-plasma, say Inyushin, Grishchenko, and their colleagues.

What generates this bioplasmic energy? How do we replenish our energy body? The Kazakh scientists discovered it's the oxygen we breathe that converts some of its surplus electrons and a certain quantum of energy into the energy body. In the silent high-frequency discharge, they could actually see this process as it occurred.

Breathing, it seems, charges the entire bioplasmic body and renews our reserves of vital energy and helps to equalize disturbed energy patterns. Of course, the Indian philosophy

NEW FRONTIERS of the MIND

1

1
Group of Soviet parapsychologists discuss records of recent telepathy tests. From left to right: psychic Karl Nikolaiev, biologist Edward Naumov, unidentified scientist, bio-physicist Yuri Kamensky, and telepathist and university student Alex Monin.

2
Wolf Grigorevich Messing, the Soviet Union's most celebrated psychic, was tested by Joseph Stalin—and passed.

3
Nelya Mikhailova, the Russian PK medium, and some of the objects she has moved with her PK power.

2

Начало пробуждения испытуемой

ритм испытуемой

Начало мысленного приказа на пробуждение

ритм врача гипнолога

4

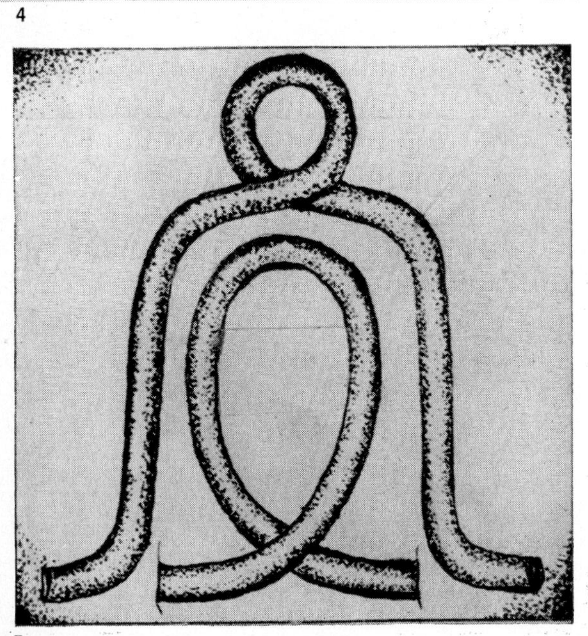

5

4

Hypnosis by telepathy: this Russian chart depicts the alpha brain waves of the subject (top two lines) and the hypnotist (two bottom lines) as charted by the EEG. The "X" in the third line marks the beginning of the hypnotist's mental command for the subject to awaken; the "X" on the top line records the point (only a short time later) when the subject begins to obey.

5

Design for the new Soviet dowsing rod.

6

Pattern of energy discharge from the skin of the human chest. The flares change color and pattern as health and mood change. According to some Soviet doctors, the points on the skin where the brightest flares emerge may correspond to acupuncture points as charted by Chinese medicine.

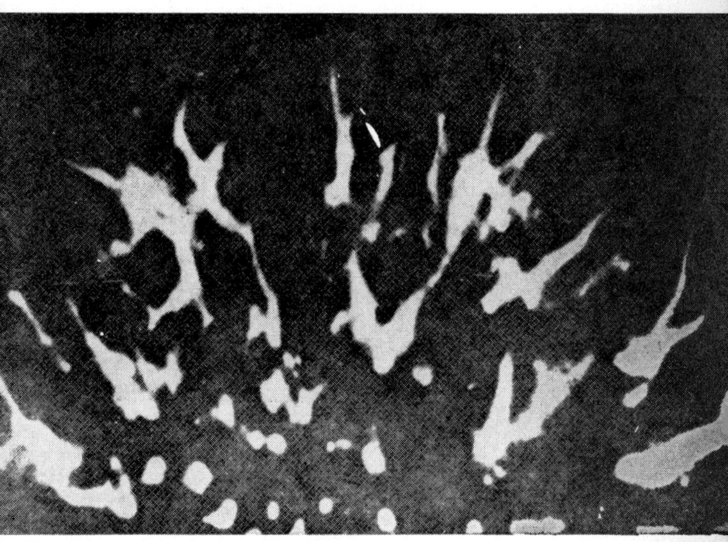

6

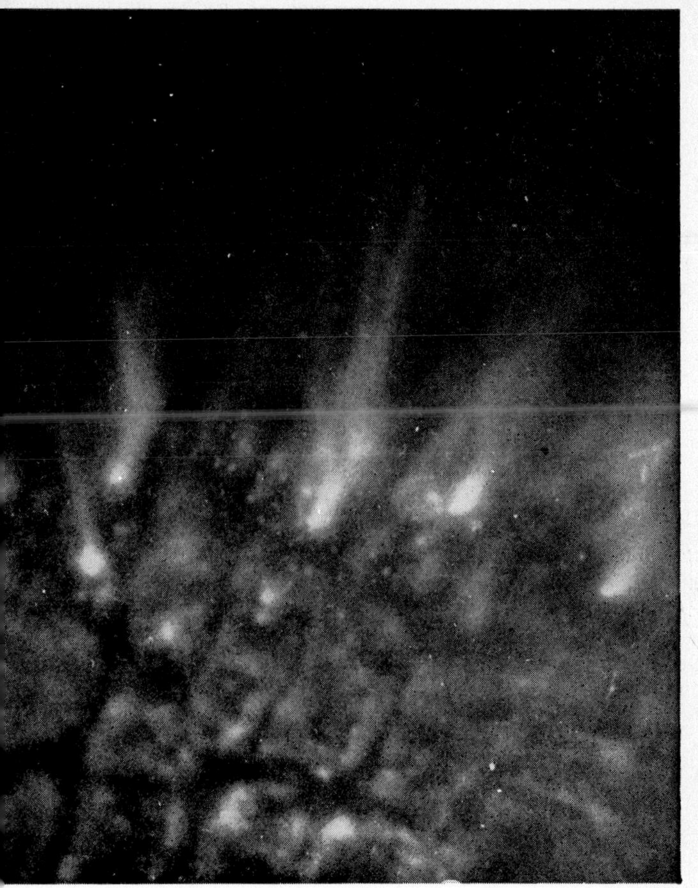

7 Each of these pictures shows a human fingertip magnified fifty times. Picture shows that of a healthy man, calm and even-tempered.

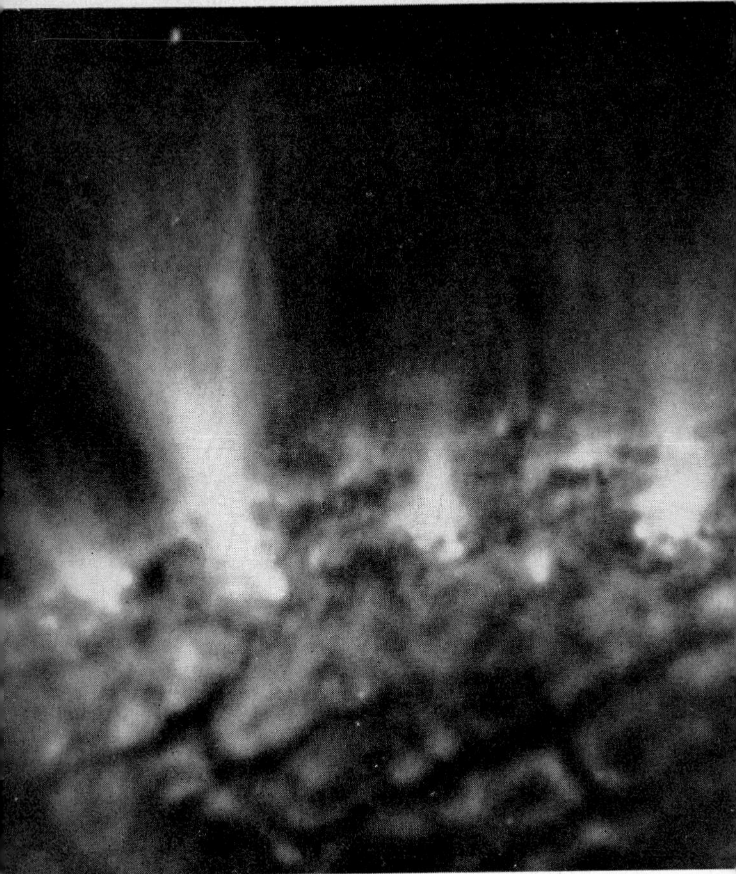

8 Photo shows the finger of an overtired, emotionally tense individual. In a state of fatigue, more energy seems to leave the body.

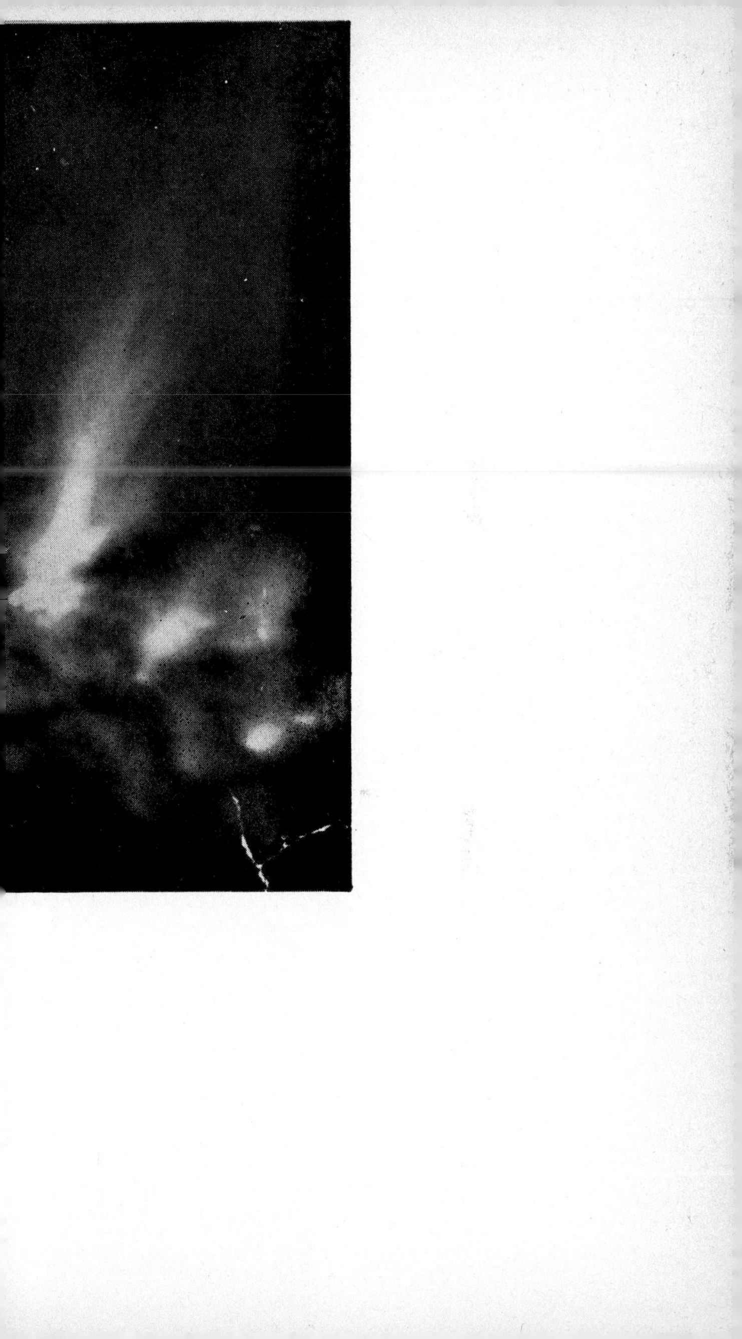

9
Lilac buds as seen in a regular photograph.

10
The same buds photographed in a field of high-frequency electric current. Plumes of light pour out of the buds in a luminous crown, or halo.

11
Each bud has been cut in half. The radiant crown still shines, this time even clearer. The energy discharges from the center.

12
The buds have been cut off entirely. Energy continues to pour out of the plant, like a Roman candle, seeming to follow a specific path through the plant.

9

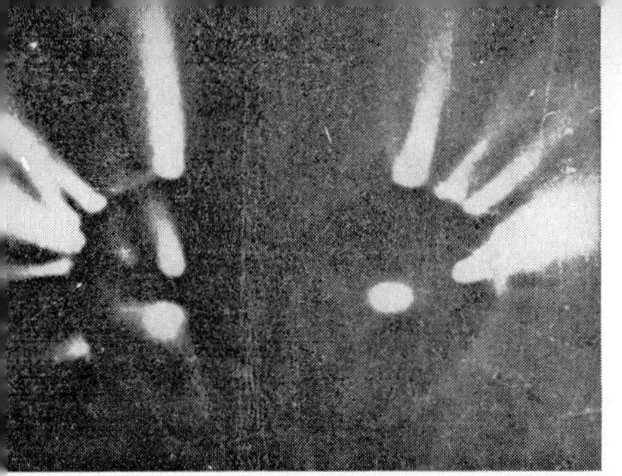

10

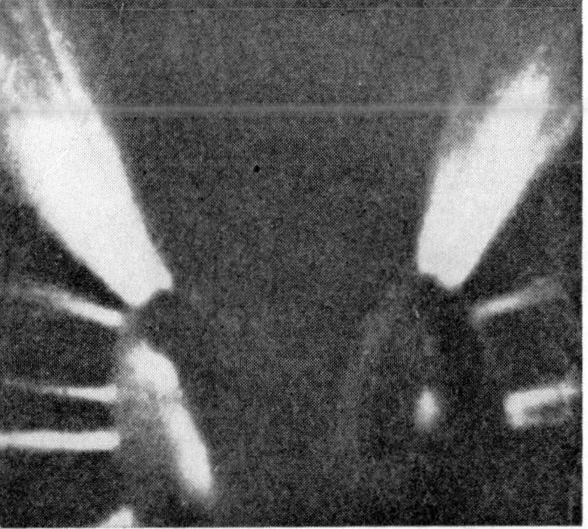

11

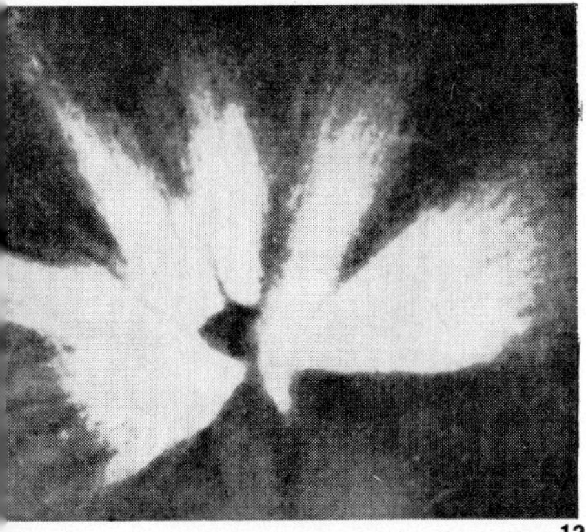

12

14

13
The radiant crown of two whole buds. Occasionally, little circular fireballs shoot out in different directions and quickly vanish from sight.

14
A leaf just torn from a plant sparkles and glitters.

15
The same leaf, withering, shows how the energy of life begins to fade prior to death.

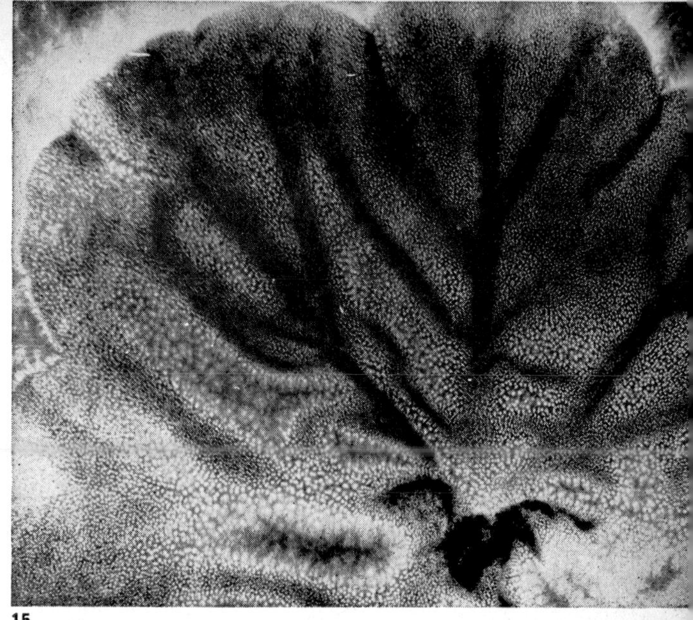

15

13

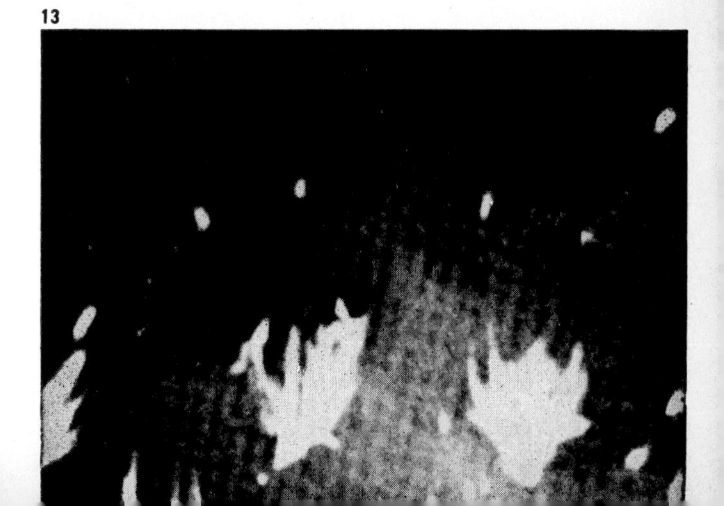

16
Acupuncture points, which if stimulated, supposedly heighten psychic sensitivity.

17
Bretislav Kafka (1891–1967), famous Czech sculptor and pioneer explorer of the psychic realm.

18
Clairvoyance, Hypnotism, and Magnetism at the Service of the Military, reveals how the Czech Army used psychic powers to effect some of its brilliantly successful campaigns.

19
Soldier dowsing.

16

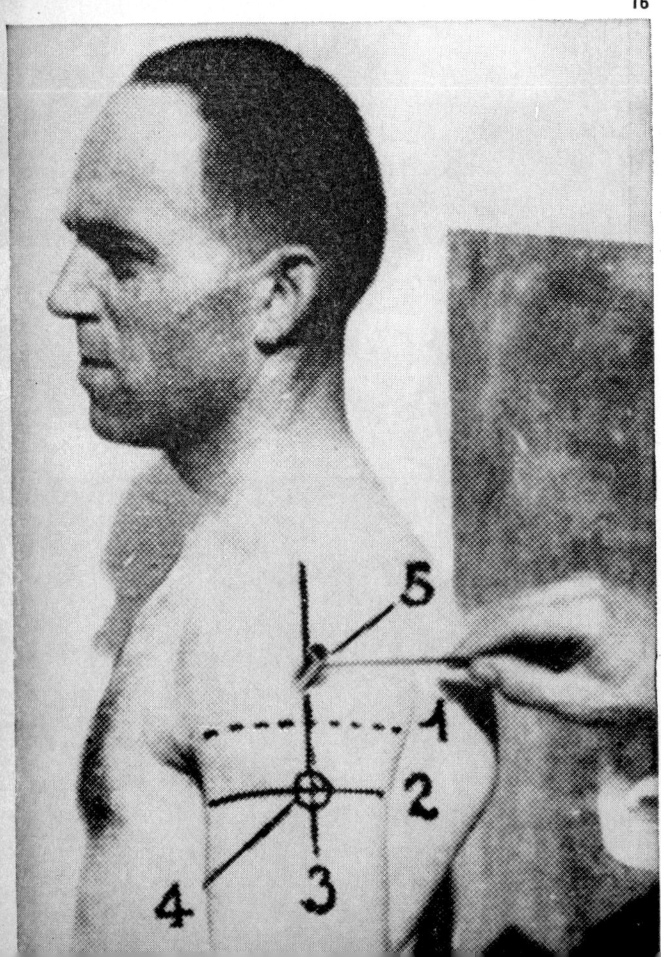

17

18

SVAZEK XXIV EDICE „SPIRIT". SVAZEK XXIV

JASNOVIDNOST

Hypnotismus a magnetická léčba
ve službách militarismu.

Dle vlastní prožité prakse podává

KAREL HEJBALÍK.

*

1925.

19

20 Dr. Zdenek Rejdak, prominent Czech parapsychologist.

of Yoga has always maintained that breathing charges the whole body with "Vital Force" or "Prana" and Yoga prescribes specific breathing exercises for good health.

Now the biologists at the Kazakh State University began to understand *why* breathing ionized air has "a high medicinal effect for many kinds of disease." Many diseases were shown to begin when the supply of bioplasma deteriorated, the Soviets say. Soviets found even spraying a wound with ionized air would greatly speed healing as the negative ions helped restore the plasmic body to equilibrium.

"With this concept of the biological plasma body, we can open new paths to understanding the growth of cancer, tumors and other forms of disease," wrote the biologists.

The scientists also studied the impact of different colors on the "bioplasma". Each color, they found, changes the activity of the bioplasma and calls forth specific oscillations in it. For instance, blue seemed to intensify the discharge of luminescence. Perhaps the basis of eyeless sight lies in the reactions of human bioplasma to color. They found too that weak magnetic fields stabilized the luminescence of the bioplasma.

At the parapsychology conference in Moscow, we met Dr. V. Inyushin, one of the scientists from Alma-Ata, who conducted some of this research. In between urging us to come to Alma-Ata to see their work and wondering why American biologists and biochemists were not involved in parapsychology research and why none were sent to the conference, he explained, "The Kirlian discovery has opened up the possibility of studying the plasmic states of the organism. It is through the biological plasma body that we react to all cosmic occurrences. When there are disturbances of the sun [or solar flares], our biologists have charted all kinds of biological reactions in humans, plants, and animals," said Dr. Inyushin. "These disturbances of the sun cause changes in the whole plasmic balance of the universe and in turn affect the bioplasma of living organisms. This results in physical changes we can see."

The Soviet findings coincided exactly with what Eileen Garrett, the medium, had said. And it makes you wonder if the Soviets are beginning to uncover in the working of the bioplasmic body some new scientific bases for another ancient system of thought: astrology.[61] Soviet cosmic biologist Dr. Chijevsky did extensive work on the impact of the 11½ year solar flare cycle in human life.[19-21, 304]

For centuries, many psychics have claimed that it's possible to separate the "astral body" from the physical body at will. Some psychics maintain they can not only move this energy body but even travel in it. Soviets are currently studying Yogis who claim to do out-of-body travel.[24] At times of crisis, trance, coma or under the influence of anesthetics, it is said that this energy body may spontaneously eject. Dr. Charles Tart of the University of California, Davis is beginning to do tests on out-of-the-body travel.[408] Harold Sherman, author, psychic and director of the ESP Research Associates Foundation in Arkansas, has attempted to do studies of people who claim to have had this experience.

At death, this energy body is supposed to leave the physical body. Mediums report, "The etheric body or energy body interpenetrates the physical body—it's an exact duplicate. At death we just emerge from our flesh covering and continue our life as an energy body." [335]

It's unlikely that the Soviets are about to probe the afterlife. It's also unlikely that the Soviets' bioplasma body is the whole explanation of so-called astral travel. But in the course of their extensive research with the Kirlian process, the Soviets have many times photographed the moment of death. Little by little as a plant's or animal's physical body dies, Russians saw sparks and flares of the bioplasmic body shooting out into space, swimming away and disappearing from sight. Gradually there was no luminescence at all coming from the dead plant or animal. Meanwhile, biological field detectors at a distance continued to detect pulsating force fields from the now dead body. Is this energy coming from the dispersing bioplasmic body? Perhaps with the aid of Kirlian photography a little more of the mystery of death can be unravelled.

Valentina Chrisanfovna Kirlian and Semyon Davidovich Kirlian have made it possible for everyone to see at least part of the aura. They have photographed it seems, the legendary energy body, our second, subtle body. As the Curies found a new, whirling universe inside a lump of radium, so the Kirlians have found "Whole galaxies of lights,—blue, gold, green, violet" and "a fire world, great channels of blazing, glittering light" in living things, in us. Of all the new and unusual we encountered behind the Iron Curtain, the Kirlian discovery seems to us potentially the most important. We'll never be able to think of ourselves or anyone else in quite the same solid, opaque, inert terms that we did before seeing the brilliant, beautiful Kirlian pictures.

The implications of the assertion by Soviet scientists that an energy body or astral body exists are vast. There is hardly any area of our thought: philosophy, science, art, religion, medicine, that won't sooner or later be affected by the concept that we have not one, but two bodies. We've called it the secondary body. Perhaps it is the primary body. Perhaps, through it we are linked with all things in the universe more vitally than we ever imagined.

For parapsychology too, the understanding of man's energy body may be the key to centuries-old mysteries. It seemed Mrs. Garrett had been right about the existence of a human energy body, its characteristics, the impact of the solar system on it. Was she right in stating this energy body is the medium of psychic happenings?

The Kirlians had given parapsychologists an amazing new exploratory technique and they immediately put it to use in exploring the energy body and ESP. The adventure was just beginning. . . .

18

THE ENERGY BODY AND ESP

An energy body, a second body, a subtle, sensitive body that reacts almost immediately to a shift of thought or mood, or to changes in the environment. This is a brand-new idea in Soviet biology. It's so new that the shock waves haven't been felt in other areas of science. But the aura and so-called astral body have long been dumped in the province of the parapsychologists and they were quick on the uptake.

"This discovery of an energy circulating in the body, neither blood nor electrical, is extremely important for parapsychology," reputable scientists told us. It might provide the long-awaited clues needed for a sensible explanation of a host of supernormal happenings, from dowsing to telepathy to psychic healing.

HEALING

Aside from the "witches" who heal, mainly in Siberian villages, the Soviet Union has some well-known and respected psychic healers who, it is claimed, can cure all kinds of illnesses by the laying on of hands. Two very well-known healers from the city of Tbilisi, capital of the Soviet Republic of Georgia, are Comrade Kenchadze and Colonel Alexei Krivorotov.

Krivorotov, now retired from military service on a pension, has worked for over seven years as a psychic healer in conjunction with his son, a medical doctor. Soviets report he is particularly successful at curing back ailments, radiculitis, infections, and many illnesses of the nervous system.[89] Healing isn't instantaneous but takes about a month of treatments.

A patient, having been carefully examined and diagnosed

by the young Dr. Krivorotov, is placed in a chair. The colonel stands behind the sick person holding his hands about five centimeters from the patient's body. Starting from the head, he works his way down the back. Patients usually report feeling great heat radiating from the colonel's hands, although his hands do not touch them. If an inner organ is diseased, patients often report feeling tremendous heat pouring from the spot, almost, they say, as if the organ is being choked. Krivorotov can feel this warmth radiating from the patient and can diagnose exactly where the illness is. Throughout a healing treatment, patients claim they feel Krivorotov's hands burning through them. Yet tests showed no change in temperature of either the patient's or Krivorotov's skin. In fact, Krivorotov's hands were cool to touch. Many patients reported this burning feeling stayed with them for up to two days after the treatment, yet medical tests again showed the temperature to be normal.

"I think the energy is coming from some outside source," Colonel Krivorotov says. Often while he cures patients, observers hear noises that sound like small explosions or discharges that seem to come from the space between Krivorotov's hands and the patient.

Three years ago Soviet scientists decided to test Krivorotov using the Kirlian photography method. A month of extensive experiments took place. Results weren't published, but we were told by a reliable source that the high-frequency photos of Krivorotov's hands as he healed showed a complete change in the energy patterns coming from his skin. "Before," "During," and "After" Kirlian pictures showed distinctive characteristics. The brightness of the emission and the strength of the flares from his hands depended on whether Krivorotov was tense or relaxed. At the moment when he seemed to be causing a sensation of intense heat in a patient, the general overall brightness in Krivorotov's hands decreased and in one small area of his hands a narrow focused channel of intense brilliance developed. It was almost as if the energy pouring from his hands could focus like a laser beam.

The Kirlian technique also showed variations in the pain the patients were experiencing; bright, intense colors for strong pain; pastel colors as pain diminished. Valentina Kirlian was the first person to produce evidence that pain and injury set bold, bright color emanating from the body. She literally fell into her discovery. One day she tripped in the lab, hit the floor, and wrenched her leg. She didn't call for help. Instead she called for her husband to help her get a look at her leg in the high-frequency fields. They saw unusually vivid colors.

Besides pain, sudden, strong emotions also bring changes of color and light emanating from the body. If a person is angry or exhausted, the Kirlian apparatus reveals that increased light pours from the body in a distinct pattern. These changes in the color and intensity of light seem to affect your own physical body. Could they affect other living things too?

Dr. Bernard Grad of McGill University in Montreal may have a clue. Grad painstakingly proved if a psychic healer held water in a sealed flask and this water was later poured on barley seeds, the plants significantly outgrew untreated seeds. But—and this is the most intriguing part—if depressed psychiatric patients held the flasks of water, the growth of the seeds was retarded.

Dr. Grad suggests, that there appeared to be some "X factor" or energy that flows from the human body to affect growth of plants and animals. A person's mood affected this energy. This previously unacknowledged "energy" has the widest implications for medical science, from healing to lab tests, Grad says.[305]

Perhaps what the Kirlians are photographing streaming from the healer's hand and the increase of bright flares they see in angry or fearful people is the "X" energy that Dr. Grad described. The Kirlians photographed the bright energy streaming from healer to patient. Maybe their apparatus can also show us exactly *how* the energy flowing from the hands of an emotionally depressed person can affect water and plants.

The preliminary work with Kirlian photography so far seems to indicate that psychic healing involves a transfer of energy from the *bioplasmic body* of the healer to the *bioplasmic body* of his patient. Changes on this level eventually reflect in the physical body and supposedly heal it. Discovery of how the bioplasmic body works could help us develop new forms of healing based on balancing these energies in the bioplasmic body, possibly with negative ions, electromagnetic pulses, or oscillating magnetic fields. Medical diagnosis may also get a big boost from Kirlian photography. A recent series of diagnostic tests with the Kirlian technique at a Sochi sanatorium were, reportedly, a success.

Psychics are said to be able to work their "wonders" on other than living things. A short while ago, Dr. Jacques Errera, Councillor on Nuclear Matters to the Belgian government, became involved in work with a healer who held his hands over a piece of fresh meat. This "treatment" by the healer seemed to preserve the meat. It did not decay or deteriorate for a month though it was not refrigerated.[162] Some sort of X energy was involved. Could it be the same energy the Kirlians photographed streaming from the hands of Colonel Krivorotov?

In the USSR, Dr. Peter Kapitsa, son of the famous physicist who developed Russia's atomic and hydrogen bombs, is one of the scientists interested in the study of this X factor that Dr. Errera had mentioned to him. We met Dr. Kapitsa in his office at the Institute for Physics Problems in Moscow. "We have not set up any experiments yet on this phenomenon," Kapitsa told us, "but I am very interested in this type of research because we are beginning to encounter problems of this nature in various areas of scientific research here."

The Kirlian study of the energy body has led to unexpected and promising developments in another form of medicine, perhaps even more unusual to us than psychic healing. The Russians loaded our luggage with Soviet books on acupuncture, a centuries-old Chinese system of medicine that effects cures with needles.

"It's important, the newest thing in ESP research," the Russians told us. Maybe it was a great revelation, but the only response they got from us was blank looks. All either of us knew about Chinese medicine was the name of it. Even that took a while coming over as the Russians manfully struggled to tell us in English, "There's an important connection between 'Chinese holes' and ESP!"

It seems in the realm of aura, energy body and perhaps telepathy there may be a connection between acupuncture and ESP. It's a strange story. The pieces of this fantastic puzzle began to fall into place in the 1950s.

THE ENERGY BODY AND ACUPUNCTURE

Dr. Mikhail Kuzmich Gaikin, a Leningrad surgeon, gazed intently at the myriad patterns of lights sparkling out of Kirlian's hand and his own hand under the impact of high-frequency fields. Dr. Gaikin had read about the Kirlians in the *Literary Gazette* in 1953. Something about the picture accompanying the article set an idea ticking in him. He made the long trip to Krasnodar, southeast of the Crimea.

The Kirlians showed Gaikin pictures of a man's body that looked like a carnival of light. Next, in the high-frequency field, Gaikin saw an unbelievable display of fireworks in his own hands—great channels of violet fiery flashes blazed turbulently. There were silent yellowish-red and blue lights like "dwarf stars." There seemed to be craterlike depressions from which erupted not fiery lava, but radiance like arctic lights. Some of these lights seemed to shoot off into space.

"Where is this caravan of lights coming from? Where is it going?" Kirlian asked Gaikin. "Why are the yellowish-red and the blue lights always paired? And why are they different sizes? Why are the large flares violet? It seems to us this colored panorama of lights must be subject to some law. Maybe the mysteries of living nature are coded into the colors of these lights."

Gaikin mused—could these flares be electricity from the nerves? But the signal flares didn't correspond to nerve endings in the skin. Moreover, these same flares poured out of plants and plants don't have a nervous system. There seemed to be no difference between the cells that glowed and those that did not glow.

The pattern of lights he saw in the human body reminded Gaikin of something he'd come across in China. As chief surgeon on the Zabaikal Front in 1945, Dr. Gaikin had seen Chinese doctors cure what he'd always considered incurable diseases—rheumatoid arthritis, epilepsy, types of deafness. The doctors used the ancient Chinese form of medicine—acupuncture. (John Hersey in his book *Hiroshima* reports acupuncture will even cure the effects of nuclear radiation.) How does it work? Gaikin asked the Chinese.

"An energy we call Life Force or Vital Energy circulates through the body on specific pathways," the Chinese told him. "This Vital Energy can be tapped at seven hundred points on the skin that were mapped out thousands of years ago." The Chinese inserted fine needles at those points to correct imbalances in this supposed primary energy flow, and thus apparently cured disease.

"You see," they said, "these seven hundred points on the skin are in *communication* with organs deep inside the body and with the whole mental and physiological state of a person. Changing the energy flow on these points changes the Vital Energy deep inside the body."

Dissection showed no trace of the pathways of this so called Vital Energy. It didn't make sense to Gaikin, trained in Western medicine. But one thing did make sense to him. Patients got better. He studied acupuncture, tried it, and it worked. In the last two decades thousands of Soviet and European doctors have tested acupuncture and are using it today.

In the Kirlians' tiny room, as Gaikin stared at the pictures of a human being under high-frequency fields, it seemed his hunch had paid off. The spots where lights flared most brilliantly appeared to match the acupuncture points the Chinese had mapped out thousands of years ago! Gaikin was excited. Just possibly the Kirlian discovery might give the first scientific confirmation of this five thousand-year-old system of medicine. Maybe there was also a relation between the channels of swimming light the Kirlians saw and the pathways of Vital Energy described by the ancient Chinese.

The Kirlians were intrigued too. Chinese medicine with its unusual ideas about the nature of the human body might lead to the overall theory they needed to tie together their many seemingly unrelated discoveries.

The Kirlians learned a lot about acupuncture. And so did we (See Appendix A, 9.) After going through Russian, French, and British works on the subject, we began to get a clearer idea of why our Russian friends were excited about acupuncture, why they thought it might give a better understanding of the Kirlian discovery as well as of certain psychic events. Can acupuncture, for example, help explain the different *colors* of the flares that they see flashing from living things?

According to the Chinese, man's body has two kinds of energy: electrical and "Vital." The Vital Energy, is *not* electricity but behaves similarly. Like electricity, it is polarized into positive and negative. Is this a clue to the two basic colors, blue and reddish-yellow, that showed up in living things in the Kirlian photos?

Acupuncture, it seemed to some Russians, might help unlock the medical meaning in the Kirlians' pictures with greater precision than the general study of the aura. Chinese medicine states that points on the skin connect through pathways of Vital Energy to internal organs. For instance, a point on the inside tip of the little finger of the right hand is on the energy pathway leading to the heart. These points seem to show up in the Kirlian pictures as flares of brilliant light. If the intensity, color and location of the flares can be interpreted, doctors might have a window on the condition of deep internal organs like the pancreas or brain that are often difficult to diagnose.

Of all the strange phenomena they'd encountered with their high-frequency device, the Kirlians were most impressed by the ability to see disease *ahead of time*. Here was something that acupuncturists seemed to know all about. There's even an old aphorism in Chinese medicine, "The superior physician cures *before* the illness is manifested. The inferior physician can only care for the illness which he was unable to prevent." The Chinese believe the highest healing science deals with this invisible level of energy. A skilled practitioner, through reading of pulses, determines if there is any imbalance in the counterpart body of energy. He can tell whether there will be a breakdown in an organ long before this energy imbalance translates itself into a crippling physical fact. He then attempts to rebalance the energy flow and prevent the oncoming disease. (In ancient China, "medicare" subscribers paid the acupuncture doctor to keep them from getting sick. If they did fall ill, the doctor paid them!)

The Kirlian pictures coupled with the knowledge of acupuncture lead perhaps to a new perspective on some kinds of precognition. Every organ in the body, according to acupuncture theory, communicates its condition via the energy pathways to the skin in the form of energy patterns. A clairvoyant may look at you and prophesy, "You are going to get tuberculosis in about two years." Instead of seeing around the corner of the future, the prophet may be aware of problems already in your energy body or he may see these problems reflected in changes of color in your aura.[404]

So far, coming from left field, the ideas of acupuncture seemed to tally with what the Kirlians had observed experimentally. It was bizarre. And the parallels went even further. The Kirlians had found that emotions, moods, thought all seem to have a drastic effect on these energy pictures of ourselves.

In Chinese medicine, they learned, you are always viewed as a whole—a concept which includes body, mind, and environment. The Chinese say that both habitual states of mind and sudden moods reflect in the Vital Energy. According to them, it is this energy that links the mind and the physical body. This is the *modus operandi* of psychosomatic illness, the means by which the mind affects the body. A negative depressed state of mind acts on the Vital Energy like a toxic substance, they say, and will eventually manifest itself as illness. Conversely, the Chinese say, a malfunction in the body cauld cause a mental illness. Correcting the Vital Energy imbalance in the body can correct the condition of the mind. (For this reason, acupuncture has become an adjunct to psychotherapy in the Soviet Union.[246])

It may have been more than moods that caused changes in the lights flaring from the Kirlians' hands. Acupuncturists believe Vital Energy in the body links man with the cosmos. If there is a change in the universe and environment, a *resonance* is produced in the Vital Energy of the human body which in turn affects the physical body. In this way the body adjusts to changes around it. The Vital Energy, the Chinese say, is affected by a host of things: the seasons, cycles of the moon, tides, thunderstorms, strong winds, and even levels of noise. Supposedly an illness and its treatment can be affected by any of these changes in the environment. Eventually the State University of Kazakhstan affirmed that the bioplasmic body *is* affected by changes in the atmosphere, just as acupuncture theory predicted.[60]

Thanks to the alert Dr. Gaikin, the unlikely happened and acupuncture and Kirlian photography got together. First of all, the combination led to a landmark advance in the sort of medicine used by millions of people throughout the world. One of the great problems of acupuncture has always been locating exactly the tiny (less than a millimeter wide) treatment points on the skin. After studying the Kirlian process, Dr. Gaikin and engineer Vladislav Mikalevsky of Leningrad invented an electronic device that pinpoints the acupuncture points within a tenth of a millimeter. It's called the "tobiscope." [27]

Russia heralded this invention. The Soviet government displayed the tobiscope at Expo '67 in Montreal just as it played up such other advances of Soviet science as the Vostok spaceship and the atomic icebreaker *Lenin*.

The Soviets are serious about acupuncture. (See Appendix.) They study it at top institutes like the Gorky Medical Institute and the Kirov Institute of War Medicine in Leningrad; their scientists have rolled up a great deal of experimental data on acupuncture; they've shown that whatever this energy is, it does not travel on the skin, but does take a deep interior pathway. Acupuncture has been amped-up, modernized, combined with EEGs, electrocardiograms, etc.; in the USSR and Europe acupuncturists not only use needles to stimulate the points on the skin but also employ static electricity, sound, cortisone, and adrenal cream for massage.[17, 246-247]

Acupuncture lit up by Kirlian photography may lead to new forms of medical treatment, but there is a larger, perhaps ultimately more beneficial, implication in this mating of the ancient and the modern: a more unified view of man. This is a view of the human being linked to the cosmos; a view of man aware of and reacting, via his secondary or bioplasmic body, to changes in the planets, environment, and weather, as well as to illnesses, moods, and the thoughts of others; a view of man as an enmeshed, integral part of life on earth and in the universe.

Acupuncture with its mapped points also provided a fully developed method for finding out just *how* the bioplasmic body was reacting to all these changes around us.

The parapsychologists seized on the possibility and the strange sounding idea of acupuncture as an ESP research tool was born.

ACUPUNCTURE, TELEPATHY, AND THE BIOPLASMIC BODY

Whatever telepathy is—a physical wave or a nonmaterial thing—when it reaches you, it has to stimulate you physically for you to get the message or see the vision. In the United States Douglas Dean's years of research at the Newark College of Engineering have shown that when a telepathic message comes through to you from someone, there's a change in blood volume in your body. Your conscious mind is not aware of this but a plethysmograph, which reveals changes of blood volume in the thumb, can measure this change unerringly.[286-288]

At Rosary Hill College in Buffalo, New York, Sister Dr. Justa Smith found after extremely sophisticated scientific research that psi can even affect enzymes.[399] The latest Russian research in Leningrad had supposedly shown that changes in brain waves coincide with telepathy reaching the body. Again, you may not necessarily be conscious of this change.[151-152] Research on humans with the polygraph (lie detector) also gives some indication of just exactly when ESP reaches the body, although again knowledge of it might not be conscious.[340]

Telepathy seems to have something to do with the entire body. ESP seemed to come in on all levels of the body's physical activity. Years ago Mrs. Garrett said the energy body or human double "is the medium of telepathic and clairvoyant projection." Was she right? Could "the medium be the message"?

The Soviets wondered if the energy body picks up the telepathic message first, then reflects it in our physical body. They needed a way to clearly measure the effect, if any, of telepathy on the bioplasmic energy. They couldn't use Kirlian photography. It's dangerous to put the entire body in high-frequency fields for any length of time. They turned instead to the ancient route to bioplasmic (or Vital) energy. Acupuncture landed in the world of electronics.

An up-and-coming young physicist, Victor Adamenko, invented an improved version of the tobiscope to locate acupuncture points. Then he invented a new apparatus, the CCAP—Conductivity of the Channels of Acupuncture Points. (See Chapter 12.) The full explanation of how and why the CCAP works is complicated. Put simply, it uses a strategic combination of acupuncture points to measure the changes of the bioplasmic energy in the body. Variations in energy can be graphed and intensity of reaction shown on a numerical scale.[173]

We saw some data on this and a very reliable source gave us the following report. A group of Moscow researchers decided to use the CCAP in ESP testing. They attached a control group and an experimental group of volunteers to the machines. Then the volunteers were hypnotised. A doctor in a distant room in the institute attempted to send telepathic suggestions to specific volunteers. As his thought pulsed out, scientists intently watched the graphs of the CCAP. To their amazement, the needles flickered back and forth on the numerical scale as the intensity of the doctor's thought commands varied. Telepathy was affecting the bioplasmic energy of the subjects' bodies!

It seems telepathy is picked up by the bioplasmic energy.

The scientists' great leap of imagination had paid off. The ancient canons of acupuncture had led them to a new way of charting telepathy. Did the ESP message go first to the bioplasmic body and then the physical body? Could they chart the precise pathway of different thoughts on acupuncture maps of the body? Do different thoughts have different intensities? These are a few of the questions that opened before these Russian researchers. These young scientists already have some objective, scientific proof that bioplasmic body has a very intimate connection with a whole bagful of unexplained psychic happenings.

POINTS THAT MAKE YOU PSYCHIC?

Make yourself psychic with acupuncture? Some Communist scientists think it's possible. Mediums say you can expand your consciousness via the human energy body. Evidence seems to suggest that often telepathic information appears to be picked up by our bodies but never reaches our conscious awareness. By stimulating certain centers in the body with drugs or exercises, it might be possible to make conscious the incoming ESP. Indian philosophy as well as many clairvoyants hold that psychic force functions through certain glands—mainly the pituitary and the pineal.

We met scientists in both Czechoslovakia and Russia who suspect that since specific acupuncture points can command the bioplasmic energy flow passing through organs, glands, and the brain, possibly psychic force can be stimulated with acupuncture.

We were shown several photographs by scientists detailing acupuncture points on the upper arm. "By stimulating these points with needles a person's psychic ability may be heightened," they said. "But don't try it unless you have a trained acupuncturist."

THE AURA, ENERGY BODY, AND PLANTS

The Kirlian process has produced some very strange pictures of plants. Multicolored lights shine from plants like a luminous coat of arms identifying each species.

But in the Kirlian pictures you can also see something else invisible to all but the psychic eye: rays of energy, whirling fireballs of light that shoot out of a plant into space. Using the Kirlian method, scientists photographed a lilac stem with two buds. In the first picture they saw plumes of light pouring out of the buds and small spikes of light like a luminous crown. Then they cut each bud in half. Still the radiant spikes showed, this time even clearer. They lopped off the buds completely. Now great beams of energy shot from the end of the stem pouring out of specific pathways. The plant's stem shone like a Roman candle.

And there was another mystery. From time to time, little circular fireballs would shoot out in different directions and quickly vanish into space.[9] The Kirlian plant work rang a bell with some Soviet scientists and has led them to delve back into the famous discovery of radiations from living matter made in the 1930s by the well-known Russian, Dr. Alexander Gurvitch.[306] (See Appendix A, 8.)

Being very aware of the Kirlian photography of plants,

the Soviets we met were voraciously interested in another kind of plant work. They pumped for details on the surprising work of Cleve Backster that's caused a sensation in America. Backster, owner of the Backster School of Lie Detection in New York and a recognized expert with the polygraph, announced in 1968 that plants have emotions, memory, and ESP! Throughout several years of careful research, Backster found plants record a measurable reaction on a lie detector when any living thing dies in their presence. Plants seemed to recognize their owners and to respond to thoughts and emotions of people around them. Backster says, "It seems to indicate some sort of 'primary perception' or consciousness in every living cell." [269-270]

Is the energy streaming out of plants in the Kirlian photographs the medium of the plants' perception? Is it the bioplasmic body of plants that reacts to the death of living things around it?

Mrs. Garrett, who visited Backster's lab, remarked to us, "I can tell how a plant is reacting by changes in the 'surround' or aura of the plant, just as I can see the auras of people."

Perhaps, one day, research with the Kirlian apparatus on the energy body of plants will help explain the highly researched impact that PK, thought, prayer, and music seem to have on plants.

A WINDOW ON THE UNKNOWN

"Man is much more than a machine!" Soviet scientists told us fervently, and Kirlian photography shows we exist simultaneously in more dimensions than we'd realized. The sparkling fact that the energy body exists is a discovery that sends out tracers in all directions—tracers that are bound to set smouldering some new ideas about ourselves.

This bioplasmic body that we're all supposed to have reacts to thought, emotion, sound, light, color, magnetic fields, any subtle change in the environment from the grass we walk on to the planets we rarely notice. A fresh slant on astrology? On biorhythms? Yes, but perhaps there are also implications too for medicine, psychiatry, even sociology and philosophy. Here is the almost unexplored world of our subtle interaction with everyone and everything; this is the world of "plasma," of the shifting "tissue" of the universe connecting all to all, and we, according to the Russians, are part of the tissue.

The Kirlian discovery has across-the-board implications for psychic things too. Psychic healing of body and mind may prove to be a matter of balancing the energies of the bioplasmic body. Once understood, this kind of healing could be done with precision, not in the current hit or miss fashion. If telepathy moves in your bioplasmic body it may make comprehensible why ESP seems to be picked up by your whole physical body, why blood and brain waves react to telepathy whether you're getting any conscious message or not. Then there is eyeless sight and dowsing. So far, no one can really explain why the dowsing rod dips to water and fingers are able to know colors. Perhaps the bioplasmic body is the missing link that will lead to an explanation of these and other out-of-the-way abilities like Nelya Mikhailova's PK. (See Appendix A, 4.)

The Kirlian effect and the discovery of an energy body by Soviet biophysicists also provide independent confirmation of the extensive research on the existence of a "counterpart body" done at the Delawarr Laboratories in Oxford, England. The pioneering research of George de la Warr in the field of biomagnetics has been largely ignored in the West, but the Communists have shown great interest and even dispatched a Soviet scientist to visit the Delawarr Lab several years ago. The work of George and Marjorie de la Warr has vast implication for parapsychology and for the understanding of the mysterious "force" which permits perception at a distance by any living cell.[289-293]

The scientists who have examined Kirlian photography are reputable people in the pure sciences in Russia, and most of them have no connection with parapsychology. A major university published detailed scientific reports mapping the bioplasmic body. There will have to be more research inside and outside of Russia before we can say definitely that the Soviet scientists have correctly interpreted the Kirlians' beautiful pictures.

However, the Kirlian discovery promises to give us some

long-awaited answers and to raise a new generation of questions.

"It's fantastic—it's a fire world!" And most extraordinary, it's part of every human being. As Semyon Kirlian said, "This is a beginning and it's not little."

19

A SOVIET WITCH PREDICTS

A witch in a suburban Moscow apartment block? During preparations for the fiftieth anniversary of the Soviet revolution, author and *New York Times* editor Harrison Salisbury, wrote about a well-known Moscow witch.[392] The witch predicted, "The Bolshevik revolution will not live to see its fiftieth birthday." Of course, Salisbury says, space-age Muscovites don't believe in keepers of the cauldron, yet the witch's words "had a sour effect." The sophisticated Soviet also says he doesn't really believe in the soothsayers who predict each year whether war will erupt. They see the military future in white mushrooms sprouting at the feet of pale birch and dark green pine trees. A scarcity of mushrooms bodes well for peace.

Crystal gazers and wizards, witches and sorcerers, the wise ones who talk to the animals of the forest, the crafty ones who'll dry up a neighbor's cow or weave a web to restrain a wandering mate—the Soviets may be able to arc cosmonauts off to the moon, but they haven't been able to totally disperse the higgledy-piggledy crowd that dances on the good black Russian earth to the light of the occult moon. The "magics," as one Russian friend called them, aren't overworked, but they've lasted better in Soviet cities than the world's other oldest profession. Here and there, out in the country, the magic folk arts shuttle and spin their exotic charms. It's not surprising that the old cajoleries linger on. Russia has always been intimate with the unseen, been ravished by it, been tempted to try and control its forces. The basic yen remains from the college professor to the scruffy gypsies in Soviet parks offering to read any palm that crosses theirs with rubles.

According to the English witch Sybil Leek, there are organized witch covens in Russia which are in worldwide underground communication with witches in the West.

Through a fortuitous leap of events—and not, we hope,

through sorcery—we met a Russian witch. ("Witch" was *her* name for herself, not ours.) We'll call her Zima, a woman whose path we crossed, fittingly enough, in Kiev, capital of the Republic of the Ukraine and once the capital of all Russia. A thousand years ago, when Moscow meant a muddy trading post on the banks of a northern river, Kiev, mighty in Byzantine blues and golds, in learning and commerce, ruled a sumptuous territory. Long ago disjointed from power, today Kiev is a relaxed, gracious city which in the summer becomes a music-filled resort town.

Our witch agreed to meet us one evening in a park on the palisades bordering the Dnieper River. With friends, we scrambled up what seemed like a vertical park to some benches overlooking the river spreading out far below. A woman waited on a bench. Hair braided and pinned into a damp-looking chignon, wearing a blouse and skirt, freckled and tan, she looked like other middle-aged, comfortably built vacationers.

"Ah, here you are!" She laughed because we were all puffing. A Russian friend helped with the translation and we were introduced to Zima. "I am a witch," she said, "yes." She was also an animated talker. In the area of the occult, Zima explained, she had some experiences as a child, "but I didn't learn to use my powers until after I grew up. It all happened because a very favorite relative of mine was sick. Not just sick physically; she was totally demoralized. It looked like she wouldn't even be able to finish school. The doctors gave up. Everybody gave up," Zima sighed.

"But I kept having a feeling that perhaps the witches in the country, people who had the old knowledge, could help. I traveled to the villages across Siberia. Oh," she exclaimed, "there are a great many witches and sorcerers there! I talked to everyone I could find, I began to learn."

Zima thinks her trip into the "old knowledge" paid off. When she returned to her city with some potions and some knowledge of psychic healing, the very favorite relative recovered. After that Zima was on her way into witchcraft, not for money, like many Russian witches, but for her own self-development. (Zima is college educated and, oddly enough, works in a technical field.)

"A medical doctor who was a very learned man gave me this," Zima said. She held out an exquisite little carving, the lines of which almost seemed to crackle with motion—a sacred object, not Christian, from a much older religion. This was Zima's connection to one of the gods. "A smiling god. He's very powerful. It's through him my information comes." We were allowed to look, but not to touch.

The gods are all around us, Zima told us. "A few times I've been able to just catch a glimpse of them in the air. They're very beautiful. A lot of people don't think they exist. But it doesn't make any difference. They're here."

Zima's use of the symbol to connect with her god and make conscious her psychic impressions is similar to the Washington psychic Jeane Dixon's use of a crystal ball and to more technologically oriented psychics who speak of watching "a blank TV screen in my mind." However, Zima usually *hears* much of her information. "I am able now, though, to see pictures of the future in water. They're stills. They don't move yet; I'm told they will eventually if I train."

Does she foresee precisely, or in symbols?

"Sometimes things come symbolically. I don't know why but whenever I see soldiers in the uniforms of the Napoleonic wars, it means death is involved."

We wondered how a Russian witch would feel about parapsychology. Would she look down on it as child's play, a johnny-come-lately? Zima thought parapsychology was great. She'd read about the psychic Karl Nikolaiev. "It's about time scientists got around to investigating these things. If only they'd started such a science sooner. Now let people shake their heads when I see things."

"People" seemed to mean, in particular, Zima's relatives, many of whom apparently are Party members. Having Zima and all her gods in the family seemed to be headache number one, two and three. "My family calls me a witch too, but to them that means crazy. It sends my cousin into a rage!" Zima laughed rocking back and forth. "He even tore up occult material I was studying and I found him trying to flush it down the toilet. But I got more. It's because of him I'm so interested in this new science of parapsychology." Zima grew suddenly solemn. "What will he say when science proves you can read thoughts and see the future? Eh?" Zima poked one of our companions. "So, maybe *I'm* not so crazy. Maybe *they're* wrong," she said, jolly again.

Would she answer some questions for us about the future?

"Ah," Zima sucked in her lips as if she was actually tasting the idea. "Yes, all right," she said, finally taking the little carving back out of her vividly embroidered bag.

We asked what would happen in the American presidential election. (This was July 6, 1968; we'd heard no news of America for over five weeks except of the assassination of Robert Kennedy.) Elbows on her knees, Zima concentrated on the swirling lines of her symbol.

"He says that America will move to the right." Do you mean the Republicans will win, we asked, or what?

Silence. Zima "listened" again. " 'It will move to the right,' he repeats. And that is the only thing that will save America. America will be saved. Things will probably get worse there, but it will be far, far better than any place else." It's sticky to decide what "right" means in either the lexicon of an ancient smiling god or a Soviet citizen, but no synonyms were forthcoming, so we went on to ask about the race problem.

"It will get more calm," she said. "There will be fewer riots, but still a strong struggle forward."

What about Canada? "Canada will be split up. It will divide. But the people won't feel it much."

And world problems. "China wants to be friends with America. You may not believe this now, but you will see. Russia and China will be split very wide, much worse than now. And," she said, grinning broadly, "he says that one day, Russia and America will be friends—one day!

"Here in Russia," she continued more somberly, "trouble is coming. It may last even as long as fifteen years. After that, many of the new ideas that are talked about now will be given a chance. We will understand the power of the mind better. Fifteen or twenty years from now parapsychology will be very important. Many people who are in this field today will have high posts then.

"The masses in Russia will not be permitted to read your book on ESP. But the chosen few here *will* see it and they *will* read it."

Zima made a few personal predictions about our own futures. She also saw a rather exotic, not run-of-the-mill accident involving a friend of ours that subsequently came true.

"Enough, enough," Zima said. "My friends here would keep me talking all night. I don't know if what I just told you was right or wrong. You'll have to see. I'm surprised that the god spoke to me at all. This morning I was so upset. There was a lot of unpleasantness. Usually when that happens, I get nothing for days. But I did swim and swim today and water always helps me attune again."

We're going to have to wait and see how correct Zima was on personal predictions involving ourselves because they're not "scheduled" to happen for a few years yet. So far as Zima's predictions of international events are concerned, to be fair we should point out that they have less of the educated guess to them than they would if made by a Westerner. Soviets get infinitesimally little news about world events or even about the moves of their own country on the world stage.

Since Zima made these predictions back in the summer of 1968, the United States elections took place and as every one knows a Republican was elected President. The race riots since then have not been as severe as in previous years, while the struggle forward continues in a more constructive vein. On the international scene, China for the first time has extended feelers toward the West and has prepared to establish diplomatic relations with Canada.

It wasn't until several months after we met Zima that Russians got the first trickle of news about armed clashes with the Chinese on their eastern borders. The reports came as a tremendous shock to the average Soviet citizen. Since then, conflict along the Sino-Soviet border has steadily worsened with armed clashes spreading from far eastern Khabarovsk all the way west to Central Asia. Inside Russia, anti-Chinese propaganda has grown virulent and Radio Peking is now jammed in Russia by the government. China has launched an all-out anti-Soviet campaign.

It looks like Zima's prediction that things would get worse in Russia is coming true. Within months after we met her the Neo-Stalinists had made a comeback; liberals were purged from important positions; the few outspoken dissenters have been sent to forced labor camps. Maybe Zima is right and it will be more than a decade before new ideas take root in the USSR.

Zima wouldn't come with us for a late snack. "I'm a vegetarian, it helps with my powers." We shook hands. Our witch patted us both on the arms. "Remember, ask the gods, all you have to do is *ask*. They'll do anything for you." Then Zima went off into the night, clattering down the steep path in her sandals.

Whatever else she is, Zima is an immensely appealing woman, eccentric, individualistic, with a mind full of tracers that shoot off in all directions, yet brimming with that all-so-human *simpatico* many Russians bathe you in.

FOLK HEALERS

Like Zima, witches have always tried to foretell the future. Infinitely more alluring to most Russians, however, was the idea that witchcraft could bring them a ruble-laden, romance-filled, and, most importantly, a ripsnorting healthy future.

The Soviet press inveighs against healing witches, yet *Komsomolskaya Pravda*, the youth paper, did advise its readers: if you fall sick in the country and there is no doctor for miles, don't be too proud to go to a well recommended sorcerer for the emergency. Perhaps it's not such bad advice. Concocting their remedies, Russian witches built an extensive folk pharmacopoeia which Soviet science is now beginning to explore to its own rich benefit. For instance, they discovered there are powerful antibiotic actions in special compounds of strawberries and raspberries which the witches had often prescribed.

The mercurial Soviet scientists are into another exotic old form of healing too, nicknamed "Flower Therapy" by Dr. Nikolai Yurchenko. After fifteen years of study at a sanitorium in Sukhumi, Dr. Yurchenko believes that specific plants and trees help specific illnesses—*actually*, not just psychologically. Being near deep red roses supposedly strengthens the nervous system. Another scientist, Akaki Kereselidze of the Georgian Institute of Subtropical Farming, foresees scientifically planned healing parks for specific ailments. If you want to live to a grand old age then you must, he says, "be surrounded with beauty of a useful sort, and not of an idle type."[421]

There were and still are, it seems, many quacks among the witching doctors. In the mid 1960s the Soviet magazine, *Krokodile* harpooned a sorcerer of Bashkir. He treated his patients by having them gulp down chicken droppings and cough up a twenty-eight dollar fee. Sometimes, *Krokodile* reported, even army colonels and university graduates journeyed thousands of miles for this dubious magic in a barn. In 1968 the Soviet paper *Trud* wrote of dozens of people beating a highway to the door of an apparently more effective village healer, sixty-nine-year-old (although she says she's ninety) Ekaterina Zlobine. She lives in the Volgograd region and diagnoses citizens by holding onto their right thumbs. Her treatment is a prayer and a bunch of miracle grass costing eight rubles. Ekaterina's magic has brought her a television set, a refrigerator, and her own private taxi, plus the devotion of her fellow villagers, who sell lodgings and food to her patients. The official police explanation for leaving her alone is that she is too old to bother. On the other hand, nobody has said that she didn't cure, at least, some people.

According to Zima, there are still some cackling hag-type witches around, sour and scary as Baba Yaga, the witch of Russian fairytales who lived in a hut mounted on monstrous chicken legs. "A malicious witch lives near my aunt," Zima told us. "I rarely go there, she sets up such a bad vibration. And this witch is always doing unpleasant things like telling people when they'll die." This is the sort of witch one would use to make a neighbor's pig scrawny.

The witches' power over the health of livestock was often more prized than her healing of humans. In *Doctor Zhivago,* Boris Pasternak evokes a proud Russian witch, Kubarikha, living with the partisans in a snow-laden Siberian forest. Zhivago watches as Kubarikha incants a get-well spell (the kind that is still used) for a scabby cow. "Beauty" the cow will recover, Kubarikha assures the animal's owner; then in a moment of generosity, the witch reveals a glimpse of the invisible world wheeling about their ears. There, those twisted twigs, Kubarikha points. You think they're nothing. But really a water sprite is making a garland. She stares into the motionless, dark pines around the clearing. She sees a raging battlefield coursing with the hosts of Evil and Good. Kubarikha knows that whirling snowspouts are werewolves seeking lost warlock babies, that the red flag, the banner of the partisans, is actually the death woman's purple kerchief luring the young to be killed and shaking pestilence on the land. Pasternak gives Kubarikha a beautiful song to sing, a song of love and life to the Rowan tree. It vibrates in the listening Zhivago, eventually leading him to again seek his own lost life.

Besides witches, other unorthodox healers live in the USSR. In Moscow we were told that doctors are scrutinizing a psychic named Rozova who can clairvoyantly "see" and expertly diagnose a variety of illnesses. This woman says that disease microbes "tell" her their names. A number of psychic healers surfaced in the 1960s, many in the far-off parts of the USSR. One highly revered healer was at the Moscow Conference with us. "He's well over ninety," our Soviet friends whispered insistently. He looked about sixty-five.

Perhaps the greatest folk healer was Karl Ottovich Zeeling. "A man with hair, white as the moon, hanging to his shoulders, a beard, kind blue eyes, and a clever, concentrated face," is how a contemporary saw him in the 1930s. The sick journeyed from all directions to be diagnosed and treated by Zeeling in the far Siberian city Tomsk. A scientist described the healer working: "Zeeling, a big, fine-looking man, extended his hand. He knows nothing about the fully clothed patient, yet his hand researches easily, circulating well above the body.

" 'You have your appendix missing,' says Zeeling.

" 'That's right. Yesterday was my first day up after the operation,' the patient said with a big grin.

"People, sick people came into the room, one after another. Zeeling diagnoses each, gives each the exact method of cure."

Zeeling, according to a small band of dedicated biologists, could "diagnose" all kinds of things. He held his hands over eggs. "Male." "Female." Invariably, the scientists said, he knew the sex of the unborn chick. His large hands waved over covered photographs of people. Again he could always identify their sex. Zeeling, who must have looked like a holy Siberian hermit of old, brought some of the legendary magic of mirrors to life. He could correctly tell the scientists the sex of the last person to gaze into the mirror on the wall.

Before the great purges of the late 1930s, the gifted Siberian supposedly taught some of the scientists to "read" with their hands as they labored to measure the living energies coming from the healer. They concluded his gift was radiesthesia.[31]

Zeeling usually carried a prism. Looking in his triangular prism, he could "see" something no one else could, the next day's weather. One scientist remembers, "Often as the mysterious old fellow walked on the veranda, he would look at his prism and say, 'The color blue is growing. It will rain.' He was always right. Once Karl said, 'Blue! It just jumped, abruptly, suddenly; there's a huge increase. Watch the papers. There's probably been a volcanic eruption.' Shortly afterward the papers reported a strong volcanic upheaval—in the Pacific Ocean."

A now-elderly member of Zeeling's circle recently said, "To study radiesthesia when we did was dangerous. They hunted for researchers as they hunt for witches. In a savage blow in the epoch of 'the cult of personality' [i.e. during Stalin's regime], Karl Zeeling was murdered in 1937."

One surviving scientist who worked with the healer thinks Zeeling will eventually be rehabilitated as an honored early practitioner of medical radiesthesia, a new area of research. This scientist comments about his study of Zeeling's healing: "It led us to extraordinary new ideas about the nature of life, in particular about the energetical nature of *thought*—ideas leading so far that they are as yet frightful to express."

A SUPERNATURAL HOTHOUSE

From the first, Soviet authorities were literal witch hunters. They broke the backs of the beneficial occultists and the religious mystics, just as they leveled the fraudulent and the greedy. It isn't impossible to understand in part the unmerciful opposition of early Soviets to anything that seemed in the least allied to the supernatural. Old Russia wasn't just a hotbed of superstition; she was a six-thousand-mile botanical garden of superstition. Almost every grotesque known to the world and some not known elsewhere sucked up nourishment in Russia. Werewolves and were-bears prowled the forests waiting for the unwary. Vampires flickered alive with each setting sun—not chic Count Draculas, but lumbering monsters in tattered grave rags. Ghosts walked, spirits of the night howled. This wasn't legend to the people who lived it. Superstition in old Russia was as concrete and pernicious as the lice infesting most of the populace. Magic spells, amulets, potions, powders, and counterhexes were widely considered to be necessities of life.

On the brighter side, pre-Freudian sorcerers did a good business analyzing dreams. Grannies, instead of watching TV, looked at lumps of hot wax hardening in water to see pictures of the future. Many families possessed a house brownie and nymphs enlivened the countryside.

Generally, however, there was more of Caliban than Ariel in the omnipresent unseen. Judging from accounts, there were traffic jams of unclean spirits to get in and out of benighted Russians. Doctors' records of the late nineteenth century speak of women in a part of northern Russia who were all periodically possessed by screaming demons who drove them to beat everyone in sight, break dishes, froth, dance, and curse until they keeled over and the demon fled. The society expected this possession and, probably as a result of this, it occurred more or less annually.

Both men and women had to look out for the incubi and succubi—demon or spirit lovers. Dr. Leonid L. Vasiliev mentions a succubus case reported to him in the 1920s. Meanwhile, thousands of Holy Fools wandered the land, venerated by peasant, squire, and often bishop. Usually hapless idiots, their counsel was asked for by the most elevated groups. Often these unfortunates had a "disciple" who interpreted their babblings for the uninitiated and collected the grateful love offerings to God. Stagnating branches of the Church itself promoted belief in devils and hobgoblins and gave rise to bizarre masochistic cults and to the most peculiar flights of religious ecstasy. One aristocratic lady became known for her saintliness because she always swooned in divine ecstasy when the preposition "of" was spoken in a particular part of the Mass.

Attempting to lay a plank or two across the swamp in the late nineteenth century, Alexander Aksakov, a well-educated, well-traveled man and councillor to the Tsar, became the first psychic researcher in Russia. He brought the famous American medium D. D. Home to St. Petersburg in 1861. Americans and Englishmen argued theology, metaphysics, even theories of electricity in trying to explain Home's powers. Russians knew better. Word went round that Home acquired his powers by sleeping every night in a bed crammed full of healthy black cats.

Alexander Aksakov, who eventually became a spiritualist, did produce much interesting, perceptive research. Like Pierre Janet in France, Frederic Myers in England, William James in the United States, Aksakov helped give shape to a new field of study. Unfortunately, today he is still taboo in his own country and forgotten outside of it. Perhaps because he was Russian, Aksakov did seem to get into more way out happenings than his European colleagues. During a seance, five people testified that one of his mediums "evaporated, disappeared from the waist down." [264] This supposedly so unsettled the medium that she refused to try another seance for two years. A Lolita prototype situation reared up. A little girl spirit, the story goes, materialized only to be set upon by a few dirty old men in the dark of the seance room.

Throngs of other educated Russians enjoyed more "usual" experiences with table tipping, amateur clairvoyance, and precognition experiments. With her otherworldly leaning, Russia quite naturally took to Spiritualism when it appeared in the late nineteenth century. Even Tsar Alexander III discreetly contacted one of the Fox sisters in America, around whom the spiritualist movement was founded, to determine the most propitious day for his coronation. Shortly before the Revolution, the country listed twelve thousand organized Spiritualist circles.

CAN A YOUNG RUSSIAN WITH NOTHING BUT ESP . . . ?

Out of the chock-full and simmering supernatural of old Russia came the two most famous and most powerful occultists of modern times: Rasputin and Madame Helen Blavatsky, both of whom fired mightily the passions and the arguing instincts of their contemporaries. The Horatio Alger of Russian occultism, Rasputin bounded from a Siberian hut to the treasure crusted halls of the absolute ruler of all Russia. With the royal family in his sway, body and soul, many thought the hypnotic monk Rasputin finally ruled the Russian Empire.

And then there was Madame Blavatsky. Helen Blavatsky, bigger, bolder, brighter than life, isn't easily caught in a volume. She was a child often found hypnotizing the pigeons in the tower of her country estate and a young medium who almost ended up in jail when she helped Russian police solve a murder. How could she know so much if she hadn't been involved? But Madame Blavatasky could do just about anything. She fled her antique husband and Russia to be a bareback rider in the circus, to fight, disguised as a man, under Garibaldi, to be left for dead on the battlefield, to recover and become a dressmaker in Boston. Then she founded the Theosophical Society.

Madame Blavatsky moved her growing entourage to India. There her psychic powers ripened to perfection. She could, people said, conjure sweet perfume, fresh fruit out of the air; she could float about the whole world in her astral body; more important, she received communications from the really extraordinary departed, the great Masters of occult, hermetic tradition. Some thought she was a fake, some thought her genuine, but everyone agreed Madame Blavatsky was something else again. Of much greater consequence than her showmanship are the two huge books she wrote, *Isis Unveiled* and *The Secret Doctrine*. Purportedly the Masters helped her unfold in these works the subtle knowledge preserved from antiquity and soon to be reborn in the world. Madame Blavatsky covered worlds within worlds. Her fellow countrymen are just beginning to investigate in their own way the edge of what she touched. Before she died in 1891, Madame Blavatsky made a prediction about her native land. "When England ceases to carry the torch of democracy, out of Russia will come the greatest civilization the world has ever seen."

SHAMANS AND THE DANCE OF THE SUPERNATURAL

The *shamans,* the holy men or "witch doctors" of Siberia, could supposedly communicate telepathically, see clairvoyantly, travel out of their bodies, predict the future, and heal the sick. They did not use psychic talent for its own sake. *Shamans* were the mainstays, the social pivots of their peoples. As their talent could mean life or death to the tribe, it was not a position lightly come by. If you felt the calling, you retired to the woods to learn. Periodically the apprentice underwent extreme examinations. He would be pushed through a hole chopped in the winter ice of a Siberian river and told to surface through another many yards upstream. The idea was that bad apples would sink. He had to grasp supernormal powers to survive; it was also believed the wicked could not attain the highest knowledge and would be phased out in final tests. According to anthropologist Gerald Heard, only one bad apple ever got away. He murdered his guru halfway through the course and put his power to work expanding in other ways. His name was Genghis Khan.

Shamans took drugs and flung themselves into sacred dances to catapult into the psychic. The fire blazed, the drum beat, the *shaman* danced faster and faster until he collapsed in a trance. Singing and drum brought him round and again the *shaman* danced, leaping, stamping, a fury of motion until his body fell to the ground and he, hopefully, shot out into the world of the unseen. Dancing into psychic powers has sprung up elsewhere in Russia. Country witches often do a slow dance to help secure their spells. Rasputin, a hybrid of *shamanism* and Christian mysticism, was famous for frenzied all-night dancing that seemed to leave him buoyant and his onlookers exhausted.

There is another Russian who also seems to have leapt into the psychic through dance, Nijinsky—the great Nijinsky. The most meticulous audiences of Paris sat and watched as the curtains opened and suddenly a human form soared and glittered and spun across the stage, dazzling them, enthralling them as if he were a real god with real wings on his heels. Even the critics wrote that Nijinsky never exited like other dancers; he simply seemed to float up and off behind the curtains.

People who worked with Nijinsky noticed something about his leaps that the audience missed. "It's not that he goes up higher," some said, "it's that he comes down slower!" In his book, *Between Two Worlds,* the psychiatrist Nandor Fodor speaks of an interview with his close friend, the dancer's wife Romola. Nijinsky, she said, never understood why other dancers couldn't stay up as he did, why they couldn't also control the speed of their descent. Romola once remarked to Nijinsky, "What a shame you can never see yourself dance." But he said, "I do! Always. I am outside. I make myself dance from the outside."

The idea of flying on your own has always scintillated in Russian stories that are crisscrossed with beautiful princesses swooping elegantly through the evening sky and witches who, instead of flying on broomsticks, use a mortar and pestle. They fly in the mortar and beat it onward with the pestle.

But what was the secret of Nijinsky's great leaps? Dance was a religious gift to him, a mission to express eternal truths through the body. He looked into Yoga, worked with Ouija boards, and reportedly was a good automatic writer. Speculating on Nijinsky and levitation, Dr. Fodor recalled Hindu practices that supposedly counteract gravity and the ancient saying that he who awakens the Anahat Chakra in the heart can walk on air.

The Russian inclination to think of flying out of the body through dance, to see psychic power moving through the motion of the body, may explain in part Soviet parapsychology's lifelong interest in kinetic telepathy. They try to command a person to move by telepathy, a kind of muscular ESP.

THE MYSTIC SOUL OF RUSSIA

The brilliant psychoanalyst Carl Jung wrote of the great forces energizing the unconscious psyche of a nation. Jung was speaking of pre-Hitler Germany, but his analysis is applicable to any country. Life forces denied the light of day strengthened and soared in the night of the psyche until the furies rode with the Valkyrie, according to Jung. Germany hurtled into the eye of the irrational dragging the rest of the world with her. Cases of national mania would continue, Jung thought, until we work through to a better grasp of the unknown parts of our nature. Unlike Jung, however, many opted to ignore at least the psychic side of our nature. Even Freud feared that if the psychic gates were loosed we'd be swept away on a black tide of occultism. Eventually Freud changed his mind about the value of parapsychology.

Many Soviets like Vladimir Lvov, a leading opponent of ESP research, haven't changed their minds. Lvov fears that any step away from Pavlov dogma will plunge Russia back into the old, degraded occultism. This is more than distaste for superstition. It is a real fear of the monstrous compulsions of the unconscious. Some people suggest that it is this instinctive fear of being swept away by the irrational and unconscious that at bottom motivates all committed opposition to the investigation of the nonlogical.

It is a justfiable fear in the Soviet Union. The deep psyche of Russia has lashed more violently, perhaps more extremely, than that of any other people. Until recently Russia had little rational structure to climb back on. This is the unconscious chaos that throws up an Ivan the Terrible who will one day on a whim murder ten thousand people and hurl them into the river until one could almost walk across the water on the bodies; an Ivan who will spend the following day beating his breast in church genuinely rueing his sins; an Ivan who will the next day sink back into gore. Insane is a label, not an explanation—just as "crazy" was a convenient dismissal of country witches who occasionally did see clairvoyantly what was going on in the next village. Russia still has a few witches, but infinitely more compelling to everyone, Russia still has, or at least had until this decade, her terrible Ivans, her Stalins, and her Berias.

Soviet parapsychology, with its EEG machines, information theory, and imaginative young scientists, is beginning to bring to heel the old invisible powers of the witches. But para*psychology* is a misnomer in the USSR. Unlike the West, there is little psychology in the field. This raises question marks like the white mushrooms at the feet of birch and pine. If they eventually understand one level of the unseen and not another, will the Russians simply move from the unconscious manipulations of owl and broomstick to the conscious manipulations of Faust? Or is this first study of the psychic a move toward looking within, is parapsychology, as its Soviet supporters contend, "summoned to study the full nature of man himself"?

Soviet parapsychology is on the move and so, it seems, is the Russian mind, gathering itself up for some new shift. Which returns us to the classic question most writers sooner or later echo when contemplating the land that bred Gogol and drove him to write: "Russia, are you not speeding along like a fiery troika that nothing can overtake? . . . The onlooker stands still, struck dumb as by a divine miracle. . . . What mysterious force impels this troika, these horses never seen before? . . . On you rush under divine inspiration! Russia, whither flyest thou? Answer! She gives no answer." [39]

20

ARE WE IN AN ESP RACE WITH RUSSIA?

When we finally boarded a train in Kiev heading toward the Russian border and Romania, we wondered how to sort out the "information explosion" that had rocked us during the last month. We'd met so many people, heard so many things, been loaded with so many books and reports.

We'd wondered if the Soviets were up to something in ESP. As we rolled through the Ukrainian farmlands one thing at least seemed certain. They were. Then we came to the hard question. What did that mean in Russia? And, in the sensitive era of super powers, the era of act and react, did it mean anything to America? Were we unknowingly in an ESP race the way we'd been in a space race in the early 1950s?

To get an idea of how American and Soviet psi research stack up and an idea of "what it all means," it helps to look at Soviet parapsychology as both a cultural phenomenon inside Russia and an action of the USSR on the international scene.

ESP-ionage, OR A WEAPON OF WAR

A classic Russian adventure story, *The Master of the World,* hinges on the possibility that a man possessing the secret of psi would be able to rule the world. Is this possibility well on the way to reality with Soviet leaders? Is ESP a weapon of war? All research on ESP in the USSR is, of course, ultimately funded by the government. There is every indication from multiple sources that psi research with military potential is well-financed by the Soviet Army, Secret Police, and other paramilitary agencies. Soviet scientists doing psi research in nonmilitary areas often have trouble getting money.

"Secret psi research associated with state security and defense is going on in the USSR," Dr. Milan Ryzl, formerly of Prague, reports.[382] Communist State authorities, the military and the Secret Police display an unusual, disproportionate interest in parapsychology, he says. Soviets are attempting to apply ESP to both police and military use.

"Some years ago," Ryzl says, "a project was begun in the USSR to apply telepathy to indoctrinate and 'reeducate anti-social elements.' It was hoped that suggestion at a distance could induce individuals, without their being aware of it, to adopt the officially desired political and social attitudes. There is evidence that funds given to the late Dr. Vasiliev for his laboratory were linked with some secret research entrusted to him. The dangers of possible misuse of psi should not be overlooked," Dr. Ryzl warns.

Highly placed Soviet scientists take parapsychology seriously, not snickeringly. Reports of psi research on Soviet submarines help confirm military involvement in parapsychology. There are reports of several military institutes where ESP research is being done in the USSR. We have seen confidential Western reports on Soviet attempts to train clairvoyants for spy purposes. According to W. Clement Stone [405] there is clandestine psi research going on at the Pavlov Institute of Higher Nervous Activity in Moscow, and the Durov Institute has fifty scientists studying telepathy. A Communist indicated to us that there is more psi research at secret science cities in Siberia. If even part of this is true, it's time that America knew about it.

The Soviet Union has the world's largest spy network. This penchant for spying includes gathering information on their own citizens as well as information about the rest of the world. Obviously, telepathy and clairvoyance would make ideal additions to a spy arsenal and such undercover groups are constantly said to be supporting ESP research.

Apart from the intriguing cloak and dagger of ESPionage, there is the world of fields and forces, of searching for as yet unknown energies that provides such an impetus for Soviet parapsychology. The energy behind PK has often been spoken of as the "ultimate weapon." The American psychic Jeane Dixon has prophesied that soon man will find new uses for electromagnetic fields and will harness new energies from the cosmos. Is this search for fields another reason why the Soviet military "shows a disproportionate interest in ESP"?

Said one knowledgeable Western authority, "Many of the Soviets doing ESP research are often brave and sincere, but they're the pawns of the politicians." Running like a leitmotif through all Soviet talk about ESP is the stark warning "Psi must not be misused for evil. We only hope it will not fall into the hands of those anywhere who would use it as a biological weapon." We were asked to relay this idea to America. We never heard the refrain anywhere else.

Sybil Leek, the well-known writer and member of a British witch coven, reports that underground hermetic and witch covens function in Russia. Supposedly they are in communication with British covens. "According to the information I've gotten, the United States is fifty years behind the Russians in psychic research," she says, referring in particular to Soviet military ESP.

If Westerners had bothered to read Soviet publications in the 1950s, we would have seen that much data on the development of Sputnik was published long before it shot into space and astounded the world. Today we are still not keeping up with material readily available in Soviet publications and scientific papers, particularly in the field of parapsychology. According to John Gunther, author of *Inside Russia Today*, "American sicentists remain woefully ignorant of what is going on in their fields in Russia and this can have serious practical consequences."

ARE THERE RELIGIOUS IMPLICATIONS TO SOVIET PARAPSYCHOLOGY?

The early Bolsheviks believed in a new world they could make—they were idealistic, Utopian, almost messianic in their hopes for a better world, says Dr. Nikolai Khokhlov, a Soviet defector, now a psychology professor in the United States.[320] Khokhlov points out that these early dreams almost perished. Today there is a new inner drive among young Soviets to build a better world, to realize some of the idealistic components that were part of the early Communist movement. At the same time, there has been a "religious" movement of a sort developing in the Soviet Union. As Svetlana Alliluyeva says, "People in Russia are religious, not from studying writings, but from feeling."

In a sociological poll in the USSR reported in *Soviet Life*,[159] one young Soviet commented: "The younger generation will live better in terms of material wealth, but we will have more complex problems to deal with. That is the historical trend. Where our parents had knotty material problems to solve, our tough ones will be spiritual."

Whether parapsychology will, through its new view of the nature of man, create a new kind of spiritual trend remains to be seen. If by "spiritual movement" you mean a return to organized religion and worship, you speak of something completely *outside* of Soviet parapsychology. But if by "spiritual" you mean seeking to understand man and his place in the universe, then Soviet parapsychology might be in part an expression of a spiritual movement.

POLITICAL INTERFERENCE

Beneath the stolid surface, the 1960s was a decade of great intellectual ferment, openness to new ideas, and new demands for a freer society in Russia. As part of this move into new spheres, censorship on public discussion of ESP was lifted in the 1960s and scores of Soviet publications featured outstanding articles on parapsychology by both writers and scientists. Critics of ESP often found no market for their dogmatic views.

In the 1960s the Soviet rulers began to find themselves face to face with something previously unheard of in the USSR—an opposition to certain government policies that expressed itself in open demonstrations and in openly circulated underground magazines (*Heresy, Phoenix, Syntax*).

Scientists and writers were often the most independent in their thought. Scientists are an elite and materially privileged group in Soviet society, with free access to information. Dr. Andrei Sakharov, one of the fathers of the Soviet H-bomb, winner of the Lenin Prize, in his famous manifesto "Report Against the System" sharply criticized the

Soviet regime and ideological control over intellectuals. He called for cooperation between East and West, and the convergence of capitalism and communism. Sakharov was spontaneously supported by such famous scientists as Dr. Peter Kapitsa and Dr. Igor Tamm. Young and old, scientists united. Rather than publicly attack such world famous men, Brezhnev and his cohorts tried to cut the ground out from under them. A secret meeting was held to discuss the explosive state of Soviet science. The "Stalinist" Ministry for Public Order was set up again. In 1968 the government set up new controls over the 800,000 scientists in the USSR; henceforth scientists would be required to undergo "reconfirmation" political examinations every three years to retain their posts. In Leningrad alone over one hundred scientists were fired for nonconformity with the approved line.[425]

Communist newspapers launched attacks against scientists in general, condemning their "shocking seminars," "specious theories," and "lack of a clear political line." Parapsychology was not omitted in this outburst against the scientists. The *Literary Gazette*, criticizing scientists for ESP research, set up a phony telepathy test with Karl Nikolaiev and when ESP occurred omitted the results in its negative write up. The Communist Party organ *Pravda* attacked scientists for investigating Nelya Mikhailova.

Does this mean that psi research was a many-colored flash in the pan that died with the 1960s? No. It would be very foolish to believe that, no matter what your bias toward ESP. It is unlikely that the Neo-Stalinist element will, or even wants to, halt the thrust of Soviet parapsychology. The Neo-Stalinists are not the only people in high places in Russia, and even their opposition seems to be aimed not at parapsychology but at mass discussion of ESP, much public revelation of research, and those scientists who would like to have free exchange of information with researchers in other countries. In the long run, the Neo-Stalinists who hamper a free scientific exchange in any field are only holding their own country back just as they held back their space program.

AMERICA VS. RUSSIA: A PSYCHIC COMPARISON

How does parapsychology in the West stack up with parapsychology in the USSR? Some authorities maintain, "We're thirty years behind the Russians." Others say, "But our scientific methods are much better and we have a great deal more experience." In certain ways both are right.

The Soviet government supports parapsychology research to the tune of an estimated 20 million rubles a year. The United States government budget, apparently, is zero. This book, long as it is, does not begin to cover all the material we brought back. Books have been condensed to paragraphs. And it was of course not possible for us to contact even a fraction of the scientists doing psi research in the USSR. We only scratched the surface.

1. The most important difference between American and Soviet research is that their research is angled toward *use* of psi. The aim is technological application. In America, ESP research as a whole only recently emerged from the basics of establishing statistical proof of psi's existence.

2. Psychical research in the USSR is regarded as a new field in the natural sciences linked with bionics, physiology, biology, etc. They call it "bio-information," "biotelecommunication," "biocybernetics." Psi laboratories in Communist countries are in universities, technology institutes, colleges. Psi research generally is done by pure scientists. Telepathy research is looked on favorably by many levels of scientists, from technologists to some of the elite of the Soviet Academy of Sciences. In America, ESP research has been a stepchild of psychology, at best barely tolerated by the academic community. It's been given almost no house room in universities.

3. Soviets use the team approach to ESP, gathering specialists from many different fields to provide well rounded interdisciplinary research. There is also cooperation among scientists from the Communist bloc. In the West, psi scientists tend to work singly or with one or two others in the same field. Divisiveness among Western researchers is appalling.

4. Soviets are well informed on Western research. They

know all about psychics like Cayce, Croiset, and Serios and they are familiar with serious scientific parapsychological work in the West. Westerners know little about either Soviet psychics or Soviet research.

5. Basic Soviet psi research is physiological. Western work is generally statistical, psychological, philosophical. Soviet research is highly specialized; the scope of the field is more limited. Our work is much broader, encompassing the humanities, religion, psychiatry, philosophy. Western psi research has eighty years of experience behind it, a wealth of information that the Soviets assimilated to help power their recent thrust into psi.

6. There is no specific Soviet journal devoted to parapsychology. Semi-popular periodicals carry general articles on psi; but scientific papers are published in regular Soviet scientific journals appropriate to the specific field—cybernetics, biology, etc. Soviet institutes periodically publish collections of scientific papers on work in parapsychology. In America parapsychologists have rarely been welcomed by regular science journals.

7. One can't help noticing the contagious enthusiasm of the Soviet parapsychologists, their openness to new ideas, their daring, their willingness to explore forgotten splinters of knowledge. Maybe it's the newness of the field there. Perhaps in America the long and unbudging hostility of academic and scientific colleagues has had a more stultifying effect on our parapsychologists than has the outright political repression now and then faced by their Soviet counterparts.

Some Communist scientists have psychic abilities which they don't mind talking about. Western researchers seem to be leery of admitting to psi talent. Almost all the Soviet researchers seem to have tried to develop a feeling for the psychic realm within themselves, much as our psychiatrists must learn something of their own complex being before they can work with others. The atmosphere in dealing with psychics is closer to that of the superb Russian music conservatories or ballet schools, with the scientists constantly seeking ever better ways to improve, encourage, and enhance talents rather than the skeptical, "Show me, and show me in my way" approach so often encountered in the West.

8. Until recently, the impetus behind much Western psychic research came from private individuals or foundations seeking answers about life after death or religious philosophy. This work yielded, certainly, valuable understanding of the unconscious structure of the psyche and other dimensions. "In the Communist countries, people accept parapsychology in a much more 'down to earth' way as a field of potential scientific significance," says Dr. Ryzl. The motivation is more mundane.

Our intention has not been to assess the many-pronged and in some cases extraordinary psi exploration in the West. Libraries of books have been written on it and more will undoubtedly come as work in the field picks up speed. We've simply tried to assess Soviet psychic research and the areas in which they seem to surpass us.

Trying to probe Soviet ESP and "what it all means" is extremely complex. The Soviet Union is simultaneously a country of both backwardness and stupendous progress. As more and more aspects of ESP in Russia began to unfold to us throughout the trip, we couldn't help thinking of a comment made by American impresario Sol Hurok. Famous for bringing Russian entertainers to the West, Hurok explained, "If it would be easy, everybody would be doing it." Somehow it seemed applicable to trying to understand the nature of telepathy and what the Soviets were doing in ESP. As George Kennan, former U.S. ambassador to Russia, says, "There can only be degrees of ignorance about Russia."

"One conclusion seems justified," says Dr. Ryzl, a former member of the Czech Academy of Science. "Parapsychology in the Communist countries and especially in the USSR occupies a strong position. We can expect it to be developed with determination." [382]

Prominent German parapsychologist Dr. Hans Bender, head of the Psychology Department at the University of Freiburg, has made many visits to Soviet ESP labs. As early as 1964 he told writer Norma Lee Browning, "I think the experiments in telepathy behind the Iron Curtain may be more significant than we realize." [405]

A foremost American physicist, Dr. Joseph H. Rush, referring to Vasiliev's work, wrote, "If this [Soviet] book does not spark some new lines of research in the West, the loss will be ours." [370]

The secrecy surrounding some Soviet research makes an accurate assessment difficult. However, the Soviets do seem to be many years ahead of us in certain areas of technical parapsychology. They are ahead of us in discoveries about the physical essence of the human being and how psi functions in and through us. They are ahead of us in concentrating effort on uncovering the basic energy behind psi. They are ahead of us in attempts to control certain varying factors like the influence of magnetic weather during psi tests. They seem to be ahead of us in seeking out and creating conditions that unlock the psi potential present in every human being.

There's no point in saying to American parapsychologists, "Why have you let us fall behind?" If anything, it's the pure scientists in the West who have let us down. The men and women who have devoted themselves to psychic research have been criticized and condemned enough. They don't need catcalls, they need help. They need money, well-equipped and well-staffed labs, they need recognition, they need new blood. They need to attract young, highly trained, sensitive people from all areas of science, medicine, and the humanities into parapsychology.

Wake up America? We're told that on every other newscast about a hundred different dangerous problems. But parapsychology is more than a "problem." It is a realm of new understanding. As Neil Armstrong told a joint session of Congress, "We're entering the Age of Aquarius which has so much meaning to the younger generation." The probes of psi research are part of that new age. It looks like we will have to one day back into an ESP race, the way we backed into the space race. There are bright and dark compellings in the race for outer space—benefits and knowledge to be won for people everywhere, military advantages to be exploited. The same mixture of light and dark fuels the inner space race in Russia.

"We come in the name of all humanity," said the first men on the moon. They were Americans. It seems to us the great exploration into inner space should be in the name of all humanity too. This is something the Soviets we met hope for and worry about. It would be too bad if America lost its chance to explore a vast living unknown by default. Soviet breakthroughs in psi research are in physiological and technological areas largely ignored in the West. Their researchers are hampered by political restrictions from investigating much of the fine work that is being done in the West. It seems to us that America stands to contribute the most by bringing the two halves of psi research together to make a whole.

Dr. Khokhlov, who has lived in both the East and the West, says, "The fate of the world today depends on the common understanding by the whole human race of what a human being really is, and on enlarging the common notion of man."

The Soviets are opening up man's higher sense perceptions and the untapped potentials of the human mind. How America responds to the challenge and how the Soviets use these new-found powers of the mind could change the destiny of us all.

II

BULGARIA

21

VANGA DIMITROVA, THE BULGARIAN ORACLE

We finally arrived in the cool, clear land of Bulgaria with its rolling green mountains and its legendary coast on the Black Sea. Bulgaria is known, if at all in America, for its valleys of roses that supply attar for the world's perfume and also as the proud homeland of yogurt. But there's a lot more to Bulgaria.

One of the country's "valuables" right now is Vanga Dimitrova, the blind seeress of Bulgaria. Vanga, who lives near the Greek border in the small town of Petrich, is a great psychic, on a par with Gerard Croiset of Utrecht, Holland, and Jeane Dixon of Washington. Like them, she is famous in her part of the world and crowds of people seek her help. Vanga finds missing people, helps solve crimes, diagnoses disease, and reads the past. But her greatest gift is prophecy. This middle-aged blind woman foretells the future with astonishing accuracy. And she lives in a country wise enough to appreciate her.

Bulgaria has had six thousand years to grow wise. A country in the Balkan Peninsula, about the size of Tennessee, it is bordered by Romania, Yugoslavia, Greece, and Turkey. After Bulgaria's Golden Age in the thirteenth century it fell to the Turkish Sultans. The six-hundred-year brutal Turkish domination was finally thrown off with the help of Tsarist Russia less than a hundred years ago. Next came the wild, mixed up, famous Balkan intrigues that inspired an era of spy movies and, in real life, led to nothing but chaos and reversals on all fronts for Bulgaria. The Communists grabbed power in 1944. During the following period of political stability the really grinding poverty was eliminated, the illiteracy wiped out. Now there are dozens of universities, colleges, hospitals, and medical institutes. Today Bulgaria's eight million people are probably better off than people in many parts of the Soviet Union, though poorer than many of those in the other satellites.

Our search for the story of the amazing prophetess Vanga, and of psi itself in Bulgaria, began in the capital, Sofia, a five-thousand-year-old city that gives the impression of neither youth nor age. Sofia just *is*—like nature. Her people talk of *natural* things, like psychic ability, naturally, and with more unconscious ease than people we've met anywhere else. Once you get the feeling of the country, something near the lively, harmonious note of a Greek vase, you're not so surprised that tiny Bulgaria has the modern world's first government-supported prophetess, Vanga Dimitrova. And you're not surprised that the Bulgarians have moved into broad scientific psychic research more smoothly, it seems, than anyone else.

"Vanga Dimitrova has never been a stranger in my life. Even though I've never met her, she knew my life better than I did myself." The woman who made that comment had agreed to tell us about the part Vanga played in her life, to talk about seeing the future roll out like a tapestry, as if the threads of her life had been woven before she was born.

We headed out of the Grand Balkan Hotel to our meeting. In front of us, the central square rattled with taxis and convoys of red trolleys hooked trunk to tail. Across the square stood the fourteen centuries old St. Sophia Church. To our right, like the top third of a sunken quonset hut, was a literally underground church used during the Turkish oppression. Minarets of a mosque rose just beyond and a muezzin still called people to prayer. Behind us, in the center of the hotel courtyard, were the "not-quite" ruins of a Roman bath. A welter of time, a land of heroic age, a country focusing its twentieth-century knowledge on that still point in the eye of time—the blind psychic who foresees and foretells.

"As I told you, I never met Vanga. It was my father who went to her when I was still a child of twelve." The woman opposite us was in her mid thirties. She had style and she had a good government job. Slim-legged, auburn-haired, gray-eyed, she lit up in conversation. When you knew her better, you noticed that in off moments, when she sat waiting in a lobby or a café, she had the pensive look of a statue staring into some motionless pool.

"My father was a medical doctor and a committed materialist. He went to Vanga simply because he was curious. He wanted to see how the woman acted toward the people who came to her, if she was a conscious or unconscious fraud.

"At the time, Vanga lived in the village of Petrich, as she still does. She talked to the people in her house, a peasant's cottage really, pretty small and rough. She doesn't live grandly now, but it's much better than it was. When my father arrived, the courtyard was, as always, full of people waiting to be admitted to Vanga. She came to the door and called my father—by his pet name, one that was never used outside the family. She said she'd take him first because he was the one person in the yard who didn't believe in her in the slightest. Once he was inside, Vanga told him all sorts of things about his past. My father was married three times. She described the marriages correctly, told him details, private, small things that only he, not even his later wives, knew.

"Then Vanga started speaking about the future. My father, she predicted, would die in fourteen years, in 1958, of cancer. She also spoke about my younger brother and me. Of all his children, we were his favorites. Vanga said I would make a happy marriage but that my husband would die suddenly shortly after. I would be left with a baby to raise. She said I'd marry again and this would be a mistake. It would turn out badly for me. My brother's fate would be even worse, according to Vanga. He would be killed in a freak accident when he was in his twenties.

"This experience at Petrich shook my father profoundly. Vanga had described intimate scenes in his past very clearly and in great detail. What she predicted for my father and the rest of us wasn't exactly pleasant.

"My poor father was terribly upset when he got home. He had to talk about it with someone, so he confided in my stepmother. He told her everything, but made her promise never to reveal a word of it. But of course—you know how women are—not very long afterward she told the entire story to me. I don't know, maybe she felt she had to confide in someone too.

"Many years later, my father decided he had an ulcer. He was a doctor, he should have known better, but perhaps he wanted so hard to believe that he didn't have something worse that he misdiagnosed. He had two operations. The second time they just took a look and sewed him up. He died of cancer—in 1958, on the date Vanga had predicted.

"I got married. It was a good, happy marriage. I was even happier when my first child came. Then a few months later, unexpectedly, suddenly, my husband died—still a very young man. I did remarry and it did turn out disastrously. Now, I'm divorced. A few years ago my brother ran to catch a streetcar. He jumped on—but then something went wrong. He lost his balance and fell. He was killed.

"It all happened. Everything that Vanga said would happen to the three of us did happen. She was right, I can tell you that. But I can't tell you why. I was only a child, only twelve years old, when my father went to Vanga. My whole life was spread out for her to see. Why? Was it a plan, fate, something to do with reincarnation? Why could Vanga see this? Why?"

You felt the intensity behind her question. You knew she didn't expect you to have the answer, but you had the feeling she'd go on asking that "Why?" in case someday, someplace, there was an answer.

"I don't know if you believe in God," she continued. "I don't believe in the rituals of the church, or the dogma, or the kind of picture they paint of things. But I know there is *something*. When life goes well, I say, 'Thank you God,' and when it goes badly I say, 'Help me, help me.' But I still don't know what there is that made it possible for Vanga to see my life.

"It's probably because she took my father first that she was so accurate in her predictions for my family. She's always better at the beginning of the day. It takes its toll. She's often sick too. Poor Vanga. I don't hold a grudge against her for anything. She must have a very sad life."

Vanga Dimitrova is a peasant woman, near fifty, living with her sister in Petrich, a village in the hilly country where Bulgaria borders Yugoslavia and Greece. She is far from any kind of mainstream, but as a seeress Vanga has her own kind of mainstream. Vanga's life has unavoidably intertwined with the pains, pleasures, and experiences of the thousands who have appealed to her as a last resort and with the wars, revolutions, and misfortunes of her land. "It's a great comfort to me that I've been able to help some people," says this woman, who looks like the portrait of a folk oracle come to life. Vanga always wears black and, usually, the peasant woman's shawl around her head, both of which accentuate the face, round and sightless, not a tragic face, but a plain, unadorned human face that looks as if it's been exposed to all seasons. There is a quality of blunt endurance to her short figure and to her character as well. Vanga has given psychic readings to dozens of people at a stretch. She doesn't just tackle the country locals. The parade across her threshold also includes the best educated and the most worldly, who have come to Petrich out of curiosity or desperation. They include celebrities from the West—jet-setters and famous people seeking information from a psychic uninvolved with the politics and problems of the West.

The scientists who have worked with Vanga call her "an honorable woman." She is more than a "country wise-woman," they say. She is one of the major psychics alive today.

"She's often very sad about the things she foresees for people," one of the scientists told us. "Her psychic gift makes her unhappy. But, on the other hand, she can't live without it. She can't stop. It is the *modus operandi* of her personality." The knowledge that she has helped some, that she isn't just a useless blind woman put out to sun while everyone else works, seems to shore her up against the overload of unhappy "visions"—death, disease, murder, broken homes, failing careers—that relate to the people who tramp through her living room.

Vanga probably doesn't know that the predictions she made for our friend's father came true. She probably doesn't even remember that skeptical doctor and the scenes from his life, past and future, that lit up for her for a few moments. But, unfortunately for Vanga, some of her most dramatic and tragic prophecies have centered on people close to her.

Her brother Thomas gives this account. "During the bad war years Vanga helped many people. They came to her to find out what had happened to friends they'd been separated from, to find out about loved ones in battle. They came to ask if they would return if they went to fight. Vanga told them who would die and foretold which ones would return and when.

"Early in 1944, my brother Vasil and I decided to join the partisans fighting the Germans. We went to see Vanga to say goodbye. As soon as we appeared, she began to cry and said to Vasil, "You will die when you are twenty-three years old."

" 'You can tell that to somebody else,' Vasil said right back to her. 'I don't believe it, not a word of it.'

"We spent the spring and summer together in the hills fighting the Germans. Then in the autumn, we were separated. Vasil's unit attacked the village of Foukso. They blew up a bridge and killed several Nazis. Vasil was wounded and SS men captured him."

The Germans herded all the people in the town into the central church. Surrounded by machine guns, they could only watch mutely as the Germans marched Vasil down the aisle and propped him up. Shots erupted in the old church. Vasil pitched to the floor dead. "It was October 8, 1944, my brother's birthday. On that day he turned 23."

The date of your death. Vanga's uncanny ability to see even two decades into the future is the most unusual part of her psychic talent. Neither she nor those who consult her usually have any desire to know this particular bit of information. It comes gratuitously. If she does happen to see death date, she is, supposedly, almost always right. Vanga doesn't know why the fatal day is suddenly revealed to her. "To my great regret, as I came to see more and more of other people's lives, I also often came to see the dates of their deaths. Long before it happened. I foresaw the day my husband would die even though he was still in his thirties. I saw, too, that nothing could be done to save him. His name was Dimitri Georgeyev and he was a good and kind man, but unfortunately he became a drunkard. I think really it was all the people that insisted on coming to me, hundreds of people with troubles going in and out of our house, that drove him to drinking. He died, my greatest sorrow, on April 7, 1956, just as I had foreseen. From that day I've worn black clothes. And since his death I've not been called by his last name Georgeyev. I'm known as Vanga Dimitrova."

Vanga's prophetic ability may be sensitive to death because her first recorded prediction involved a very special death to her. When she was thirteen Vanga began to have bouts of blindness. "The thought of not being able to see for the rest of my life upset me terribly. My father and the whole family tried to help as much as possible. But it was in vain." After two unsuccessful operations, Vanga went blind again when she was nineteen. "My father was told that only a certain specialist could help, so he took me to him. But it didn't work out. Perhaps if we'd been wealthier, I would be able to see today."

Vanga's sister Lubka gives a fuller account. "My father traveled with Vanga to another town. The doctor at the hospital examined her and said that Vanga's sight might be restored if he operated right away. Then he asked my father for a great sum of money. Father was a migrant worker. He could only get work seasonally. He didn't have anything like the kind of money the doctor demanded—though I know he would have given it to help Vanga if he had it."

Vanga was to be blind. The father led his daughter home. When she got there, Vanga began whispering to her brothers and sisters that she feared their father would die soon. She said she knew it. They tried to soothe her. She was just imagining morbid things because she couldn't see, they said. But her father did die—on the exact day Vanga had specified. She had exchanged one kind of sight for another.

At that time Vanga lived in a village just outside of Bulgaria in Macedonia. People began to come to the family cottage. Could they talk to the blind girl? Would the seeress help them? Soon they came from neighboring villages. In the turbulent summer of 1941, Vanga made a prediction about an unexpected turn in her own life. She told her sister Lubka, "Soon a man in uniform from another country will come. He will be the man in my life." Lubka says now, "Of course, we thought that this time she was wrong. After all, Vanga was blind."

In the fall a young soldier with a handsome black mustache arrived from nearby Petrich in Bulgaria. It was Dimitri Georgeyev who came to find out who killed his brother, "I knew," Vanga remembers, "but I didn't want to tell Dimitri. I didn't want him to take revenge. He insisted. Finally, I made him swear he wouldn't do anything to the men. I told him generally who was involved, but not the specific two in the gang who actually committed the murder."

One of the men Vanga "saw" as a murderer eventually died in a street brawl. The other, years later, supposedly confessed on his deathbed that he'd killed Dimitri's brother. But that wasn't the real point of the story. The soldier Dimitri returned to Bulgaria. Demobilized a short time later he headed right back to Vanga's. At the door he said, "Vanga, I've come here to ask you . . ."

"I'm blind, I'm not for you," Vanga broke in.

"It doesn't make any difference. I want you to be my wife."

"So I gave in," Vanga says. She and Dimitri moved to Petrich across the border in Bulgaria. The people in Petrich had gained a seeress. Boris Gurov, a middle-aged farmer, immediately visited his new neighbor. His younger brother Nikola had disappeared in 1923 when he was only fifteen. The family searched everywhere, but no clues were ever found. It still nagged Boris.

"I see him. He's alive!" Vanga told him. "I see your brother Nikola in a great town in Russia. He grew up there. He's a scientist. But . . . he isn't there now. He's a slave to the Germans. He's in a camp. Don't worry though, he'll come to you early this spring. You can recognize him by the gray uniform. He'll be carrying two suitcases," Vanga added.

It was too bizarre. Boris couldn't buy the idea that his lost brother was a Soviet scientist, much less that he was in a concentration camp at that moment. Boris went home convinced that he'd never know the truth. As a curiosity, he related Vanga's fantastic tale to his family.

According to reports, two months later, on a spring morning at dawn, a stranger stopped wearily in front of Boris house. He set down two suitcases. He didn't look familiar to anyone in the village. He didn't look familiar to Boris when he went out to speak to the stranger. It was Nikola. The younger brother had returned after almost twenty years. Nikola substantiated Vanga's vision of him.

He had run away to Russia, eventually going through school there and becoming an engineer. When war came he was swept into the Red Army and soon captured by the Germans. In the camp, Nikola finally convinced the Germans that he was a Bulgarian, then officially allies of the Germans. The Nazis let him go. He walked home in his gray prison uniform.

Is this sightless woman, living in the wild Thracian hills that are referred to by Homer and Virgil, always right in her prophecy? Can she see the future as exactly as we switch on a television set? Not quite. Some days her psychic power doesn't work. Sometimes she's wrong. She gets no particular feeling that tips her off whether her predictions are right or wrong. But—and it's a very large but—Vanga Dimitrova is more than usually right. According to documentation done by scientists, she is right 80 percent of the time. Eighty percent of what she sees clairvoyantly of the past and of what she foresees of the future is right on target, and 80 percent is no mean score in the oracular annals.

Vanga is particularly expert at psychically giving people information about missing friends and relatives. During the war a Yugoslavian woman appealed to Vanga for news of her husband who'd been reported missing in action. "He's not dead," Vanga said. "He'll return soon." He did—and at the time Vanga predicted. The circle of her fame grew wider.

More recently a Bulgarian farmer journeyed some distance to Petrich. Could Vanga help find him his missing daughter? Quietly Vanga told him the girl had committed suicide, drowning herself in a lake not far from his home. The body was later recovered from the lake.

One day a woman appeared at Vanga's door already knowing the person she wanted information about was dead. Her sister had been buried fifteen years before. But what were the real circumstances of her death? "Your sister was killed by her own husband," Vanga told her. "He managed to set up a false alibi that he'd been in Sofia at the time." According to accounts, the homicidal husband was eventually found out.

In the realm of psychic detective work, Vanga, blind, sitting in her small home, was able to give the Bulgarian border patrol enough information to lead to the capture of a mountain desperado wanted for seven murders. Bulgarian newspapers report she is often used by police to solve crimes.

Vanga says she has no control over the mental images that form in her mind's eye. They have to come naturally. "I can't force them. They may be about the past, the present, or the future." She has no way of knowing which triad of time will suddenly light up for her.

A few years ago a Bulgarian novelist took the half-day drive from Sofia to Petrich. Vanga didn't answer his questions. Instead words tumbled out of her outlining in detail a book the writer had just completed, a manuscript he'd as yet shown no one. "It's a true story," Vanga said. "Except at the end. In the book you let the girl die, which was not so in real life. She's still living. You should change the end and tell the story truthfully. It will make a better book." Vanga had been so astonishingly right about his manuscript that supposedly the writer took her advice and let his heroine live. Reportedly, Vanga told the novelist he would take a long trip to Russia and would also have two close brushes with accidental death. In time, the report goes, these predictions did materialize.

These are a very few of the accounts that have made Vanga famous in Bulgaria. Vanga is literally and figuratively a national institution. A great many Bulgarians, when all else fails, appeal to Vanga. Very few of them, no matter how horrible her predictions, have tried to foist the wicked witch image on Vanga. People mention her with interest, usually with respect. "Those stories you've heard about Vanga Dimitrova are true," a young secretary in our hotel assured us. "She's a remarkable woman and deserves tremendous credit for all the people she's helped. My sister is trying to get an appointment to see her now. It isn't as easy as it was in the old days when you could just go line up in the yard and hope for the best. Now, you have to apply to a sort of committee they have there. They give you a date and it can be a long wait."

For foreigners the cost of a consultation with Vanga is about thirty dollars. For Bulgarians, the fee is around ten *leva* ($5.00), which for many Bulgarians is the equivalent of at least a day's wages. The money does not go to Vanga, but to the state. Vanga receives a small salary equivalent to about two hundred dollars a month from the government.

Scientists later explained that the committee was set up for three reasons: to keep Vanga from being overrun by thousands of visitors; to make proper records of her prophecies; and to interview those who come. This enables the scientists to follow up her predictions as the years go by.

What do Bulgarian scientists think of this blind oracle in their midst?

The Institutes of Suggestology and Parapsychology in Sofia and Petrich are staffed with some thirty scientists who have studied Vanga's phenomenal psychic abilities using the most modern, sophisticated electronic equipment. Their chief spokesman is Dr. Georgi Lozanov, director of both Institutes. Dr. Lozanov, a physician and psychotherapist for sixteen years and a practitioner of Yoga for twenty-five years, is the pioneer of parapsychology in Bulgaria. He is a celebrated doctor, famous not only in Bulgaria but also throughout the Communist bloc countries for his discoveries about the supernormal powers of the mind. His words carry weight in Bulgaria.

Dr. Lozanov stated publicly to the Bulgarian and Yugoslavian press, "The stories about Vanga Dimitrova are not fantasies, although some of them are exaggerations. She is extraordinarily talented."

A Yugoslavian writer asked Dr. Lozanov if Vanga was the most talented prophet in the world. "It's hard to say. Precognitive abilities are like poetry. Everything depends on training and often on being able to capture inspirations in words. Sometimes Vanga works in a minute, sometimes she takes several hours. Telepathy and, on occasion, fantasy are mixed into her predictions. Yet case histories seem to show that Vanga does read the future for those who go to her personally, and even for those who do not. She has psychic capacities way beyond those of either ordinary people or most other psychics." [205]

Vanga has been a personage to Dr. Lozanov for years. "I've known about Vanga since I was twelve or thirteen. I heard so much that when I was in my twenties I decided to go see for myself. A friend, Sasha Itrech, an assistant at the University of Sofia, went with me."

The two young researchers pulled their car off the road well before the outskirts of Petrich and started walking. They didn't want anyone to have a straw of information about them. Lozanov suspected Vanga might have spies spread through the village who tipped her off about new arrivals.

"We lined up with hundreds of others," Lozanov related, "and waited a full three hours before inching to the head of the line. We didn't even talk to each other. Why should we give any listeners clues? Finally it was our turn. Sasha went in first. Vanga began by telling him his first and second name. She told him where he was born and described the second floor corner apartment where he lived at that time. Then she told him his mother's name and identified the disease she suffered with. She told Sasha the date of his father's death and named the illness that had killed him. She gave Sasha all this information as if she was reading it from a book. Then she said, 'You've been married seven years, but you have no children. You will have a child one year from now.' This did happen exactly as she had predicted.

"Then it was my turn. As I came through the door Vanga said, 'Georgi, why have you come? You're a doctor who cures with hypnosis. You want to test me. Why have you come now? You're too early. You will come again some years from now.' She seemed to imply that serious scientific study of her prophetic talent might be possible at that time. I didn't say anything; instead I tried my first experiment," Lozanov says. "Using all my will power and the little telepathic ability I possess, I imagined that I was another man, a man I knew very well. She began to foretell, but it was wrong. And she told me so. Then she said, 'Go, I can't tell you anything.' "

Lozanov remarks, "My being able to block Vanga is a very interesting thing. It was the first bit of assurance I had for my hypothesis that Vanga gleaned what she told visitors from their own minds, telepathically." Lozanov didn't elaborate his idea or show its relation to prophecy. It's easy enough to assume that Vanga draws her knowledge of your past and present from your own mind—but the future? Perhaps the seeress doesn't get her knowledge from some big outline in the sky, but in certain cases anyway, we carry our destiny with us. This goes well beyond the idea of the logical outcome of present actions or thought. What is there in a twelve-year-old girl that leads logically to the death of her husband a decade later after the birth of their first child? Even if this "design" were in the girl, how does it attach to the father standing before Vanga?

Struggling to get some understanding of prophecy, many people have tended to think of time as something that rolls to us like a pageant on a conveyor belt. Perhaps the tableaux are already there, like those in a parade several blocks away. The prophets are compared to people on top of a building; they can see further. This gave rise to the idea of the "spacious present"—the idea that some can see more of the present than others. The work with Vanga indicates we might get a further glint of understanding if we switch our perspective. Perhaps there is a seed, a pattern in us that sometimes draws our future to us, just as the acorn draws the elements it needs to become an oak. The acorn has to become an oak, but does it have to become an old one, an oak with twenty branches, fifty branches? If it puts out a branch into a power line, it will be lopped off; if it puts one out in some other direction, it will remain.

To Dr. Lozanov's mind, the theories about Vanga's prophecy are not as important at this stage as is "tremendously hard work." "Whatever prophecy is, I am sure it can be and will be explained scientifically," he says. With case histories and documentation, the theories may begin to shape more easily when experience is collated. One central question is whether what Vanga foresees can be avoided. Are her words a warning or a decree?

It's a little easier to get some glint of understanding by looking at Vanga's psychic medical work. She may not be reading embryos of time locked in the reaches of our minds that we cannot usually tap, but she may well be reading information about our physical condition that is constantly being tabulated in our unconscious. Vanga is not a healer and she can't psychically prescribe a remedy. What Vanga can do, supposedly, is diagnose a disease or malfunction. She can predict whether the sick will survive or succumb to their maladies.

Twenty years have passed since Vanga told the young Lozanov to go; she could do nothing for him. But since then, as she predicted, the right time for investigation *did* arrive and she and Lozanov have done a great deal for each other. "In the last ten years I've had hundreds, probably thousands of conversations with Vanga. She came to trust me and agreed to work with me," Dr. Lozanov says. "I've done many, many tests and experiments with her. And I've checked her background personally, trying to document the past events she's revealed to people and the future she's predicted."

The cases Lozanov checked out reflect the wide range of Vanga's gift. "Twenty-five years ago a woman from a village in Macedonia lost her son; he disappeared. He was seen playing by a river. The townspeople searched all over, but there was no trace of the boy. Even his mother finally agreed there was no hope of finding him," Dr. Lozanov reported. "This was in wartime, before liberation. Twenty-two years passed. The woman happened to go to Vanga to find out about a disease that was bothering her. 'You'll be all right,' Vanga assured her. Then suddenly added, 'and your son will return as well. I see him with a gypsy. He's grown up. If you go tomorrow morning to a certain village, you'll find him.' The woman headed straight for the village Vanga had named. And there she *did* find her son as Vanga described him. He didn't recognize her as first, but as she talked over past events, he gradually began to remember. Today they are reunited." Lozanov visited them to document the story.

"Once I went to Petrich and found several peasants from the village of N. at Vanga's," Lozanov remembers. "They wanted to know why their bees kept dying. 'Why do you come to me?' Vanga asked them. 'It would be better if you took the poison out of the beehives.' The peasants left. Later I drove out and asked them if Vanga had been right. They said yes. She'd told them who'd put the poison in the hive and he confessed when confronted with her words."

Lozanov has in his bulging files the story of a chauffeur from one of the government ministries. The chauffeur went to see her out of curiosity. Vanga told him he wasn't a good man. 'If your wife knew what you're up to she'd leave tomorrow. But that is not so dangerous. There's trouble coming on the 11th of November this year. You'll be badly hurt, but you'll live.' The driver laughed and left. On the

11th of November he crashed and was hurt badly," says Lozanov.

Vanga has said, "I'm not afraid to tell people what I see, but generally I don't like to speak about marriage problems. I see a lot of things about married men and women. I want to help, and telling them much of what I see has happened and will happen wouldn't help them."

Dr. Lozanov has also looked into some of Vanga's more bizarre psychic feats. "Vanga visited a pregnant woman in the village of P. in south Bulgaria. She told her hostess that that child to come would be killed when it was a little more than an infant. And she pointed to the house where the future killer lived. It did happen. Afterward the militia arrested the killer in the house that Vanga had pointed out."

By the mid 1960s, people were flocking to Vanga from all over Eastern Europe and finally Western Europe. A few even arrived from Australia, America, and Canada. There were too many. She was being pressed to do as many as fifty readings a day. Like other great psychics, it looked like Vanga might be broken by her gift. Multitudes of the sick, the curious, the worried—they were there every day and often as the long line wound to its end, Vanga was in a daze, her speech slurred, her prophetic images coming through blurred and confused.

But in Sofia something else was happening in the mid sixties. The farsighted Bulgarian government had decided that clairvoyance and precognition were ripe and vital fields of scientific inquiry. The government founded the Institute of Suggestology and Parapsychology which, among other accomplishments, gave shelter to Vanga and shielded her from the more exorbitant demands made on her energies. She became, in 1966, a state-employed psychic. Today, in addition to her small government salary, she's been given two secretaries and a panel to interview applicants. In addition, to study Vanga scientifically, there is a government-supported, fully equipped and staffed parapsychology lab in Petrich, a branch of the large Sofia Institute.

A Communist government supporting and studying a prophet and clairvoyant seemed extraordinary to us. Some Western parapsychologists who'd visited Iron Curtain countries four or five years ago maintained Communists scarcely dared mention the "forbidden" topic of prophecy even in private conversations. A Westerner who'd brought up precognition at a Communist conference had seemingly shocked the delegates. Yet the government of Bulgaria was setting a world precedent in studying this phenomenon of psychic prediction. "How did this come about?" we asked Dr. Lozanov when we met him at the Institute of Suggestology and Parapsychology in Sofia.

Forty-three-year-old Lozanov, with a halo of graying, curly hair, sharply arched eyebrows, and warm dark eyes edged with smile lines, radiates a good-humored, deep concern for people. He is a compact, lithe man of medium height. Although he is a master hypnotist, he does not have the compelling glance of the stereotype hypnotist. His eyes, instead of piercing into you, draw you toward him. Georgi Lozanov laughs often and long—an ongoing laughter that seems to have escaped from the joke at hand into some realm of free-floating delight. Perhaps Lozanov has found some of the delight gurus are reputed to enjoy during his twenty-five-year study of the higher philosophical forms of Yoga.

After a short conversation with him it was understandable how he'd gained the confidence and cooperation not only of Vanga but also of scores of other psychics—often such temperamental, individualistic personalities that many researchers refuse to tackle people with towering psi talent. Lozanov has combined stringent self-development through Yoga with rigorous scientific training—an extraordinary combination which has given him deep insight and rapport with the phenomenal minds of psychics.

Dr. Lozanov smiled at our question about Bulgarian interest in the paranormal. "You must remember this is a very ancient country," he said. "It is the land of Orpheus."

Orpheus, known to us as the god of music and poetry, is reputed to have actually lived in the land which is now Bulgaria. According to legend, Orpheus was a great prophet, teacher, and musician and when he sang and played the lyre, the birds flew to him, the fish left water and sprang to him, the wind and sea became still, rivers flowed upward toward him, the trees and the very stones followed after Orpheus. And when he was set upon, his body torn to bits and scattered to the four winds, the severed head of Orpheus, borne on a river, sang on.

"We've had a long tradition of occult culture in Bulgaria," Lozanov continued. "Many people here have psychic experiences—perhaps it's the atmosphere," he smiled, "but it's not so unusual. This accounts in part for the openness, the willingness to look into parapsychology.

"Actually, everyone is psychic," Lozanov added. "But not everyone is able to use psychic talent in a practical way. Anyone can sing a few notes, but someone with a gift for music will develop their talent to a high level."

"How did the government become interested in psi?" we asked.

"I did work on precognition for twenty years," Lozanov said. "I researched about sixty-five paragnosts [psychics] in Bulgaria. I knew there would be a time in Bulgaria when scientists could go into this study.

"I worked with Vanga Dimitrova for about ten years. There were many difficulties and those were tough years. Basically, I had to prove she was really clairvoyant. About three years ago there was a commission on Vanga. I welcome commissions," he smiled.

Well-aware that acres of statistics can be argued away or ignored, test results and testimonials denied, logical arguments defeated, Lozanov decided to let the commission members judge for themselves and make up their own minds through firsthand experience and evidence. "I took the entire commission, one by one, to Vanga," said Lozanov. "Before we went, some of them came to me and said, 'Why are you wasting your time on Vanga? Why don't you leave this precognition business and stick to psychiatry?' I answered, 'We'll talk about this afterwards.'

"We were in luck that day. Vanga was in top form. She proved *very* clairvoyant." Afterward some commission members came to Lozanov and said, "We *must* experiment. We *must* look into this."

The commission reported favorably on Vanga and at the time of the thaw in the mid sixties, parapsychology was okayed. Institutes of Parapsychology were founded and funded. Other scientific groups, such as the Institute of Physiology, cooperated fully on ESP research.

"Our support is from the highest levels of government," said Lozanov, "the highest. The government has given us excellent conditions for our work. We never have to worry about money here. We can go ahead on any project, in any area of paranormal. Vanga is the first clairvoyant in the world to be put on the state payroll and our government has created good conditions for researching precognition." Lozanov said this with considerable pride—pride in Bulgaria and her remarkable people to whom Lozanov is extraordinarily dedicated.

The Bulgarians are to be congratulated for having the wisdom and courage to embark on so important and valuable a field of study as this probe into the veiled realms of human existence. Many of the lives of Bulgaria's eight million citizens have been touched by the prophecies of Vanga, whether they know her or not, and it is urgent to understand more of this phenomenon. Perhaps if the Parapsychology Institute's study of prophecy leads to a breakthrough, Bulgaria will one day be credited with bringing one of the greatest understandings of all time to the world.

"People have come from all parts of the globe to consult Vanga and for many years we've sent questionnaires to more than three thousand of them regularly, to check up on Vanga's predictions. Our research so far shows that 80 percent of what Vanga predicted is right.

"It would be very daring to say definitely, 'she is precognitive,'" Lozanov cautioned. "We must avoid early statements. The feeling here is, if precognition exists in a person, then we're not afraid of what that may imply philosophically. If precognition exists, we'll find explanations. In my personal opinion, not as director of the Institute, Vanga is a paragnost; she *can* predict the future, but not 100 percent."

In general, Communist scientists feel that paranormal happenings probably occur according to specific laws which can be discovered and worked out. The Communist definition of "materialism" includes the laws of scientific occurrences, and hence, if psychic events follow laws of behavior, they can be considered as "material."

Besides case histories, how else were they studying precognition?

Lozanov's reply was not surprising. It conformed to the major thrust of research into the paranormal throughout the Communist world: an effort to understand the basic energy behind the paranormal and the relation of this energy to the human body. "We are studying the energy fields around Vanga during precognition." Lozanov told us, "and the relation of prophecy to other forms of ESP." Lozanov and his colleagues are immersed in a total study of precognition—the whole woman and the whole panorama of her psychic pronouncements. "We have complete documentation, medical and otherwise, for every day of Vanga's life over the past few years," Dr. Lozanov told us. "Why does she have good and bad days? Are there medical factors involved in her obtaining totally accurate prophecies of the future? Do biological fields around her body affect precognition and clairvoyance? Does her brain function differently from other people's brains? What of her psychological make-up? These are just a few of the things we're looking into."

He continued, "It's not possible to study all these paranormal aspects of humans without bringing in many areas of science. That's why I believe a group of many different specialists is the best method of ESP research," said Lozanov. "Our Institute has a staff of thirty scientists, all from different specialties, who work together to study Vanga and psi in general.

"The pure scientist who works on ESP often doesn't understand the psychotherapeutic aspects. It's possible some of the more complex aspects of the human psyche and the laws of suggestion might escape his notice. Everything about a human being is not quite so simple as some of these pure scientists would like it to be. On the other hand, the psychologist or psychotherapist alone may not be able to elucidate technical problems in physics or electrophysiology. When all work together, as we do here in the Institute, we can prevent some mistakes and avoid taking many wrong turns. Of course, if a researcher ever stopped making mistakes completely, there'd be no development at all!" He interrupted his vivid, brisk staccato explanation with a laugh.

The Bulgarians believe firmly in a unified, interdisciplinary approach to psi. After all, the human being is not a machine chopped up into separate, insulated parts.

"We also try to keep a good atmosphere around Vanga to protect her. Other researchers may want to work with Vanga, but so far she only wishes to work with us," said Lozanov. It's a testimonial to the fact that Lozanov has better rapport with psychics than most scientists. There are only so many hours a day, and many good psychics feel they should help people in need rather than work in a lab at abstract, dull, or painful scientific tests.

We knew something of the kind of predictions Vanga makes—dates of death, accidents to come, the various fortunes of life. "Examining thousands of Vanga's prophecies for different people, don't you sometimes see an overall pattern for people from specific areas or countries?" we asked. "Wouldn't this give you some idea of future political events or natural catastrophes to come, like earthquakes?"

"Vanga makes no political predictions," he said with some finality. "She doesn't *want* to make political predictions, *only personal predictions.*"

"Well, what is prophecy?" we finally asked. He smiled and asked us to explain it to him. Instead we asked him how Vanga explains it. Do people carry traces of their own destiny? Does the story of the future come from some other plane, from discarnate spirits, as some people think?

"Vanga tells us she is shown pictures and hears voices. She tells people what she sees and hears. As scientists, of course, we have to be *very* skeptical about these voices, but that is how Vanga says she gets information."

Is there such a thing as fate, *karma,* predestination? Are some patterns of our lives fixed? If so, why is one person doomed to tragedy, another gifted with ease and happiness? Why should Vanga predict for a pregnant woman that the child she's carrying will be killed by a man who will be staying on such and such a street. Was it the destiny of this child to be born for the purpose of being murdered?

The thousands of Bulgarians whose lives have been touched by Vanga's prophecies have been brought up short by questions like these. Some Bulgarians we spoke with outside the Institute talk of reincarnation as a possible explanation; some turn to modern science for answers. Bulgarians have been forced to grapple with some of the mysteries of human existence. How to explain the destiny of a child—the destiny of a country like Bulgaria whose people were oppressed by brutal Turkish rulers for a torturous six hundred years.

Perhaps because of its millennia of civilization, perhaps because of the long centuries of oppression, perhaps because of the harmonious atmosphere of the land, Bulgaria's small population seems to have more psychics per capita than most other places. It has telepathists, clairvoyants, prophets, healers; psychic power is virtually a national resource.

"Our occult culture goes back to ancient times," Lozanov reiterated. "From the Renaissance, we've had mystic religious societies. The most powerful of these was similar to the Albigensians in France who were stamped out by the Inquisition. But here they survived and flourished. Understanding and acceptance of the psychic element in life has filtered through our culture. Many people in our country do have psychic experiences on many different levels. We have a good 'climate' for it. You've no doubt felt this on the Black Sea coast here. There is a very spiritual ambiance, a quality of harmoniousness there."

There *is* a special quality to the Bulgarian Black Sea coast that even the more calloused travel writers notice. The good "climate" is reflected in the open-minded attitude many Bulgarians have toward ESP. We were constantly surprised to find that Bulgarians we met by chance were well informed about psi and took it all as a matter of course. "Telepathy, oh yes," said one young man we met who studied English at the University of Sofia. "A professor of mine has often mentioned telepathy. We've had discussions on it and about Aladdin's Lamp, which he believes is linked to this phenomenon. He theorized that the story of Aladdin's Lamp may have been left over from a far more ancient and highly developed civilization than ours. He thinks the Lamp represented the harnessing of psychic power for practical purposes—a thing the later, more primitive people would have called magical."

A med student told us, "People like Vanga aren't new. The Greeks had Cassandra and the Oracles of Delphi. Prophecy has always been a question that has puzzled people. There was a case history I found of a woman who needed psychotherapy. She claimed she was a countess, a French countess, who had lived centuries ago in a certain château in France. She told the psychiatrists she wanted to be taken there. As an experiment they finally decided to go. She'd never been to France before. The woman knew all the rooms in the château and described them minutely before she was taken into them. She said there was a portrait of herself in a specific place. They located the picture, a portrait of a countess who'd lived there two hundred years ago, the woman she claimed to be. They looked up all the names she mentioned in old, out-of-the-way chronicles available only in France, and the names were all there. She even gave accurate descriptions of how the rooms had looked for specific receptions and state dinners. It was all correct.

"Reincarnation . . ." he said, "It's a very intriguing idea. There's another case that sticks in my mind about a man who dreamed he had built a palace hundreds of years ago, perhaps even a thousand years ago. He described the entire plan, the location, and so forth. The man was obsessed with his palace. The clinic suggested to an archeologist that he check the spot the man had designated. The archeologists began to dig. They found the palace. It was built exactly as the man had dreamed it.

"It makes you wonder, doesn't it?" the student asked.

Today Dr. Lozanov is lifting psi ability out of the realm of mysticism in his country and bringing strict scientific disciplines to bear on it in his labs. "It can all be explained scientifically," he says.

Returning to Lozanov's work with the Seeress of Petrich, we couldn't resist asking, "Does Vanga predict for you?"

"The first time I went to her as a young man is the only time Vanga ever predicted for me," he said. "Many people think she must predict for me all the time, but now you see her own life is very closely intertwined with events in my life and the progress of the Institute. It is very hard for her to predict for herself and therefore she does not predict for me either. Besides," he grinned, "I don't need predictions."

How did you become interested in psychic things? Were members of your family psychic?

"Oh no, none of my family had the slightest interest in parapsychology." Like many boys in Eastern countries where hypnotism was early accepted, Lozanov, with his natural gift for hypnosis, took to hypnotizing his school friends. One day he asked an entranced classmate, "What is our friend doing in another part of the city right now?" They checked the boy's reply. "He was right," Lozanov says. "My classmate demonstrated clairvoyance while in trance. This made me think. I became interested in parapsychology and Yoga and I studied psychology and psychiatry at the University of Sofia."

Lozanov has traveled throughout the world in connection with his work in parapsychology and suggestology, not only within the Communist bloc countries, but also to India, Europe, Britain, America. In every country he has sought clues to the understanding of clairvoyance and precognition. He has been able to establish a warm rapport with some of the greatest prophets and clairvoyants in the world. They include some of the most famous yogis of India and Croiset of Holland, who will cooperate with him on a joint research project. Jeane Dixon of Washington, may visit Bulgaria in the near future. "Perhaps some day we will have a conference of prophets," Lozanov says with a long laugh.

Many reports and case histories involving Vanga were published in Bulgaria and recently in a five-part series in the Yugoslavian magazine *Svet,*[53, 205] but so far the scientific data has not been released. "When will you publish the research you've done on Vanga over the past ten years?" we asked.

"Perhaps in another year or so, we *may* publish. It depends. Since the authority of the Institute is involved, we're not really going to say absolutely definitely that she can predict the future," Lozanov said. "We'll say the material *suggests* paranormal abilities and then an explanation won't be needed as yet." When this study is published it will be the most extensive, detailed, all-inclusive, and (after meeting the people involved) probably the most creative study ever done on a living prophet.

Vanga is an ongoing research project for the Bulgarian scientists. But so far their careful study indicating that Vanga is 80 percent correct in her prophecy lends fire to the Bulgarian belief that Vanga is a major psychic. Vanga's 80 percent is even more astonishing because it is a scientific calculation of day by day predictions, not just a few big ones published now and then. And Vanga's triumph of foreseeing is built on specific events predicted for people she rarely knows, people who are not famous. There is perhaps less question about the purity of the psychic element in Vanga's kind of prediction than in prophecies of war in certain areas, the downfall of a world leader, the divorce of a famous movie star. The mounting sweep of evidence indicating that the blind woman of Petrich can and often does see the future makes you think, if nothing else, that we might not know quite as much about ourselves and the world we live in as textbook science implies.

Vanga has been a seeress for over thirty years. She's been blind to the everyday world as long. She can't see the beauties that abound in her land, the clear blue-green of the sea, the long rows of the sunflower crop growing tall and top-heavy, the "treasure hordes"—gold bowls, cups, jewelry that fascinates, gleaming since the third millennium B.C. And she can't see the new things that would probably seem more unusual to her—the miniskirts swinging along, the toy rocket ships, the EEG machine the scientists use on her.

But Vanga in her troubled life, like Bulgaria itself, seems to have made a special arrangement with time. She sees through time clearly. With her sightless eyes she sees, now and then anyway, what the rest of us look to blindly.

22

MISSION CONTROL CENTER FOR THE MIND

Investigation into the mysteries of the mind is thriving today in Bulgaria, but until the mid 1960s few Westerners had a chance to learn much about it or to immerse themselves in Bulgaria's magnificent heritage or even to catch more than a glimpse of its lovely countryside as they sped through the land on the "Orient Express" heading for Istanbul. Then Bulgaria, which seems to live on its own ancient internal rhythms, decided to open to the world again. In 1959 Bulgaria reestablished diplomatic relations with the United States and gradually went into the tourist industry.

As the barriers vanished and hospitality reasserted itself, we discovered that ESP research had been going along quietly in Bulgaria.[108, 166] The first question almost anyone might ask is, why? Considering the needs of this small country, why would resources and energies be channeled to psychic studies? The answer, once you investigate, is obvious: it's useful. Bulgarian inquiries into the unknowns of the mind have already brought a bumper crop of new understanding that's been put to work in psychotherapy, medicine, education, and rehabilitation.

The highly intelligent force behind many of these breakthroughs is Dr. Georgi Lozanov, who heads the Institute of Suggestology and Parapsychology. In the capital of Bulgaria, on a quiet, shaded street five minutes' walk from Sofia's central square, stands the headquarters for this new investigation of the mind—a freshly remodeled, attractive three-storied charcoal gray building on Budapest Street. We walked past the wrought-iron fence and a few casual beds of roses.

Inside the wood-paneled, books-lined reception room we were met by Mrs. R. Dimitrova (no relation to Vanga), Executive Secretary to Dr. Lozanov. "She's my right hand," he says. "She seems to know even before I do what I'm going to do next." We'd corresponded with Mrs. Dimitrova for a number of years and she'd gone out of her way to help us with translations and in locating published material on Bulgarian work. She told us in French, "It's because everyone here is so enthusiastic that they've accomplished so much." Then, explaining that she herself had just returned from a long trip to Ethiopia with her engineer husband, Mrs. Dimitrova introduced us to Franz Tantchev, information officer for the Institute, a slight, soft-spoken man with a pleasant shy smile.

They both toured us through the center and introduced us to the staff. Reflecting Lozanov's team approach to the exploration of the mind, his staff is made up of thirty scientists in varying specialties. "I have wonderful colleagues," Lozanov told us later. "They are very creative, very fine people." There are physiologists, engineers, doctors, physicists, education specialists, and psychologists who seem to work with amazing compatibility despite their vastly different approaches to psi. There are also special labs at the Institute for the study of parapsychology; for the study of the physiology of subsensory stimulation, and a third section investigating the psychology of suggestion, i.e. suggestology.

Each lab was overflowing with sophisticated electronic apparatus for physiological research. We estimated that equipment in a single room—much of it imported from Italy—probably cost over $100,000, and there were many labs. They had EEG machines, some with twelve-track channels, some eight-channel portable ones, there were video recorders, electrocardiograph instruments, oscilloscopes, special photographic equipment, photic stimulators, special rooms entirely encased in wire mesh like large Faraday cages.

"We use the portable electroencephalographs to study various clairvoyants we're working with," Mr. Tantchev explained. Supposedly they are also using EEG equipment that measures brain waves at a distance from the head, rather than with electrodes attached to the scalp. "The equipment in some of these other labs is used to try to find out exactly what happens in the brain when memory is expanded," Tantchev said.

The building in a rose garden in Sofia is a sort of mission control center for exploring the whole person. There, ESP is not considered to be just a psychological happening as it often is in the West, or just a physiological one as it often tends to be in the Soviet Union. The Bulgarians have brought the investigation of mind and living matter under one broad roof.

Dr. Lozanov orchestrates the most diverse psi research. The Institute has explored the basis of Yoga, PK, suggestion, and eyeless sight. They're studying the nature of sleep and monitoring dreams through rapid eye movements. They've explored everything from the impact of cosmic influences on telepathy to the power of mind on plants. (It made the plants grow three times higher.) They knew about the astonishing work of the American Cleve Backster, who uses lie detectors to monitor "telepathy" with plants. The Bulgarians are setting up tests to duplicate his work in their labs. They've studied mental wizards with computer-like minds who are able to calculate faster than electronic machines. In one lab they were investigating telepathy in twins, checking out reports that somehow an artificially created brain wave pattern in one twin is sometimes reflected in the second twin isolated in another room.

A short, referenceless magazine article in the West had announced that Mikhail Drogzenovich, a fifty-three-year-old farmer from the Bulgarian village of Stara Zagora could supposedly levitate—lift himself off the ground without any visible means of support. Before "scientific witnesses," the item read, the husky farmer closed his eyes and sat down in a field. After intense concentration, he apparently slowly began to rise in the air until he was about four feet above the ground. His eyes remained closed, thereby ruling out mass hypnosis of the observers. He sat in the air some ten minutes while witnesses checked that there was no rope, equipment, or mechanical devices connected to the hovering Drogzenovich. Then the farmer slowly settled back to earth. "Once I'm in the air," he was quoted as saying, "I'm unable to change my position. I get there by will power."

When we were introduced to some of the scientists on staff (who coincidentally were in the midst of studying the discoveries about brain waves made by the Leningrad mathematician Dr. Genady Sergeyev), we asked them about any work on levitation. If they'd ever heard of Mikhail, the hovering farmer, they didn't admit it. But they did say Dr. Lozanov had photographed a number of yogis in India who seemingly could defy gravity and levitate for short periods.

"The yogi he studied and filmed," they said, "could levitate while he was lying down. It seemed to us that he had somehow trained the muscles in his back to make him sort of bound or jump into the air. His whole body rose horizontally several centimeters, but he only stayed up one second."

In the Institute's library Mr. Tantchev showed us some of the new acquisitions and international journals. They have a translation department to keep them posted on all relevant research done by foreign scientists in all parts of the world.

There's something contagious about curiosity, openness, plans for exploring any kind of unknown. The allure of exploring the reaches of mind, the potentials of the human being, seemed very strong at the Sofia Institute. The Institute of Suggestology and Parapsychology, which is entirely government-supported, is more than just a research center, however. The Institute is affiliated with Bulgarian universities and has the power to confer doctorates in the natural sciences for completion of a Ph.D. program which includes training in parapsychological research. Dr. Lozanov stresses he is interested in setting up a student exchange program with any similar institute in the West.

SUGGESTOLOGY

Suggestology is a new "ology" more or less devised by Dr. Lozanov. It's a whole new kind of mind expansion. In Bulgaria it always goes along with parapsychology. Suggestology is the scientific study of suggestion. It is a method of reaching and making use of the unknown reserves, powers, and abilities of the human mind. It overlaps with parapsychology.

Many scientists when confronted with a paranormal occurrence fall back on the catchall, nonexplanatory explanation, "Suggestion." Lozanov decided to look at this "so-called suggestion" and to try to discover how it works. Through extensive experimental research he has discovered laws of suggestion which he has applied in many fields from medicine to education. Suggestology is *not* hypnosis. With suggestology you are always in the waking state and aware of everything around you.

"I don't think you can research parapsychology without knowing something about the laws of suggestion," says Lozanov. "ESP and suggestion are very closely related. It's true some apparently paranormal happenings really are suggestions in the waking state. But on the other hand, our experiments show we can increase people's ESP abilities with suggestion. The best way is to start with suggestion—so much more is known about it—and then work toward ESP.

"I had many extremely interesting conversations about suggestology with yogis in India on my recent trip there," he said. "After talking to them I felt that what I call 'the suggestive state,' rather than specific Yoga exercises, may be the key to their paranormal powers."

Speaking of what has already proved, in part, highly practical research going on at his institute, Lozanov maintains, "These new sciences of parapsychology and suggestology have many practical applications. Telepathy is an inexpensive and promising communications system for space and underwater exploration. The parapsychological phenomena can be applied to pedagogy; it can overcome language barriers; it can help in rehabilitation to overcome defects of speech, hearing, sight, and in psychology and medicine; it can give us new and very rich material for familiarizing ourselves with secret and unknown possibilities of the human personality." [66]

HEALING WITH THOUGHT

Dr. Lozanov has instituted a large-scale program of "mental healing" in Bulgarian medical clinics. "Your thoughts can 'nourish' illness," says Lozanov. "The lives of many people are full of fear—fear of death, fear of catastrophes, fear of disease, fear of life, fear of fear. . . . How few of these are really justified! Fear creates tension and poisons the climate of one's life. Life should be a ceaseless stream of happiness. But it is impossible to be happy when you are fanatically attached to things which sooner or later you must lose."

Lozanov believes the secret of physical health and longevity lies not only in exercise and the physical state of the body but also in the psychological make-up of the individual. His system of mental therapy is aimed at building up a solid psychological barrier against illness in the patient's mind. The basis of his healing system is Yoga.[222]

Yoga speaks of a vital energy called "Prana" which circulates through the body and says that thought can direct this energy, just as thought directed the energy photographed by the Kirlians. Dr. Lozanov says, "The 'miracles' a yogi achieves can be explained by the vital role played by the cerebral cortex and the force of thought or suggestion: the yogi can anesthetize himself using his thought, he can help staunch the flow of blood, he can simulate death, he can affect the walls of the heart, the blood pressure, breathing metabolism, and so on."

He explains that the interplay of the yogi's thoughts with his body can determine health, peace of mind, and longevity. If a person has some illness, he must not think of it with terror because his thoughts of fear will aggravate the disease still more. To help restore a patient's physical and mental balance, Lozanov starts not with an attempt to remove any specific symptom but with the yogic principle of deep relaxation to erase tension and fear. "It's not so much healing as it is teaching the art of living," he says.

At the Trade Union Sanatorium at Bankya in Bulgaria, a typical group session in mental healing begins with Lozanov explaining how it's possible for the mind to help heal the body. Then the psychotherapist's calm, melodious voice addresses the relaxed but fully awake patients. "Relax! deeply, deeply . . . there is nothing troubling you. Your entire body is fully relaxed. All your muscles are at rest. You are able to overcome all difficulties." After about twenty minutes of positive suggestion while the patients relax, Lozanov concludes, "You feel completely well. You sleep well; you have a good appetite."

Finally a singer begins with a melodic recitation of well-loved poetry. "It's important to fix your sights on an elevated goal to stimulate you toward creative pursuits," says Lozanov. The healing suggestions seem to catch the attention of one's innermost thoughts, according to the patients.

Among the sick there are cases of people suffering from functional disorders of the nervous system as well as various neuroses and allergies. The sanatorium officials testify that many are cured after a few sessions of positive thought patterning—the process Lozanov calls "suggestology." They cite many case histories. Tsonka M. had a neurosis for several years which had not yielded to treatment by a series of doctors, but after a few sessions of mental healing or "suggestology" she is well and fully healthy. Dobrinka P. suffered from a form of diabetes; she drank up to forty quarts of water a day. After a number of psychotherapy sessions with suggestology she is well again. "Many former patients make special trips out to the sanatorium to thank Dr. Lozanov," say the officials.[165]

Lozanov began this form of mental healing when he worked in the Department of Psychiatry of the Medical Postgraduate Institute headed by Professor Emmanuel Sjarankov. Bulgarian psychotherapists affirm that this healing method can be applied to many types of illnesses. Suggestology is already widely used in many of the country's neurological and psychiatric institutions.

Dr. Lozanov believes his mental therapy method is not only a great boon for psychotherapy but also a valuable tool for the surgeon. "The mind can anesthetize the body," says Lozanov. "Anesthesia by the mind is superior to using drugs. Not only does it make surgery painless, it decreases blood loss, speeds healing of the incision, reduces danger of infection, and there are no aftereffects. The first major operation performed with Lozanov's method of "thought anesthesia" took place in Bykovo, Bulgaria, on August 24, 1965. It made world medical history.

The patient, a fifty-year-old gym teacher, came to Lozanov's office. "I've heard that you can provoke anesthesia with the mind," he said. "I'd like to try it for my operation." Lozanov had already used this method for minor surgical procedures—small incisions and dental work. This patient required complex abdominal surgery for a large inguinal hernia. The operation would be difficult and would take at least an hour. Lozanov agreed to do it with thought as an anesthetic.

"I met the patient several times and explained my method to him. He was, I found, a highly educated man. I told him that this was *not* hypnosis: 'You will be fully conscious throughout the operation. It's *not* auto-suggestion. I will guide you the entire time.'"

Dr. Ivan Kalpov and Dr. Vasily Tanev would perform the operation. It would be fully televised and filmed for medical study. Lozanov explained his technique to the surgeons, then as nurses wheeled the patient into the operating theater, Lozanov began his thought suggestion on the patient.

As the surgeons cut a two inch incision through skin and muscles, the patient felt nothing, was fully conscious, and spoke calmly to the masked figures around the table. The surgeons cut out the sac of the hernia, then began to suture. The patient didn't flinch. He joked over the sound of the metallic clink of the instruments. Afterward he remembered clearly each step of his operation. Lozanov suggested that he decrease blood circulation to the operated area and there was virtually no blood loss. He suggested after the wound had been stitched that it would heal rapidly and without infection.

"I feel fine," the patient reported as he was wheeled back to his bed.

"There was virtually no pain during the fifty-minute operation or *after* the operation," said the director of the hospital, Dr. M. Dimitrov. "The incisions on this man healed much faster than usual." [233]

This operation using Georgi Lozanov's suggestive anesthetic (not hypnosis, they insist) made headlines in the Communist bloc countries. They had long been familiar with the use of hypnosis in medicine, but this is supposedly something different. Outside doctors, particularly from Poland, flew to Bulgaria to investigate and learn the techniques of medical suggestology. Since then, many operations have been performed using the Lozanov method of psycho-anesthesia on a fully conscious patient. "We believe the technique of waking suggestion will continue to find a wider and very useful place in practice of medicine," the Bulgarians say.[49, 147]

Lozanov's bold use of suggestology in psychotherapy and medicine aroused criticism—in particular, criticism of the hernia operation. "There was a commission," said Lozanov with a smile. "About a thousand doctors attended a conference to see movies of the operation, dispute, and discuss the procedure. At the end of the discussions I brought out the patient. He told them how satisfied he was. Three years later he's in splendid condition. What could the opposing doctors say to this man?" The film of the operation and a report on it were also presented at an international medical congress in Rome in September 1967.

PARAPSYCHOLOGY: TEACHING THE BLIND TO SEE

With the emphasis on applied parapsychology in Bulgaria, Lozanov borrowed the Soviet technique of skin sight to help the blind. Whether or not the reasons why it works are known, skin sight exists and we can use it to help people right now, he feels.

"To exclude any question of fraud and to be sure the experiments were totally reliable, I worked with sixty children who'd been blind from birth or had gone blind in infancy."

Even though they were blind, for additional insurance, their eyes were blindfolded and during most of the experiments an opaque screen was placed between the face of the child and the object examined. Over four hundred tests were done in 1964. Out of the sixty youngsters Lozanov tested, three immediately showed the ability to distinguish colors and geometrical figures by skin sight without any training. Even when the scientists concealed the patterns and colors behind glass, these three children could identify them.

"But the most important factor," says Lozanov, "is that the remaining fifty-seven children could be *trained* to learn skin sight." After several training sessions, the children gradually learned to distinguish one color from another, although they'd never seen color and had to be told the names of what they sensed. They said, "I can tell a difference, but I never knew what it was."

"Little by little, these blind children were trained to know colors, geometrical figures, and even to read," Lozanov reported in the science and technology section of the journal *Narodna Mladej.*[128] The children demonstrated their ability at a scientific meeting before physicians, psychiatrists, and psychotherapists. The examinations showed that skin vision could be trained, but just like other talents the limits of ability varied with each child. The full details of these tests are published in Lozanov's book *Suggestology and Suggestopedia.*[112] Lozanov later told us that Bulgaria's famed blind prophetess Vanga Dimitrova had also learned skin sight to help herself overcome her blindness.

SUPERNORMAL POWERS OF THE MIND REVOLUTIONIZE EDUCATION

One of the most powerful keys to many problems we face today can be expressed in one word—education. Education can help us overcome poverty, help underdeveloped countries produce food and materials. Education can help solve potential war situations by raising living standards; it can teach us something about each other and give everyone a head start in life. But for education as we know it to do this would require decades, perhaps generations. We don't have time. Even with time, education as we know it often can't penetrate the minds of the disturbed or retarded, and sometimes can't even overcome the intense boredom of the intelligent.

What if it were possible to transfer information without the circuitous paths of present ways of teaching? What if a teacher could teach a student beyond the normal capacity of his mind by "broadcasting" over the defense mechanisms of the normally unused 90 percent of the brain? A technique that could break through the barrier in the mind that prevents us from making use of the major part of our intellectual capacities would be revolutionary.

But that's exactly what Dr. Lozanov believes he has created—a teaching method that speeds up learning fifty times, increases retention, requires virtually no effort on the part of the students, reaches retarded and brilliant, young and old alike, and requires no special equipment. It sounds fantastic, but the Bulgarians have thousands of controlled test results to prove they've found such a method. At the Institute of Suggestology and Parapsychology, records reveal that hundreds of people from all levels of society learned entire two-year language courses in as little as twenty days. Small experimental groups are mastering courses in basic mathematics, physics, chemistry, and biology in a matter of weeks.

"It's not hypnosis or sleep learning. It's far more practical than that. The student is fully awake and in complete control of himself," says Dr. Lozanov. It's a kind of mind to mind contact between teacher and student, based on Yoga techniques, and Lozanov calls it, "Suggestopedia."

In a typical classroom at the Institute, twelve people —students, housewives, laborers, professional people, old and young—relax in reclining chairs that resemble airplane seats. The room looks more like a lounge than a classroom. The lighting is subdued to enhance the calming effect. The students are listening to music, gentle soothing music. They look as if they were at a concert, completely wrapped up in the harmony of sounds.

In actuality this is a French lesson. Against the background of Brahms or Beethoven, the voice of the teacher seems sometimes businesslike, as if ordering work to be done, sometimes soft and calming, then unexpectedly hard, commanding. Her voice repeats in a special rhythm, on a special scale of intonation, French words, idioms, and their translations. But the students aren't really listening. They've been warned *not* to pay attention, not to think about whether they hear the teacher. "Relax. Don't think about anything." Their conscious minds are to be totally occupied with the music.

The next day surprised students discover that even though they were sure they'd learned nothing, they remember and can easily read, write, and speak from 120 to 150 new words absorbed during the two-hour session. In the same way the toughest part of the language course, the grammar rules, painlessly take root in the minds of music-lulled students. Within a month students with no prior knowledge of a language have accepted two to three thousand vocabulary words and have a good grasp of the grammar. Tests a year later show they still know all the material learned in this incredibly effortless way.

How does it work? Lozanov based his method, which can help you learn five to fifty times faster, on the Yoga technique of relaxation—*Savasanna.* Using suggestion and autosuggestion, muscle tension is relaxed and the brain relieved of the usual anxieties and stresses. In this relaxed "free state of consciousness," or meditative state, fatigue quickly vanishes. Freed from all distractions which hamper its functioning, the brain resembles a sponge able to absorb knowledge of all kinds. The secret of the technique is that material dosn't reach the memory in the ordinary way, because the student doesn't participate consciously in the process. Instead, the student has "a calm, intuitive perception of the material presented."

During the time the teacher intones words against a musical background, there seem to be distinct physiological changes in the body and changes in the brain waves. The alpha rhythm of rest predominates in the brain. Memory and intelligence show improvement for some time after a suggestopedia session.

Suggestology has begun to reveal something about the marvelous nature of memory itself. "Man's brain remembers a colossal quantity of information—even how many steps it took you to walk to the bus stop. These 'unknown perceptions' show us the subconscious has startling powers. There's nothing supernatural about expanding memory or receiving telepathic information," according to Lozanov.

Science has long known of individuals with super memories like Mikhail Kuni in Russia, who at a glance can remember a page full of material, verbatim. Lozanov's suggestology, it seems, is capable of giving many of us jet speed memories.

Once the mind is opened in this reverielike state, Lozanov found that the capacity to remember seems almost boundless, there is no apparent cutoff point. "It's as easy to remember one hundred words as fifty. We decided to see how far we could go and formed classes of volunteers. In a single session of only fifteen minutes we taught fifteen lessons from a French grammar book containing about five hundred new words. Immediately after, we gave a written test and three days later another test. The results were excellent—extraordinary. All the words had been retained," Lozanov says.

In *Suggestology and Suggestopedia* Lozanov reports results of some of these tests with complete scientific data. With suggestopedia the Bulgarians have expanded time in a very real sense, teaching you in a minute what usually takes many weeks to learn. Anything this good sounds like it must be illegal or unhealthy. "There's no strain at all," students testify; "you don't get tired mentally or physically." Many pupils attend evening courses at the Institute after a long, full work day. They often arrive tired, sometimes with headaches. "The meditative sessions leave you feeling great, wonderfully refreshed and invigorated," both students and attending scientists assert. "It even cures headaches." Lozanov adds that, unlike hypnosis, this new method of the mind can be used on anyone. Medically trained personnel are not necessary, regular teachers are used, and there are no psychological or legal problems as there can be with hypnotism.

Suggestopedia has worked wonders for some time in Bulgaria. In the early 1960s Lozanov perfected his method. Then more years of tests were carried out at the Medical Postgraduate Institute, the Science and Research Institute, and the Institute of Pedagogics. Lozanov's assertion that he could improve a person's memory capacity by more than 50 percent using suggestology immediately aroused a yammer of protest from the skeptics. Rather than debate endlessly, sparring with reams of statistics, he used the personal approach. "There was a commission."

Lozanov gathered the commission members in a Sofia hotel. There, each day, they relaxed in a state of waking reverie and listened to language lessons. At the end of several weeks, despite many firm beliefs that they couldn't learn a thing in this effortless fashion, they emerged fluent in a foreign language they'd not known before. What could they say? They'd learned despite themselves. In 1966 the Bulgarian Ministry of Education founded the center for suggestopedia at the Institute of Suggestology and Parapsychology. It teaches regular classes and studies physiological and psychological processes responsible for this phenomenal expansion of mind and memory.

"We're still exploring, still experimenting, still changing the method," said Mr. Tantchev. "Every day we discover new things about how suggestopedia works. Classes now run four hours a day: two hours for the suggestion session, one hour for the practice and tests, one hour for new material. Students come six days a week for three months. At the end of that time they have the equivalent of a two- or three-year course, a six-thousand-word vocabulary, and a complete grasp of grammar. They can read, write, and *speak* fluently. Tests a year later show students retain all they learned in this course.

"The next course begins in October," said Franz Tantchev, a specialist in languages. "You should come back and see us then. If you took the course, you'd really understand why we're so excited about it."

Over fifteen hundred people from all walks of life, ages ten to seventy, have taken the program at the Institute. Another five thousand are on the waiting list. University students in particular constantly phone, begging to be let into the program. "This interest is easily understood considering the results," said a linguistics professor from the University of Sofia, now herself a practitioner of the method.

If you've ever tried to learn a language or cram your head full of the basic facts necessary for any discipline, suggestopedia sounds too good to be true. But it *is* true. The Bulgarians have volumes of tests and graphs and multilingual students to prove it. You *can* lean back, relax, listen to music, and learn without effort and without even realizing it. "The possibilities of using suggestopedia on a mass scale are very promising," Lozanov says. "It's inexpensive and ideally exportable."

Right now we need a leap into bold new ideas and methods that work in education even more than we need to develop the intuitive side of our nature. Suggestopedia could be a real head start; it could catapult the undereducated ahead in a year instead of a decade. Perhaps it will do away with the old "environment-versus-heredity" argument about the limits of human potential because suggestopedia by-passes the conscious limits of the mind and opens up its vast powers. College students are rattling the universities refusing to put up with centuries old, obsolete, life consuming ways of learning. Suggestopedia could help demolish "fact factories." With basic knowledge quickly and painlessly instilled, schools could increasingly become places of creative teaching and thinking.

Educators from many parts of the world have gone to Bulgaria to study the claims of suggestology. They've returned to India, Germany, and Russia to found their own institutes of suggestopedia.

The education-conscious Soviets were among the first to seize on Bulgaria's suggestopedia. The Moscow Foreign Languages Pedagogical Institute's resounding success with the Lozanov method made headlines in *Pravda* in July 1969.[207] "You can learn a language in a month," they enthused, and an impressive group of Soviet professors praised suggestopedia. In the West, UNESCO and the Ford Foundation have expressed interest and the New York State Medical College at Albany invited Dr. Lozanov to lecture there, which he did in September 1969. Dr. Lozanov's new book on Suggestology published in Bulgaria and Russia, may soon be available in English. There have been many articles on suggestopedia in the Bulgarian press.[4, 43, 153, 164, 221, 223] In English, *Bulgaria Today* tells of the country's new teaching method.[222]

Lozanov's suggestopedia, taken from Yoga, adapted to our modern needs, is a genuine form of mind expansion. It's revolutionary—evolutionary, perhaps. What powers, what talents will surge into being as more of the mind is freed? The Bulgarian Institute of Suggestology and Parapsychology is trying to map out the new realms. Suggestopedia may be one of the most useful contributions Bulgaria has made to the world.

EXPLORING PSI

Can you send a verbal message telepathically, a line of poetry, a distress call, stock market quotes, anything at all? Like the Soviets and others, Dr. Lozanov is developing a telepathic coded message system which the Russians reported in *Komsomolskaya Pravda,* October 9, 1966. Unlike the others, however, Lozanov doesn't have to use involved hardware like EEG machines to register his telepathic messages, because he doesn't rely on small, unconscious, physical reactions to get the message through.

Lozanov's first telepathic code receiver, a young Bulgarian man, sat in front of two telegraph keys, one by his left hand, the other by his right. The sender, some distance away, telepathically commands the receiver to press either the right or left key. This is automatically recorded. As a metronome clicks, the sender repeats each telepathic command ten times. The receiver must get six of these for the symbol to be considered received. In this sort of code when the receiver presses the left key it might be considered a dash, and the right key a dot.

Dr. Lozanov reported at the 1966 Parapsychology Conference in Moscow that out of 1766 individual commands sent telepathically, his subject received 1215 or about 70 percent right. "Chances for this to have happened by coincidence are less than one in a million," he said. "With this telegraph method, we sent not only individual words but also phrases and entire sentences. Sender and receiver were separated by several rooms." [110]

Lozanov places great stress on ESP tests that can easily be demonstrated at any time on demand. "We demonstrated this test many, many times," he said, "to scientists and doctors."

Since then Lozanov has carried out literally thousands of telegraph tests with coded ESP messages. One of his ESP subjects is a girl who once was one of his patients. "She demonstrated very high telepathic ability," he says. "When I tried her on the telegraph tests, she got the message immediately. She got very high results—about 80 percent on the tests. I did one month of tests every day with her." The ESP tests with code and keys usually run several hours. "We found we could transmit long segments of information with this method."

Lozanov believes this mode of telepathy, which is essentially transmitting to someone the impulse to move in a specific direction, a kind of kinetic telepathy or muscular ESP, is a major step toward making telepathy something we can put to use. "Telepathy *can* be used practically," he says. What he's done is to give a practical turn to experiments in telepathic command of a person's movement—the kinetic ESP that has so long intrigued the Soviets.

Where has Lozanov found talented psychics for his ESP tests? In addition to studying Vanga and other topnotch psychics in Bulgaria, he also trains average people to become psychic.

"We found while using suggestology that some people became telepathic," he says.

The Bulgarian scientists decided to further explore some of the techniques they'd been using in suggestology. Could the same techniques be directed specifically to increasing ESP? They tried group experiments on sixty to seventy people at a time. First they were given ESP tests to check on the level of natural ability. Then a carefully prepared program of suggestion was given the fully awake group. Check-up ESP tests followed after several sessions.

"We found you can improve the abilities of a whole group of different people all at one time with the suggestion method. Telepathic and clairvoyant ability can be cultivated and trained by suggestology," says Lozanov. "The laws of telepathic phenomena appear to conform with those of clinical suggestion in the awakened state."

It's not surprising. The free floating, untroubled state of consciousness basic to suggestology seems identical to the state of mind usually considered necessary for good reception of telepathy and clairvoyance. Physiological studies show alpha waves predominate in the brain during suggestology and, according to Lozanov, alpha waves help in receiving telepathy. "There's a very close connection between ESP and suggestion," says Lozanov.

Being an expert hypnotist well-acquainted with the work of the Russian ESP pioneer Dr. Leonid Vasiliev, Lozanov naturally explored the classic Russian sleep-wake test—causing someone at a distance to lose consciousness by telepathic command. As early as 1945 Dr. Lozanov set up large-scale long distance sleep-wake experiments. "In this state of telepathic hypnosis, the subjects know about events happening at great distances from themselves. We find this clairvoyant ability in 'sleeping' subjects can be trained and perfected too."

Dr. Nikolai Kamenov, a member of the Bulgarian Academy of Sciences, and Dr. Milan Ryzl, the Czech biochemist and parapsychologist, witnessed Lozanov's expertise with telepathic hypnosis. These tests took place in 1964 at the Bulgarian Medical Postgraduate Institute in the Department of Psychiatry where Lozanov worked before directing his own institute. Lozanov's subject was "Dusko," a tall, well-built, dark-haired young man. Dr. Ryzl had already run a batch of preliminary tests of Dusko's ESP ability. Ryzl asked him to guess colored cards concealed in opaque envelopes. He was able to, well above chance.

The three scientists and Dusko sat chatting in the office. Lozanov explained that the investigations of Dusko's psychic ability were still at the preliminary stage and that ideal test conditions to get the most out of Dusko's gift had not yet been developed fully. Ryzl slipped Lozanov a note. It read, "Nevertheless, make him go to sleep telepathically!" To be sure there was no previous agreement between those present, Dr. Kamenov added to the note, "Put him to sleep from another room after five minutes have elapsed."

Dr. Lozanov made an excuse and went out of the room. Ryzl and Kamenov continued to talk animatedly with Dusko. Five minutes passed. Fifteen seconds later, Dusko suddenly stopped talking in mid sentence. Within thirty seconds he was calmly asleep in his chair. Dr. Kamenov snapped several photographs while Ryzl took down scientific observations on Dusko's condition. Kamenov went to the room where Lozanov sat, photographed him, and silently gave him a note: "Wake him exactly two minutes from now."

Kamenov again sat down near Dusko. Exactly two minutes later Dusko woke up, by some sort of telepathic alarm clock, and resumed his conversation. The experiment was repeated twice. "Dr. Lozanov has successfully demonstrated hypnosis by telepathy," Dr. Ryzl stated.[66, 376, 377]

At the Medical Postgraduate Institute, under the leadership of Professor Emmanuel Sjarankov, Dr. Lozanov spent half his working time on research into skin sight, telepathy, and clairvoyance. "I did a great many experiments to try to clarify the telepathic interrelation between two hypnotized subjects and also the ESP connection between the subject and hypnotist."

The idea of electromagnetic waves carrying telepathy, he

thinks, is contradictory to his own observations, but he feels sooner or later we'll discover some physiological principle connected with telepathy.

Lozanov is also opposed to the thesis that ESP is a throwback, an ability of our primitive ancestors that shrivels in civilized man. "On the contrary," says Lozanov, "it is the most cultivated, artistic types of personalities—the writers, painters, and artists—who have this ability. With modern man it is more a question of an artistic inspiration in realizing the telepathic connection."

Talking with Lozanov at the Institute in his large, airy office brilliant with color and flowers, we asked, "Do scientists here believe ESP is entirely a physical phenomenon?"

"That's one of the main unknowns in parapsychology," Dr. Lozanov said. "In India I asked the yogis the very same question. Indian yogis themselves have varying ideas. Some think psi is purely physical—some of them are very materialistic," Lozanov added in an aside. "Others think it's mental. Some think both. The connection between mental and physical has yet to be found. For future parapsychological research, this connection is the key to great success."

"What's the view of your Institute?"

"Our scientists are working on many experiments, but we have no official hypothesis. We don't publish our experiments. We'll publish our work when we can *demonstrate everything*." Official demonstrations before scientific commissions have been the building blocks of Lozanov's spectacular career—the open sesame that gets ESP accepted even by the skeptics.

"It is possible in principle for us to demonstrate ESP on demand now. It *must* be possible to demonstrate it at any time, and we will be able to demonstrate it very soon. We don't know all the laws yet. Twenty years ago hypnosis was in the same position—it could not always be demonstrated. Today it can, because we know the laws. In the same way we need to discover the laws of psychic forces."

In his forty-three years, Dr. Lozanov has accomplished an enormous amount. He has evolved radical new concepts of the mind's powers, tested and demonstrated them scientifically, and gotten these ideas and techniques accepted all over the world. Despite his rapidly growing world fame, he is startlingly modest and free from egotism. "This is not the time for personalities in the field," he says. "It's the time for very hard work."

When he is not on whirlwind trips through America, India, Germany, Russia, where he is supervising the setting up of new suggestology institutes, he sometimes works eighteen and twenty hours a day at the Institute, often sleeping there as well in order not to lose time. Lozanov is totally dedicated to helping people and seems to care little for the material things of life.

"The key thing is that doctors and psychiatrists should be able to help everyone who needs help. Money is not the important thing," he says. He refuses to set up a private psychiatric practice on the side, which under Bulgarian law he is allowed to do. "In the same way," he says, "suggestology and suggestopedia should be given to the world and not kept for the benefit of just a few."

Dr. Lozanov is particularly loyal to the people of Bulgaria and proud of their accomplishments. We came away from Bulgaria with an impression of an exceedingly likable, intelligent, committed man.

Another major part of Lozanov's work has been informing the public about ESP through radio, television, lectures, and demonstrations. During a broadcast on Radio Sofia he assured the public: "Telepathy has already abandoned the scrolls of the ancient mystic and occult schools and it's coming out in the open under sunlight in the hands of the contemporary magicians—the men of science. This has been the path of many scientific discoveries, which have set free the age-old wisdom of the masses from the fantastic tinge given it by various epochs." [108]

For parapsychology today in Bulgaria, the emphasis is *not* on secret societies or religions and certainly not on mysticism. In an age of science, the Bulgarians have turned the full spectrum of science, from psychology to physics, on ESP. The inquiry is serious, but not somber. These researchers seem to have a warmer understanding of psi than many others; the people seem less embarrassed or horrified if ESP sparks in their lives. The evolution of inquiry into psychic realms has been less jagged than in most countries. Of course, there are people hostile to ESP in Bulgaria and there are skeptics—in the best sense of the word—even among the parapsychologists themselves.

But the "good climate" is reflected in the surprisingly broad perimeter of Bulgarian parapsychology; in the Sofia Institute, with its large staff of *full-time* scientific psi researchers; and in the top-flight quality of men like Georgi Lozanov. He may be the best known, but there are many others who are attracted to the field.

If Vanga Dimitrova has taken a private look ahead, we can't help wondering just what surprises she has foreseen coming to the rest of us from Bulgarian parapsychology in the years to come.

III

CZECHOSLOVAKIA

23

THE PSYCHIC LIFE OF CZECHOSLOVAKIA

"There's dancing in the streets of Prague!" our Bulgarian friends rushed to tell us one morning in late July 1968. They'd been up all night listening to the exhilarating news from Czechoslovakia on their shortwave radios. It was a remarkable bulletin about the usually reserved Czechs and a city often described by tourists as sober and gloomy. But this was the brief springtime of Czech freedom, and they were celebrating. But soon the Bulgarians relayed a more disturbing news item: "All Soviets are forbidden to go to Czechoslovakia." "This means trouble," they said.

It had taken days even to get reservations on a plane to Prague, but as we boarded the huge Caravelle jet in Budapest, we realized we'd missed a bulletin or two. There were only five other people aboard. And when we reached the very "mod" new Prague airport, we were the only ones to disembark—the others went on to Paris.

At our Prague hotel Western newsmen explained there'd been another confrontation that day between the Soviet and Czech leaders, but the Czechs had come out on top in this preliminary round, making only a few concessions. Optimism returned to the country. Only a few ominous notes—like the reports of Westerners who'd seen the huge masses of troops supposedly on "maneuvers" in Czechoslovakia; or the clairvoyant mentioned in Slovak newspapers who predicted, "Blood will run in the streets before autumn."

In actual fact it was only a matter of weeks before Soviet tanks would roar through the ancient streets of Prague. We would have only a short time to probe some of the most fascinating and baffling phenomena we uncovered on our psychic odyssey.

The story of what is happening today in the realm of the psychic is closely bound with the history of Czechoslovakia, the civilization of Czechoslovakia, the very streets of Prague itself—Gothic, Romanesque, Baroque, Renaissance, Rococo—streets that seem to have been sculpted rather than built.

Modern Czechoslovakia (the size of New York state, with a population of 14 million) was carved out of the Austro-Hungarian Empire in 1918, and is a jigsaw puzzle of Bohemia, Moravia, Silesia, and Slovakia. Prague, the capital of Bohemia, goes back millennia. The first university in the Germanic Roman Empire was founded in Prague in 1348 during the Golden Age of Bohemia under Charles IV. By the time of King Wenceslaus in the thirteenth century, the Czechs were already among the most civilized peoples in Europe.

By the twentieth century Czechoslovakia was one of the leading industrial nations of Europe. Then came World War II and Nazi domination. In 1948 the Communists in the country staged a coup and seized power. For about a decade Czechoslovakia was a Stalinist police state.

Yet despite it all, Prague endures—Prague a city which has been called "kingly," "indescribable, incomparable in the splendor of its churches"; "the equal of Florence" (Pope Pius II); "the Northern Rome" (Auguste Rodin). In so old a city, steeped in music, laden with art treasures, leading center of Renaissance science, it is not surprising that some of the ancient knowledge should survive.

ALCHEMY

Crossing the Vltava (or Moldau) River via the Charles Bridge, which is itself a museum of statues, we come to the brilliant complex of buildings, gardens, museums, and churches known as Hradcany which combines at once the present government, the President's residence, the historical, spiritual, and cultural heritage of Bohemia and Czechoslovakia. The heights are crowned with Prague (Hradcany) Castle and the magnificently beautiful Gothic Cathedral of St. Vitus. And here, built into the walls and fortifications of Hradcany, is "Golden Lane," the houses of the ancient alchemists—colleagues of one of the most famous alchemists of the Renaissance, Emperor Rudolf II.

"Isn't that a quaint legend?" ask the tourists. But alchemy has never left Prague. Alchemy is built right into the Czech character, the way the alchemists' houses are built right into the fortifications of Prague. The alchemists still work in Czechoslovakia. Equipment for them is made in some of the famous Bohemian crystal factories. French physicist Dr. Jacques Bergier confirmed the continued existence of alchemy in Czechoslovakia. He had been contacted personally by three Prague alchemists.[343]

Alchemy has long been misunderstood in the West as some sort of maniacal desire to turn base metals into gold. In actuality, for the alchemist, power over matter and energy is only a secondary goal. The real aim of the alchemist's activities (which some think stem from the ancient science of a long-extinct civilization) is the transformation of the alchemist himself, his accession to a higher state of consciousness. Everything is oriented toward the transmutation of the man himself, toward his spiritual liberation and his fusion with "divine energy." One of the greatest psychiatrists of our time, Dr. C. G. Jung, felt alchemy might be one of the keys to understanding the strange workings of the mind.

In the course of working toward a higher degree of consciousness, the alchemist was to learn, as a by-product, the true nature of the universe, how to control all matter, the secrets of generating and liberating energy, the universal cure of all illness, and the secret of indefinitely prolonging life.

Could alchemy contain fragments of a science that has been lost to us? Could the ancients have known things our modern technologists only recently have begun to uncover? German engineer Wilhelm König, hired by the city of Baghdad to build sewers, discovered in the Baghdad Museum some flat stones found in Iraq and classified vaguely as "ritual objects" which were in actuality electric batteries that had been in use *two thousands years before Galvani.*[343] What else labeled "objects of worship" in our archeological museums will turn out to be highly sophisticated technological components?

The Communists believe there is a close connection between traditional alchemy and avant-garde science. For some time now the scientific press in the USSR has openly been taking a great interest in alchemy and is undertaking historical research.

We have it on reputable authority that there are thriving hermetic groups now inside Russia. These Soviet students of hermetic knowledge happen to be Soviet scientists, and they are poring over ancient alchemical manuscripts which have reached them in the form of Xeroxed copies. Some of these ancient texts—Arab manuscripts of the twelfth century, for instance—contain data on chemistry, jet propulsion, and designs for rockets used for bombardment.

Soviet space pioneer and developer of astronautics K. E. Tsiolkovsky, revealed in his diaries (finally published in 1959, some time after his death) that in creating the space rocket he had followed the ideas of Roger Boscovitch, a Yugoslavian trained in alchemy who lived in the eighteenth century. Aside from Boscovitch's elucidation of the techniques of rocketry and interplanetary travel, his works also provide the modern explanation of radioactivity, demonstrations of the existence of planets in orbit around stars, statistical mechanics theories not developed in the West until the twentieth century, and a unitary theory of the Universe—a single equation for mechanics, physics, chemistry, biology, psychology. His work covers quantum theory, wave mechanics, and the atom formed of nucleons. (For details see Boscovitch's correspondence in Bestermann collection, Paris, France.) Tsiolkovsky's urgent appeal to Soviets to investigate ESP may well have derived from his readings of Boscovitch's penetrating studies.

While no systematic study of the 100,000 books and manuscripts on alchemy we have in the West has ever been done by our scientific experts, the Communists are eagerly examining these old texts which cram Prague libraries. Here among the time-worn buildings of Prague, the lore of the alchemists still lingers. Prague, whose rooftops indent the sky like notes on a music staff, notes that perhaps transcribe the formula of some harmonic modulation whose vibrations are able to transform matter—for the alchemists encoded their secrets not just in manuscripts, but in architecture and in *forms*.

What secrets have the Czechs found? What alchemy have they explored? We were to find things here that bordered on the edge of the fantastic.

It was in Prague that the famous cabalistic rabbi of the sixteenth century, Rabbi Yehuda Low, supposedly created the "golem"—a small clay or wooden figure of a human being which, it is said, he endowed with life. The golem could carry messages and perform tasks. How was this little statuelike figure endowed with life? Low said energy could be infused in matter by the aid of a combination of letters forming the word *Shem,* one of the names of God. The *Shem* was written down and inserted into the golem, which brought it to life and action. (Applying the ideas of American physicist Charles A. Muses,[369] this might mean that the frequencies of vibrations which comprise certain sounds—even spoken words—could be infused in wood or clay, possibly giving the material magnetic or electrostatic properties capable of acting on other substances.)

The legend has it that Rabbi Low used his golem as a servant on weekdays and extracted the *Shem* from the golem on the Sabbath so it could rest. Once the Rabbi forgot, and supposedly the golem ran amuck in the streets terrifying the people. Low caught the golem, and extracted the *Shem* from it in front of the synagogue. The golem fell to pieces. Its remains are said to be still found among the debris in the attic of the synagogue. Rabbi Low is also credited with having performed alchemical wonders before alchemist Emperor Rudolf II.

The legend of the golem has sunk deep into Czech culture, inspiring many of the modern writers such as Karel Čapek. *R.U.R.*, one of his internationally successful plays, was about near-human "robots" who revolt against man.

Today in Czechoslovakia we found scientists who have delved into ancient texts and have come up with a process not unlike the one the fabled Rabbi Low may have used to impregnate wood or metal with biological energy.

Yet another important area of alchemical tradition was the necessity to know precise planetary aspects before undertaking a scientific project. Alchemy required astrological knowledge. And today in Czechoslovakia there is a Center for Scientific Astrology financed by the Communist government.[149] Here the science of cosmobiology or astrology is employed in medicine and psychiatry. Astrology is the Czech answer to the Pope's birth control ban. "Astrology," they told us, "can be used for contraception. It can even be used to choose the sex of your child."

Given the psychic traditions of Czechoslovakia's past, it followed naturally that the people of the country would take a visual interest in questions which are now part of scientific parapsychology.

Dr. Karel Kuchynka (Ku-kin-ka), now seventy-eight and one of Czechoslovakia's pioneers in parapsychology, explained:[92, 162] "Neither official science nor official religions could give the final answers to the secrets of life or the universe. In our country you find representatives of every nuance and religious sect—there are anthroposophists, theosophists, spiritualists, adepts in ancient magic, adepts in the sciences of early Egypt, alchemists (even the world's oldest and largest group of followers of the Maharishi—long before the Beatles heard of him!). This almost general tendency I think is a result of the subconscious structure of the Czech soul, which gave birth to the great religious movements and reforms, especially those of Bohemia in the Middle Ages." (Here Dr. Kuchynka was referring to the movement founded by the Czech religious reformer John Huss, a century before Luther.)

"The critical and meditative character of our people increases even more this interest in paranormal phenomena. Thus the soil here in Czechoslovakia is more favorable for psi than elsewhere." For example, from the 1920s till the German invasion, one of the most popular major weekly magazines in Czechoslovakia ran a regular column on scientific research in parapsychology.

Dr. Kuchynka described research on psi at the University of Prague carried out at the very beginning of the twentieth century by neurologists, psychiatrists, engineers, chemists, medical doctors, and biologists. Files and files of research exist on telepathy as a crimesolver, on psychometry, on psychics and graphoanalysis, on PK, on clairvoyance, on poltergeists, and so on. Czech scientists were among the first to extensively study famous mediums of the time, such as Rudi Schneider, Madame Silbert, and Stefan Ossowiecki.

Numerous international conferences were held in Czechoslovakia on parapsychology. At one of them a "tribunal" of the elite of Czech scientists and intellectuals all testified that under the very strictest experimental conditions, the medium Madame Silbert caused a bell in the well-lit room to move without any direct contact, apported watches, rings, and other objects, created luminous phenomena in the room, caused bells to ring at a distance, moved a heavy table, and, most amazing of all, created the engraving of the name "Nell" and a small triangle on the inside of a closed watchcase and on the inside of a closed cigarette case filled with cigarettes.

Among the famous Prague psychics studied by Czech scientists was Adolf Fencl-Bilovsky who gave life readings, rather like Edgar Cayce. However, he didn't go into trance to do it. Picking up a sheet of paper on which an infant had scribbled, he would detail the child's future, his or her talents, mental abilities, future illnesses, and the line of work the child would go into. The life readings were kept on file and the person's destiny later checked against them. "Every characteristic indicated by the psychic corresponded perfectly to the truth," says Dr. Kuchynka.

"We studied other psychics, too, who could determine the details of a person's life through a photograph. Mr. Kordon-Veri was given a small picture of someone totally unknown to him. He depicted minutely the region where the photo had been taken, indicated that the person in the photo was ill and was in that particular region because of the illness. He said he heard the words 'Velebit' and 'Rabe.' This was all correct—the picture was of a Czech musician who during her illness was staying in the Velebit Hotel on the Island of Arbe (which is Rab in Czech) on the Adriatic Sea. The description of the surroundings of the hotel corresponded precisely to the reality. Holding a sketch of the same person in his hands, the clairvoyant declared, 'This woman has the talent of a genius in music, but she is seriously ill and is about to die or is already dead.' At that very moment, 11 p.m., the musician was already in agony and died the next day at six in the morning."

Dr. Kuchynka recalls many long-distance ESP tests in which drawings were transmitted telepathically; also a test with the celebrated Polish clairvoyant Stefan Ossowiecki (Os-soviet-ski) of Warsaw. Ossowiecki was visiting the famous Czech resort of Marienbad. The scientists decided to test his clairvoyant rapport with a person totally unknown to him. A journalist in Cracow prepared a drawing at his home and sent a sealed copy to the scientists at Marienbad. Then, four hundred miles away from Ossowiecki, he drew the same picture in the sand. To exclude any possibility that the envelope might be opened or that someone might peek at the sketch and tell Ossowiecki, the journalist decided to add a few details to his picture in the sand.

At a given moment Ossowiecki began tracing a sketch in sand at Marienbad. Then a bit later he added an ellipse and a figure inside it. Then he rubbed it out and replaced it with a "W."

Afterward the commission confirmed that Ossowiecki had reproduced the journalist's drawing exactly. The journalist explained that he had drawn an ellipse first with a figure in it, then erased it and replaced it finally by a drawing with the letter "W" in the ellipse. Even this change had not escaped the clairvoyant.

Dr. Oscar Fischer of Prague had also worked with the famous clairvoyant Eric Hanussen. Under Hitler, Hanussen gained wealth and power as a psychic and astrologer. In the 1930's Hanussen was assassinated by the Nazis because he could clairvoyantly see the Nazis' many secret projects and this seemed dangerous and inopportune to the Fascist hierarchy, according to Dr. Kuchynka.[92, 119]

So widespread was the understanding of parapsychology in intellectual circles in Czechoslovakia that even the Rector of the University of Brno (the third largest city in the country) chose for his installation speech this topic: "Man has more than the 'doors' of his senses. Today there is no doubt that in certain psychophysiological conditions, the psyche of man can influence the psyche of another man even without the intervention of sense perception." This was the famous Czech biologist and physiologist Dr. Eduard Babak.

"I think the importance of parapsychology for us lies precisely in its possibility of elucidating by its discoveries the true nature of man and of showing that man is linked to the cosmos more closely than he'd ever supposed," says Dr. Kuchynka.

The use of ESP in Czechoslovakia has not been limited to university researchers and private groups. The Czech military revealed in their journal *Periscope* (1966) that they had frequently used psi for war. One particular troop from the Czech Army, which had scored phenomenal successes during the entire 1919 campaign between Czechoslovakia and Hungary, admitted much later that their secret weapon had been ESP.

A former army man confirmed the report for us. "We used clairvoyance to great advantage in the campaign against the Hungarians in 1919. We'd put soldiers with psi ability into a trance and they'd tell us the exact position of the Hungarian Army, help us locate soldiers we'd lost, and so on. I'll never forget one occasion when the psychic said, 'I see the Hungarians right now! There's about 150 of them. They're bathing in a river and poorly guarded.' He gave us the exact location. We set out. Fifty of us captured a whole unit of 150 *nude* Hungarians!

"We also used dowsers in World War I to help us locate traps, weapons, drinking water, and to track the enemy precisely." He showed us photos of the Czech troops working the typical forked twig dowsing rod. "Of course, psi was also used by the partisans in Czechoslovakia during the last war."

The Czech military published a handbook on ESP for the army in 1925 called "Clairvoyance, Hypnotism, and Magnetism" by Karel Hejbalik.

"At first ESP was used by the Czech soldiers unknown to the commander," says Hejbalik, "but at Kremnica, Colonel B., who understood psi, took command of three units and one battalion. He put psychic soldiers into deep hypnosis to improve their telepathic ability, then commanded them to do clairvoyant reconnaissance."

The colonel and all the officers involved in the campaign are still alive and were interviewed by Czech parapsychologists. "The information the clairvoyant soldiers gave us was always correct," they said. "On this basis we could go into action. It was a great advantage in battle. The clairvoyant research party safeguarded the troops in action."

The historical records bear out the effectiveness of psi in battle, says the Czechs. "The Czech army achieved extraordinary results with psi which have been concretely confirmed in fighting practice," says Czech Army Journal *Periscope*.

According to Miroslav Ivanov, in his book *Not Only the Black Uniforms*, psychics were used for warnings, news about concentration camps, immigration, and partisan groups during World War II and the Nazi occupation. "Many facts given us by the clairvoyants were right. The abilities of telepathists were used in war with excellent results to get information about the enemy, his intentions, his bases, his aerodromes."

Says the 1966 issue of *Periscope*, "Imagine an army organization with a staff of clairvoyants who would follow the layout and intentions of the General Staff of a foreign army, and locate all military bases. It could turn ESP from a military weapon to a *peace* weapon!"

Today, through the Communist world, military interest in ESP runs high.

"Only during the German occupation was our official research in parapsychology stopped," says Dr. Kuchynka. "The Germans forbade our universities to continue this work."

But it would appear that research and interest in the paranormal during those years just went underground and never completely stopped. Today, under Communism, the work has openly resumed. Every facet of the whole panorama of psychic research can be found in Czechoslovakia: reincarnation studies, alchemy, statistical ESP testing, LSD and ESP, PK research, telepathy, studies of mediums, poltergeists, investigations of hauntings, "psychotronics"—a new form of parapsychology research on a new form of psychic energy. A Czech doctor, once one of Stalin's physicians, wrote us that he was even investigating the research done by Aksakov in Russia. (See chapter 19.)

English journalist Theo Lang of the British *Sunday Mirror*, who went to Czechoslovakia to investigate Czech psi research, reported he was "absolutely astonished" at the acceptance of psychic research by modern scientists as well as by the general public. "Czech physicists, physiologists, biochemists, and others I interviewed seemed to calmly accept another world—a world of spirits, ghosts and poltergeists, and to believe that it could be investigated and charted."

Dr. Vladimir Drozen, Director of the Faculty of Pedagogy at Hradec Králové University told him, "The existence of this psi field is not contrary to any known law of physics." [299]

PSYCHOTRONICS

"We've changed the name 'Parapsychology' to 'Psychotronics' here in Czechoslovakia. With a new name totally unconnected with any hint of the occult, we've now gotten the cooperation of serious scientists for psi research." It was Dr. Zdenek Rejdak (Ray-dek) speaking, Scientific Secretary of one of the most active and most respected Czech parapsychology centers, the Czechoslovak Coordination Committee for Research in Telepathy, Telegnosis, and Psychokinesis.

A tall, genial man with a great thatch of blond hair, Dr. Rejdak, though only in his mid thirties, has had many years experience as a psychic researcher. Apart from being a psychologist with the military, a specialist in physiology, and a prolific writer, Rejdak worked for sixteen years in parapsychology with Brĕtislav Kafka, a highly unusual researcher.

"Psychotronics is, in essence, the bionics of man. We're trying to study the psi phenomenon *in* man, and secondly as an energy on its own," Dr. Rejdak told us. (Bionics is a new science of systems which function like living systems.)

The group of Czech scientists he heads does wide-ranging psi research; produces films on psi; runs an ESP Lecture Program at the People's University of Prague with scientists from East and West as speakers; and just published a first-in-the-world international anthology of scientific papers on psi by both Communist and Western researchers.[185]

Dr. Rejdak is something of a Renaissance man with a shrewd knowledge of many areas of science as well as the arts, literature, and music. He believes in the interdisciplinary approach to psychotronics (parapsychology). "Discoveries in psi will benefit every other field of knowledge," he says.

In 1968 the Czech group issued a manifesto (see Appendix C). In the West it appeared in the English *Paraphysics Journal,* and in the Communist world it was presented at the International Parapsychology Conference in Moscow.

Instead of the "dual" nature of man and the universe postulated by contemporary science, the Czechs suggest man is of a three-fold nature and the cosmos is "triadic." The third aspect of Man and the Universe, they say, is a new form of energy—"psychotronic" energy.[23] Psychotronic energy may carry telepathy, may be the basis of PK, clairvoyance, healing, and any paranormal phenomenon where there's no physical or biophysical explanation.

"We're trying to discover the nature of the energy that causes psychic phenomena and we're trying to isolate this 'psychotronic' energy," Dr. Rejdak said. The results of their startling research are detailed later.

"We have the support of the Central Committee of the Communist Party, and the Czech Academy of Sciences virtually unanimously approved research in psychotronics," he said. "They've made available to us all the resources of the universities. If we want to make an EEG study of a medium, for instance, the neurophysiology department and scientists from other departments of the Charles University all cooperate and loan us the equipment and technicians."

Like the Soviets, the Czechs employ the most modern scientific research instruments in their study of psi. Current work includes novel experiments: the attempt to telepathically communicate sweet or sour tastes. They are also doing extensive research on PK. The group is producing three new films on parapsychology covering dowsing and telepathy. They are also studying famous Czech clairvoyants, psychics, healers, and dowsers.

New instrumentation isn't the only new thing to come to ESP in Czechoslovakia. Czech scientists are also applying new mathematical techniques. An American scientist who works for a government agency recently reported that Czech scientists applied information theory to telepathy in an unusually successful way.

The Czechs thought about "noise," the amount of interference in a communication system. They decided to assume telepathy was a communication channel with a noise level so high that nearly all the message was drowned out. Information theory has techniques to overcome the noise problem, calculations that, among other things, tell how many repetitions of a single bit of information are necessary for proper reception. Applying these, the Czechs asked two people to try and telepathically send binary (two-symbol) coded messages back and forth, with a computor working out the necessary formulae of information theory.

The American scientist reports that the Czechs "demonstrated something like *98 percent reliability of pure telepathy communication.* In other words, something better than the reliability of field communication by field telephone or radio transmitters." Data on the tests appeared in *Analog.*[281]

REINCARNATION RESEARCH

To get an idea of the background of the current explosion of psi research in Czechoslovakia, we talked to many people in other fields. By chance we encountered a private group doing reincarnation "research." They were all well-off Czechs with responsible jobs in business and industry. Most of them had traveled widely not only in the Communist world but outside it as well.

"We've done life readings for many people here," they told us. "We have mediums who are highly skilled at reincarnation research."

From what we heard, some of their material is similar to the life readings of Edgar Cayce or the work of British medium Joan Grant, whose novels detailing past lives in Egypt, Rome, Italy, and England surprised scholars with their accuracy.

Much of the current data involves past lives in Egypt and Atlantis. "We checked out Egyptian life readings and we were surprised to find the data was pretty accurate. That encouraged us to go further." The Czechs we talked to assured us the mediums who described life in the courts of early Egypt had never been to Egypt, nor did they have any access to scholarly material locked in museums in Egypt, much of which is in hieroglyphs only a few scholars in the world can decipher. Yet supposedly, when the details of the Czech material were examined by Egyptologists, they found it accurate.

Neither Soviets nor Czechs seem to find the idea of Atlantis hard to believe. Dr. N. F. Zhirov, foremost chemist and member of the Soviet Academy of Sciences, recently published a scientific study, *Atlantis: The Basic Problems of*

Atlantis, giving evidence of the existence of a lost continent. The book was well received by the Soviet scientific establishment. Soviet physicist Dr. N. Ledner, another Atlantis supporter, has collected cultural, historical, and scientific data on Atlantis for twenty years.

The continent of Atlantis was supposed to have existed in the middle of the Atlantic Ocean before 9,000 B.C. and allegedly was highly developed technologically. (Dr. Manson Valentine and Dr. Dimitry Ribicoff of Miami's Palm Beach Atlantic College reported in early 1969 that they had found portions of 15,000-year-old ruins in the sea near the Bahamas. "They may be part of Atlantis," they said.)[403]

The Czechs, who'd never heard of Edgar Cayce, gave us data on Atlantis that strangely enough tallies with Cayce's accounts. Even the unusual names of Atlanteans match.

"Hitler," the Czechs said, "was an Atlantean." They wrote down the name he supposedly bore in Atlantis, then scribbled it out with disgust.

Czechoslovakia felt the Nazi fury long and painfully. In Lidice, every man, woman, and child in the entire town was systematically murdered by the Nazis. Every building and house was broken stone by stone, stick by stick until Lidice was "wiped from the face of the earth."

The Czechs, we found, knew about some of the dark psychic aspects of the Nazi movement which most Westerners are not aware of. "Your historians have tried to explain Hitler with the logic of cause and effect—with winning elections—or by a diagnosis of madness. Hitler was, in fact, a very skilled practitioner of the occult. The Nazi movement was deeply involved with the *black arts* of the occult," the Czechs said.

It is not generally known in America that Hitler was a clairvoyant and a medium. He was born in Braunau am Inn in Austria, a town long famous for the tremendous number of mediums it produced, particularly Rudi and Willy Schneider who astounded all Europe with their psychic feats. Hitler had the same wet nurse as Willy Schneider. Hitler was apparently trained in mediumship by Professor Haushofer of the University of Munich, who is said to have been initiated, during a stay in Japan, into one of the most important secret Buddhist societies.

Hitler is credited with accurate clairvoyant predictions about the course of the war and even the death of Roosevelt, according to author Louis Pauwels and physicist Dr. Jacques Bergier in *The Morning of the Magicians,* a long-time best seller in Europe.

Hitler, it seems, not only surrounded himself with astrologers, clairvoyants, and prophets, he was one himself. Those close to him attest he seemed on occasion possessed by dark, "outside personalities" and spoke with their voices, according to Pauwels and Bergier. Hitler talked of Ultima Thule, the magic center of a vanished civilization; of Shamballah, the legendary underground camp in the Himalayas whose forces of violence and power control humanity; of Agarthi, another legendary underground Himalayan city of goodness and meditation. He dreamed of beings—half-human, half-spirit—who would place a reservoir of energy in Nazi hands to dominate the world. Although they sound like the fantasies of a madman to most of us, these ideas were derived from Tibetan magic. So was the swastika. Many Nazis were initiated into secret occult societies all over Germany and trained in Eastern black magic. It was to purify the world for the coming of a race of Man-Gods, of Supermen, which Hitler predicted was coming, that incredible millions were slaughtered and that the Nazis so willingly worked the gas ovens. The entire world reeled under the impact, not of a madman, but of a "black" magician, said some of our Czech friends. "Hitler was a practitioner of the black arts of the occult. If we are to avoid falling into the grip of these Dark Powers again," they said, "we must begin to understand psi, we must discover what forces can be unleashed by the human mind, what incredible energies it controls."

As we were leaving, some of the Czechs in the group demonstrated their tour-de-force knowledge of astrology. Doing the complicated mathematical calculations of an astrology chart in their heads, they prepared accurate charts and did a quick astrology reading.

BRĚTISLAV KAFKA, PIONEER PARAPSYCHOLOGIST

One of the most colorful and famous psychic explorers in Czechoslovakia died at the age of seventy-six only a short time before our visit. His name is Brĕtislav Kafka. "His ideas have been the source of much of our current research into psi," Czech scientists told us. They showed us his picture, a heavyset man with a face lined like a Bohemian wood carving.

Kafka was one of Czechoslovakia's famous sculptors. His magnificent carvings in stone and wood adorn many of the buildings and cathedrals in Prague, such as the superb Gothic St. Vitus Cathedral beside Prague Castle. But while his hands worked a special alchemy with stone, his thoughts turned to the true dream of the alchemist—the transformation and liberation of the human personality and the releasing of dormant psychic forces.

Having become wealthy as a sculptor, he set up his studio a few miles outside Prague and there began his incredible voyages into the mysteries of the powers of the mind.

He chose psychically sensitive people as his subjects and he paid them out of his own pocket. Some were employed as his assistants in the studio. Just as the sculptor's chisel in his hands had sought and released the multitude of forms concealed inside the plain blocks of wood and marble, his mind sculpted new personalities from the plain, simple people who worked for him. He determined to create phenomenal psychic powers in them.

There in the Bohemian countryside—a landscape where statues of baroque saints guard crossroads, where St. John of Nepomuk protects bridges against floods, where paintings of St. Florian guard against lightning—in this countryside, inside a sculpture-cluttered studio, some strange scenes took place. Some assistants were put into lifelong hypnotic trances from which they were never to emerge. Some were hypnotized for ten to fourteen years. Others were placed in very deep states of waking hypnosis lasting from twelve to fourteen hours each day.

In Kafka's unique parapsychology lab, the hypnotized subjects were trained in ESP until their psychic faculties were perfected. After extensive psi training with hypnosis, the subjects reportedly got phenomenal results, scoring generally around the 90 percent level, according to Dr. Rejdak, whose reports on Kafka appear in the military annual *Periscope*.[178]

Kafka chose seven top psychics from a great number of sensitive people. They took part in various experiments. For instance, on June 18, 1925, Kafka and his psychics were in the town of Krásno and Bečva in Czechoslovakia. The expedition of Roald Amundsen was on its way to the North Pole. Kafka commanded his psychics to clairvoyantly see what was happening at the North Pole.

"There's a terrible fog and a strong wind at the Pole," they said. "No one from the expedition has gotten here yet. The storm is too severe to reach the Pole by air."

On the 20th of June the Czechs heard the news. Amundsen had returned with one airplane without having reached the North Pole.

During World War II, Kafka used his well-trained psychics to follow the progress of the war, the decisions of the generals, and the changes on the front lines. Kafka would put a psychic into trance and command him to tell what he saw on the front. Then another psychic with no knowledge of the first psychic's report would be clairvoyantly dispatched to the same area. Usually the reports of all the psychics jibed, and Kafka had an overall picture of what was happening hundreds of miles away.

Kafka also pioneered influencing sleep telepathically, carrying out scores of experiments in which ESP messages were received by sleeping subjects.

There were experiments, too, on the powers of hypnosis. In one unusual test a man was kept in hypnotic trance in one room for three weeks without food. "You are in a beautiful garden," he was told. "This is an orchard laden with fruit. You may pick and eat all you wish. Would you like this apple?" said Kafka, reaching for an imaginary apple.

"No, I'd like that one on the other branch," the man replied.

Kafka pretended to pick it for him and the man devoured it with gusto.

Throughout the three-week period the man felt himself in the best of health.

"All his physiological functions were diminished to the absolute minimum," current Czech scientists told us. "There was no need even to use the toilet." At the end of the three-week phase without food in the garden of fantasy, not only was the man well, but he *"gained weight,"* they said.

Dr. Rejdak told us, "Kafka believed there was a third form of energy in addition to those we know, and that humans are able to draw on this energy reservoir when they wish to. They are also able to obtain this same energy from other people."

We've heard of religious mystics who've lived on nothing but communion for years. "Would this be similar?" we asked.

"Most likely. Kafka believed it was possible to have the energy transfer from person to person or even from animals to humans. He would send a person who was fatigued out to lie underneath a cow. He said you could draw energy and strength from living things around us."

Dr. Milan Ryzl, a former Prague biochemist, recalled some of the background about Kafka for us. "Some of the subjects were trained to become healers. Others were trained to develop clairvoyance and various psychic powers. He had one assistant there—a man who became famous as a powerful healer—but he spent all his time in the hypnotic state. After several years of this rather grim training, Kafka would take him out for a walk and he'd say to him, pointing to a tree. 'Look at that bird.' The assistant would look at the bird selected and it supposedly would fall from the tree, dead." According to Ryzl, the assistant had a powerful physical effect on other animals as well.

Kafka believe that all living things—plants, animals, and people—are encased in an envelope of energy, or aura, the same energy revealed in the Kirlian photographs.

"He discovered the 'sensitives' or psychics have a much thinner aura or energy shield around them. You see, they have less covering, less protection. That's supposedly why they are sensitive," Czech researchers explained. Kafka found sensitives reacted far more strongly to weather changes than average people. He thought the protective shield of energy had something to do with telepathy messages reaching a psychic.

Exploring this living energy—psychotronic energy—is one of the main thrusts of Czech research today. And Kafka's method of giving people a new psychic dimension to life via hypnosis, of creating clairvoyants and psychics by hypnotic training, is being explored by Dr. Milan Ryzl.

24

DR. MILAN RYZL
CREATOR OF PSYCHICS

Milan Ryzl, who comes over like a fully plugged in switchboard crackling with ideas, projects, commentary, and questions, looked speculatively at the young secretary sitting opposite him in his ESP lab in Prague. "We're going to try and find out, Josefka, if a prophesied event can be changed, can be *interfered* with. What I mean is," Ryzl said, "what if you were able to foresee a terrible car crash involving someone you knew? Does this have to happen? Or could your warning help the person avoid his fate? If the future can be changed, how much can it be altered—completely, partially, or what?"

The girl, known as J.K., whom we call Josefka, didn't have ready answers to the old conundrums of prophecy. Ryzl didn't pause long enough to let her try to think of any. He hoped she'd come up with answers in a different way. He hoped Josefka could use her psychic ability to predict a small piece of the future for him—a tidbit to put through his scientific mill.

"We used to be told that natural science could answer all questions," says biochemist Ryzl. "But it is not adequate to answer the eternal mysteries, the deep problems of philosophy, and the questions of religion. That's why I went into parapsychology. I want to explore some of these age-old questions scientifically."

To probe the mysteries of time, he set up an intriguing chore for Josefka. "Tonight, I want you to try to foresee something for a friend, something you wish she could avoid. Then we'll try to tip your friend off and see what happens."

Josefka, a strong featured but attractive brunette, relaxed as Ryzl led her into trance. The girl she'd decided to predict for lived fifty miles away, outside of Prague. In trance Josefka, "an honorable girl, gentle and sensitive, but with a strong will," usually followed Ryzl's instructions without a ripple. But now she began to get angry, her voice choked up. "She shouldn't go!" Josefka shifted restlessly in her chair.

"What are you seeing?" Ryzl asked.

"I see her, she's wearing a two-piece suit. She's talking to a man, I don't know him . . . he's a stranger to her too. They're in a restaurant. He wants her to go off with him . . . on a motorcycle. *She shouldn't go!*"

In Josefka's hypnotic vision, the friend climbed precariously on a one seater cycle with the stranger and racketed into the country night. "They've stopped. They're quarreling. Now they're going on—no, they've stopped again." The quarrel got worse. "He's torn her skirt . . . Oh my God!" Ryzl suddenly heard a blow by blow description of a lovers' lane rape.

Ryzl got more of a prophecy than he had bargained for. To Josefka, awake now but half crying, still in the throes of what she'd "witnessed," the experience had leaped far beyond any scientific experiment. "I don't care how silly it sounds. I'm going to phone and tell her first thing in the morning."

"Of course, we couldn't say ESP," Ryzl remembers, "so Josefka told the girl she'd had a horrible nightmare." Before Josefka related much of the "nightmare" on the phone, her friend interrupted.

"You're too late! It's already happened—last night."

The girl had been waiting at a cafe for her boyfriend when a man approached her, saying he'd been sent to give her a lift to where the boy was. According to Ryzl, everything Josefka described in trance was right: the color of her friend's suit, the torn skirt, the motorcycle, the looks of the man, the quarrels on the road, and, finally, the rape. Josefka hadn't looked into the future as Ryzl hoped, she'd given him a live broadcast. She "oversaw" the abduction at the time it was actually playing out fifty miles away.

More astonishing still, Josefka was not a medium or a psychic Ryzl had chanced to find. Josefka had no psychic ability when she first met Ryzl a few months before. Dr. Ryzl had *made* her clairvoyant with a unique training system he'd devised.

"That was certainly a fine case of clairvoyance on

Josefka's part, but it won't hold water with scientists. The people involved weren't about to sign affidavits proving the accuracy of the clairvoyance—not in a rape case," Ryzl said with a wry smile. "But it did happen."

Ryzl does, however, have file cases full of precisely documented ESP experiments, enough to make him the best-known Communist parapsychologist. (See Bibliography.) Some of his internationally published papers involve Josefka, one of the so-called "ordinary" people he taught to be psychic. With a quick eye and a quick comment for what's going on about him, the forty-one-year-old Ryzl is a man of many personalities. There is the electric, free-wheeling Ryzl—even his hair, full and wavy, has an electric, half-tamed look—who'll take a chance and bet on a horse one of his psychics sees winning a race. This is the one-step-ahead-of-the-pack Ryzl, who managed to get out of Czechoslovakia in late 1967 during the hardline Novotny regime, bringing with him to America not just a hastily packed suitcase, but also his wife, his two sons, his assistant, his library, and his car.

Then there is Ryzl the careful, methodical scientist who has produced some of the finest contemporary ESP work done anywhere. While still in Prague he became a research associate of the Duke Parapsychology Laboratory and the only Communist to ever receive the McDougall Award given by the Parapsychology Association of Durham, North Carolina, for distinguished work in the field. Ryzl speaks Russian, English, German, Czech, and reads even more languages. Since the late 1950s, Ryzl (who often visited ESP groups in Russia, Bulgaria, even India) has been a connection—for a time, the only connection—between psychic researchers in the East and West.

He's also been the man to see if you want to connect to your own psychic powers. He created a psychic system which supposedly gave off-the-street volunteers a wide-awake, working sixth sense. "I believe most people have latent psychic ability," Ryzl maintains. "The problem today is to devise methods of evoking this talent and bringing it under conscious control."

Sixth sense: Ryzl says it often and means it straight. He'd like to equip all of us with ESP that we could use as handily as we use our other senses. Dr. Leonid Vasiliev, Russia's pioneer parapsychologist, called Ryzl's method for nurturing the sixth sense one of the most promising developments in parapsychology. In a grand, years-long experiment, Ryzl attempted to evoke a psychic sense in five hundred students. Fifty of these Czech volunteers, according to the reports, did become psychic in one way or another.

How did Ryzl do it? He followed the lead of his extraordinary countryman, the sculptor Brĕtislav Kafka. He moved into hypnosis. He designed his psychic training method to ease people one step at a time from the reasonable into the seemingly unreasonable.[379] Hypnosis let him transfuse the student with confidence, let him circumvent the logical mind, chattering with arguments and qualms.

Josefka was one of the people who responded to Ryzl's ads for volunteers for a scientific experiment and also to his technique. "At our first meeting, Josefka seemed to be the sort of person I wanted," Ryzl, the Pygmalion of Psi, told us. "She proved a good hypnotic subject. She'd never had any psychic experiences and wasn't much interested in the field. Actually, people who are don't make very good subjects. They're always trying to figure out if anything is happening. But I do need people who understand that a scientific experiment is a specific thing to be worked through faithfully to the end. Josefka was fine on that account too. She's a highly reliable type, of Czech-German background, supposedly a descendent of Haydn, and she had a lifelong interest in medicine. Only unfortunately family circumstances kept her from entering medical school."

For over a month Ryzl used his three weekly sessions with Josefka to gain absolute hypnotic control over her. One afternoon Ryzl, with a penchant for unstodgy tests, moved his experimenting to a crowded trolley clanging along Prague's noisy, cobbled streets. As the trolley stopped at an intersection, Ryzl turned to Josefka and murmured his "sleeping draught," a hypnotic command word. "Take off your ring," he ordered the instantly entranced girl. Thirty seconds later, the trolley reached the other side of the intersection with Josefka again awake. She didn't realize anything had happened. She couldn't imagine where her ring was.

In the lab, as Josefka sat under his hypnotic sway, Ryzl trained her to visualize—to see, for instance, an imaginary yellow tulip with uwavering clarity, as if it were spotlighted in a dark room. Like many Communist researchers, Ryzl believes the ability to visualize sharply is central to good psychic performance. "To make up for all the shortcomings of the male race," he presented the entranced Josefka with a beautiful imaginary bouquet of deep red roses. He treated male students to cheesecake visions of Czech actresses—or, if they were technologists, to close-up hallucinations of the latest model car. One of the secrets of his success is that Ryzl tries to suit his method to the individual, not twist the person to the system.

As volunteers watch their bright hypnotic hallucination, Ryzl begins his psychic sleight of hand. He asks them to see other things—not illusions, but real things you're not supposed to be able to see—a clock completely hidden behind a screen, or what the people upstairs are doing at the moment.

One volunteer, a premedical student at Charles University, astounded Ryzl as he tried to lead him into ESP. On the first try, the boy correctly identified all twenty-five hidden ESP cards! "His performance was so amazing that I decided to give him a posthypnotic suggestion to remember what he'd done. That was my big mistake. He was horrified! Psychic things aren't supposed to happen. It was impossible. How could I have made him do such an unnatural thing? He couldn't get away from me fast enough. I never saw him again."

Generally, Ryzl has to talk students into clairvoyance rather like a control tower talks a pilot, flying blind, into the field. "You see a brightness, a sort of fog. You're doing fine. Now the fog is beginning to clear. You're beginning to make out an object." Trying to solo into ESP, people circle the target verbally. One woman said, "I see a sort of luster . . . a metallic color . . . and angles." The angles grew clearer. "I just said crossed pencils. I do get the impression of two things crossing, but they're not pencils. The ends far from me are pointed. I can't get the near ends sharply yet . . . there seem to be two circles projecting from a fog. It's a pair of scissors!" She was right.

Students are very often wrong. Right or wrong, Ryzl pumps them to overflowing with confidence-building suggestions. If a person can't seem to switch on clairvoyance,

Ryzl tries autoscopic vision. Eyes closed, entranced subjects are commanded to get up *mentally* and walk away from themselves. "Turn around, see yourself, wait until you can see your face, your shirt, your fingernails." Ryzl asks the person who thinks he's standing outside of himself to check the time on his watch, describe the number of cross-pieces on a chair in the corner. The subject does. Ryzl praises him lavishly, though he knows unconscious memory is probably at work, not ESP. The next sliding step is unmistakable psychic. "Now take a look and describe the furniture in the next room." The door is shut, the student has never seen the side room. From "standing outside," it's an easy step into "traveling clairvoyance." Says Ryzl, "I lead the student on an imaginary trip to the place I want him to see psychically. In the United States, I might say, 'You see skyscrapers. Now you're walking along Broadway. Turn right at 44th Street, go to the third building. . . .' "

Ryzl led Josefka on an imaginary clairvoyant trip across Prague. She went along the narrow streets, past the pastry shop, the tobacco store, the drugstore—thin stone buildings, all ornamented as though the coiling and stretching of some deep kinetic urge couldn't resist shaping plain stone into ribbons, cherubs, bows, drapery. Josefka hurried on in her imaginary walk across streets, past apartment houses with cobbled courtyards, by unexpected niches in building walls filled with small clumps of fresh flowers "in memory of ——, murdered on this spot by the Nazis." Finally, in her traveling clairvoyance, she climbed the stairs to her own apartment. Ryzl led her into the kitchen to see what her mother was doing. "These experiences seemed so real," Josefka reported. "It wasn't at all like seeing a movie. I felt I was really there. It seemed I could touch the kitchen table, smell the food." The Czechs label these tactile and other nonverbal impressions "groping at a distance." Ryzl reports Josefka and some of her fellow students were able to clairvoyantly drop in on kith and kin and determine correctly what they were doing.

Whether his psychics are attempting to see across space or across time, Ryzl tries to have them "see" scenes as they would really look in everyday actuality. "When a psychic sees symbolically, there's a great problem with interpretation." And there always has been, since the days of the dramatic muddles over the Delphic Oracle.

Whenever he can, Ryzl tries to show students that this "weird" psychic sense is an asset. Three months after taking up her psychic education, Josefka one day complained, "I've lost my apartment keys." Putting her in trance, Ryzl told her to look back in time and see what happened to them. As though describing a film, Josefka told him, "It's morning. My grandmother is taking the keys out of my purse." Eventually she "saw" the old lady put them on a shelf in the cupboard. Arriving home, Josefka found her keys exactly where she'd seen them clairvoyantly. On another occasion, anxious to get hold of her mother, Josefka phoned home. No answer. "Concentrate," Ryzl commanded, "and tell me the precise minute your mother is going to get in." Later, curiously, Josefka dialed home at the time she'd predicted psychically. "Why, hello," her mother answered. "I've just come through the door."

When he's trying to lure his volunteers into a sixth sense or when he wants to study ESP as "an individual, unique, and more or less creative act," Ryzl uses the qualitative approach. Even when he introduces the typical statistical tests to students he often uses them informally, more concerned with teaching than proving. Ryzl, however, knew quite well that if he wanted other parapsychologists—particularly those in the West—to give his psychic training system a tumble, he'd have to rack up a stack of solid statistical proof that a volunteer had indeed become psychic. (His most extensively documented prodigy, Pavel Stepanek, a wonder medium to scientific hardliners, is covered in the next chapter.)

Ryzl documented Josefka's psychic proficiency after six months of his course. He used ESP cards wrapped inside several thicknesses of stiff, opaque paper. Neither Ryzl nor Josefka knew which symbol was in a particular package. Ryzl double-checked each wrapped card to be positive there were no sensory clues. Then he handed the packets, one at a time, to the entranced Josefka. Speaking slowly, Josefka made her guesses: "Circle . . . star . . ." She ran through 250 cards. Chance expectation is fifty correct answers. Josefka scored 121 hits. There is less than one chance in a trillion that she could have done this accidentally.

But was it Ryzl's technique that activated Josefka's sixth sense? He asked her to guess 250 more cards when wide awake. She scored at chance level. During her psychic training, Ryzl gave Josefka various statistical tests. Another particularly impressive one involved cards behind a screen. Ryzl wanted Josefka to tell him two things clairvoyantly. Does the sealed envelope contain a card? If so, what symbol is on it? On this occasion, Josefka's ESP clicked off when it came to identifying symbols, but flowed freely in determining whether a thick, opaque envelope she could neither see nor touch was full. Out of five hundred guesses in this simple heads-or-tails test, by chance you should get half, or 250, of the answers right. Josefka scored 314 correctly.[372] The odds against doing this by chance are greater than a million to one.

Josefka apparently learned to tune in psychic talent under Ryzl's hypnotic control. What good was it? It was about as useful as a dummy's ability to talk sitting at the knee of the ventriloquist. Ryzl's professed aim is to give people a fully integrated sixth sense. There were two ways, Ryzl thought, to make Josefka a round-the-clock psychic. Either she must gain conscious mastery of her new ability, or she must go through life in a trance.

He tried the more bizarre, but easier alternative first. One wintry evening he told the hypnotized Josefka, "I want you to remain in light trance until you return here tomorrow evening. But," cautioned Ryzl, "act just as you would in the waking state." None of Josefka's family or co-workers realized the girl walked, talked, and ate with them in trance, although her mother did ask if anything were wrong. "You look so sad," she said. "No, nothing's wrong," the entranced Josefka assured her. Even Ryzl wasn't positive his hypnosis had stuck when Josefka walked into the lab the next day. He described her as reminiscent of a slightly drunk woman concentrating hard on the proper actions.

A test showed her still under hypnosis. "It would be impossible to live like that!" Josefka exclaimed when she was finally set free. Life had seemed as drab as flat paint.

All the highlights vanished. And Ryzl saw that the entranced Josefka also lost her own sparkle. He abandoned any idea of sending psychic zombies into the world.

Transplanting control of the new sixth sense from Ryzl to the student is a delicate operation. Ryzl tries to teach the individual to get himself into the state of consciousness needed for ESP—an "active mental inactivity." Josefka found she had to balance on a gray thread between sleep and wakefulness. All thought inhibited, she must wait patiently, passively for the psychic impression to appear. After the images formed, she must switch on the active, critical side of her mind to evaluate and report on what filled her psychic screen. Some people lose their ESP when Ryzl can no longer instill confidence hypnotically. Others find their psychic ability freezes into specific channels. Ryzl thinks the risk is worth taking. "The integrity of the personality is preserved. And students who can manipulate their own states of consciousness are better able to interpret complicated clairvoyant scenes."

Josefka began to find she was, at times, psychic as she went through her day coping with the logistics of big city life in Prague. She began occasionally to tune into her friends' thoughts telepathically. "It's really funny," Josefka confided to Ryzl. "Sometimes I have to try not to laugh at some of the thoughts I get. You see, they usually have nothing to do with what we're talking about. I get the other things that are going through their minds."

Josefka's employers benefited from the new abilities she acquired at her psychic night school course, though she probably didn't tell them about it. One day after rummaging through the office files, searching for some important, missing papers, Josefka realized that if she did possess the vaunted sixth sense, this would be a good time to use it. She summoned her clairvoyance and got a picture of the documents. Quietly she slipped on her coat and headed for a branch office a few miles away. This office had been completely refurnished since her last visit some months ago. According to Ryzl, Josefka walked straight to a desk she'd seen clairvoyantly, opened the drawer, and picked up the lost documents.

"Once in a while, Josefka thought her sixth sense was a nuisance. She'd foresee something unpleasant and then have to wait for it to happen. She also felt strange about confessing to her friends that she had this new talent, but generally she seemed to enjoy it," Ryzl told us.

Another subject, Mrs. Adolphaba, apparently enjoyed a newfound ability to identify anything wrapped up in a box. In 1965, an ABC television crew from America descended on Ryzl and his students in Prague to film a segment for a documentary on ESP. Happily ignoring the whirring cameras and the Laocoon coils filling the usually placid lab Mrs. Adolphaba successfully identified for the Americans three out of four objects they'd presealed in boxes. But shortly afterward, Mrs. Adolphaba left Ryzl for "personal reasons"—probably her family's objections, he says.

Ryzl found not everyone was delighted when he bestowed a new sense on them. "People were afraid they'd be thought strange; a few thought some other parapsychologist might pay them more. There was one girl who was shaping into a good clairvoyant, then she got engaged. Her fiancé absolutely refused to allow her to see me. He thought I was some kind of a vampire. Others left because they were too busy, many of them were students at Charles University. Their ESP suffered during exams, as it always does when people are worried, overworked, tired."

Most of Ryzl's volunteers wound up with just the five senses they started with. He reports that fifty of the five hundred people he tried to train did develop ESP.[379] Thirteen of these people showed psychic ability on a level with Josefka's—telepathy, precognition, clairvoyance, and traveling clairvoyance. "That figure of five hundred trainees is a little misleading. I had to include in that everyone I worked with, even people who only showed up for two or three sessions. It took a year of training before Josefka could manipulate her own clairvoyance.

"Unfortunately, Josefka left too, just as we were beginning to get somewhere in precognition experiments. Her grandmother died suddenly. She'd been brought up by the old woman and it was a bad shock. Josefka rushed right into an unfortunate marriage. She's divorced now. She came to tell me that she wanted to get back into psychic work—but then, soon after that, I left Czechoslovakia."

Why did Ryzl leave? He was on the staff of the Czech Institute of Biology. He was a member of the Czech Academy of Science. He headed a parapsychology research group. He had a special room fitted as a lab in his apartment; he lectured on his psychic system to psychology classes at Charles University.

"It's true, I was in a very good position. I had started a new center. I could do more or less anything I wanted in psychic research," Ryzl admits. "In the beginning, in the late 1950s, it hadn't been so easy. There was tremendous opposition. And the skeptics did not criticize on scientific grounds. They argued against parapsychology on political, ideological grounds. There was a great deal of mudslinging." By the time Ryzl left, at the end of 1967, thanks in part to his own work and the publicity he'd given parapsychology in Russia and the West, the Czech government turned a beneficent eye on parapsychology. Ironically, it was because the dictatorial Novotny regime felt so warmly toward the field that Ryzl says he had to leave. "The authorities are certainly interested now. The Czech secret police visited me. This was before Dubcek. They wanted me to report to them on the psychic research going on in the countries I visited. They wanted me to look for information. I am a scientist, not a spy. They were so insistent, I decided I'd try to get out and take my chances in America."

While he worked in Czechoslovakia, Ryzl did more than his share proving the existence of ESP. His work is the best documented, at least publicly, of any Communist researcher. Yet Ryzl, like most men on the way up in the Communist field, is more interested in using psi than in validating it *ad nauseam*. When the eyeless sight craze ruffled through Russia, Ryzl immediately tried his brand of eyeless sight in a Prague home for the blind. Apparently he wasn't much concerned about fields or forces or skin sensitivity. Everybody had heard about the Soviet eyeless sight readers. Popular belief in it seemed just what Ryzl needed to "trick" blind children into seeing clairvoyantly. He hypnotized blind grammar school boys and girls. "Run your fingers over this case," he commanded, presenting a heavy metal pocket watch with the lid closed. "Your fingers can easily feel where the watch hands are. Tell me what time it is." To the delight of everyone, the children did, well above the possibilities of chance. They may have thought they were finger reading like Rosa Kuleshova, but it sounds like old-fashioned ESP was giving them the time of day. Ryzl, who exudes excitement and makes tests seem more like adventures than a task, fired up a young prodigy.

"It was very funny. I went back to the school and got quite a surprise. One of the boys told me he could do what I did. Apparently, playing parapsychologist, he managed to hypnotize another blind boy. He did pretty well with his experiments too. He got the hypnotized child, while the teacher watched, to identify the color of spools of thread that the teacher made up for them."

Ryzl tried more sporting uses of psi. "I wish you had the same kind of lottery in the United States that we have in Prague," he said after questioning us about the New York State lottery. If we had a lottery like the one in Czechoslovakia, there might be a lot more people crowding into the labs for psychic experiments. "There are forty-nine numbers in the Czech lottery. If you guess six of them, in any order at all, you get a big prize, about $10,000. For five right numbers you get about half that, and so on down the line. It's a perfect setup for a precognition test, don't you think?

"We signalized the numbers of the lottery into symbols and asked Josefka, Pavel Stepanek, and other psychics I'd developed to try to foresee the winners. The first week we got only one right, then the next week, three. The next try we got four numbers right. And we won a good sum. To do this really properly, you should get a lot of psychics trying to predict the right numbers and average their guesses. That way individual error is cut way down."

Ryzl is a healthy believer in motivation. Before leaving Prague, he called for the government to support gifted psychics as they do other talented people. "If psychics had recognition, if they didn't have to worry about an unrelated job, they'd be much better able to help explore their own gifts."

Perhaps because Ryzl didn't believe in motivating other parapsychologists to get in on the lottery business, he didn't document his ESP lottery experiment *in toto*. Instead, he set up the kind of standard precognition tests most researchers are used to.[372, 381] He'd trained Josefka for over half a year. She could more or less assume the state of mind required for ESP on her own. Ryzl simply instructed her, "I want you to tell me in order now the symbols my assistant is going to pick *next week*." Ryzl wrote down and locked away the ten thousand symbols Josefka reeled off. Days later, his laboratory assistant, using scientifically controlled randomized techniques, also recorded ten thousand symbols. In four hundred runs of twenty-five calls, Josefka averaged 5.79 hits per run. Odds against doing this prophecy by chance are greater than a million to one.

It seems Ryzl had taken an ordinary girl and pushed her to the point where she could see the supposedly nonexistent future. To predict an earthquake or an assassination is a lot more exciting than Josefka's symbol-guessing, yet her accomplishment is almost more enigmatic. The abstract, colorless, completely unemotional nature of the test obliterates any thought of the educated guess. It's hard to believe there are great stirrings in the substrata of earth or consciousness converging on the choice of ten thousand symbols next week. Why would the mind leap ahead to grasp the right symbols?

Precognition is key to the mysteries of psi in Ryzl's opinion. "It's why I can't believe in the theory that electromagnetic waves somehow cause psi. They can't explain prophecy. Some people, particularly in Russia, speak of a psi field. But what is that? And how would it explain prophecy? I believe the answer lies in a new understanding of space and time. And I think it is very deep." In a slightly different vein, Ryzl said, "The findings of parapsychology indicate that there must exist some higher realities lying over our material life."

In 1968, when he worked for a time at Dr. Rhine's Foundation for Research on the Nature of Man at Durham, Ryzl tried precognitive tests on girl students of Duke University. Like Josefka, some scored significantly. Ryzl doesn't mention taking any high-scoring coeds off to the races to help him make his way in the new world.

"I took Josefka to the races, but she didn't really enjoy them much because I had her in trance. I asked her to look ahead and see what winning numbers would light up on the board after the race. It was comical. She was right, but we lost our bets. Josefka correctly saw the column of numbers running down the right-hand side of the board. In this particular race, two horses tied for first. Instead of being in the usual column, their numbers were put side by side across the top of the board, a place I hadn't directed her to see in her vision."

Ryzl still turns over in his mind the idea of interfering with a predicted event in the future. "Josefka and I did a series of informal tests. She predicted, noting it on a piece of paper that I couldn't see, whether I would get up and leave the room or remain in my chair. Then I flipped a coin. Heads I left; tails I stayed. We did this a number of times and she was right. Then, just to see what would happen, I decided I would stay in the room no matter which way the coin came up. And this time, interestingly, Josefka couldn't predict my movements at all. She said nothing come to her, she felt blocked." Interference with the future is something Ryzl plans to work on in America. "I suppose some events cannot be prophesied and some cannot be changed. But I suspect that many can be altered if enough minds are channeled toward them."

While still in Czechoslovakia, Ryzl brought his scientific sights to bear on realms as intriguing and elusive as prophecy. Dr. Ryzl wrote about these unusual investigations in an Indian Journal.[374] "We carried out these experiments in a Prague parapsychology lab. Subjects with reliable psychic abilities attempted to perceive various formations and processes which cannot be perceived by normal senses, but which are postulated by religious and occult doctrines—for instance the so-called 'astral body,' substantiality of 'soul,' the survival of the 'soul' after death, reincarnation and so forth."

Ryzl emphasizes he is fully aware that in the present state of knowledge about psi faculties it would be premature to draw extensive inferences from the experiments. "Nevertheless, many times, statements made by psychic subjects contained information that rationalized well with the often heterogeneous allegations of occult and religious systems."

He goes on to say that if any conclusions can be drawn from these deep ventures into the psychic realm, the main one is that the world we perceive normally is only a single component of a greater whole. He suggests there exists another reality beyond our senses, our present day instrumentation, and perhaps beyond the mathematical picture of the world drawn by theoretical physics. He will need new terms and new scientific coordinates to explore this further reality, Ryzl thinks.

"I realize I will be criticized for mentioning these experiments," Ryzl wrote, "but I do so to state my conviction that parapsychology bids fair to find the connecting link between empirical natural sciences and religion—i.e., to find a possibility of integrating religion as a 'science dealing with supersensory entities' with the natural sciences." If this goal is realized, Dr. Ryzl sees the development of parapsychology leading toward findings as revolutionary if not more revolutionary than the advent of Copernican cosmogony or the splitting of the atom.

What about Ryzl's psychic training system as a means of helping parapsychology on its way? Certainly it is an important attempt to find a practical route to psi, to increase our ability to know. Even though Ryzl has departed from Czechoslovakia, the Communist world still considers his method one of the two viable ways of developing needed psychics. (According to Dr. Sergeyev of Leningrad, another way of finding people with ESP is to test for an unusually large difference in electrical potential between front and back of the brain. The two methods could naturally be combined.) Most Western scientists, so far, seem more interested in studying the card-guessing ability of Ryzl's most famous trainee, Pavel Stepanek, than in trying to develop new psychics. Probably many researchers would not be successful with Ryzl's technique—simply because they are not Ryzl.

The personality of the experimenter in a hypnotic system is inextricably combined with the success of the project. Ryzl is a lively, ebullient, brimming enthusiast who gives you the feeling ESP is neither frightening nor impossible. Just as some patients and some psychiatrists don't click, the personalities of some researchers may not be the right ones to fuse ESP with Ryzl's methods. Furthermore, Ryzl says, "Hypnosis is certainly not the right technique to use on everybody. I only found it successful with 10 per cent of my people. We must develop other methods for evoking psychic ability too."

What will ESP be used for? "To make money, and as a

weapon," Ryzl states flatly. In this, he's much more cynical than most American researchers, but Ryzl—a Czech—perhaps has reason. He once remarked casually that psychic abilities on a large scale would certainly bring about some novel social, psychological, and legal problems. "In the long run, of course, psi will mean much more than a tip on the market or a military weapon. It will revolutionize life generally."

When he arrived in America, the Bulletin of Rhine's Foundation for Research on the Nature of Man quoted Ryzl: "The developments in the natural sciences, and, of course, the whole trend of the development of modern civilization have given emphasis to the material and technical aspects of life. In today's civilization man is drawn more and more away from his inner life. In my opinion, parapsychological research could reverse this trend and direct man's attention also to other aspects of his cosmic existence and to other forces and components of his personality." [295]

The exploration of the potentials of psi for each individual is just beginning. Ryzl is packed with novel ideas, with energy; he's a comer, adept at both fancy footwork and solid research; he also has a better grasp of psi trends in the Communist world than anyone else in America. His defection went generally unheralded in the West, but caused reverberations in the Communist bloc. Ryzl may prove a very fortunate addition to America, particularly if he and others are right in believing the inner space race is on.

25

PAVEL STEPANEK, AN ANSWER FOR THE SKEPTICS?

"Pavel Stepanek's achievement is one that has rarely, if ever, been equaled in the history of parapsychology," says foremost American parapsychologist, Dr. J. G. Pratt.[277] "We have no hesitation in saying that the results [of tests with Stepanek] provide evidence of ESP," he and Dr. Jan Blom of Holland declared.[352]

"ESP Proof From Prague?" chimed in British science magazine, *The New Scientist*.[274] Pavel Stepanek is the first psychic in twenty years to be written up in an establishment science journal such as *Nature* (Vol. 220, 1968).

Pavel Stepanek can demonstrate ESP on demand! said an international band of researchers. A new star subject has been discovered in Prague! [390] Tested and vouched for by parapsychologists from a multitude of countries, research on Stepanek now occupies volumes of the world's parapsychology journals.[348-349, 388, 390]

Who is this darling of the parapsychologists, this *wunderkind* of psi, this cipher known in the annals of psychic research as "P.S." as if he were a rare atomic element or a postscript to a letter? When we finally reached Prague, it was a relief to meet the man behind the scientific symbology.

Blond, with blue eyes and turned-up nose, Pavel, usually beaming, comes over as someone out of a more innocent era, a little bit like the true-hearted woodsman of children's stories. In addition to his old-fashioned niceness which makes it hard enough to suspect him of guile, Pavel Stepanek is probably the world's most stringently, exhaustively tested psychic—in one department. Pavel is an ESP card whiz. If there was a seal of approval in psi labs, he would have it.

When we met in Czechoslovakia, Pavel asked us to sign

his memory book. Handwritten testimonials and remembrances of visits slant across its pages signed by generally hardnosed scientists. During the 1960s over a dozen parapsychologists from England, India, America, Sweden, Japan, and Holland journeyed to Czechoslovakia to meet Stepanek, Dr. Ryzl's most famous psychic student. Pavel has never refused to put his gift at their disposal, sometimes even taking vacation days from his job to do it. To hear the grateful scientists tell it, the most amazing thing about Stepanek, a bachelor in his late thirties, is his modest, ever cooperative, unmediumistic personality.

There may be no such thing as undeniable proof of anything, but the successful parapsychological work with Stepanek seems undeniable. This unassuming, slightly shy Czech is proving a *bête noire* to people who believe ESP can't exist.

Stepanek, the lab psychic of the century, had his "greatness" thrust upon him. "It was in the summer of 1961," he said. "A friend told me about the experiments Dr. Ryzl was doing. People ask me now why I decided to volunteer at Ryzl's lab. It was curiosity, plain curiosity that got me there."

Curiosity got him there. Then Ryzl took over, prodding and coaxing Stepanek through his hypnotic-into-psychic course. After a few months, a psychic sense did begin to emerge in Pavel. Sitting in trance, his usual smile relaxed, Pavel began to answer correctly, "circle, star, wavy lines," when Ryzl asked, "which ESP card is behind the screen?" Pavel's developing sixth sense fastened on the hidden cards so sharply that Ryzl tried a new test—a tightly controlled model experiment.

Pavel simply had to tell if the black or white side of a card was upward inside an opaque envelope. In a separate, closed-off room, Mrs. Ryzl, also a psi experimenter, prepared the cards. First she turned to the Prague telephone book as a source of random numbers—odd numbers signified one color up, even the other. She randomly inserted the cards in snug envelopes and clipped them shut. These covers were strictly opaque; even when she held an empty one in front of a lamp, no light shone through.

Mrs. Ryzl took the randomized cards to her husband in the experimental room. He began cutting the deck with an unusual formula that he alone knew, based on the time of sunrise and sunset in Prague. When the tests began, neither the Ryzls nor Stepanek had any sensory way of knowing whether black or white faced up inside the envelopes. Holding the deck behind a screen, Ryzl picked up the top card. The entranced Pavel made the first of a decade of card guesses to come.

He was a grand success. After each run through the deck, the Ryzls repeated their painstaking randomizing procedure so that Pavel eventually made two thousand calls. Probability dictates a thousand correct. The odds are a billion to one against getting 1,114 cards right. Pavel Stepanek did.[391]

Ryzl's training apparently kicked over Stepanek's ESP. But there was a big difference between Stepanek's new psychic power and that of other successful students. His clairvoyance didn't spark off in all directions. It ran like a river right toward ESP cards. As far as enhancing life goes, this kind of a sixth sense didn't seem to do much for Stepanek. But it was a golden opportunity for Ryzl. The faithful Stepanek might be just the person Ryzl needed to build airtight, undeniable proof that a student had become psychic under his hypnotic training. Could Stepanek's clairvoyance light on or light up hidden cards when he was not in trance?

"Stepanek actually took longer to display clairvoyance under hypnosis than many students, but he learned to assume conscious control of his psychic talent very quickly," Ryzl relates. In a little more than a month they were ready for a new series of tests.

Mrs. Ryzl again helped her husband prepare a complex, randomized batch of cards. This time when Ryzl went into the large airy testing room, he didn't hypnotize Pavel. He didn't even give him a word of encouragement. Ryzl just sat down and let Stepanek touch each sealed enevelope briefly with his fingertips. Pavel gazed into space "with an air of workman-like concentration," then guessed. He was doing more than guessing, the Ryzls discovered. He was psychic. The clairvoyance stuck even when he was wide awake. The odds against guessing as well as he had by chance were about twelve thousand to one.[391]

Stepanek was on his own as a psychic; Ryzl never again

gave him hypnotic help. Instead he gave him an awful lot of card tests. Stepanek is an ESP statistician's dream. Ryzl's barrage of figures startled researchers in the West. Here was a young Czech scientist who claimed he'd found a non-mystical, repeatable, more or less scientific, and above all successful program for training psychics. And he had a high scoring card guesser to prove it. The first foreign parapsychologist to land in Prague was Dr. J. G. Pratt, an experienced investigator who'd run some famous card experiments of his own when he worked with Rhine at Duke University. Pratt designed card tests for the Czech bachelor. Pavel showed his mettle and came out psychic [387] "on demand," says Pratt, "and under conditions that would normally be expected to inhibit success."

Next, three Dutch scientists, J. T. Berendregt, P. R. Barkema, and J. Kappers, made the flight to Prague. Ryzl turned his prize pupil over to them totally. Stepanek gave fine psychic scores on the complex card tests the three Dutch visitors devised.

Then a new mystery developed. Ryzl had determined statistically that Pavel reacted in a particular way to some cards more often than others.[389] The Dutch used some of these favored cards from past tests, put them in new envelopes, turned them over between runs. There seemed to be no possible way for Stepanek to know when a favorite came up. Still he guessed them in a consistent pattern. "It's as if he put a psychic mark on the card," says Ryzl, "as though some unknown force helps him attune to one card and not another." The tuning to certain cards is known as the "focusing effect" and right now it may be leading to an important breakthrough in parapsychology. The Dutch naturally wondered if there was something different, like the rate of heat absorption, about the favored cards that made them identifiable even through envelopes.

Professor J. Kistemaker of the Laboratory of Mass Separation, the Netherlands, and Dr. J. Blom of the Phonetic Laboratory of the University of Amsterdam checked the physical properties of the decks. The cards, they reported, are all alike. They could find no differences. The thorough Dutch also asked a world champion magician, Fred Kaps, is he could duplicate Pavel's card calling, under identical conditions, with his magic. Kaps, at length, told them his bag of tricks couldn't match Stepanek's ESP performance.[385]

Stepanek seemed to be a man for the long haul. He's kept right on racking up impressive scores on the tests. Yet, as a psychic, he's a sort of Johnny-one-note. "It's a curious thing," Ryzl says, "Stepanek's clairvoyance always moved in that one channel, etching it deeper and deeper. Apparently this single ability to score well on the tests satisfies whatever motivation or need he has for a sixth sense."

Roman Catholicism is alive with meaning for Stepanek and he practices it faithfully. "Czechoslovakia is still a very Catholic country," he told us. Did he ever have a mystical experience? Did he ever have any kind of psychic experience in his whole life, apart from the cards? "I personally think there may have been one thing that happened to me that was ESP," Stepanek told us. "It was during the war when I was a boy. One morning I woke up with a strange feeling, a sort of presentiment. I felt terribly restless. I told my mother I just couldn't stay in the house. I went out, across town to my aunt's home. All of a sudden the sirens went off. Planes came over. It was Prague's first air raid. There was no damage to our house or anything like that. It's just that I seemed to know something bad was going to happen."

Stepanek has read accounts of other psychics, the famous ones who pick up thoughts, find lost children, help solve crimes. "I'd really like to try to do more with my ESP," he admits. "Maybe I can someday. But the scientists have asked me not to try anything else until they're through with the cards. So . . ." Pavel smiled and shrugged.

As the mid sixties approached, more scientists went through Czech customs toting suitcases filled with yellow and white, green and white, black and white cards. Carrying green and white cards was Dr. John Beloff of the University of Edinburgh. Working with Beloff, Stepanek turned in one of his few negatively significant psi scores.[384] He scored less cards right than you should by chance. Unconsciously he used clairvoyance to miss. That a desire to miss should begin to stalk Pavel's subconscious isn't surprising. When Beloff put his deck on the table Pavel had already run through 42,598 certified and published card guesses and many, many more unofficial calls.

Twenty thousand guesses before, scientists were wondering how Stepanek had managed to keep on identifying ESP cards so long. Almost all good card subjects lose their ability as time wears away in the laboratory. Perhaps it's plain boredom, perhaps as some Soviet researchers claim it's because the ESP cards done quickly cause a blur in the telepathic brain wave pattern. Or perhaps some other facet of the test levels out and extinguishes card ESP even in the most renowned psychics. A major part of the Stepanek personality, however, is a desire to please, and, unlike everybody else, he seems to get a kick out of card tests. The Duke Parapsychology Laboratory next dispatched John Freeman, an American and Miss B. K. Kanthamani, an Indian, to Prague. As Freeman and Miss Kanthamani calculated the calls he made on several card runs, Stepanek paced restlessly, chainsmoking American cigarettes. Finally the scientists emerged from their inner sanctum. Pavel's salad days had returned. Again his cheerful self, Stepanek left the lab knowing he was scoring at the ten-thousand-to-one level.[386]

At this point, Ryzl had proved about as much as he could with Stepanek. His own tests, coupled with the validating work of others, built his proof, pristine and sturdy as the superstructure of a skyscraper. He had developed a psychic. Beyond the necessities of currently acceptable proof, Ryzl doesn't seem avidly interested in card tests as he pursues psi. "You don't really know when clairvoyance is occurring during card tests," Ryzl points out. Only the ghostly after-image of ESP appears in the statistical calculations. An individual call may be a lucky guess or it may be a flash of clairvoyance. Ryzl proved his point almost too well. Stepanek, the bird in the hand, has been much more researched and discussed in the West than Ryzl's training technique. It's easier to get a handle on Stepanek's black and white ESP than to adapt Ryzl's ways to hatch psychics of your own. And many researchers may not be overly interested in the basic emphasis of Ryzl's system which, more than breeding lab specimens, leans toward developing a psychic quality in people, sparked with all the uncontrolled loops and surprises of life itself.

To continue showing his stuff, Stepanek needed a new mentor. Fortunately, he found one in the empathetic Dr. Pratt, now of the University of Virginia. Pratt visited Prague numerous times, carefully charting clues to the workings of Pavel's gift. Then, in 1968, something "wonderful" happened to Stepanek.

"I was so excited when I got home I ran through the door and shouted, 'Pack my bags, mama! I'm off to America!' My parents were really surprised. They never dreamed that these scientific experiments I was involved in would lead to a trip to America. Neither did I. It was a wonderful experience.

"In some ways I guess I had more fun on my trips because I went as a psychic. It started even before I left Prague for the first time, when I went to the American Embassy for a visa. 'What is the purpose of your trip?' they asked. ESP, I answered. There was a long pause.

"I traveled by ship and met so many different kinds of people. I had a day in New York. In America the thing that impressed me most was the lights," Pavel said. "Everything is all lit up at night there. We don't have anything like that here. It was so beautiful to see. While I was staying in Virginia at the University, I took a Greyhound bus to North Carolina to visit Dr. Rhine's Foundation."

Pavel is an enthusiastic, happily impressionable tourist and loves to reminisce about Times Square, Bloomingdale's Department Store, President Jefferson's home in Charlottesville, country music, and the people he met—third generation Czechs living in Virginia, and various parapsychological luminaries.

Ryzl hoped to give his volunteers a sixth sense to transform their lives. Stepanek's grooved right into cards and stuck. But indirectly, and perhaps in a less disconcerting way, the ESP Ryzl bestowed on Pavel has transformed his life. In the spring of 1969 Pavel made his third trip across Europe to spend a month in America. In the university library where he works as a clerk, Pavel is the only person who's seen the United States. Even Ryzl never traveled to the West until he left for good.

"Did you see my movie?" Stepanek asked us, referring to a film of him guessing cards with Dr. Pratt. "I heard it was shown at the Moscow Parapsychology Conference."

We told him he looked good in it. "I never expected to be a movie star," Pavel laughed. "Particularly not in Moscow!" Stepanek obviously enjoys his burgeoning fame, openly, the way you'd enjoy basking in the sun in your yard, without any feeling of afflatus.

What do his friends think of Stepanek's psychic adventures? "Sometimes I talk about it a little with the person who told me about Dr. Ryzl—but the rest of my old friends are married now. They have their own concerns. It's different for a person alone in the world, like me . . . nobody in Prague knows about my ESP."

In his many tests with Dr. Pratt, Pavel's ESP has shifted out of simple card guessing to a far more obscure and, some think, far more important phenomenon.[274, 353-55, 350] Pratt is wholeheartedly on the trail of the "focusing effect," Pavel's ability to relate clairvoyantly to favored cards, to seemingly know when favorites are presented no matter how well they are wrapped. Pratt discovered that Pavel not only had favorite cards, but that he also began to focus on certain envelopes that held cards, even though there were no visual, no physical clues, no differences at all. These envelopes were put inside covers. Still Pavel could focus on his favorites. Eventually, some of the covers also showed focusing and these were then fitted into jackets. In recent tests, Pavel has been presented with packages containing card, envelope, cover, and jacket, one inside the other.

Obviously it takes a group of experimenters and computerized calculations to get the trees out of the forest of statistics, the trees being whichever of the four elements Pavel is focusing on.

Focusing is a new discovery. What is it? Ryzl thinks Pavel may leave a sort of psychic mark on guessed cards that he later recognizes clairvoyantly. Some researchers believe Pavel, like every other long-distance card guesser in history, is bone bored, but rather than clicking off clairvoyance, unconsciously invents busy work. After years of research on Pavel's focusing, Dr. Pratt thinks it might be a clue to some unknown "psi field."

Is there a psi field around objects and around people? Is it some peculiarity of psi fields that enables mediums to tune in to some objects and not others? Such a field is implied by psychometry: a psychic holding an antique locket, a pen, or any object belonging to an unknown person may suddenly tune into events in the person's life or even the long closed histories of past owners of an old object. It's as if things carry invisible traces of experience, just as Pavel's favorite cards seem to. Pavel's focusing, if ever explained, might help unlock many conundrums in ESP.

Focusing is obscure and complicated, but it seems to be proving something to scientists. Studies of Stepanek's ESP have finally cracked the scientific journals for the first time in twenty years. Researchers are beginning to ask, "Is ESP scientifically respectable at last?" Whether it's guessing or focusing, Pavel seems to stand for proof that's hard for many rigid establishmentarians to ignore.

Pavel with his singular ESP is an important psychic. He's managed to keep on clairvoyantly identifying cards longer than anyone in history. He's provided parapsychologists with contemporary proof positive. In this there may be an archetypal tale. The shy, unassuming man with his simple gift knocks at the impregnable castle. Today it looks as if the gates of the scientific establishment that never opened to his more splendiferous colleagues are opening to Pavel Stepanek. For that alone he deserves a niche in the history of psychic research. Even the scientists agree it couldn't happen to a nicer person.

26

ASTROLOGICAL BIRTH CONTROL

The full moon like a glowing jack-o'-lantern rising above the tree tops; the cool sickle moon riding with the high stars; no moon, the moon invisible but real and turning and moving the rhythms of the sea, of trees, of oysters, and perhaps of all of us. Czechoslovakia has a science center, complete with computers, volumes of mathematical data, minute medical information, that is very much concerned with the moon and the planets. But there isn't an astronaut or a space capsule mock-up in sight. The scientists at this center are gynecologists and psychiatrists.

Led by Dr. Eugen Jonas (pronounced Yoan-ash), these M.D.s are trying to eliminate a great deal of woe right here on earth. To do it, they're dispensing "prescriptions" based on the position of the moon, the sun, and the planets; in other words, these Czech doctors are using astrology. Their astrological advice is coming from the Astra Research Center for Planned Parenthood in Nitra, founded in 1968 by the Czech government.[1, 125, 220A] Dr. Jonas struggled for over a decade to bring in his far-ranging discoveries in medical astrology.[63] It was worth fighting for.

The Astra Center of Czechoslovakia believes it has found a way to:

- ★ Ensure safe, reliable birth control without pills, contraceptives, or operations;
- ★ Help many seemingly sterile women become fertile;
- ★ Help women who have had nothing but miscarriages deliver full-term babies;
- ★ Help ensure a healthy baby, eliminating birth defects and mental retardation;
- ★ Allow parents to choose whether they will have a girl or a boy.

It's quite a claim, but the Czechs seem to be on to quite an extraordinary way of solving a lot of tragic problems.

Dr. Jonas, a psychiatrist, is no fly-by-night fortuneteller. A slight man with a gentle smile, Dr. Jonas looks as if he's stayed up late for a long time poring over his calculations. International conferences have asked Jonas to present some of his hard won findings—The Czech Academy of Science Conference on Biorhythm in Prague, the Brussels Conference on the Influence of Planets on Man, 1968. The International Society for Planned Parenthood with UNESCO is studying Jonas' work. The Max Planck Institute at Heidelberg asked to see his statistical findings.[62] Academician Petrov Maslaskov of Leningrad's Institute of Gynecology is leading the exploration of the Jonas discovery in Russia. Top-ranking scientists from various fields in Czechoslovakia and Hungary who've taken the trouble to examine Jonas' research have gone to bat for him. Birth control via astrology seems to work.

Dr. Jonas, from Slovakia close to the Hungarian border, began his uphill fight in 1956. Hungary passed a law legalizing abortion. Jonas, then a young psychiatric doctor, began to wonder, "Couldn't there be a less traumatic way of going about birth control?" He'd noticed in his practice that women of high nervous sensitivity seemed to experience a recurring cycle of heightened sexual desire. This high point came on different days for different women. But, and this was his first clue, it recurred in all of them about every thirty days.

On the side, Dr. Jonas had studied both astronomy and astrology. He knew science has recently established that the moon influences humans in a variety of ways, from an increase of arson at full moon to a decrease in the birth of children at times of new moon. Jonas also knew that outstanding scientists of other centuries from Hippocrates to Kepler and Leibniz practiced astrology. The old astrologers have always maintained that fertility periods have something to do with the waxing and waning of the moon. Obviously, it was more complicated than the idea that all women's fertility period simply followed the phases of the moon.

Could Jonas find anything in the hoary tables of astrology that would help in the modern birth control struggle? Combining his psychiatric observations and birth data of particular women with the calculations of astronomy and astrology, he waded into a mass of figuring. Jonas found something—a planetary configuration, a key. This is an individual pattern that, basically, involves the relationship of the sun and the moon at each woman's birth. Once you find this calculation, Jonas discovered, it's possible to go on and figure out the days that a woman can conceive during her entire lifetime. If she avoids intercourse on these days, she can forget about unwanted pregnancy. If she longs for a baby then she must make the most of these fertility days.

Jonas compiled his figures, tables, case histories, and mailed his thesis to the Hungarian Academy of Science and the Czech Academy.

"We can't ignore the statements of Dr. Jonas even if we know that the old astrology went the way of all speculation," wrote Dr. Jirim Malkom of the Prague Gynecology Clinic in reply. "The movement of the stars is a precise time indicator; we use it to mark our time. It is not completely out of consideration that it also has some influence on the human organism. In case Dr. Jonas wishes to explore the old experiments of astrologers and to present new discoveries from them, it is all right."

It was all right. Jonas had permission from the authorities to continue his research and to send them his findings "by registered mail." Fine, but where was the backing to make the research possible, the large groups of patients needed for control tests? Jonas continued on his own until, in 1960, Dr. Aurel Hudcovic invited him to try and prove his theories at the Bratislava Clinic of Gynecology.

Here Dr. Jonas' good news discovery began to make a lot of people happy. Strings of girls or boys tend to run in some families. Many parents wind up with a brood of seven boys when all they really wanted was two boys and a girl. "Astrology allows parents to choose the sex of their child," Dr. Jonas claimed. At the Bratislava clinic he worked out the individual calculations for eight thousand women who wanted to have boys. Ninety-five percent got their made to order boy! A committee of gynecologists a short while later asked, "Can you work your astrology backward? If we tell you the date of intercourse, can you tell us what the sex of the child was?" Jonas tried and came up right 87 percent of the time. More recent tests seem to indicate parents now using Jonas' system can determine the sex of the child they will have with 98 percent accuracy. Full scientific data on Dr. Jonas' work with this medical astrology are included in his book, *Predetermining the Sex of a Child.*

It was nice he could help parents get the girl or boy they wanted. But Jonas was disturbed by much more difficult, tragic problems facing parents. Studying over five thousand case histories, he found that, excluding hereditary problems, dead, deformed, or retarded children were invariably produced when a woman conceived during certain oppositions of sun and moon or major planets in her individual chart. "Women who are born during the opposition of sun and moon, in other words at full moon, must take particular care not to conceive when this pattern recurs. They run a great risk of having unhealthy, deformed babies."

Dr. Jonas told F. Rubin of the *British Astrology Journal* about Mrs. V. Petrovis of Nitra. "She'd had three stillborn babies in a row. She finally delivered a live child, but it was deformed and three months premature. We prepared calculations for her and found something unusual. There were only four times during the year when she could conceive a normal healthy child. Carefully following our calculations, Mrs. Petrovis did produce a completely healthy, full-term baby. Mrs. Petrovis is just one of many similar cases."

Hoping to wipe out many defects in children, Jonas got permission from Dr. Lubomir Hanzlicek, Director of the Prague Institute for Psychiatrical Research, to carry out "cosmobiological" studies in the wards.

Meanwhile Dr. Kurt Rechnitz, a university professor and former director of the Budapest Obstetric Clinic in Hungary, was intrigued, and excited by Dr. Jonas' contention that astrology could be used for safe, reliable birth control. What a boon it would be if Jonas were right! Rechnitz plunged into medical astrology himself, compared mothers' charts, conception periods, and eventually amplified Jonas' system. As a test, Rechnitz did the required figuring and prescribed astrological birth control for 120 women who did not want children. None got pregnant. The Jonas-Rechnitz system is now being tested in Hungary and Czechoslovakia.[176]

By the mid 1960s Dr. Jonas had amassed an impressive

volume of statistics and case histories. His bank account was less than impressive. He spent a great deal of his own money buying up rare astrological texts. He'd traveled abroad talking to gynecologists, astronomers, physicists, and astrologers, trying to put everything they told him together. "One great problem," Jonas says, "is that gynecologists know nothing of astronomy. Astronomers haven't the slightest information about obstetrics, and both groups believe astrology is the worst sort of superstitious nonsense." A committed, studious man, Jonas knew he needed big-time backing if he was going to put his discoveries at the service of womankind. He gathered up his research and his courage and applied to the federal Health Ministry for a lab and a salary. Newspapers in Slovakia began to tell the Jonas story. Circulation doubled, tripled. One writer, Martina Janosovova, revealed that a single item on Jonas she'd written in the Slovak newspaper *Slovenku* resulted in her personally getting thousands and thousands of appeals for help. A year later the mail was still coming in, like this letter:

"As this is a matter of my happiness, I'll be frank. Before I was married, I had an abortion. Now after three years of marriage I seem to be barren. The doctors say both my husband and I are completely healthy. I decided to have a child at any price. I even tried being unfaithful to see if I'd become pregnant though I love my husband. Life without a child is not worthwhile. If only you could help me . . ."

Another woman wrote, "In 1966 I gave birth to a boy. I was very happy. But happiness didn't last long. The baby died in three months. I suffer this sorrow more and more because it doesn't seem possible for me to get pregnant. Tell me the address of Dr. Jonas. We will be thankful forever."

"Help us," "If only," "Please," "We beg you!" The Czech radio network was inundated with pleas after broadcasting a short account of Jonas' experimental work. But at the TBC Psychiatric Clinic in Sokolov, where he was a chief doctor, Jonas was hearing different sorts of comments. "You should stop treating patients and get treated yourself," one of his colleagues told him. "There's no future for you if you don't give up this astrology." When Jonas persisted in trying to get backing for full research of his findings, his doctor colleagues labeled him a "nut." Astrology could not have any bearing on medicine. They closed ranks and prevented him from taking exams for further degrees in psychiatry. Jonas took a leave of absence and headed for Hungary.

He returned with a document signed by a board of Hungarian doctors certifying his sanity. "A piece of paper doesn't prove you're sane," his former colleagues retorted —not if he persisted in fighting for his discovery. The ministry of the State Government of Slovakia sent a letter to the federal government attesting to Dr. Jonas' sanity. The Federal Health Ministry told Dr. Jonas "keep working" —but no support was forthcoming. A member of the Central Committee of the Czech Communist Party became interested in Jonas. He looked over his reports, then intervened, making it possible for the doctor to take his advanced exams. He passed with flying colors.

Despite the efforts of some medical colleagues, the embattled Jonas and his unorthodox discoveries were getting known. His book *Predetermining the Sex of a Child* was translated into six languages. His research work received attention in Hungary, England, and West Germany. The Germans even offered to give him a computer to assist his research. In his own country, scientists in and out of medicine rallied slowly around him. Finally, in 1968, the Czech Ministry of Health founded the Astra Research Center for Planned Parenthood at Nitra. Director Jonas had, at last, the staff and equipment he'd long dreamed of.[12] The government authorized the use of newspaper questionnaires. From just two newspapers, seven hundred readers sent in the detailed forms. Analyzed, this data further affirmed Jonas' ideas. In 1968 case histories and a description of the Jonas system were presented by Dr. Zdenek Rejdak in the magazine *Signal*.[182]

One woman who appealed to Astra for help after reading about it in the news was an obstetrician in Prague. She wanted to have a boy. The institute did her chart and calculated which days would ensure the conception of a boy. But, they warned, because of unusual configurations in her cosmic chart it would be difficult for her to carry a child. She ignored the warning, got pregnant, and had a miscarriage. She wrote Astra again and asked when they thought it would be possible for her to conceive a full-term baby boy. They sent her the information. Again she miscarried. Trying to understand why, the institute investigated. "I didn't really follow your plan," the doctor finally admitted. After all, she was an obstetrician, and the whole idea sounded too unbelievable. She's decided to try again for her boy with Astra's help.

Hippocrates, the "Father of Medicine," supposedly said, "The man who does not understand astrology is to be called fool rather than physician." It's unlikely the Jonas discovery will turn the family physician into an astrologer, but obstetricians at least may come to understand there are more variables to think about with their patients than they've realized before.

In Nitra, at Jonas' research center, large controlled tests are under way. Astrological calculations were done for volunteers, one group agreed to have intercourse only on the supposedly infertile days, and the other only on the predicted fertile days. Within a year or so, Jonas believes, this experiment will either prove his astrological birth control ideas and his system for choosing the sex of the baby, or will be the end of it. Other two-year-long experiments are running in Germany.

Individuals can apply to Astra for help. They submit the date, place, and, if possible, the time of their own birth and are given "cosmograms." The simplest of these are for birth control. Those to help women with a history of still births, miscarriages, or deformed babies require much more complex calculation. So far, Astra claims that with the help of the precise computers, they are just about 100 percent correct in the birth control cosmograms and 98 percent correct in their other work.

Why does the position of the moon, the sun, and perhaps the major planets at a woman's birth later affect her own child bearing? Nobody knows really. Scientists speculate about radiation on cells, or on the imposition of some pattern or rhythm, or about the idea that we are somehow in a dynamic relationship to everything in the universe.[42] Dr. Rechnitz of Hungary says that the phases of the moon may, possibly, build up tensions in the nervous system and affect a woman's hormones. "It's not surprising," according to obstetrician Rechnitz, "that this relationship to the moon was observed by a psychiatrist not an obstetrician." Rechnitz goes on, "Professor Pfaff of Erlangen, Germany, was the last professor of astrology; from then on this area was completely overridden by charlatans, which is a great pity because, as Jonas' discoveries prove, these are laws that should have been investigated to the roots."

Cosmobiology is a new science just taking off in Europe and America. Perhaps one day it will answer the "whys" of Jonas' discovery. But all we really need to know at the moment is whether the Astra system works. If it does, as early evidence indicates, these wondrous calculations can be put to work immediately.

Dr. Jonas' medical astrology is nothing but good news. Unlike most modern scientific discoveries, there seems to be no dark side associated with it. What a wonderful benefit it would be in the area of birth control alone. The Czechs point out it is 98 percent effective—as good as "The Pill." [62] There are no side effects, no nausea, no headaches, no nervous tension, no weight gain, no worry about possible serious long-term effects. And there are no monthly purchases to make. It is more effective than contraceptive devices. It's certainly a lot easier on a woman than having an abortion.

Birth control via astrology could be *the* answer for today's embroiled and embittered Roman Catholics.[126] If the Pope sanctions that theologically sound but highly ineffective rhythm method, it's hard to see how he could object to the astrology system.

But the Astra system is not just good news for people who wish to avoid unwanted children. It's just as happy a discovery for people who do want children. Parents could choose the sex of their child if they wished.[122] Barren women can, they say, be helped, the real unhappiness of still births and miscarriages in great part wiped out. "Children will not come into the world deformed, mental retardation could be reduced on a wide scale, if the theories of Jonas continue to check out and are applied." [62] How can anyone object to testing a system, no matter how unorthodox, if it promises to alleviate the suffering and sorrow of children. And there's no danger to anyone in experimenting with Jonas' medical astrology. Understanding of this sort of astrology could be a comfort also to parents haunted with the question, "Why is my child retarded? What did we do?"

In all directions, Dr. Jonas' discovery sounds like a positive good. Speaking of it, one Czech writing in their newspaper *Pravda* said, "To everyone who likes children—this would be the basis of a happy life."

Jonas' struggle to again put astrology to work for humanity on a sound basis seems to have paid off. Sparked by his success, scientists in Czechoslovakia and Hungary have begun to look into astrology—or as it is now often called, astrobiology—to see if it can be of help in other areas of medicine,[25, 245] in science [6, 44, 97, 183] and in human relations.[174]

Massive tests to prove once and for all if Dr. Eugen Jonas' surprising discoveries are genuine are now under way. We hope you'll be hearing a great deal more of him in the years to come.

27

PYRAMID POWER AND THE RIDDLE OF THE RAZOR BLADES

For some five thousand years, people have been speculating on the meaning of the Great Pyramids of Egypt—one of the seven wonders of the world and one of the strangest works of architecture in existence. What was the purpose of this structure, the largest man-made building on earth? It is thought to be a burial tomb for King Cheops, but no remains were found in it. According to the American psychic, Edgar Cayce, the actual construction and engineering of the pyramid were worked out by Hermes, a descendant of Hermes Trismegistus.[366] The Great Pyramid, which sits in the desert near Cairo, covers thirteen acres, measures a thousand yards around the base, and is built of huge blocks of limestone weighing as much as fifty-four tons each, yet each of these blocks was fitted into the pyramid and adjusted to within a half-millimeter like a jewel in a precision watch.

And there's another startling fact about the pyramid: Czech patent 91304 was issued on a model of the Cheops Pyramid in Prague. Pharaohs being in short supply nowadays, the Czechs had something else in mind for the pyramid.

In Prague, while visiting some friends, we noticed a small cardboard model of the Great Pyramid sitting on top of a bookcase, the same kind of pyramid which is pictured on the U.S. one dollar bill. Inside there was a razor blade balanced on top of a matchbox. Finally our curiosity overcame us and we asked about it.

"Would you like to know one of the secrets of the pyramids?" our hosts asked us, with big grins.

"Of course."

"Well," they began, "one of the secrets of the pyramid is the *shape!*"

We vaguely recalled that Edgar Cayce had reported that the secrets of the pyramid are written in the language of mathematics, geometry, and astronomy as well as in the symbology of the kinds of stone used. Cayce maintained that for those who could read it the Great Pyramid was a record in stone of the history and development of man from earliest times to 1998.

"But what does the shape of the pyramid do?" we asked.

"It generates energy," the Czech said straight-faced.

Was it a joke? If not, how come the Czechs were so familiar with the "secrets of the pyramids"?

They told us. Some years ago a Frenchman, a Monsieur Bovis, had visited the Great Pyramid in Egypt. A third of the way up the structure is the pharaoh's chamber. Tired with the heat, Bovis entered. He found the air unusually humid. But there was something else in the room that surprised the Frenchman, something that had no connection with the pharaohs. There were garbage cans in the chamber containing cats and other small animals that had wandered into the pyramid, lost their way, and died. "There's something strange about those animals," Bovis thought. "There's no smell of decay from them." The animals were dehydrated, *mummified* despite the humidity. It struck him as very odd.

"Could it be," he wondered, "that the shape of the pyramid alone could guarantee that the pharaoh's corpse would be preserved even if the intricate embalming failed?" He noted that the ratio for the dimensions and also the bearings of the base were correct to 5 seconds of a degree on the north-south, east-west axes—the most accurately oriented building known to engineering science. "This is certainly not by accident," he decided.

Bovis made a model of the Cheops pyramid, with a base about one yard in length. He oriented it squarely on the north-south axis and a third of the way up in this structure he placed a dead cat. After a time it mummified. Gradually he experimented putting different types of organic matter under the pyramid, particularly organic matter that decayed quickly. From these experiments Bovis concluded there must be something about the pyramid that stops decay and causes quick dehydration.[181]

The published reports of Bovis' research drew the attention of Mr. Karel Drbal (pronounced Dre-*bal*) a Prague radio engineer who had pioneered radio and television in Czechoslovakia. "Why did the pyramid have this effect of mummifying organic matter?" he wondered.

Drbal did several experiments himself with small models of the Cheops pyramid and concluded, "There's a relation between the *shape* of the space inside the pyramid and the physical, chemical, and biological processes going on inside that space. By using suitable forms and shapes, we should be able to make processes occur faster or delay them."

This fact had already been discovered by a French firm that patented a specially shaped container for making yogurt. The shape enhanced the process.

The world-famous breweries of Czechoslovakia that originated Pilsner and Budweiser beer were also aware that the form of the container can affect the contents. One of the Prague breweries had tried to switch over to barrels with angular sides and found that the quality of their beer was not as good, despite the fact they'd used all the same methods of processing used with the round barrels.

Some time later Mr. Drbal remembered an old gambit some of his friends in the army had used when they wanted to tease one another. At the time Drbal was in the service, soldiers still used straight razors. If you wanted to get someone mad all you had to do was put his razor on the windowsill at night so it was in the light of the full moon. It became blunted. We now know, the Czech told us, that the polarized light of the moon has an unfavorable effect on the sharpness of the blade because polarized light vibrates in one direction only.

But there is no polarized light under a pyramid. However, Drbal wondered, could the shape itself accumulate electromagnetic waves or cosmic rays or some other unknown energy waves which might be around us all the time? The energy accumulating in the pyramid might be the basis of the effect the pyramid had on physical, chemical, and biological processes.

The edge of a razor blade has a crystal structure which is "alive." After use, this sharpness becomes deformed, but the deformation needn't be permanent. Some materials are able to return to their original form after a time, even in their crystal structure. Theoretically, Drbal figured, if a blade is of very good quality steel, as long as it is not damaged mechanically and if it is not used for a time, it might return to its original sharpness.

Drbal used a new Zenith blade five times. He placed it under the model pyramid. Then he used the blade three more times. It did not become blunt. He continued to keep it in the pyramid between shaves and he was surprised to find he could shave over fifty times with the same blade. He began a lengthy series of tests with the blades and pyramids and found he could shave with some of them as many as *two hundred times*.

He concluded that the environment inside the pyramid makes the crystals in the blade return to their original form faster and hence the blade becomes sharp again.[192]

Soon the cardboard Cheops pyramid as a razor blade sharpener was launched! "This was back in the 1950s when we couldn't get imported razor blades, so you see the sharpener was working miracles with our inferior Czech razor blades," the Czechs joked. Soon word of the razor blade sharpener spread to Russia and Soviet soldiers began setting up pyramids in their barracks. Getting a decent razor blade in the USSR was so difficult at the time it had become the constant complaint of Soviet newspapers and satirical magazines. (Some Russians think it still is a problem.)

"Why don't you patent the pyramid?" Drbal's friends suggested for fun. He contacted the patent office, which as he points out, "doesn't shock easily. They often see 'perpetual motion machines.'"

The patent office worried over the new patent. They corresponded with Drbal for weeks. What could they do if the blades really got sharp? Finally, the chief engineer at the patent office built a model pyramid himself. He got the same results as Drbal and everyone else who tried the pyramid. It worked.

The patent office of the Czechoslovakian Republic in 1959 issued patent number 91304 on the Cheops Pyramid Razor-Blade Sharpener to Karel Drbal of Prague. Shortly after, a Czech factory began to manufacture miniature cardboard pyramids that sold for a while on the market. Today they are making and selling styrofoam ones.

In Prague we met Karel Drbal, a slim man with angular

features, now in his sixties and retired on a pension. Charming and urbane, he explained in superb French that he had been born in Vienna where his father worked for a time. Later he himself worked in Paris for seven years. Besides being an engineer and a pianist, Drbal has long been interested in parapsychology and has been an active investigator.

"What sort of energy in the pyramid could cause meat to mummify and razor blades to sharpen?" we asked him. He told us about the Abbé Moreux's book *The Mysterious Science of the Pharaohs,* and showed us a book he'd acquired in Paris many years ago called *Ondes des Formes* (*Waves from Forms*) by L. Turenne, an engineer and former professor of radio. Various forms, Turenne asserts—such as spheres, pyramids, semi-spheres, squares—act as different types of *resonators* for the energy of the cosmos, the sun, and the energy all around us. Just as the special shape of a violin gives tone and quality to a bow touching a string, the special shape of a pyramid apparently is a resonant cavity for the "live" crystals of a razor blade.

"What effect do these different forms have on human beings? After all, we spend most of our lives inside box-shaped buildings or cars with semi-spherical or oblong roofs."

"Some of these forms are very healthful for humans. The sphere shape, for instance, has a good effect," Drbal told us. "So does the pyramid form. Some researchers believe if hospitals were built in this form patients would get better faster. A semi-sphere, on the other hand, exerts an unhealthy effect on the organism."

Buckminster Fuller's remarkable geodesic bubble would apparently be a healthy environment. Architects in Saskatchewan, Canada, have created trapezoidal rooms and unusual corridors in a hospital for schizophrenics and found that the new environment was beneficial for them. However, no one here had been thinking in terms of some form of energy being channeled by the forms.

"It's a difficult theory to explain and we still don't have all the answers."

The Czechs are having a lot of fun with their razor blade sharpening pyramid. But behind the fun and games, there are questions that intrigue some scientists. What is going on under the pyramid anyway? Nothing at all should be happening to razor blades or small dead animals plunked under a cardboard Cheops pyramid.

Scientists at the Charles University, we learned, were exploring the force from the pyramid that would mummify meat. In the chapters on the Kirlian discovery, we mentioned the fact that psychic healers have displayed the ability to mummify meat within a very short time with some sort of "X" force that seemed to flow from their hands. The phenomenon has attracted the attention of many scientists throughout the world, such as Dr. Peter Kapitsa in Russia, Dr. Jacques Errera of Belgium, Douglas Dean of Newark College of Engineering. Does the energy in the pyramid have anything to do with the energy healers project that also mummifies meat? Is it similar to a magnetic phenomenon? Does it have anything to do with PK?

Later, at the Delawarr Laboratories in England, we saw that with new sophisticated instrumentation it is possible to graphically chart the patterns of the wave fronts of sounds. Certain combinations of sound yield precise geometric forms. For example, the final chord from Handel's "Hallelujah Chorus,"—five notes comprised of five different frequencies—had wave fronts which when superimposed formed a five-pointed geometric star. What do we still have to learn about form and proportion? Are all forms in our world actually the result of combinations of vibrations of various frequencies, as American physicist Charles A. Muses suggests? [369]

Some Americans have speculated that the pyramid form may be a kind of gigantic lens which is able to focus some unknown energy by its shape.[162] In optics, as apparently with the pyramid, shape and form are all important. Others have noted the resemblance of the pyramid form to the form of crystals—for instance the magnetite crystal (lodestone) which looks like two pyramids placed base to base, and have suggested that the energy of the pyramid might have something to do with a magnetic phenomenon.

We returned to engineer Drbal and the pyramid form. What other uses could it have?

"Many more uses are still to be discovered, but something I've been thinking about lately is the form of hats," he said with a smile. "Why are the traditional witches' hats in the form of a cone? Think of the unusual shape of the hats used in many religious ceremonies. Perhaps there was a reason for these forms. I began to experiment with hats made in the shape of a pyramid. The people who've tested them so far say they relieve headaches," he told us. "If nothing else, at least people get a kick out of them. Of course, each hat has to be made specifically for each person," he explained. And who knows, he may soon have a patent on his "Magic Hat."

Does the pyramid itself really work as a razor blade sharpener? One of the first things we did when we returned

How to construct a Cheops pyramid razor blade sharpener. Each side is an isosceles triangle with equal sides of 8⅞" each. Base should be 9⅜". The finished pyramid should stand six inches tall. (Dimensions for larger pyramids—see p. 376.)

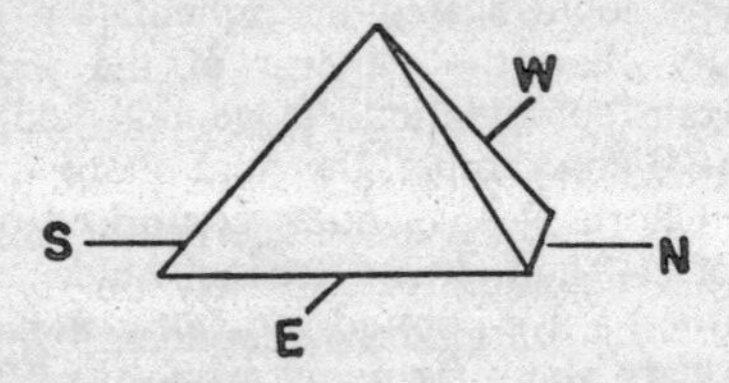

A. Place the pyramid on the Earth's North-South magnetic axis.

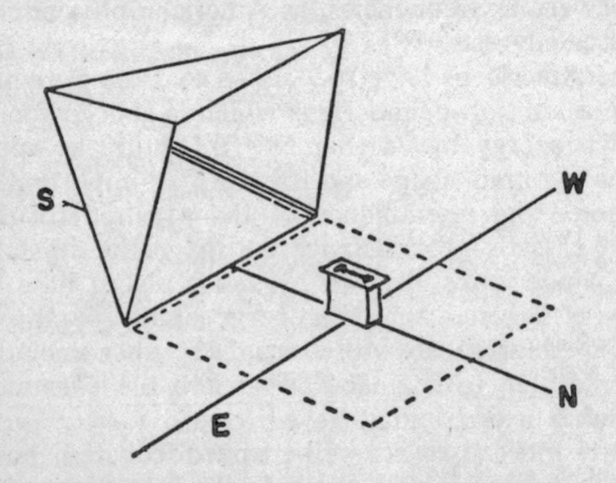

B. Razor blade should be placed in the exact center, on a match-box or other base that stands exactly 2 inches tall.

home was build cardboard models of the Cheops pyramid. Soon our friends were putting together pyramids too. We can attest that the used razor blades sharpened up again and remained sharp if kept in the pyramid between uses. We had best results with plain Gillette blue blades. It doesn't seem to work as well on stainless steel.

If you'd like to see for yourself how the pyramid works (see diagram), cut four triangles of heavy cardboard (not corrugated) with the base 9⅜ inches and both sides 8⅞ inches. Tape the sides together with adhesive tape so that the pyramid stands 6 inches high measured from the tip of the point.

Trace the outline of the pyramid base on a large sheet of paper. Draw two lines dividing the square into four quarters. Orient the north-south line precisely using a compass to find true north. Place an empty matchbox or holder 2 inches high (one third the height of the pyramid) on the center of the north-south axis. Place a razor blade that's been used several times on the north-south axis on top of the matchbox. The sharp edges should face east-west. Place the pyramid over the blade so the point is directly above it. Use the pattern on the paper underneath as a guide. The pyramid and blade must be precisely on the north-south axis; otherwise the sharpening effect doesn't work properly.

The pyramid should not be set up on any electrical device. The used blade should remain under the pyramid for about six days before being used again. After that it can be used every day if always kept in the pyramid between uses.

Object	*Initial Weight*	*Days in 6" high Pyramid*	*Weight After*	*Dehydration†*
Hen's egg (with shell)	52 grams	43	17 grams	66%
Hen's egg (without shell)	33 grams	19	15 grams	53%
Portion of veal stomach	33 grams	9	10 grams	70%
Windpipe of sheep	23 grams	6	10 grams	50%
Fish (not cleaned)	35 grams	13	10 grams	71%
Brain of a sheep*	93 grams	49	33 grams	75%

* Placed in a pyramid 10 times the usual volume. (For larger amounts of meat, pyramid must be larger.) The brain decays very easily, but at no moment while under the pyramid was there any trace of decay, says M. Martial. † The average amount of dehydration on organic matter in the pyramid—66%.

We have not had time yet to test for ourselves the power of the pyramid to mummify, but we have the results of tests done by Monsieur Jean Martial (p. 373).

Does the pyramid have other uses besides food preservation and razor sharpening? Could it speed the growth of plants, purify water? Does the energy of the pyramid have anything to do with psychic force? We don't know yet.

The Czechs postulate two kinds of generators of what they call "psychotronic energy"—cosmic generators and biological generators. In their view a pyramid is a cosmic generator.

Students of alchemy maintain that ancient Egyptian scientists coded information into the architecture of the pyramid. Architecture, they felt, was a more permanent and ideal form of communication for initiates than writing. Researchers into alchemy have deduced that secret methods of liberation of energy have been known for thousands of years.

Whatever this strange energy associated with the form of a pyramid is, it baffles modern scientists and throws into utter confusion the readings of modern electronic equipment.

At the Ein Shams University near Cairo, a group of scientists embarked in 1968 on a million dollar project to x-ray the Pyramid of Chephren at Gizeh near Cairo. This pyramid, which was built by Cheops' brother Chephren somewhere between 2200 and 2700 B.C., stands near the Cheops pyramid and is nearly identical to it in size.

Computers and space age electronic equipment ran twenty-four hours a day for more than a year recording on magnetic tape the pattern of cosmic rays reaching the interior of the pyramid. The scientists hoped to find secret vaults inside the 6 million ton mass of the pyramid. The cosmic rays strike the pyramid uniformly on all sides and if the pyramid is solid, should be recorded uniformly by a detector in the chamber at the bottom. However, if there were secret chambers above the detector, more cosmic rays would come through hollow areas than through solid areas. Thus the scientists might be able to locate secret vaults or even the tomb of Chephren himself inside the pyramid.

In early 1969 the project reached a climax. The latest

IBM 1130 computer was delivered to the Ein Shams University Computer Center. Thousands of man-hours were spent on the research and the scientists made hundreds of reels of recordings from the pyramid. Finally, in July of 1969, Dr. Amr Gohed in charge of the installations at the pyramid made a startling report to *The Times of London*. The scientists had reached an impasse. Whatever was happening in the pyramid, said Dr. Gohed, "defies all the known laws of science and electronics."

John Tunstall, a reporter from *The Times*, flew to Egypt. He watched as Dr. Gohed ran one of the tapes from the pyramid through a computer, which traced the pattern of cosmic ray particles on paper. Dr. Gohed then selected a recording made the day after the first tape had been made and put it through the computer. The recorded pattern was totally different. "This is scientifically impossible," he said.

But it was happening before the scientists' eyes. The first recordings had raised hopes of a great discovery of secret chambers or tombs. But now these recordings were found to be only a jumbled mass of meaningless symbols.

"Has all this scientific know-how been rendered useless by some force beyond man's comprehension?" Tunstall asked.

Said Dr. Gohed in *The Times*, "Either the geometry of the pyramid is in substantial error, which would affect our readings, or there is a mystery which is beyond explanation—call it what you will, occultism, the curse of the Pharaohs, sorcery, or magic, *there is some force that defies the laws of science at work in the pyramid.*" 413

It seems our modern scientists and all their space-age equipment had come face to face with the same phenomenon the Czechs had long known about—"pyramid power." It was this mysterious energy which the Czech researchers began to explore further.

PYRAMID SIZE CHART

Height	Base	Sides
V 5	z 7,85	b 7,47
10	15,70	14,94
15	23,56	22,41
20	31,41	29,89
25	39,27	37,36
30	47,12	44,83
35	54,97	52,31
40	62,83	59,78
45	70,68	67,25
50	78,54	74,73
55	86,39	82,20
60	94,24	89,67
65	102,10	97,14
70	109,95	104,62
75	117,81	112,09
80	125,66	119,56
85	133,51	127,04
90	141,37	134,51
95	149,22	141,98
100	157,08	149,46

All figures given in centimeters.

28

PSYCHOTRONIC GENERATORS—PSYCHIC MACHINES?

The next thing that we saw, the climax of our stay in Czechoslovakia, sounds fantastic and is fantastic—but it may be genuine. We were confronted with a gallery of objects—burnished and gleaming, rough and pebbled, steel, bronze, copper, iron, gold—"psychotronic generators" that do the impossible. We saw them demonstrated in a film shown by Czech scientists at the International Parapsychology Conference in Moscow. We held these psychotronic generators, heavy in our hands. We worked one of them ourselves.

What are they all about? There isn't an easy answer. The Czechs start out explaining them this way: "Human beings and all living things are filled with a kind of energy that until recently hasn't been known to Western science. This bio-energy, which we call psychotronic energy, seems to be behind PK; it may be the basis of dowsing. It may prove to be involved in all psychic happenings. The psychotronic generators draw this bio-energy from a person, accumulate it, and use it. Once charged with your energy, the generators can do some of the things a psychic can do."[186] That was the first door they opened for us into the mystery. There were corridors to come.

The psychotronic generator, or Pavlita generator as it is sometimes called after its inventor, sprang in part from antique manuscripts and forgotten discoveries, old learning combined with the knowledge of modern science. The idea of a bio-energy is an old one.

The ancient Chinese said that you are not a machinelike collections of parts, but a powerhouse of unusual energy. They called it Life Force or Vital Energy. The universe, too, they said, is suffused with Vital Energy, and thus you are linked with the cosmos.

Next door in India, the ancient Hindus spoke of this vital force in you which they named Prana. Modern Yoga is based on the idea of Prana. But if this vital or "X" energy is more than a philosophical concept, how come no one in the West ever stumbled across it?

"They did," the Czechs said. Many "discoverers" caused a momentary flurry with their new energy, then were forgotten or, at best, remembered as brilliant cranks as Western science hurried on to its great technological flowering. The chart shows only the most famous discoverers. There have been many others. They all came to their finding by different paths, they all gave "it" a different name, but surprisingly, they very often agree on the characteristic of this supposed energy in you.

DISCOVERER	NAME OF X FORCE
Ancient Chinese	Vital Energy
Ancient Hindu	Prana
Polynesian Huna	Mana
Renaissance	
Paracelsus	Munis
van Helmont	Magnale Magnum
Eighteenth to Twentieth Centuries	
Mesmer	Animal Magnetism
Reichenbach	Odic Force
Keely	Motor Force
Blondlot	N-rays
Radiesthesists	Etheric Force
L. E. Eeman	"X" Force
Current Medicine	Psychosomatic [?]
Contemporary Communist World	
Soviet scientists	Bioplasmic Energy
Czech scientists	Psychotronic Energy

Today in the Soviet Union groups of pure scientists are looking into a "new discovery"—a vital, previously unknown energy connected with living beings. Bioplasmic energy is their name for it. But the Russians have a big plus going for them. Thanks to the Kirlian discovery (detailed in chapters 16, 17, and 18), bioplasmic energy can be seen by anyone in photographs and electron microscopes. It can be scientifically observed and studied as it swirls in sparkling flares of color. Twentieth-century scientists, with their tracking and charting devices, lifted the atom of the ancient Greeks out of the realm of philosophy and into the realm of the actual, making it a practical energy. Perhaps the Soviets starting with the Kirlian apparatus will do the same for the vital energy of ancient cultures. Or perhaps the Czechs will, with their psychotronic generators. They too have made the rediscovery.

Robert Pavlita, gray-haired in his mid fifties, is an inventor and design director for a large Czech textile plant. In person, very much the no-nonsense, efficient businessman, Pavlita has for thirty years worked privately on psychotronic generators. He believes they run on this newly discovered energy. In the mid sixties, Pavlita's name reached the West amid a mishmash of confusion. "Czech businessman is fine PK medium." Then, "Pavlita has no PK ability." Is he or isn't he? Sitting in parapsychology offices in America, there was no way to tell. The story behind the reports shows how the confusion got started. After thirty years of experimenting, Pavlita went to Hradec Králové University, east of Prague. An electrophysiologist, a physicist, and eventually the entire physics department tested him.

The scientists set up experiments with a device designed by Pavlita. Inside a tightly sealed metal box a spike revolved, run by an electric motor beneath. On top of the turning spike the scientists had balanced a copper strip. It looked like a letter T. The only other thing inside the box was a small metallic object in one corner, not connected to anything. The revolutions of the copper strip going round and round were recorded photoelectrically.

Pavlita, as the scientists watched, stood about six feet away from the contraption. He concentrated, stared hard at it. Suddenly the copper strip stood still, as though some force were holding it, counteracting the turning rod. What could it be? The entire device was even magnetically screened.

Pavlita continued to stare. The witnesses watched intently. Slowly, the copper strip began turning—this time in the opposite direction. It looked as if some invisible force inside the sealed case were pushing it, spinning it in opposition to the revolving rod that held it. For two years the scientists tested Pavlita.

"PK! A fraudproof demonstration of PK," wrote British journalist Theo Lang, who'd heard of Pavlita and flown in to witness a demonstration.[299] The scientists agree it was a fraudproof demonstration of *something*, but what? They couldn't find any known force that could cause the strip to stop and reverse as Pavlita stared. It sounds like PK, but it isn't—not exactly.

Pavlita maintains he is a technologist operating a form of energy, clicking it off and on, directing it, as any technologist would direct an energy like electricity. The small unconnected device inside the sealed box is a psychotronic generator. Supposedly, as Pavlita stares, his bio-energy is drawn into the generator, which accumulates it and directs it. The Czechs believe many people could have PK ability this way, with the generator functioning as go-between.

Pavlita's early "PK" test was a demonstration that this so-called vital, psychotronic energy could be harnessed and directed at will. But all its discoverers claim this is a vast universal energy. The Czechs told us, tried to show us, that even at this stage of discovery they can do much more than just duplicate PK.

The prime question for all the Westerners who've come up against this vital, or psychotronic energy, for the past five hundred years is, what does it do?

Paracelsus, the Renaissance alchemist and physician, reported this energy radiated from one person to another and could act at a distance. He believed it could purify the body and restore health, or could poison the body and cause disease. Dr. van Helmont the seventeenth-century Flemish chemist and physician believed the energy could enable one person to affect another at a distance. The famous German chemist, Baron von Reichenbach, said the energy could be stored and that substances could be charged with it. Unknown to Reichenbach, the Polynesian practitioners of Huna agreed that the vital energy could be transferred from humans to objects.

Other researchers into this now and then rediscovered human energy reported that it could even *move* objects at a distance—in other words, PK. According to the British medical magazine *Lancet* for July 30, 1921, Dr. Charles Russ, M.R.C.S., showed the Ophthalmic Congress at Oxford in 1921 that with a proper apparatus a person could cause a solenoid to move by gazing at it. There were other doctors with similar devices and ideas, particularly in

France. One was Dr. Paul Joire who designed a special device with a needle that turned when a human stared or stood near it. He called the unknown force that caused the reaction, "emanations from biological systems".

Through the years, varied researchers came up with "facts" about this supposedly nonexistent energy. It could be reflected, refracted, polarized, and combined with other energies. It could—many reported—create effects similar to magnetism, electricity, heat, and luminous radiations, but was in itself none of these. It conducts slower than electricity, but can build up something similar to an electrostatic charge. It was said this odd energy from humans could be conducted by paper, wood, wool, silk, and many substances that are electrical insulators. And this fabled energy that flowed from people seemed to be somehow involved with psychic things.[337]

It really does sound like the creaking plot of an old mystic horror movie—the secrets of the ancients revived. The flickering occult shadows that seem to automatically attach themselves to such an idea may be one reason our scientists have never given the matter a serious look. But the Czechs are willing to examine *facts*. After hearing experimental reports on the psychotronic generators, the Central Committee of the Czech Communist Party a few years ago approved research. It's also backed by the Czech Academy of Science.

In Moscow, at the session of the Parapsychology Conference held in the Czech Embassy, we were introduced to the world of the psychotronic generator. The leader of the Czech delegation, Dr. Zdenek Rejdak, who works for the military, explained, "Everybody has psychic abilities, but most of the time we are unaware of them. The psychic force lies dormant or is blocked, making telepathy or PK a rarity. To cause psychic powers to work, we need something to evoke them or to reinforce them. If we assume human or other living things give off a certain energy, then we might be able to accumulate it. If so, we can have work carried out by the energy. ESP needn't be a rarity then. It could work all the time and under any conditions." [188] Later he told us, "I've heard that the United States is also thinking about making machines to do this."

The Czechs showed a very memorable documentary film

created by one of their major movie studios. Like the tour-de-force Czech films that have dazzled crowds across America, this science film was artistically executed, right down to the electronic music. The content, for a science film, was even more dazzling. One after another, the camera lit up what seemed to be modern sculptures—gleaming forms that could have been created by Brancusi, or more intricate ones, perhaps by Dali. Other objects looked like precision-cut components for machines that hadn't been invented yet, spare parts from 2001. Still other small metal and wood scultpures were reminiscent of these "ritual objects" set out by the museums of the world, from the British Museum in London to the little, dusty museums of Asian Turkey and southern Egypt. But these are not sculptures; the objects aren't in a museum. This is an ordinary apartment in a small town in Czechoslovakia. The devices sitting on the table supposedly collect psychotronic energy given off by living things. The human beings donating their "energy" to the generators in the film are the designer Robert Pavlita and his daughter Jana.

"The generators accumulate human energy," we were told during the film. "Then they carry out work. There are different types of generators for different types of work." We're shown a rotor being turned by an electric motor. Robert Pavlita and his daughter Jana place a needle on the revolving rotor. A psychotronic generator is aimed at the needle. The supposedly nonexistent energy makes the needle stop turning.

Next, we cut to an apparatus that looks like a fat screwdriver. Just as Nelya Mikhailova apparently builds up some sort of energy that attracts matches, glass, bread, this Pavlita generator draws small bits of substance to itself. "The force of attraction depends on the amount of energy accumulated in the generator," the Czechs state. It looks like electrostatic energy—the force you get when you rub a comb on wool, turning it into a "magnet" that picks up paper and other light things. Static electricity doesn't work under water. The Pavlita generator is placed in water; still it attracts and lifts bits and pieces of nonmagnetic material.

As if to confirm our feeling that these generators are reminiscent of something seen before, the film shifts to scenes from ancient Egyptian texts. The eye of the camera focuses and stays on the Egyptian ankh, the sacred symbol of life.

It is reported that commissions of experts from the Czechoslovakian Academy of Science and the University of Hradec Králové—physicists, electronics experts, radio technicians, electrophysiologists, and mathematicians—all investigated the psychotronic generators. We're shown a generator whose force turns a small blade. They've tested to eliminate static electricity, air currents, temperature changes. The blade turns. The blade doesn't react to a strong magnet. The experts test with magnetic fields. They make no difference. The "vital energy," that supposedly philosophical concept, continues to turn the blade. We see them cover the entire device with a glass cylinder. Nevetheless, it moves. We're told they've suspended it in water. Still it revolves.

Apart from the film, Dr. C. Vesely, an electrophysiologist, Dr. Jiri Macko, a physicist, Dr. Peregrin and Mr. H. Kuksin, who tested and studied Pavlita's equipment at Hradec Králové University, declared in a interview, "the experiments have excluded any conceivable physical agent —even heat." Several members of the Academy of Science reported, "We must continue to explore this energy."

Dr. Julius Krmessky, an outstanding Czech mathematician and physicist, tackled this unexplained energy radiating from humans and published an important scientific paper for the Chair of Physics of the Pedagogical Institute of Trnava in 1963. Krmessky calculated the force required to make the blade turn at 1.2×10^{-3} dynes. "It can't be heat or air," he reports. "The radiation goes right through glass, water, wood, cardboard, any type of metal—even iron—and its strength doesn't diminish at all. Furthermore, the *mind* seems to control this energy." [90]

Returning to the film, the camera shifts to pans of bean seeds divided into experimental and control groups. Another psychotronic generator, a studded metal square supporting a coiled, borelike neck, is directed at one of the pans of seeds. Days later, the plants developing from the "radiated" seeds are easily seen to be almost double the size of those from the "untreated" seeds. This is something we have seen before, notably at McGill University in Montreal. In an excruciatingly well-controlled series of tests, Dr. Bernard Grad showed that seedlings watered with a flask of saline solution previously held in the hands of a well-known healer grew fuller and higher plants than seeds watered with unheld saline solution. The Czechs had said that their psychotronic energy was the "X" force behind many psychic mysteries.

The film gave close-ups on other tests, pointing to practical uses for psychotronic generators. Sealed bottles of dye-filled polluted water from a textile factory are irradiated with psychotronic energy from the Pavlita generators. In twelve hours the water is clear. The pollutant seems to have crystallized and fallen to the bottom of the flasks. A signed, official chemical analysis of the water by an independent laboratory flashes on the screen. "This purification of polluted water could not have been done by a chemical purifier," it concludes. What was not said in the film, but told to us later by one of the scientists involved, is something more extraordinary. "Analysis found that whatever the energy was, it has caused a change in the actual molecular structure of the water itself! The two hydrogen atoms spread further apart."

This rang a bell too. We'd been told by a reputable scientific source in the United States that a well-known American lab studied water that had been held in a sealed flask by a healer. Word had it that there seemed to be a molecular change in this water, a spreading of the bonds between the hydrogen and oxygen.[162]

"This is only an infinitesimal part of the Pavlita experiments conducted by the inventor and many other scientists in Czechoslovakia. The psychotronic generators have obtained results in telekinesis, telepathy, clairvoyance tests." *Telepathy?* But that was the end of the movie.

None of the Westerners (ourselves very much included) seemed to know what to make of this Merlinlike Czech with his artful device, that seemed to have few if any moving parts, yet drew a wondrous, invisible energy from human beings. What could one say to these reputable, solid Czech scientists speaking so earnestly of their psychotronic energy? The Western scientists cautiously observed, "This deserves serious interest."

What did the Russians think? Soviet scientists had already seen this film a few months earlier. Years ago some of their researchers postulated the idea that they needed to discover a new form of energy to explain supernormal events. And of course, most of the Russians present knew in detail the research being done on the bioplasma body, discovered by the Kirlians—something that Westerners had no idea of.

Dr. Genady Sergeyev, the Leningrad neurophysiologist commented at the conference, "The Pavlita work shows it is possible *to transfer energy from living bodies to nonliving matter*. The most important influence of this energy is on water. In fact, we use this very principle in the development of detectors that examine the fields around Mrs. Mikhailova during PK." Both Sergeyev and Rejdak talked about electronic bioplasma in the human body as the basis of PK and this psychotronic energy.[198]

Later we learned a Russian scientist after seeing the Pavlita film had tried to build a generator on his own. "He made it out of the wrong material," said Dr. Rejdak. "It was very crude, but it did work. He wanted us to tell him a lot more about the generators after that."

We wanted to be told a lot more too. When we got to Prague we inundated the scientists with questions about Pavlita and psychotronics.

THE SECRET'S IN THE FORM

"I first met Robert Pavlita about four years ago," Dr. Rejdak told us. "Word of his generators had somehow reached England. A British journalist came over, saw a generator in action, and wrote quite a story. Of course, our press got wind of it and rushed into print with a rash of controversial articles. It caused a tremendous sensation. You see, the government [the old Novotny regime] didn't know anything about the generators. They were as surprised as the public. The whole subject of Pavlita and biological radiation was hushed up, and a number of scientists, including myself, were asked to investigate. Following our reports, Pavlita has been rehabilitated."

Rejdak is nicely qualified to investigate. Apart from being a psychologist, he has also specialized in physiology and worked in parapsychology for years with the famous Czech sculptor and psychic researcher Břetislav Kafka. His judgment seemed well-respected by other scientists in

Czechoslovakia and the other Communist countries. What had he uncovered in his investigations of Pavlita that convinced him it was not fraud?

Before we could even get to that question, we wanted to start at the beginning. "Where did Pavlita get the inspiration for his generators?" We wondered if the Egyptian scenes in the movie could possibly have been meant as more than an artistic touch.

"Pavlita got the idea from studying many very old texts." Which ones? The Czechs smiled and shook their heads. "We're sorry, we can't tell you that yet." This didn't give us much to go on. Czechoslovakia is awash with forgotten treatises and antique books. Manuscripts that haven't been thumbed for centuries wait in the state libraries and in the collections of the medieval castles and even still turn up in second-hand bookstores.

"One of our main problems with the psychotronic generators right now," the Czechs went on, "is that they are not fully patented yet. Naturally, Pavlita doesn't want to let the plans get out."

Robert Pavlita realizes the value of patents. Years ago he invented a new process for the textile industry. Royalties still roll in from the Socialist bloc and Western Europe, particularly West Germany. "Fortunately Pavlita was able to use these rather considerable royalties for his research into psychotronic energy. No one else would finance the work at the beginning."

The Czechs weren't about to give us a do-it-yourself generator kit. But they were willing to open doors trying to give us a sensible view of psychotronics. The next door they opened is the most mind-teasing.

"The secret of the generators is their *form.* That's the key thing Pavlita gleaned in his studies. It's the shape that let's you accumulate this energy and turn it to whatever purposes you want." Now we understood why they were so hooked on the light-hearted pyramid razor blade sharpener. There, too, the "secret" is supposedly the form.

"In some ways the principle of the generators is like art. You make generators out of one sort of material to do one thing and out of a different sort to do another. It's the juxtaposition of materials within a specific form that makes it work. Pavlita uses copper, iron, gold, steel, brass, various kinds of metals, and sometimes even wood. Most generators are a carefully formulated combination of metals."

"When we first saw these generators," said Dr. Rejdak, "some of the other scientists were baffled. But I happened to be familiar with the research done by Reichenbach, and I realized Pavlita's work was along the same lines. It's an extension of Reichenbach's idea of an odoscope, but modernized and far, far more sophisticated." (Reichenbach invented an odoscope apparatus which supposedly could collect what he called odic force, "an all-pervasive energy.")

"Aside from generators that accumulate energy from living things, we also have generators that accumulate 'cosmic' energy or energy from the environment. The pyramid's an example of a generator that works on 'cosmic' energy."

Apparently, the Czech psychotronic energy (like the old Chinese Vital Energy) springs from living things and from the cosmos, as do in-the-environment "cosmic" electricity and bioelectricity from the human body.

If you had a generator, how would you charge it with your own energy?

"The energy doesn't come from a particular organ in your body. It comes from your entire force field, so to speak. Many of the generators have a certain staring pattern carved into them to help concentration and conduction of the energy."

Here's another old idea, the staring pattern that is now tacked up in rooms across America as a result of the influx of Eastern philosophy, the staring pattern that is said to boost concentration and release psychic or spiritual power. The Czechs maintain that this power, handled correctly, can amp up a geranium plant or run a small motor.

Do you have to keep a specific thought in mind while trying to charge a generator? "No. You don't have to think anything in particular or will your energy into the generator. Staring in pattern is enough to direct the force, if the generator is properly made. Now, we've developed automatic generators that work without staring. We believe they can collect biological energy from anything living—human, animal, plant. Tests are scheduled to see if they can accumulate energy from something as basic as a fertilized egg."

If energy is really being drawn from you, don't you get tired?

"There's only a very silght aftereffect, but it's stronger if emotion is involved. There are changes while you're charging it." The Czechs did EEG tests on Pavlita's daughter while she charged a generator. They found an "unusual pattern." Soviet scientist Dr. Genady Sergeyev, who flew in and tested Robert and Jana Pavlita with EEGs and other monitoring devices while they charged generators, said there was a change in the structure of the biological fields around their bodies. He reports, "There was unstable, cold electronic plasma in the brain. During certain phases of brain activity, magnetic, electric, and other types of waves were given off."

"Look," said the Czechs, "you can try a simple test for yourselves before we leave for Pavlita's." Dr. Rejdak dug a box out of a drawer in his desk. Inside the box was a small round stick of wood about four inches long that looked like a cuticle stick, pointed at both ends.

"This was made two years ago, under pressure, by a special process. It was charged by a generator so that it is able to channel the biological energy of a person."

He handed the stick to one of us and scattered, on the coffee table, small fragments: aluminum, salt, tin, stone, iron, crystal, etc., about the size of one's little fingernail. Some were magnetic, some weren't. We looked over the stick—no trace of adhesive or anything else on it. No friction was applied. Neither Rejdak nor either of us rubbed it on anything. We touched a fragment of crystal, prodded it.

The crystal clung. With the crystal still attached, we moved the stick over a circle of metal. It stuck to the crystal. Moving the stick over the table, one item after another eventually clung to it, until they hung from the stick in a small daisy chain. It was like playing Nelya Mikhailova, PK medium. Or was it some obscure workings of static electricity?

"Everybody thinks of static electricity," the Czechs agreed, "which is why we've done so many tests to prove it isn't. Psychotronic energy, the energy you're using in a small way right now, has many similarities with electromagnetic energy, which is natural. But psychotronic energy itself is much more subtle," Dr. Rejdak told us. "This stick, by the way, doesn't work as well when you're tired."

How long does a charge stay in a generator?

"The generator that speeds plant growth, once charged, works steadily for three days. That's about the longest at the moment. We have one designed to turn a small electric motor. The first day it requires a charge of half an hour. Then, a few minutes every day and the generator will turn the motor about fifty hours."

If you owned a psychotronic generator, what else could you do with it? Would it actually be what Marshall McLuhan calls "an extension of man"—in this case an extension of your psychic faculties? If they operate on the energy that is supposedly behind supernormal happenings, would a generator be "psychic"?

The Czech scientists, who seem eminently sane and responsible people, said, "Yes." They showed us small segments of film to back up this "yes." One generator, they said, could do that most classic of all ESP tests, the card test.

This "telepathic" generator has a rotating pointer on top. ESP cards are arranged in a circle beneath. The generator is the "receiver." In another room sits a person who will send. He holds the pack of twenty-five cards shuffled and randomized. The sender turns one card at a time face up and concentrates on its pattern. In the first room, the pointer of the generator slowly turns and stops, directed at the card with the same symbol the sender is looking at. As the sender goes through the deck, the generator continues to swing from card to card as an observer notes down is "choices" in order.

What kind of ESP scores does the generator get?

"It is always 100 percent correct. The generator never makes a mistake."

It was a funny looking creature to be the ESP subject of the century! But it isn't a subject, it's a machine, though rather unlike the kind of machines we're used to. Even familiar machines like computers can be programmed to identify a specific symbol when it's encountered. The "only" difference is that the psychotronic generator, because it works on another kind of energy, recognizes symbols across space, through walls, when a person stares at them.

Engineer Drbal, the specialist in electronics, tried to clarify. "All forms, whether sculptures, designs, rooftops of buildings like the pyramid—all forms have wave fronts. So do the patterns on the ESP cards." Supposedly, when a person thinks about this pattern on the card, it seems to intensify the wave front. The generator is designed to pick up this pattern. That's the hypothesis, anyway.

"Instead of cards being placed under the pointer, we can put a potato, an apple, various vegetables and fruits. Another set is placed in front of a person in a separate room. As the person selects each, the revolving pointer on the generator also turns to indicate the matching vegetable." Their generators, the Czechs added, could also distinguish blood samples and match a child with his parents.

In the United States Cleve Backster, head of the Backster School of Lie Detection in New York, has found that organic matter—plants, fruits, vegetables, blood samples—seems to have a form of "primary perception." They communicate, sometimes across vast distances. And they "recognize"; even cell scrapings from a person's mouth "recognized" their owner according to the polygraph tracings.

Have the Czechs with their generators succeeded in isolating whatever basic factor it is in living things that's capable of "perceiving" and "recognizing" at a distance?

Pavlita's generators turn wheels, step up plant growth, purify polluted water, perhaps changing its molecular structure. "It's all done by psychotronic energy." Well, if it actually is a real energy, what happens if you aim it at people?

"That depends on the kind of generator. Some, we believe, could speed healing of wounds and recovery from various illnesses. Others have a harmful effect. We tested the force of one type of generator, for example, on the brain. Pavlita's daughter Jana offered to be the guinea pig. At a distance of several yards, we beamed this energy from a generator toward her head. The EEG showed it caused a change in her brain waves. Jana became dizzy—her spatial orientation was affected, and she began to swirl around.

"There have been various experiments on lower forms of life. Snails for one, were subjected to the psychotronic force. It caused them to withdraw into their shells and go into a state similar to hibernation. We've also tested insects."

They showed us photos of the generator used. It looked like a chunky metal doughnut with a slice through it on one side. The metal circle was held up on a rod and a base, like a mirror. "We placed flies in this generator. They died instantly."

If psychotronic energy could kill flies, could it kill bacteria or diseased cells in the body? Could it alter genetic material—DNA and RNA? Before we could go further into this death ray for flies, several more people arrived to join our group.

A VISIT TO THE CZECH MERLIN

Our convoy of cars drove through the suburbs of Prague, out into the Bohemian countryside and headed east toward the small town where Pavlita, our modern-day Merlin, lived.

The man driving our car had been introduced as a composer. "I'm a specialist in criminology," he told us. "I've worked quite a bit with the police in the past, before I took up composing full time." He was the heir to a very distinguished family name, known far beyond Czechoslovakia. His father was one of the country's famous composers, his grandfather was renowned as the architect of some of the grand buildings of the Austro-Hungarian Empire. This moderately well-known son wrote show tunes, "songs with *plenty* of melody."

What did he know about Pavlita? Not very much, but he'd come up against enough frauds and clever swindles in his police work. If there was something funny going on, he assured us he'd spot it.

"I have heard that Pavlita is a medium who does PK, moves objects. That's something I'd like to see."

It seemed Pavlita caused confusion on his home turf too. We'd heard Dr. Milan Ryzl say in the United States before we left that he'd found no evidence of PK and that Pavlita's claims were probably a self-delusion. He mentioned that uncontrolled air currents could be expected to produce Pavlita's results. Quite possibly in the early tests before Ryzl left Czechoslovakia in 1967, there may not have been controls that completely excluded any chance of air movement affecting the turning of a strip of foil on a rotor. But air currents have nothing to do with purifying water, improving plant growth, or "magnetizing" bits of glass and metal. And Ryzl, busy with his own psi work in Prague, was never one of the principal investigators of Pavlita. Certainly a good deal of evidence must have been amassed before Pavlita was officially rehabilitated, which didn't occur until after Ryzl had left.

We tried to explain to our companion that we'd heard Pavlita wasn't exactly a PK medium, but he'd built generators that supposedly worked on the human energy that caused PK. "That's even harder to swallow!" That much we all agreed on. "I always try to keep an open but skeptical attitude toward everything in ESP," he went on. "I can't say it's impossible, still . . ." He reached into his raincoat pocket. "I hope I don't spoil anybody's afternoon." He produced two "supermagnets." "Maybe we can find out a little more about the ways of the generators with these. I intend to try them on the Pavlita machines."

We'd been speeding over hill and dale for hours, past neat villages of red-roofed, stone houses built close to the road, through spas, heavy with dark green leaves, baroque fountains, and statues in the town squares. Occasionally our friend pointed to turrets and dragon-teeth walls on the summit of a distant hill and gave us a short history of some of the medieval castles Czechoslovakia is famous for.

What had gotten him interested in parapsychology? "I said I was a skeptic about most things, and particularly about parapsychology, but I couldn't help getting interested in the subject. Quite a long time ago, my mother consulted a psychic. The woman told her a quantity of things that would happen in the future, not just to my mother, but also to me. They happened. I decided to consult the psychic myself. She described the woman I was engaged to at the time, but told me we wouldn't marry. She said I'd marry someone else; she told me where and how I would meet my wife, what she'd look like, and that the marriage would eventually fail. She was right. She also described in detail a future accident in which I'd break my leg. There was much more, but it was all correct. Sure, some of it must have been coincidence or suggestion, but not all of it. I guess I'm skeptical too about passing it all off with an easy, but nonsensical explanation."

Finally, we reached a small town and pulled to a stop on

a street lined with tall old shade trees and four-story buildings standing wall to wall. As in many Czech towns, classical sculpture and colorful painted frescoes wound around the building. A carved stone figure, like a miniature Atlas, supported the rooftop at the corner and surveyed the crossroads with wary eyes. The street was deserted, misty with a fine rain. A tall, athletic-looking man, with dark eyes and even features, came out of a building entrance to greet us. Robert Pavlita was casually dressed in slacks and a plaid sport shirt. He could have been an American executive relaxing on a day off.

Upstairs in the apartment, Pavlita's nineteen-year-old daughter Jana led us into the bright, spacious living room furnished with blond, industriously polished Scandinavian-style furniture, a grand piano, and many paintings. She left us around the dinner table and almost instantly reappeared with coffee and cake. Jana was a pretty girl, delicate and chic in a white flowered miniskirt, her reddish hair styled in a short high-fashion cut. A Czech friend had described her as "very docile" and observed that she worked a heavy schedule on generator research without, it seemed, a murmur of complaint and without much time for anything else. That afternoon she seemed slightly unnerved at finding herself the hostess of our polyglot group.

There seemed to be very little frivolity about Robert Pavlita. He came over as a man who has no time to waste, who's used to getting straight to the point and dispatching matters. After a brief conference with Dr. Rejdak, he brought out a few of the seventy or more psychotronic generators he'd designed. He set them on the table and let us examine them. "They're beautiful," one of the Czechs commented. And they were. Most of our companions had not been introduced to the wonders of Pavlita before, either.

We picked up the first generator. It looked like a small abstract figure of an ancient fertility goddess—a rectangle of metal for the head and a trapezoid of iron for the body, with bosomlike projections on it. Although it stood only six or seven inches high, it was enormously heavy. Etched on the "head" was a staring pattern, a vertical zigzag design. For different functions, the "head" segment could be removed and other components substituted. How do you charge it? Pavlita showed us how he held it, his thumb on the conical projections on the front and one of his fingers on a similar projection on the back. As you moved your eyes along the zigzag pattern in a sort of figure eight, the device supposedly picked up and accumulated your bio-energy.

Circular-shaped generators, like small suns, sat on the table: a circle of black iron dappled with speckles of gold or brass, others with diamond-shaped designs cut into them. Some were ice smooth, some rough like a wrought-iron gate.

"What got you into this?" we asked Pavlita.

"I've always been interested in the idea of another form of energy," he said. "Even when I was just a boy at school." He'd been educated in a technical school and after graduating, his genius for invention quickly led to new processes and new machines for industry.

As he chain-smoked, Pavlita explained some of the things the generators could do. "Every motion a person makes in a room leaves a pattern, a trace. The generator is able to pick up this trace at a distance of several rooms. Even moving one's hand in a circle over a table creates enough of a trace for the machine to pick up and identify."

One of the Czechs tried to explain to us in slow, careful English. "This trace he is speaking of is a form. It is not an energy, as we know it. They think what occurs is that a sort of indentation is made into the surroundings. This is the trace."

The composer-criminologist didn't buy this idea at all, or much else that was being said. Pavlita showed him privately a huge book of pictures and reports in one corner of the room.

"This energy is a real energy," Pavlita said, "a genuine force of nature." When Jana was a small child, he and his wife discovered she'd gotten into the room where they kept the generators. Thinking the bright objects must be toys, Jana began to play with them. "We caught her, but not before the little finger on each of her hands became paralyzed," Pavlita said. "Fortunately it was only temporary."

While the groups wrangled over various theories of how the generators worked, Pavlita set up an experiment in the kitchen for just the two of us to see. It was a well-lit, ordinary kitchen. He put a circular collar of copper about ten inches in diameter and five inches high on the table. There was an inch-wide gap between the two ends of the collar. A small tubular generator, which simply seemed to be a hollow piece of metal, with no moving parts, no wires, was attached vertically to the collar beside the gap. He put a small metal ball on top of the tube. Inside the collar, a tin wheel resembling the spokes on an umbrella was poised on a needlelike stand.

Pavlita set up a glass shield between himself and the device. He took off his watch. He reached around the glass and adjusted the metal ball. Then he drew his hands back behind the barrier and began the charging process by gazing at a pattern on the generator, moving his head slightly up and down. He called to Jana to join him. She stood behind him, directed her gaze to the generator, and moved her head gently from side to side. They did not seem to be straining to force this charging process.

In less than a minute the generator was charged; slowly the tin wheel began to turn. It turned as if pulses were being directed at it, then faster and more smoothly. We didn't detect any draft of air, any heat wave that could have caused the motion. There were no magnets in sight, no wires, nothing attached under the table. No scientist would accept this as a test, but it was a very much out in the open, sharply illuminated demonstration. The Department of Physics of the University of Hradec Králové, which had examined some of the Pavlita devices, as well as experts from the Czech Academy of Science, agreed that normal physical causes had been fairly ruled out in controlled tests. Then, how did it work?

Dr. Rejdak explained that copper seems to attract this psychotronic energy and that the copper circular collar seemed to polarize, one side positive and one side negative. Presumably, the interplay of force from the two poles caused the wheel to be attracted, then repulsed, forcing it to move.

Pavlita cleared the table and came back with another type of generator. This one was a long hollow rectangle of steel about seven inches long and an inch or two in width. He attached a conical aluminum tip to the bottom end. "The tip can be of wood, plastic, anything nonmagnetic," he said. When he was done, the generator looked like a pudgy ballpoint pen.

The other guests joined us. Pavlita scattered fragments of nonmagnetic substance onto a sheet of glass. Various people tested them with a magnet. When they were satisfied that magnetism had no effect on the fragments Pavlita picked up the generator, placing his fingers on two metal circles on the back. He moved his thumb back and forth over a scalloped opening in the front, as if he were playing a clarinet. He touched the tip to a piece of copper. It picked it up. He carried the copper to pieces of crystal, silver, aluminum. They all clung together in a stack from the generator. "The energy is going into these nonmagnetic substances," he said. "Now that we've put a charge on them, anything will pick them up." He asked us for a match.

We produced some wooden ones we'd bought in Romania. He put a match near a piece of aluminum, near other little chips. Our match attracted them and, with prodding, picked them up and stacked them. He asked us to hold a magnet over the pieces. It had no effect. It did not attract them. These little chips of nonmagnetic metal and crystal, once charged with psychotronic energy from the generators, would also attract or repel the pole of a suspended magnetic needle.

Pavlita put a sheet of glass on a stand and held a formidable horseshoe magnet, about five inches long, underneath it. This time he scattered magnetic fragments on top of the glass and moved the chips about with the magnet. Then he pointed his generator at them. The generator easily picked them up despite the force of the magnet attracting them beneath. His generator also drew the pieces directly from the magnet.

Next, Pavlita dumped all the nonmagnetic substances into a glass dish of water. (Electrostatic energy doesn't work under water.) The generator not only picked up each substance, it also appeared to make the water itself cling to the tip of the generator in a narrow column. The composer brought his supermagnets into play The little fragments didn't budge. He tried it on the tip of the generator; no attraction. Pavlita said his device would even attract cloth and jokingly used it to draw the edge of the composer's handkerchief from his pocket.

And that was enough experimenting, our host decided. By this time Mrs. Pavlita had arrived home. A small, warm, bustling woman, she shook hands warmly and insisted we stay for supper.

On the long black drive back to Prague through pelting gusts of rain, great sprays of lightning lit the sky like heraldry against a backdrop of frowning fortresses and ancient castles. It brought to mind some of those late night movies of Dr. Frankenstein's laboratory as he tries to infuse life into an inanimate creature. Could this strange psychotronic energy succeed as Frankenstein's "lightning" did? Could it endow the inanimate with motion?

Have the Czechs isolated the energy that allows Nelya Mikhailova to cause nonmagnetic objects to move at a distance? Have they captured in a generator the "X" force from the healer's hands that causes wounds to heal, plants to speed their growth?

Does man have powers he never dreamed of, energies that can be isolated and used? Maybe this psychotronic energy is a key to ghosts and even to the supposed ectoplasmic substances emitted by mediums. The Czechs have only reported on the uses for psychotronic energy that they feel they've confirmed. To their mind, this is just the beginning of a discovery—an awesome discovery. We heard much speculation. And we talked finally about the future which the Czechs looked to so hopefully and about philosophy and history.

"In Czechoslovakia, history certainly repeats itself," one of the businessmen said. "For centuries about every fifty years somebody invades us. Do you really think that's about to change?" he asked with a cynical laugh.

But Czechs we met elsewhere, in restaurants, in shops, on buses, everywhere, told us again and again, "The Soviets will never invade." Many of them kidded us about being worried. "What are we guilty of? We are not leaving socialism. All we're trying to create is socialism with a human face. We're trying to guarantee freedom of the individual, freedom of speech, freedom of inquiry. The goals of the Czech experiment are the goals of the whole of human society."

In another kind of experiment during that brief Czech springtime, we had seen the psychotronic generators. What are they all about? Even the Czechs don't claim to know all there is to know about their new energy. The cardinal point in their minds is that Pavlita's generators demonstrate that an unknown energy does exist, subtly intertwined with human beings.

If it is real, if it continues to check out, in twenty years this account will read like the report of two primitives trying to describe a television or a phonograph. If before the patents were secured, we chanced in on a private demonstration of Mr. Edison's talking machine ninety-five years ago, we'd probably have written about a bizarre, almost unbelievable machine. It could, as Caruso sang in the room, somehow capture his voice in hairlike grooves on a circle of wax. A week later this circle could be put on a rotor, a sort of metal arm would trace the grooves, and, as if time didn't exist, we would hear Caruso sing out his aria like a conjured ghost. What's more, it was reported that the wax would stay charged with the voice for a long time, perhaps even for years.

The very few—two or three—Western scientists who have seen Pavlita's generators are wary of them. No one likes to wear a historical dunce cap like the members of the French Academy who bodily threw Mr. Edison's agent and his talking machine out of their chambers. They knew, after all, that wax can't talk, that the whole thing was a cheap ventriloquist's trick. Yet no one, particularly scientists, likes to be fingered as gullible either.

Many others have announced the discovery of a new form of vital energy through the years and it's come to nothing—just as America was discovered many times before Columbus made it stick. Is Pavlita a fraud? Is he a Norseman whose sightings will fade in the fogs of time and obscurity, or is he a Columbus?

A few days after we left Prague, the Soviet Union invaded. They brought in more heavy war equipment, according to the Czech television men, than even Nazi Germany used to occupy the country. Helmeted Soviet soldiers were squatters on the castle heights overlooking the city where we'd seen long-haired hippies painting Art Nouveau designs on the sidewalks: curlicues of LOVE and the injunction "Make Love Not War." Soviet tanks turned the street sullen where we'd talked over the plans the Czechs had for psychotronics in the bright, opening months to come. There would be many tests. And besides, reports and documentation, theories and films would be presented in the scientific councils of the West as well as in the Communist countries.

And now? The new energy may disappear under a new iron curtain. The Czechs told us there were isolated people in Europe and America working quietly on this "vital energy." Perhaps someone here will come up with a psychotronic generator that passes all the tests Pavlita's did. Or perhaps, hard line or soft line, the Czechs will decide they have a good thing going and let the rest of us know more about it.

It's our opinion that the Czech scientists believe they're onto something. They're secure enough in this belief to announce their discovery to outside scientific conferences. It is also our opinion that the generators work. The question is why, on what energy? Is it Prana, the Vital Energy of the Chinese, the bioplasmic energy of the Kirlian effect?

The discovery of a new-old form of energy, a vital energy, a more intimate energy than electricity or x-ray is a scintillating idea. It asks for a leap of the imagination. It implies a landing place outside the rings of current scientific knowledge, a landing place where mind and energy are no longer irrevocably split apart, but instead interact to work their wonders.

Is psychotronic energy the subtle, vital energy that mystics, mediums, and philosophers have posited and that scientists recently have looked for behind psychic happenings? Pavlita's generators reverberate in the mind like gleaming question marks against the now muted Czech countryside.

29

IMAGE, ENERGY, POTENTIAL

What we encountered taking shape—fantastic and strange as some of it seemed—in three very different cultures is at bottom the tangible manifestation of a universal thrust and longing.

We're in the space age whether we like it or not. Our energies are turned to outer space and quite obviously also to inner space. Awareness seminars, meditation, consciousness expansion, the age of Aquarius—the thrust inward is the propellant of the era.

"Human society today is faced with the dilemma of a breakdown or a breakthrough in human consciousness to match the breakthrough in science and technology," states Dr. Shafica Karagulla in *Breakthrough to Creativity*.[318] Director of the Higher Sense Perception Research Foundation in California, Dr. Karagulla, a widely honored neuropsychiatrist, is exploring the ability of sensitives to "read" aura and energy body. She is not typical. While the inward-into-more urge has taken hold in the academic-scientific disciplines in Czechoslovakia, Bulgaria, and Russia, in America it is generally on the "outside."

Maybe we should be "stockpiling" psychics. Discoveries in psi, as the Communists understand, can, like most other advances, be put to anti-human uses. Cold war gamesmanship, however, isn't the loudest message we got from Communist parapsychology. What came over is threefold and pro-human, pro-people.

Discovery of the energy behind psi "will be comparable to the discovery of atomic energy," Dr. Leonid Vasiliev said. Igor Shishkin, a bright young Soviet mathematician, recently compared discovering the theories of psi to the discovery of the theories of relativity.

Exaggerated? As you get into Communist parapsychology, you begin to get a feeling for what they mean, something more vibrant than abstruse formulae. The Communists are looking past the isolated wonder—the sugar bowl on parade, images coming in on nothing from Siberia—to a world just beyond the horizon of our perception. Dr. Genady Sergeyev, Dr. Nikolai Kozyrev, the Czech psychotronic scientists, and many others are trying to move in on a world of energy that can really do things. They are trying to give us a handle on a world we already live in, but that few can perceive or manipulate. Past that, what areas of a grand design—universal mind, the construct of being—they may stumble into is a widening question.

Vasiliev saw something even more revolutionary than a new energy coming with psi—"the direct experience of another person." We never know if another is acting, Vasiliev points out, or if another could convey what he's experiencing even if he wanted to. Psi seems to be a mind-link, a body-link. The full, direct experience of someone else is an awesome potential.

Forcing human potential into human action here and now is the drive of Communist parapsychology. To them psi is practical, it can make us *more*. They are working on ways of using psi: to improve intellectual, artistic, inventive ability; to communicate in space and undersea; to help locate minerals and water; to predict pieces of the future; to command another person's behavior at a distance; to see at a distance; to treat the living force fields around the body. That's just the beginning.

As these scientists plunge into their practically pointed psi research, a sense of living unity, of infinite movement and variety, is beginning to emerge from the cocoon of the unknown and the unseen. This is man, a being of energy in a galaxy of energies, dynamically linked to all life and to the forces of the universe.

Overall, Communist parapsychology can be summed up in three words: Image, Energy, Potential. The world of psychic research in Czechoslovakia, Bulgaria, and Russia is made of efforts to key into a new dimension of universal energy, efforts to unlock the boundless unused potential of the human being. As a by-product, Communist parapsychologists are bringing into view what may be the most important aspect of all: a more profound image of just what a human being is.

For all its promise, opposition to psi research is still potent in the East as well as the West. Yet:

"We have a good climate for the psychic in Bulgaria."

"There is much talk in the Soviet Union about studying the latent powers of man's psyche which science has demonstrated are unusually great."

"There is a spiritual tradition in Czechoslovakia that leads to scientific inquiry into the psychic realm."

Interest in studying the psi dimsension has also begun to stir in Poland, Romania, East Germany. (See Appendix D.)

Is America's heritage really so sterile, have we been devoid of visionaries and dreamers, devoid of interest in the "world unseen?" Have we really become more naively materialistic than the Communists?

Viewing the opposition in America, psychiatrist Jule Eisenbud, in his book on thought photography, *The World of Ted Serios*, remarks, "I suspect that if resistance to psi ever will be overcome, it will not come from staid, patient work in laboratories or any number of talks to scientists or the educated public, but from a general groundswell from the ranks of a population that is exploding in more ways than one."

Communists scientists take psi research seriously. It is not a joke. It is not the province of the wafty few. Isn't it about time we looked into this unknown side of being? Now, today and tomorrow, is the time for bold, uncompromising research. And it is the time for all of us, on every level, to stop being cowardly, to have the guts to follow the life-giving dictum, Know Thyself. This is not a matter of intellectual curiosity. This is not a matter of proving our open-mindedness. This is a matter of survival. Humanity is in a life-death struggle—Eros versus Thanatos, Freud called it. The psychic dimension has life force, it is the home of creativity and inspiration. It has freedom and life to give to those who will take it. That is why some of the most splendid minds of this country—Madame Curie, Carl Gustav Jung, Franklin D. Roosevelt, William Butler Yeats, Thomas Edison, Winston Churchill, Albert Einstein —were actively interested in the psychic spectrum. Parapsychology as the orderly study of this dimension, stands at a juncture, like the capstone of a pyramid, where the humanities, religion, science, and the arts can meet.

We can't all try to check out Communist experiments or convince authorities to do it for us. But we can create a climate. Dr. Karagulla uses sensitives drawn from the top echelons of business, medicine, technology. Can't we at least be tolerant of their kind of abilities, so they are not always and necessarily "Anonymous"? Can't public opinion aid scientists who feel they must work in the field anonymously? If something that might be psychic happens to us, we can take off the "plain brown wrapper." We can admit it to ourselves, to others, admit it to the mainstream of life.

Psi doesn't belong only in the lab. If any of the hundreds who have pondered it are right, psi is a human potential. It belongs to everybody.

The Communist parapsychologists still have a lot to buck. The opposition they face, in some cases, can be much more directly lethal than it is in the United States. But if there's anything the highly educated, highly individual collection of people we met has in common, it is outspoken enthusiasm, openness, and a sort of *simpatico* for the psychic.

What researchers East and West are trying to bring in seems worth the daring and the effort. Eileen Garrett, in *Awareness*, describes it as "discovering the fringes of an anciently existing evolutionary field." This outstanding psychic *and* outstanding business woman continues, "The human consciousness is rapidly freeing itself from the restrictions of form. . . . Man's next step to freedom would seem to be possible only in the areas of consciousness. Presently, in the infinites of space-time, man may travel in consciousness wherever he will—if he will."

In 1962 Dr. Leonid L. Vasiliev was finally able to publish *Experiments in Mental Suggestion,* his long-suppressed book on his psychic research. He wrote:

"I did the best I could, let those who can, do better."

The challenge is there, the adventure is underway. A universe is waiting that doesn't know north, south or East-West. As the Walrus said, "The time has come."

APPENDIX A

1. Force Field Research in Russia

Research on force field detectors is being done in Leningrad at the Laboratory for Biological Cybernetics in the University of Leningrad Physiology Department. The research group led by Dr. Vasiliev's successor, Dr. Pavel Gulyaiev, uses extremely sensitive high-resistance detection electrodes to chart the force field or "electrical aura," as they call it.

The Soviets report that muscular reactions which accompany even a thought can be detected and measured and that the signals in the electrical aura reveal a great deal about the state of the organism. Dr. Gulyaiev feels that this force field may be the means by which communication between fish, insects, and animals occurs.

The Soviet research is directed toward using the force field detectors for medical diagnosis and PK. The signals generated by a thought could be picked up at a distance, amplified, and used to move objects.

Dr. Gulyaiev's "electro-auragram" device is so sensitive it can measure the electrical field of a nerve. The nerves of a frog, for instance, have an electrical field of twenty-four centimeters. A nerve from the human heart has a field of ten centimeters. The electrical emanations around the body change according to health, mood, character. The distance at which this field can be measured depends on the amount of tension generated. (See Parapsychology Newsletter Jan.-Feb. 1969, May-June 1969.)

2. Sergeyev Detectors

The Sergeyev detectors apparently measure the human force field at a distance of four yards from the body. Although we were told that data concerning construction of the Sergeyev detectors was not available, having been classified by the military, a recent communication from behind the Iron Curtain indicates some details have been published by the Soviet Academy of Sciences. An American space expert has suggested that the Sergeyev detector may be similar to the Cristofv Field Intensity Meter or the Cristofv "anti-fatigue device" (*Product Engineering,* July 4, 1966 and February 13, 1967) or similar to magnetic field detectors in use in space research. (See Schafer, W.—"Further Development of the Field Effect Monitor", Life Sciences, Convair Division of General Dynamics, Report A 67–41582, pp. 125–126.)

2A. Force Field Detectors

At the University of Saskatchewan, Canada, research is also being done on measurement of human force fields at a distance. The Canadian group, headed by the well-known Dr. Abram Hoffer and Dr. Harold Kelm, is working with a detector (invented by an American, David Thomson) consisting of two capacitor plates, a preamplifier, and a line recorder like that of an electrocardiograph. This detector charts the body's invisible electrical "aura" or force field at a distance. For instance, as a patient walks into a room, the detector determines at a distance whether his anxiety level is high, medium, or low.

Inventor Thomson, assisted by Dr. Jack Ward of Trenton, New Jersey, discovered that a person's force field detects the frequencies of the force fields of other people at a distance and is affected by them. Says Thomson, "People's force fields immediately sense fear, aggression, panic, or friendliness in another person." To prove his point he built a transmitter to send out "anxiety waves"—an electromagnetic field like that of an extremely anxious human. People reacted sharply to them. Thomson reports he could clear a crowded room in fifteen minutes flat by turning on the transmitter.

Thomson also built transmitters to send out "calm" waves which duplicate the force field of a relaxed, cheerful person. Thomson says the transmitters might be used to calm frightened children or nervous hospital patients. (See *Maclean's* magazine, Sept. 1968.)

Results at the University of Saskatchewan, Dr. Hoffer wrote us, are "quite encouraging." The National Aeronautics and Space Administration is also doing research on force fields.

For parapsychology, these force field detectors and transmitters could be very important in helping to increase a person's psi or dowsing ability. The research also provides new scientific proof that the force fields of *observers* and *experimenters* may have a profound effect on psychics and tests of psychic ability.

3. Notes on Dr. Genady Sergeyev's PK Tests with Nelya Mikhailova

Tests in EEG chamber, Registration: EEG; electrocardiograph; force field detectors four yards from the subject.

There is a large gradient between the electrical characteristics in the forward part of Mikhailova's brain versus the back part of the brain (fifty to one), whereas in the average person the gradient is four to one. The usual force field around Mikhailova's body is ten times weaker than the magnetic field of the earth.

During PK, her pulse rises to 240 per minute. There is activation of deeper levels of the occipital lobe and reticular formation. This enhances polarization in the brain between front and back, says Sergeyev. When the gradient between front and back of the brain reaches a certain level, and there is most intense activity in the occipital lobe, radiation of electrostatic and electromagnetic fields is detected by the force field detectors four yards from the body. Disturbance of the magnetic fields during PK is of a stocastical character with a parametrical resonance on a frequency of five cycles. Heartbeat, brain waves, and force field fluctuations are in ratio. The fields around the PK medium are stronger further away than close to the head. Mikhailova appears to focus these force field waves in a specific area.

Spin waves in the fluctuating force field of the medium

may influence molecular activity of substances and also the activity of the brain itself, according to Sergeyev. Magnetic waves exist separately from the electrostatic waves and they may reduce friction between the object and the table during PK. In connection with magnetic waves, unmagnetic material can become magnetic. (These effects were proved ten years ago by Zelin, says Sergeyev. The theory of magnetic interaction is discussed in a book *Spin Waves* by Akeezer and others.) The most favorable time for this occurrence is when it is coordinated with magnetic disturbances of the earth.

4. Theory of PK

Sergeyev bases his theory of PK on the idea of an unhomogeneous plasma field in the body which the Kirlians of Krasnodar (Chapters 16, 17, and 18) have photographed and measured and which is now being researched at the Kazakh State University by Dr. V. Inyushin, *et al.* According to the Kazakh biologists, this bioplasma generates some of the biological fields around the body which the Sergeyev detectors measure. Mind and emotions have a powerful effect on bioplasma and in turn on the force field. Sergeyev hypothesizes that under certain specific conditions, this bioplasma could be the cause of psychokinetic phenomena. In a recent scientific paper he gives conditions under which the changes of the bioplasma appear or disappear. ("Invisible Fire," in *Telepathy, Telegnosis, Dowsing, and PK,* ed. Z. Rejdak. Prague: State Publishing, Svoboda, 1969–70. See also Inyushin in bibliography.)

5. Czech Report on Nelya Mikhailova

by Dr. Zdenek Rejdak and
Dr. Ottokar Kurz,
from Czech *Pravda,* June 14, 21, 1968
Part of report was translated
in *Paraphysics Journal,* Vol. 2 No. 3

"After the PK experiments, Mrs. Mikhailova was very exhausted, her pulse almost imperceptible, with poor mobility, and general depression visible on her face. According to Dr. Zverev's report, the loss of weight after thirty minutes of PK tests amounts to 800–1,000 grams. The EEG showed an intense emotional excitement. The electrocardiogram presented an arrhythmic action of the heart; it was impossible to differentiate the P and T waves and heart chamber complexes QRS. High percentages of blood sugar were recorded. The symptoms as a whole remind one of a stress alarm reaction in the organism, but the manner in which these changes take place in the case of Mrs. Mikhailova is not usual in the normal praxis. The function of the endocrine system was disturbed; physiological measurements showed a weakening of the organism. The faculty of taste discrimination was diminished, sleep disturbed, pains in arm and leg muscles were reported, also vertigo and malfunction of coordination.

"Laboratory experiments: PK phenomena took place in an insulated electroencephalographic chamber, Mrs. Mikhailova was able to displace light objects of plastic material and metals of weight from ten to fifty grams. At the moment of occurrence of phenomena, registrations were observed by means of several electrodes, in EEG, and cardiographic apparatus and also recordings were obtained by an apparatus at a distance without direct contact, indicating an electrostatic fluctuating field; the latter appeared at the moment of brain tension.

"An analysis of the electrical signals on the skull surface indicated that the energy level of the signals was considerably lower than the energy level of electrostatic field fluctuations recorded from a distance. At the same time, however, there existed a significant correlation, within 5 percent between the parameters of the electrical bioturbulence and the electrostatic turbulence. It appeared that at the instant of PK phenomena, there was a marked correlation between these informational characteristics and at the same time there was a concentration of energy in the direction in which the subject's gaze was fixed. It was further found that the frequency of the heart pulse could be increased fourfold under these conditions. The modulation rhythm of the intermittent electrostatic field was associated in geometric ratio with heart and brain frequencies, suggesting the heart can influence the frequency-function of the space-field modulator. . . .

"We have outlined only very partially some of the results of Dr. Sergeyev's research, showing that apparatus can detect and record the extraordinary character of these phenomena based upon the human organism."

6. Re: Nelya Mikhailova—Some Further References

Articles on Nelya Mikhailova (Ninel Kulagina) appeared in *Leningrad Pravda,* January 21, 1964, February 23, 1964, and March 15, 1964, *Izvestia,* Nov. 28, 1964, and in *Smena* on January 24, 1964. A report of Dr. Leonid Vasiliev's research with her appeared in *Smena,* January 16, 1964, called "In the Moscow Lecture Hall." First reports of her PK ability appeared in *Moscow Pravda,* March 17, 1968—"When Apples Fall" by Lev Kolodny (translated in *Journal of Paraphysics,* Vol. 2, No. 4, Downton, Wiltshire, England). "Phenomenon of Psi" by Vadim Marin, *Moscow Komsomolets,* April 7, 1968. "Miracle in a Sieve" by V. Chijov, *Pravda,* June 24, 1968 (translated in *Journal of Paraphysics,* Vol. 2, No. 4); *Evening Leningrad,* April 16, 1968. *The International Herald Tribune,* March 25, 1968 also ran an article on Mikhailova.

Czech scientists Dr. Ottokar Kurz and Dr. Zdenek Rejdak discussed test with Mikhailova in "About Telekinesis," Czech *Pravda,* June 14, 1968, and June 21, 1968. "Telekinesis or Fraud?" by Dr. Rejdak appeared in *Journal of Paraphysics,* Vol. 2, No. 3, 1968. See also "The Kulagina Ciné Films" by Dr. Rejdak, *Journal of Paraphysics,* Vol. 3, No. 3, 1969; "Notes on the Kulagina [Mikhailova] Films" by B. Herbert, Vol. 3, Nos. 3 & 4, 1969; subsequent issues carry further reports.

An article on PK with radioactive material: "Isotopes at the Service of Parapsychology," *Knowledge Is Power,* No. 9, 1967.

Three scientific papers by Dr. Sergeyev, including his work with Mikhailova, appear in *Telepathy, Telegnosis, Dowsing, and PK,* Prague: State Publishing, Svoboda,

1969–70. Sergeyev and Pavlova's two books are also relevant. *Statistical Method of Research on the Human EEG*, Leningrad: Academy of Science USSR, Science Publishing, 1968, and *Questions of the Applied Analysis of Chance Processes*. Moscow: Soviet Radio Publishing, 1968.

7. Emotions and Bioplasma

Dr. Inyushin describes the impact of emotions on animal bioplasma, as seen via the Kirlian method of high-frequency fields. Rabbits, when alarmed, showed radical changes in bioplasma radiation. A condensed bioplasma was generated. The radiations given off by the bioplasma were dark with intense flares of a purplish color. Under normal conditions, the flares are bluish and the bioplasma density evenly distributed in a complicated configuration. Inyushin states the Kirlian techniques could be applied in parapsychology to determine the psychic state of a subject and whether or not psi experimental conditions are suitable. V. M. Inyushin, in "Biological Plasma of Human Organisms and Animals," *Telepathy, Telegnosis, Dowsing, and PK*, ed. Dr. Z. Rejdak, Prague: State Publishing, Svoboda, 1969–70.

8. Mitogenetic Radiation

"*All* living cells produce an invisible radiation!" Russian scientist Dr. Alexander Gurvitch electrified the world with this announcement in the 1930s. He revealed research that sounded like PK between plants.

He chose the root of a freshly sprouted onion to be a "sender" and mounted the root in a tube like a "biological cannon." Gurvitch pointed the root tip at another onion root, the "receiver," also in a tube but with an area exposed on its side. After three hours, Gurvitch counted the number of cells in the exposed area of the "receiver" and the number in its covered side. There were one fourth more cells in the part exposed to the "biological cannon." The onion root must be radiating some sort of energy!

Gurvitch installed sheets of quartz between the onion

sender and onion receiver. Still the strange energy poured through. He tried yeast as a "receiver." The rate of yeast budding increased 30 percent. So did the growth of bacteria.

In humans Gurvitch found muscle tissue, the cornea of the eye, blood, and nerves were all "senders" of what he called "mitogenetic radiation." Cancer tissues would radiate, but not the blood of cancer patients. Hospitals in Europe began to use this blood test to diagnose. Illness affected the radiation, they found. When a sick person held a yeast culture for a few minutes, it was enough to kill vigorous yeast cells.

In New York, *Harper's Magazine,* July 1934, hailed Gurvitch's discovery—"Life whose wheel is driven by light may also be a generator of light. This is the amazing concept posed by a series of experiments in a Russian lab."

Gurvitch couldn't see the radiation from living things. He could just tabulate its effects. No one else could see what Gurvitch had found or understand what caused results to vary. Gurvitch came up with a theory of biological force fields but it was soon forgotten.

Then the Kirlians flicked the high-frequency switch on plants. Everyone could see odd rays and plumes of light beaming out of the plants. Today, scientists at the Kirov University of Kazakhstan are taking another look at Gurvitch's discovery. Their biologists state, "Now there is a new possibility of verifying the ideas of A. G. Gurvitch resting on the concept of biological plasma as the medium in which the force of this field expands."

Kirlian photography may prove there *is* a radiation coming from living things that can influence other living things.

Gurvitch's discovery brings up scores of questions in other fields too. Energy pours from plants—fresh fruit, vegetables. What does this imply about living foods? Does this energy in plants constitute the real value in food and do our chemicals, fertilizers, sprays, and additives destroy it? Perhaps Kirlian photography could be a great boon in research on nutrition, agriculture, horticulture, and related fields.

9. The Kirlian Effect

For much background data on the Kirlian Effect we are indebted to many private conversations with Soviet scientists. The following articles and scientific papers explore the Kirlian discovery further.

Kirlian and Kirlian, "Photography and Visual Observation by Means of High-Frequency Currents," *Journal of Scientific and Applied Photography*, Vol. 6, Issue 6, 1961. I. Belov, "The Borders of the Unknown," *Inventor* No. 6, 1964. I. Belov, "Flares Illuminating the Unknown," newspaper article, USSR, no source. I. Leonidov, "Signals—Of What?" *Soviet Union*, No. 145, 1962, reprinted as "Russians Photograph Life and Death," in *Fate*, September 1962.

Inyushin, Grishchenko, *et al.*, "The Biological Essence of the Kirlian Effect," *The Concept of Biological Plasma*, Alma-Ata: Kirov State University of Kazakhstan, 1968.

Inyushin, V. M., "On the Question of the Biological Activity of Red Radiation," Alma-Ata, 1965. "On the Energetic Structure of the Organism," Material Scientific Conference, Alma-Ata, 1966. "On the Question of Studying Luminescence in a High-Frequency Field," *On the Biological Influence of Monochromatic Red Light*, Alma-Ata, 1967. "On the Bio-energetic Aspects of the Influence of Light Energy on the Living Organism," *Some Questions of Theoretical and Applied Biology*, Alma-Ata, 1967.

Grishchenko, V. S., "Fourth State of Matter," Paris, 1944.

Juravlev, A. E., "Living Luminescence," Science Publishing, 1966.

Keldysh, L. V., "Superconductivity in Nonmetallic Systems," *Progress of Physical Science*, Vol. 86, No. 2, 1965.

Meshcheryakov, K. S., "On the Laws of Interaction of Mass and Energy in Cells," *Biological Influence of Monochromatic Red Light*, Alma-Ata, 1967.

Pressman, A. S., *Electromagnetic Fields and Living Nature*, Moscow, Science, 1968.

Szent-Gyiorgyi, A., *Bioenergetics*, Physmatgiz, 1960.

Frank-Kamentski, D. A., *Plasma, Fourth State of Matter*, Gosatomizd.

Chijevsky, A. L., *Air Ions and the National Economy*, Gosplanizdat, 1960. A study of the impact of solar radiations on biological activity appears in *Earth in the Universe*, Moscow: Myicl, 1964.

Chinovet, A., and S. Buxbaum, "Plasma of the Solid Body," *Progress of Physical Science*, Vol. 90, No. 1, 1966.

Articles regarding the relationship of the Kirlian Effect to Acupuncture:

Varsemova, D., "New Arm of Ancient Science," *Literary Gazette*, No. 16, May 1963.

Dyal, Igor, "700 Enigmatic Points," *Literary Gazette*, No. 24, 1967.

Raikov, V., and Adamenko, V., "Questions of Objective Research of Deep Hypnotic States," *Therapy of Mental Disease*, Moscow: Society of Neuropsychiatrists, Sechenov Medical Institute, 1968.

Further material on acupuncture:

Drabkina, S., "Tobiscope," *Sputnik*, No. 5, 1969.

Vogralik, Vadim, "Pinpricks for Health?" *Sputnik*, July, 1969 (in English).

Vogralik, V. G., *Principles of the Chinese Medical Method*, Gorky, 1961.

Bon-Kan, Kim, *The Kyung-rak System, Scientific-Material Basis of Acupuncture*, Pyong-yang: Academy of Medical Science, North Korea, 1963 (in Russian).

Dr. Wu, Wei-p'ing, *Chinese Acupuncture*, Rustington, England: Health Science Press.

Lawson-Wood, D. and J., *Five Elements of Acupuncture and Chinese Massage*, Rustington, England: Health Science Press.

Bach, Marcus, "Acupuncture—An Ancient Method of Healing," *Fate*, Dec., 1968.

Becker, Raymond de, "Les grandes médecines anciennes ne sont pas méprisables," *Planète*, Mars, 1969.

McCullough, C., "The Army Makes Them Hear," Toronto Globe and Mail, June 7, 1969.

Moss, Louis, *Acupuncture and You*, Citadel, New York, 1966.

Inglis, Brian, *Fringe Medicine*, Faber, London, 1964.

Inyushin, V., "On the Bioenergetic Aspects of the Influence of Light Energy on the Organisms of Animals," *Some Questions of Applied Biology*, Alma-Ata, 1967.

APPENDIX B

Re: Soviet Theories of PSI

Dr. Ippolit Kogan has variously applied his mathematical training to parapsychology. For example, he devised logarithms to determine the degree of "rightness" in reception of a telepathic image. A psychic may not say, "a red pot," but may say "metallic, six inches wide, red." Different qualities can be assessed for correctness. To circumvent an obstacle to electromagnetic theorists—the fact that telepathy does not seem to diminish with distance—Kogan thinks of telepathy in terms of information rather than energy. An analogy: If you're using light as an energy, a flashbulb, to expose film in a camera, then you must be fairly close to the light source. If your purpose is information, such as you get from a buoy light, then it makes no difference whether there is a blinding flash or a tiny flicker miles away. This line of thinking is applied to telepathy to explain why it does not *seem* to diminish with distance. Kogan has mathematically demonstrated that in *principle* telepathy could move on exceedingly long (more than a mile) waves. He admits paradoxically these would only explain telepathy between people in very close proximity, not across distances. He also does not rule out that other than electromagnetic forces may be involved. Some of Dr. Kogan's original work including his mathematics is available in English—see bibliography.[73–79, 416]

Leningrad mathematical physicist Igor Shishkin, who called Kogan's "the most expert defense of the electromagnetic viewpoint," is typical of a larger group of Soviets who look beyond the electromagnetic spectrum. A few think the energies of the atom are the "mechanism" of psi.[127] But most look to an unknown force or field—something pervasive, perhaps similar to gravity, Vasiliev said.[45, 46, 237] Like many Soviet physicists, Shishkin is working on a theory of fluctuations. The work of some of the Soviet "Fluctuation" theorists is presented in English translation, *Synchroton Radiation* by A. A. Sokolov and I. M. Tunov, Pergamon Press, London.

Applying fluctuations theories to psi, Shishkin draws on the work of the Soviet theoretical physicist Terletsky and on the work of de Broglie and others to form his hypothesis: telepathy moving faster than the speed of light through fluctuation in a theorized field. A short paper presenting Shishkin's novel ideas is available in English.[203-04]

APPENDIX C

The Czech Manifesto presented in 1968 at Moscow Parapsychology Conference

Psychotronics

Recently in Czechoslovakia a group of theoretical and practical workers in the field of parapsychology have coined the new term *psychotronics* in place of *parapsychology*. The first to employ this term was Fernand Clerc, the French scholar. In a report in a radio-technological journal he touched upon the possibility of causing by an act of will a drop of water to turn to the right or to the left as it fell on the edge of a razor blade. He, however, has not treated the phenomenon any further.

Choosing to employ the said term, the above workers argue as follows:

1. The term "parapsychology" appears improper and inadequate for a scientific discipline.
2. The term "psychotronics" shows that the issue in point is phenomena associated with the psychic aspect and nervous system of man and other living beings, on the one hand, and phenomena of an energetic character in its own right, on the other. It is this very form of energy that is spoken of whenever certain physical or biophysical phenomena defy explanation by the familiar forms of energy. It seems to be a form of energy far more subtle than eletromagnetic waves, and always associated with the psychic component and the psychic impulse. It appears that various transformations and transmutations of this form of energy into familiar forms of energy are not to be ruled out. Since this form of energy is likely to be superior to the forms of energy hitherto known, it may, in conformity with the laws of transformation, be

reduced to lower forms of energy in the same way as electromagnetic energy is transformed into corpuscular energy when a gamma ray is traversing a strong nuclear field.
3. This new term "psychotronics" is general enough to include all pertinent phenomena under research, present and future.
4. Inappropriate terms such as "parabiological," "paraneurophysiological" phenomena can be dispensed with.
5. In Czechoslovakia and frequently elsewhere in the world as well, there still lingers behind public opinion the view that it is the "better" run of occultists who are dealing with parapsychology. This view is apt, not infrequently, to discourage serious scientists from cooperating with workers in telepathy, telegnosis, telekinesis, and the like.

An approximate definition of the new term may be:
Psychotronics is, in essence, the bionics of man. Its main objective is to complete the set of laws governing the animate and inanimate world with new psychic, physical, and biological knowledge derived from certain extraordinary manifestations of the human psyche. Further, the objective is to seek the practical consequences of the problems involved by using either man as intermediate link or by eliminating man and using an artificial synthesis—e.g., by devising a "generator" of the energy used by man in telepathic transfer, once definite evidence has been produced that none of the familiar forms of energy,—electromagnetic, gravitational, or other—is involved. That is why it is one of the main objectives of psychotronics to search for the characteristics of this new form of energy, for working purposes called "psychotronic energy," with the "psychotron" as its unit, after experimental evidence of the existence has been produced. It is a further task of psychotronics to pass on newly acquired knowledge to other scientific disciplines, such as psychology, physics, medicine, philosophy, and the like, to contribute to building up as complex a picture of scientific knowledge as possible.

It is furthermore the opinion of the mentioned workers that by establishing and defining the new form of energy,—psychotron energy,—de Broglie's "dual" conception of the electron (which may appear to exist as either matter or as wave) may be extended to a "triadic" conception expressive of the animate and inanimate world of matter in motion in its totality. There would be then every reason for acknowledging cosmic "triality" as the supreme law of nature and the existence of man.

By laying down the parameters of the new form of energy, the conception of matter in motion will be given a third aspect. The definition of matter in motion will be determined by laws far more complex than those at present. Again, it is important not to lose sight of the fact that the introduction of the new term "psychotronics" and the definition of the new approach may prove of use for a coming to terms with those scientists whose attitude toward the issue at hand has so far been skeptical.

APPENDIX D

Parapsychology in Other European Communist Countries

Romania: Perhaps the best-known person interested in parapsychology is Dr. V. A. Gheorghiu, a specialist in experimental hypnosis with the Psychological Institute of Bucharest. Dr. Gheorghiu has visited Soviet and West German psi centers and gave a paper at the International Parapsychology Seminar in Moscow, August 1966. He reported on unusual experiments in "Parapsychology and Hypnosis —They Are Related."

Poland: From the end of the nineteenth century until World War II, Polish psychic research, founded by the famous Julius Ochorovicz, was among the most active and far-ranging in Europe. There were five major research centers. This wealth of investigation halted with the war and political upheavals. After that, until recently the only person publicly in the field was Dr. Stefan Manczarski, head of Poland's team for the International Geophysical Year, 1957. Now psi seems to be making a comeback.

Inquiring about present research, we received this reply from Dr. Franciszek Chmielewski, President of the Polish Copernicus Society of Naturalists:

"We have the Bio-Electronic Section of the Polish Copernicus Society of Naturalists: The main topics of the Section's present activity are: (1) electric phenomena in living organisms; (2) higher nerve activity in connection with parapsychological phenomena and hypnosis; (3) the influence on living organisms of all kinds of cosmic and earth radiation.

"Among the associates of our Bio-Electronic Section are many specialists in radiesthesia, hypnosis, and clairvoyance. Apart from the Section, there are in Poland many scientists whose great interest is radiesthesia—for example, the priest,

Mr. Jan Podbielski, and many whose interest is parapsychology—for instance, Professor Stefan Manczarski."

Dr. Chmielewski included this list of scientific reports:

S. Manczarski: 1/ "Question of Telepathy in Radiotechnical Studies," *Telecommunication Review,* Nos. 10, 11/12, 1964; Nos. 1/2, 3, 1947.

2/ "Application of Cybernetics and Radiophysics in Parapsychology," *Telecommunication Review,* No. 11, 1961.

3/ "Today and Tomorrow of Teletransmission." Report delivered at Symposium of Polish Academy of Science, Warsaw, December 4–6, 1963.

K. Jach: 4/ "Researches of Telepathy Phenomena in Connection with Hypothesis of Electromagnetic Waves." Unpublished.

K. Borun: 5/ "Telepathy: An Area in Science," *Almanac Of Worker,* 1962.

In connection with Poland, one other man should be mentioned. Stefan Ossowiecki (1877–1944), Russian-born of Polish parents, early discovered his outstanding psychic talent, which he then developed with the aid of a Russian-Jewish holy man. Jailed for political crimes in 1917, Ossowiecki moved to Warsaw on his release four years later. A chemical engineer, a deeply religious man, he never accepted rewards for the use of his all-round psychic talent. A fine telepathist, he was also an outstanding clairvoyant, specializing in reading messages sealed in double envelopes and *lead tubes.* Apart from many Polish scientists, the great researchers of the era—Richet, Osty, Geley, Dingwall, von Schrenk-Notzing, Vasiliev—successfully tested Ossowiecki's telepathy and clairvoyance. He is also said to have been able to influence telepathically the thought and action of another and to accomplish "astral projection."

As Germany invaded Poland, Ossowiecki was given a visa and urged to flee. He preferred to stay. During the war he put his talents to their finest use: helping the underground, giving information on lost and imprisoned people. Holding a scrap of clothing, he told where victims had been executed, where they were buried. Documented accounts speak of him locating specific bodies in mass graves layered with the dead. On the day of the Warsaw Uprising he remarked, "I see that I shall die a terrible death. But I have had a wonderful life!" Shortly, the Nazis machine-gunned Stefan Ossowiecki to death. The manuscript of his last book burned with his body. He is remembered as an expertly tested and proven psychic and a man of enormous compassion. There will soon be a book about Ossowiecki to acquaint Americans with his extraordinary life.

We did extensive interviews with a Polish scientist and other Poles visiting the West who spoke of current psi research. With the reversals that struck Poland early in 1968, they asked us to omit the material they'd given us. Suffice it to say they are interested in every area of psychic research.

Hungary: Work goes on in medical astrology. Among the many scientists in the field are Dr. Kurt Rechnitz, a university professor and former director of the Budapest Obstetric Clinic, and Dr. Endre Magyari of Budapest. We have no reports of current psi research, although Hungary —like Poland—showed activity in the field prior to the war.

East Germany: We heard simply from other Communist scientists. "There is work there." Jack Pollack in *Croiset* speaks of the Nazis confiscating the extensive files and the funds of both the Dutch *Journal of Parapsychology* and the Dutch Society for Psychical Research. Not returned, they "may be either in East Germany or elsewhere behind the Iron Curtain," Pollack says.

Partial Bibliography and References

All publications are Soviet unless otherwise noted. Those in English are marked with an asterisk. The numbers refer to references given throughout the book.

1. ABSOLON, Amand, "Organization of Activities in the Astra Research Center," *Papers on Scientific Astrology*. Bratislava: Pressfoto, 1969. CZECHOSLOVAKIAN
2. AGREST, Modest, "Visits to Earth by Inter-Planetary Beings," *Literary Gazette*, 1959.
3. ANFILOV, G., "Thought Transference—Is It Possible?" *Znanie-Sila*, No. 12, 1960.
4. ASSENOV, K., "Suggestopedia," *Stoudentska Tribouna*, Sofia, Dec. 14, 1965. BULGARIAN
5. ASTROV, M., "Again About Telepathy," *Znanie-Sila*, No. 1, 1966.
6. BARNA, Balogh, "Relations Between Astronomy and Ancient Astrology." *Papers on Scientific Astrology*. Bratislava: Pressfoto, 1969. CZECHOSLOVAKIAN (Hungarian author.)
7. BASHKIROVA, G., "The Little Girl Sensation," *Znanie-Sila*, No. 9, 1964.
8. BATENOV, A., "Experimental application of Bio-Physical (dowsing) method in Search for Water in the Desert." Paper presented: Symposium on Dowsing headed by Dr. A. A. Ogilvy, Chairman of Geo-Physics Dept., Moscow University, April 11–12, 1968.
9. BELOV, I., "The Borders of the Unknown," *Inventor*, No. 6, 1964.
10. ——— "Flares Illuminating the Unknown." No source. USSR, 1961.
11. BICARD, V., "Communications Between Height and Stability of Color Barriers." *Questions of Complex Research in Dermo-Optics*. Sverdlovsk: Pedagogical Institute, 1968.
12. BILIK, Stanislav, "Problems of Dr. Jonas Solved by Computers," *Papers on Scientific Astrology*. Bratislava: Pressfoto, 1969. CZECHOSLOVAKIAN
13. "Bio-Communications," *Moscow Pravda*, March 22, 1967.

14. BONGARD, M. M. and SMIRNOV, M. S., "About the 'Dermal Vision' of R. Kuleshova," *Biophysics*, No. 1, 1965.

*15. ——— "Telepathic Experiments, Necessary Requirements," *Journal of Paraphysics*, Vol. 2, Nos. 3, 4, 5. (Downton, Wilts., England.)

16. BONDAREV, B. V., "Results of Experiments in Bio-Physical (dowsing) Methods on Mineral Deposits in Central Asia." Paper presented at Symposium on Dowsing headed by Dr. A. A. Ogilvy, Chairman Geo-Physics Dept., Moscow University, April 11–12, 1968.

17. BON-KAN, Kim, *The Kyung-rak System, Scientific-Material Basis of Acupuncture*. Pyong-Yang: Academy of Medical Science, North Korea. 1963. (In Russian.)

18. BOULE, P., "It is Necessary to Study Facts," *Science and Religion*, No. 7, 1965.

19. CHIJEVSKY, A. L., "L'action de l'activité périodique solaire sur les phénomènes sociaux," *Traité de Climatologie Biologique et Médicale*. Paris: Masson, 1934. (Soviet author.)

20. ——— "L'action de l'activité périodique solaire sur les épidémies," After Berg, *Symposium Internationale sur les Relations Phénomenales Solaires et Terrestriales*. Brussels: Presses Académiques Européennes, 1960.

21. ——— *The Sun and Us*. Moscow: 1963.

*22. CHIJOV, V., "Miracle in a Sieve," *Pravda*, June 24, 1968. Translation: *Journal of Paraphysics*, Vol. 2, No. 4. (Downton, Wilts., England.)

23. CVEKL, J., "Psychotronics and Philosophy," *Telepathy, Telegnosis, Dowsing, Psychokinesis*. Prague: Svoboda, 1970.

24. DOBROVICH, A., "Do you want to Get Away from Yourself?" *Znanie-Sila*, No. 6, 1969.

25. DOBSA, Istvan, "Astrological Diagnosis of Difficult to Diagnose Diseases," *Papers on Scientific Astrology*. Bratislava: Pressfoto, 1969. CZECHOSLOVAKIAN (Hungarian author.)

*26. "Does Extra-Sensory Perception Exist?" *Sputnik*, Feb., 1968.

*27. DRABKINA, S., "Tobiscope," *Sputnik*, No. 5, 1969.

*28. DVINSKY, E., *Durov & His Performing Animals*. Moscow: Foreign Language Press.

29. DYAL, Igor, "700 Enigmatic Points," *Literary Gazette*, No. 24, 1967.

30. EFIMOV, V. V., "Energetics of Nerve Processes." Paper presented: Seminar Technical Parapsychology Section affiliated All Union Engineering Institute, Moscow, March 29, 1967.

31. "Experiments in Radiesthesia." Siberia: 1962.

*32. "Extra-Terrestrial Civilizations?" *Soviet Union Today,* March, 1968.

33. "Eyeless Sight," articles on: *Technology for Youth,* No. 4, 1963; Nos. 2 & 5, 1965.

34. FESENKO, R. A., "Survey of Work Done at Parapsychology Center of the University of Utrecht," Paper presented: Seminar of Technical Parapsychology section affiliated All Union Engineering Institute, Moscow, Feb. 4, 1967.

35. FIDELMAN, V., "Methods & Results of Telepathic Transmission of Numbers." Paper presented: Congress on Scientific Problems of Telepathy, A. S. Popov Radio Technology Institute, Moscow, Feb. 22, 1968.

36. FIGAR, S., "The Application of Plethysmography to the Objective Study of So-Called Extra-sensory Perception," Journal of the *Society for Psychical Research,* (London), Vol. 38, 1959. (Czech author.)

37. GELLERSTEIN, I., "Not a Question of Belief," *Nedelya, Izvestia,* 196?

38. ——— "Don't Set Limits to the Search," *Science and Religion,* No. 3, 1966.

*39. GOGOL, Nikolai, *Dead Souls.* New York: Pantheon Books, 1948.

40. GOLDBERG, I., "On Recognition of Indications of Color Through Metal Shields," *Questions of Complex Research on Dermo-Optics.* Sverdlovsk: Pedagogical Institute, 1968.

41. GOLIKOV, H., YANVAREVA, E., VORONOV, A., "A Memory of Leonid Leonidovich Vasiliev," *Herald of Leningrad University,* Biology Series, Part 2, No. 9, 1966.

42. GOLOVANOV, L., "The Rhythm of Life and Rhythm of the Cosmos," *Papers on Scientific Astrology.* Bratislava: Pressfoto, 1969. CZECHOSLOVAKIAN (Soviet author.)

43. GORANOVA, A., "Suggestopedia," *Zemedelsko Znami,* Sofia, Dec. 9, 1965. BULGARIAN

44. GULAS, Stefan, "Astrology and Economics," *Papers on Scientific Astrology.* Bratislava: Pressfoto, 1969. CZECHOSLOVAKIAN

*45. GULYAEV, P., "Psi Phenomenon, A Reality," *Soviet Review,* June, 1961. (Soviet author.)

*46. ——— "Cerebral Electromagnetic Fields," translation: *International Journal of Parapsychology,* Vol. 7, No. 4, 1965. (Soviet author.) (New York)

47. ——— "Frontier of Bionics," Leningrad University, April 1967, No. 24.

48. GURVICH, G., "Bioinformation in the Development & Forming of the Organism." Paper presented: Symposium on Parapsychology & Health, Section of Technical Parapsychology, affiliated All Union Engineering Institute, Moscow, April 24, 1967.

49. "Healing Session," *Večernji List,* (Zagreb) Sept. 18, 1965. YUGOSLAVIAN

50. HOLODOV, U. A., "Man in a Magnetic Web," *Znanie-Sila,* No. 7, 1965.

51. "Horizons of Science." Lecture on Parapsychology & on UFOs. (20 pp.) USSR: 1968.

52. "Horizons of the Future." Lectures on Parapsychology & Myths, Harmony of the Cosmos, Science, Religion & Morals—the Necessary New Religion. (45 pp.) USSR: 1968.

53. HRISTOV, E., "Parapsychology and Vanga," *Pogled Newspaper,* June 6, 1966. BULGARIAN

54. HROUSSANOV, G., "Science and Dreams," *Zemdelsko Znami,* Sofia, June 5, 1965. BULGARIAN

55. "Hypnosis without Hypnosis? Suggestopedia," *Znanie-Sila,* No. 3, 1968.

56. "In the Moscow Lecture Hall," (Ninel Kulagina), *Smena,* Jan. 16, 1964.

57. INYUSHIN, V. M., Three Papers on Basic Research in Biology, *Questions of Theoretical & Applied Biology.* Alma-Ata: Science Publishing, Kazak SSR, 1967.

58. ——— "Possibilities of Studying Tissues in High-Frequency Discharge," (Kirlian effect), *Biological Influence of Monochromatic Red Light.* Alma-Ata: Kirov University, 1967.

59. ——— "Biological Plasma of Human Organism with Animals," *Telepathy, Telegnosis, Dowsing, Psychokinesis.* Prague: Svoboda, 1970.

60. INYUSHIN, V. M., GRISHCHENKO, V. S., et al., *On the Biological Essence of the Kirlian Effect,* (*Concept of Biological Plasma*). Alma-Ata: Kazak State Kirov University, 1968.

61. "Is the Moon to Blame?" *Soviet Union,* No. 202, 1966.

62. JANOSOVOVA, Martina, "Nevertheless It Moves," (Medical astrology), Pravda (Czech) May 24, 1968. CZECHOSLOVAKIAN
63. JONAS, Eugen, "Fundamentals of Applied Astrology," *Papers on Scientific Astrology*. Bratislava: Pressfoto, 1969. CZECHOSLOVAKIAN
64. KADIKOV, Igor, "The Miraculous—Hearing & Voice," *Baikal,* No. 4, 1968, Buryat Autonomous Republic, USSR.
65. KAJINSKY, B. B., *Biological Radio-Communication.* Kiev: Ukrainian Academy of Science Press, 1962.
66. KAMENOV, N., "A Successful Telepathic Experiment in our Country," *Evening News,* Sofia, Dec. 12, 1964. BULGARIAN
67. KAMENSKY, Yu., "Let the Light Shine," *Science and Religion,* Sept., 1966.
68. ——— "Methods and Results of Telepathic Transmission of Images." Paper presented: Symposium on Parapsychology & Health, Section of Technical Parapsychology affiliated All Union Engineering Institute, Moscow, April 24, 1967.
69. KAPACHOWAS, V., "Application of Bio-Physical Method for Engineering Geology." Paper presented: Symposium on Dowsing headed by Dr. A. A. Ogilvy, Chairman of Geo-Physics Dept., Moscow University, June 20–21, 1968.
70. KITAIGORODSKY, A., "What Is Telepathy?" *Literary Gazette,* Nov. 26, 1964.
71. ——— "The World is Full of Strange Things," *Znanie-Sila,* No. 6, 1965.
72. ——— "It's Not Necessary to Fear Facts!" *Znanie-Sila,* No. 1, 1966.
*73. KOGAN, Ippolit, "Is Telepathy Possible?" *Radiotechnika,* No. 1, 1966. Translation: *Radio Engineering,* Vol. 21, pp. 75–81. New York.
*74. ——— "Bio-Information, Today and Tomorrow," *Komsomolskaya Pravda,* Oct. 9, 1966. Translation: *Journal of Paraphysics,* Vol. 2, No. 1. (Downton, Wilts., England.)
*75. ——— "Telepathy, Hypothesis & Observations," *Radiotechnika,* No. 1, 1967. Translation: *Radio Engineering,* Vol. 22, pp. 141–44. New York.
76. ——— "Information Analysis of Telepathic Experiments," *Radiotechnika,* No. 3, 1968.
77. ——— "Research on Telepathy as a Channel Transmitting Information," *Annotated Reports,* 24th All Union

Scientific Session, published by A. S. Popov Scientific Radio-Technology Institute, Moscow, 1968.

78. ——— "Informational Aspects of Telepathy," Manuscript. (pp. 28) 1969.

79. ——— "Informational Aspects of Telepathy," *Telepathy, Telegnosis, Dowsing, Psychokinesis.* Prague: Svoboda, 1970.

*80. KOLODNY, Lev, "When Apples Fall," *Moscow Pravda,* March 17, 1968. Partial translation *Journal of Paraphysics,* Vol. 2, No. 4. (Downton, Wilts., England.)

81. ——— "The Compass of Karl Nikolaiev," *Moscow Pravda,* July 17, 1966.

82. ——— "Wireless Telegraph, Number Two," *Moscow Pravda,* April 9, 1967.

83. KONSTANTINOV, B., "Sixth Sense," *Izvestia,* No. 28, 1964.

84. KOSITSKY, G., "Is it Possible to Transmit Thought?" *Health,* Journal of Ministry of Public Health, Nov., 1961, No. 11.

85. KOTIK, I. G., *Direct Transmisison of Thought.* Moscow: 1912.

*86. KOZYREV, Nikolai, "An Unexplored World," *Soviet Life,* November, 1965.

*87. ——— "Physical Peculiarities of the Components of Double Stars," *Royal Belgium Observatory Communications,* Series No. 17, 1967.

*88. ——— "Possibility of Experimental Study of the Properties of Time," *Joint Publications Research Service,* Department of Commerce, U.S.A., JPRS No. 45238, May 2, 1968.

89. KRIVOROTOV, V., "Bio-energetical Influence on the Organism of Man in Healing." Paper presented: Conference of Technical Parapsychology Section affiliated All Union Engineering Institute Moscow, June 20–1, 1968.

*90. KRMESSKY, J., " 'Radiation' from Organisms," *Journal of Paraphysics,* Vol. 3, No. 4. (Downton, Wilts., England.) (Czech author.)

91. KRUPNOV, A. "Individual Peculiarities of Heights of Color Barriers," *Questions of Complex Research on Dermo-Optics.* Sverdlovsk: Pedagogical Institute, 1968.

92. KUCHYNKA, Karel, "L'aperçu de l'activité dans le domaine de la parapsychologie en Tchécoslovaquie depuis la première guerre mondiale," extract: *Giornale Italiano Por La Ricerca Psichica,* Rome, 1964. (Czech author.)

93. KUNI, Mikhail, "Potentials of Human Memory," *Technology for Youth* No. 1, 1964.

*94. KURZ, O., "The Hranice Case," *Journal of Paraphysics,* Vol. 2, No. 5. (Downton, Wilts., England.) (Czech author.)

95. KURZ, O., and Rejdak, Z., "About Telekinesis," *Pravda* (Czech), June 14 and 21, 1968. CZECHOSLOVAKIAN

96. LAVROV, A., "The Unexplained—For the Time Being, Yes," *Smena,* No. 2, 1967.

97. LEMHENYI, Zoltan, "Connections between Astrology and Hatha Yoga," *Papers on Scientific Astrology.* Bratislava: Pressfoto, 1969.

*98. LEONIDOV, I., "Signals—Of What?" *Soviet Union,* No. 145, 1962. Reprinted as "Russians Photograph Life and Death," *Fate,* Sept., 1962.

99. LEONIDOV, L., "Reserves of Homo Sapiens," *Smena,* Oct. 20, 1965.

100. Letters to the authors.

101. LEVY, V., "In the Studio of the Hypnologist," *Znanie-Sila,* No. 5, 1964.

102. "Lozanov, G." articles on: *Zdraven Front,* May 1, 1965. BULGARIAN

103. ——— *Komsomolskaya Pravda,* July 13, 1966.

104. ——— *Moskovskaya Pravda,* July 14, 1966.

105. ——— *Otechestven Front,* Sofia, July 24, 1966. BULGARIAN

106. ——— *Mlada Fronta* Rijna 15, 1966. BULGARIAN

107. ——— *Technicheski Avangard,* Sofia, Oct. 14, 1966. BULGARIAN

108. LOZANOV, Georgi, "Telepathy," reprint of talk on *Radio Sofia,* Oct. 15, 1963.

109. ——— "Suggestion and Parapsychology." Paper presented Seminar of A. S. Popov Radio-Technology Institute, Moscow, Aug. 13, 1966.

110. ——— "Hidden Channels of the Mind," *Komsomolskaya Pravda,* Oct. 9, 1966.

111. ——— "Parapsychology in India." Paper presented: Seminar of Technical Parapsychology Section affiliated All Union Engineering Institute, Moscow, May 26–9, 1967.

112. ——— *Suggestology and Suggestopedia.* Sofia: Institute of Suggestology, 1969. BULGARIAN

113. LVOV, V., *Evening Leningrad,* April 17, 1968.

114. MARIN, Vadim, "Phenomenon of Psi," *Moscow Komsomolets,* April 7, 1968.

115. ——— "Clearly I See The Future." Moscow, 1968.

*116. MASHKOVA, V., "Sharpsighted Fingers," translation: *International Journal of Parapsychology,* (New York), Vol. 7, No. 4, 1965. (Soviet author.)

117. MELNIKOV, E. K., "Results of Bio-Physical Method in the Yakut Republic." Paper presented: Symposium on Dowsing headed by Dr. A. A. Ogilvy, Chairman of Geo-Physics Department, Moscow University. April 11–2, 1968.
118. MESSING, Wolf, "I Am a Telepathist," *Smena,* No. 14, July, 1965.
119. ——— "About Myself," *Science and Religion,* Nos. 7 & 8, 1965.
*120. ——— "The Mind Readers," *Sputnik,* No. 1, 1966.
121. MEZENTSEV, V., "No, It is Not Mysticism," *Science and Religion,* No. 7, 1965.
122. MIAVEC, Martin, "Influence of Female Genitals on the Development of Sexes," *Papers on Scientific Astrology.* Bratislava: Pressfoto, 1969. CZECHOSLOVAKIAN
123. MIKOV, E., "Psychophysical Preconditions of Telepathic Abilities." Paper presented: Conference of All Union Astro-Geodesic Society of Moscow, Oct. 31, 1966.
124. MILASHEVICH, V., "Clairvoyance and Hypnosis," *Science and Religion,* No. 7, 1965.
125. MINARIK, Stefan, "Development Perspectives of Astra Research Center," *Papers on Scientific Astrology.* Bratislava: Pressfoto, 1969. CZECHOSLOVAKIAN
126. MITOSENKA, Jozif, "Humanae Vitae Encyclical and Dr. Jonas' Revelations," *Papers on Scientific Astrology.* Bratislava: Pressfoto, 1969. CZECHOSLOVAKIAN
127. MITSKEVICH, A., "Thermodynamics—Information and Thought," *Technology for Youth,* No. 9, 1966.
128. MOMCHEV, "Skin Sight in Bulgaria Too—A Visit to the Experimental Parapsychologists," *Narodna Mladej,* Science section, April 26, 1965. BULGARIAN
*129. MORALEVICH, Y., "Biowave Communication," *Sputnik,* No. 2, 1968.
130. NAUMOV, Edward, "Brain Reserves," *Science and Religion,* No. 3, 1966.
131. ——— "What Is Parapsychology?" *Moscow Pravda,* Aug. 14, 1966.
132. ——— "Extra-Terrestrial Civilizations and Parapsychology," *Moscow Pravda,* March 14, 1967.
*133. ——— "From Telepathy to Telekinesis," *Journal of Paraphysics,* Vol. 2, No. 2. (Downton, Wilts., England.) (Soviet author.)
134. NAUMOV, E., and FESENKO, R., "What We're Working On Now," *Science and Religion,* Sept., 1966.
135. ——— "Ahead the Unknown," *Komsomolskaya Pravda,* Oct. 9, 1966.

136. NAUMOV, Pavel, "Methods of Training Telepathic Abilities." Paper presented: Congress on Scientific Problems of Telepathy, A. S. Popov Radio-Technology Institute, Moscow, Feb. 22, 1968.
137. ——— "On the Question of Wordless Transmission of Information," *Annotated Reports,* 24th All Union Scientific Session, published, A. S. Popov Scientific Technical Society, Moscow, 1968.
138. "Nelya Mikhailova," articles on: *Leningrad Pravda,* Jan. 21, Feb. 23, Mar. 15, 1964.
139. ——— *Smena,* Jan. 24, 1964.
140. ——— *Evening Leningrad,* April 17, 1968.
141. NOVOMEISKY, A., "Again about the Nizhni-Tagil Riddle," *Science and Life,* Feb., 1963.
142. ——— "The Role of the Dermo-Optic Sense in Cognition," *Questions of Philosophy,* July, 1963.
*143. ——— "The Nature of the Dermo-Optic Sense," translation: *International Journal of Parapsychology,* (New York), Vol. 7, No. 4, 1965.
144. ——— "Changes in Dermo-Optics Sensitivity in Various Conditions of Illumination," *Questions of Complex Research on Dermo-Optics.* Sverdlovsk: Pedagogical Institute, 1968.
145. NOVOMEISKY, A., BICARD, V., KRUPNOV, A., "The Location of the Color Barrier on the Basis of Residual Radiation." Ibid.
146. NOVOMEISKY, A., and YAKLOV, B., "On the Possible Sensibilities of Dermo-Optic Sense in Man." Ibid.
147. "Operating Through Suggestion in Awakened State," *Rabotnichesko Delo,* Sofia, Aug. 25, 1965. BULGARIAN
148. OSTROVSKY, B., "Why Do the Cells Shine?" *Znanie-Sila,* No. 9, 1967.
149. *Papers On Scientific Astrology.* Bratislava: Pressfoto, 1969. CZECHOSLOVAKIAN
150. PARNOV, Ye., "The Neutrino—Why Not?" *Science and Religion,* No. 3, 1966.
151. PAVLOVA, L. P., "Results and Discussion of Experiments with the Nedra-20." Paper presented: Seminar of Technical Parapsychology Section affiliated All Union Engineering Institute, Moscow, August 4, 1967.
152. ——— "Some Electroencephalographic Indices in Experimental Research in Bio-telecommunication." Moscow: 1967.
153. PEKAREVA, D., "In the Dispute with Mysticism," *Rabotnichesko Delo,* Sofia, Feb. 23, 1967. BULGARIAN

*154. PLATONOV, K. K., *Psychology As You May Like It.* Moscow: Progress Publishers, 1965.
155. POPOVKIN, Victor, "Thought Transmission Moscow-Novosibirsk," *Komsomolskaya Pravda,* July 7, 1966.
156. ——— "Isotopes at the Service of Parapsychology," *Znanie-Sila,* No. 9, 1967.
157. ——— "Wizard Rod, Myth or Problem?" *Znanie-Sila,* No. 12, 1967.
158. ——— "Le Congrès de Moscou sur la Télépathie," *Planète,* Paris, July-Aug. 1968. (Soviet author.)
*159. POZNER, V., FILINOVICH, Y., SHARAPOV, Y., "Soviet Youth Answers Gallup Poll Questions," *Soviet Life,* Nov. 1965.
160. PRESSMAN, A. S., "Of Course Telepathic Phenomena Exist," *Nedelya, Izvestia,* 196?
161. ——— *Electromagnetic Fields and Living Nature.* Moscow: Academy of Sciences USSR, Science Publishing, 1968.
162. Private communication to the authors.
163. *Questions of Theoretical and Applied Biology.* Alma-Ata: Science Publishing, Kazak SSR, 1967.
164. RADEVA, Marie, "The Possibilities Offered by Hypnopedia," *Evening News,* Sofia, May 8, 1965. BULGARIAN
165. ——— "Psychotherapy Heals and Fortifies," *Evening News,* Sofia, Aug. 14, 1965. BULGARIAN
166. ——— "What is Parapsychology? Telepathy—Science and Communication," *Otechestven Front,* Aug. 22, 1965. BULGARIAN
167. ——— "Preparation of Moscow-Sofia Telepathy Experiment," *Otechestven Front,* Aug. 24, 1966. BULGARIAN
168. "Raikov," articles on: *Technology for Youth,* No. 5, 1966, and *Soviet Union,* 1968.
169. RAIKOV, V., "Medical Aspects of Experimental Research on Telepathy in Hypnosis." Paper presented: Seminar of Bio-Information Section, A. S. Popov Radio-Technology Institute, Moscow, Feb. 25, 1966.
170. ——— "Development of Psychic Phenomena With Hypnosis." Paper presented: Seminar of A. S. Popov Radio-Technology Institute, Aug. 13, 1966.
171. ——— "Reincarnation by Hypnosis," *Science and Religion,* No. 9, 1966.
172. ——— *Znanie-Sila,* No. 11, 1966.
173. RAIKOV, V., and ADAMENKO, Victor, "Questions of Objective Research of Deep Hypnotic States," *Therapy*

of Mental Disease. Moscow: Society of Neuropsychiatrists, Sechenov Medical Institute, 1968.

174. RAISZ, Sandor, "Human Relations in the Light of Astrology," *Papers on Scientific Astrology*. Bratislava: Pressfoto, 1969. CZECHOSLOVAKIAN (Hungarian author.)

175. REBINDER, P. A., "To Advance Means to Search," *Science and Religion*, No. 3, 1966.

176. RECHNITZ, Kurt, "The Significance of Lunar Phases Theory for Regulation of Conception," *Papers on Scientific Astrology*. Bratislava: Pressfoto, 1969. CZECHOSLOVAKIAN (Hungarian author.)

*177. REIN, Y., "Kozyrev," *Soviet Life*, November, 1965.

178. REJDAK, Zdenek, "Parapsychology, War Menace or Total Peace Weapon?" *Periskop*, Prague, 1966. CZECHOSLOVAKIAN

179. ——— "Psychotronics and Parapsychology." Paper presented: Seminar of Technical Parapsychology Section affiliated All Union Engineering Institute, Moscow, May 1–4, 1967. (Czech author.)

*180. ——— "Telekinesis or Fraud?" *Pravda* (Czech) June 21, 1968. Partial translation: *Journal of Paraphysics*, Vol. 2, No. 3. (Downton, Wilts, England.)

181. ——— "From Cheops Pyramid to Razor Blades," *Signal*, (Prague) No. 34, 1968. CZECHOSLOVAKIAN

182. ——— "Astrological Birth Control," *Signal*, (Prague) No. 35, 1968. CZECHOSLOVAKIAN

183. ——— "Scientific Astrology and Psychotronics," *Papers on Scientific Astrology*. Bratislava: Pressfoto, 1969. CZECHOSLOVAKIAN

*184. ——— "The Kulagina Cine Film," *Journal of Paraphysics*, Vol. 3, No. 3. (CZECH author.)

185. ——— Editor: *Telepathy, Telegnosis, Dowsing, Psychokinesis, Papers of Czech and Foreign Authors*. Prague: Svoboda, 1970.

186. REJDAK, Z., and DRBAL, Karel, "On the Third Form of Energy," *Periskop*, (Prague) 1967. CZECHOSLOVAKIAN

*187. ——— "Telegnosis and Psychokinesis," *Journal of Paraphysics*, Vol. 2, No. 2. (Czech authors.)

188. ——— *Psychotronics*. Prague: 1970. CZECHOSLOVAKIAN

189. REPETSKY, L., "Biotelegraph," *Leningrad Banner*, April 2, 1967.

*190. REPIN, L., "The Living Organism and the Magnetic Field," *Sputnik*, No. 4, 1967.

191. ROMANENKO, A., and SERGEYEV, G., *Questions of the Applied Analysis of Chance Processes.* Moscow: Soviet Radio Publishing, 1968.
192. SAFONOV, V., "Razor Blades and the Cheops Pyramid," *Moscow Komsomolets,* May 26, 1968.
193. "Scientists Speak Out," *Moscow Pravda,* March 17, 1968.
194. SERGEYEV, Genady, "Perspectives for Using Automatic Processes for Controlling the Brain during Telepathy." Paper presented: Seminar of Technical Parapsychology Section affiliated All Union Engineering Institute, Moscow, Feb. 11, 1967.
195. ——— "Use of Principles of Bio-Information in Diagnosis." Paper presented: Symposium on Parapsychology and Health, Technical Parapsychology Section affiliated All Union Engineering Institute, April 24, 1967.
196. ——— "Experimental Research on Telepathy." Paper presented: Seminar held by Prof. Ya. Terletsky, Chair of Theoretical Physics, Moscow University, June 6, 1967.
197. ——— "On the Nature of the Experimental Research of Dr. Zdenek Rejdak." Paper presented: Seminar of Technical Parapsychology Section affiliated All Union Engineering Institute, Moscow, Dec. 3, 1967.
198. ——— "Invisible Fire," *Telepathy, Telegnosis, Dowsing, Psychokinesis,* Prague: Svoboda, 1970. CZECHOSLOVAKIAN (Soviet author.)
199. ——— "Some Methodological Parapsychological Problems," Ibid.
200. ——— "The Voice of the Brain," Ibid.
201. SERGEYEV, G., PAVLOVA, L., ROMANENKO, A., *Statistical Method of Research of the Human EEG.* Leningrad: Academy of Science USSR, Science Publishing, 1968.
*202. SHEVALEV, A., "From Sensational Uproar to Serious Research," translation: *Journal of Parapsychology,* Vol. 7, No. 4, 1965.
*203. SHISHKIN, Igor, "The Nature of Telepathic Transmission," *Journal of Paraphysics,* Vol. 3, No. 1. (Downton, Wilts., England.) (Soviet author.)
204. ——— "Telepathy's Physical Essence," *Telepathy, Telegnosis, Dowsing, Psychokinesis.* Prague: Svoboda, 1970.
205. SIMOVET, Dragomir, "Series on Bulgarian Parapsychology," *Svet,* (Belgrade) Nos. 533–537, Jan.-Feb. 1967. YUGOSLAVIAN
206. SIMAKOV, Y., "Mother and Child: Mysterious, Imperious Communications," *Znanie-Sila,* No. 6, 1969.

207. SIMUROV, A., "Is It Possible To Learn a Language in a Month?" *Pravda*, July 27, 1969.

208. SKURLATOV, V., "Can You Do Anything?—Preview of the Film 'Seven Steps Beyond the Horizon,'" *Technology for Youth*, No. 5, 1969.

209. SLOBODNIAK, A. P., *Psychotherapy, Suggestion and Hypnosis*. Kiev, Gosmedizdat, 1963.

210. SOCHEVANOV, N. N., "Research of Elector-Physiological Effects of Dowsing Rod." Paper presented: Seminar of Bio-Information Section of A. S. Popov Radio-Technology Institute, Moscow, April 8, 1966.

211. ——— "Physical Interpretation of Czech Psychotronic Phenomena." Paper presented: Seminar of Technical Parapsychology Section affiliated All Union Engineering Institute, Moscow, Dec. 3, 1967.

212. ——— "Data on Bio-Physical Effect in Field and Lab." Paper presented: Symposium on Dowsing headed by Dr. A. A. Ogilvy, Chairman of Geo-Physics Dept., Moscow University, April 11–2, 1968.

213. ——— "Perspectives for Study of Bio-Physical Method." Ibid.

214. ——— "Bio-Physical Phenomenon, Natural Evidence, Hitherto Unknown," *Telepathy, Telegnosis, Dowsing, Psychokinesis*. Prague: Svoboda, 1970. CZECHOSLOVAKIAN (Soviet author.)

215. SOCHEVANOV, N., MATVEEV, V., MELNIKOV, E., "Physiological Reaction of Man to Water and Minerals in the Earth—The Problem of the Dowsing Rod." Paper presented: Seminar of the All Union Astro-Geodesic Society of Moscow, Oct. 31, 1966.

216. SOUKAREBSKY, Lazar, "Biological Information Rather than Parapsychology," *Science and Religion*, No. 3, 1966.

217. ——— "Afterword," *Moscow Pravda*, July 17, 1966.

218. ——— "Spontaneous Telepathy and Its Biological Significance." Paper presented: Congress on the Scientific Problems of Telepathy, A. S. Popov Radio-Technology Institute, Moscow, Feb. 22, 1968.

219. ——— "Telepathic Information as a Biological Problem," *Annotated Reports*, 24th All Union Session, published A. S. Popov Radio-Technology Institute, Moscow, 1968.

220. STOYCHEV, I., "Baffling Possibilities," *Zhenata Dnes*, Sofia, No. 1, 1967. BULGARIAN

220A. SZABO, Ivan, "Astrology in Slovakia and Astra," *Papers in Scientific Astrology*. Bratislava: Pressfoto, 1969. CZECHOSLOVAKIAN (Hungarian author.)

221. TASHEV, T., "Studying Foreign Languages Through Suggestion," *Troud,* Sofia, Dec. 9, 1965. BULGARIAN
222. TASHEV, T., NATAN, T., "Suggestology," *Bulgaria Today,* No. 9, 1966.
223. TECHEVA, E., "A Method Which Can Transform Education," *Nasha Rodina,* No. 4, 1966. BULGARIAN
224. "Telepathy and Electronic Machines," *Moscow Pravda,* March 22, 1967, *Evening Moscow,* Feb. 14, 1967.
225. TERLETSKY, Y. A., "About the Possibility of the Existence and Properties of Emanations Accompanied by Negative Energy." Paper presented: Seminar held by by Prof. Terletsky, Chair. of Theoretical Physics, Moscow University, June 6, 1967.
226. "Topics of Moscow Parapsychology Seminars, Conferences, Symposiums—1965–68." Moscow: 1968. (9 pp.)
227. TOPORKOV, V., SIMONOV, P., ERSHOV, P., "Open Letter to Dr. Vasiliev," *Soviet Culture,* Dec. 16, 1965.
228. TSIPKO, A., "Let's Awaken Talent," *Komsomolskaya Pravda,* Nov. 12, 1966.
*229. ——— "Art Instruction Under Hypnosis," *Sputnik,* May, 1967.
230. TUGARINOV, V. P., "Concerning Some New Problems of Consciousness," *Herald of Leningrad University,* Series Economics, Philosophy, Law, No. 11, 1964.
231. ——— "Thinking Cybernetic Devices," *Herald of Leningrad University,* Series, Economics, Philosophy, Law, No. 17, 1966.
*232. "Twentieth-Century Mystery," *Sputnik,* Dec. 1967.
233. "Unusual Case in Medical Practice," *Sofia Pravda,* Aug. 27, 1965. BULGARIAN
234. USHKOV, D., "The Reading of Thought and Telepathy," *Science and Religion,* No. 7, 1965.
235. *USSR Academy of Sciences Reports,* Vol. 172, Nos. 4–5, 1967. (Tunguska meteorite.)
236. VASILIEV, Leonid, L., *Suggestion at a Distance—Notes of a Physiologist.* Moscow: Gospolitizdat, 1962.
*237. ——— *Experimental Research of Mental Suggestion.* Leningrad: University Press, 1962. Translation as: *Experiments in Mental Suggestion.* Hampshire, England: Gally Hill Press, 1963. (Institute for Study of Mental Images, Church Crookham.)
*238. ——— *Mysterious Phenomena of the Human Psyche.* Moscow: Political Literature Publishing House, 1964, 3rd edition. In translation: New Hyde Park, New York: University Books, 1965.
*239. ——— "Vasiliev Recalls Ossowiecki," International Journal of Parapsychology, Summer, 1965. (Soviet author.)

240. ——— "Unusual coincidences," *Science and Religion,* No. 7, 1965.
*241. ——— "Can We Control Inspiration?" *Soviet Life,* March 1966.
242. ——— "Telesuggestion," *Telepathy, Telegnosis, Dowsing, Psychokinesis.* Prague: Svoboda, 1970.
243. VARSEMOVA, D., "New Arm of Ancient Science," (Acupuncture) *Literary Gazette,* No. 16, May, 1963.
244. VILKOMIR, I., "On the Parapsychological Phenomena of Edgar Cayce." Paper presented: Seminar of Technical Parapsychology Section affiliated All Union Engineering Institute, Moscow, Feb. 4, 1967.
245. VOCASEK, Z., "Possibilities of Utilization of Dr. Jonas' Revelations about the Moment of Conception and Determination of Sex in Investigation of Causes of Down's Syndrome Appearance," *Papers on Scientific Astrology.* Bratislava: Pressfoto, 1969. CZECHOSLOVAKIAN
246. VOGRALIK, V. G., *Principles of the Chinese Medical Method, Acupuncture.* Gorky: Gorky Publishing, 1961.
*247. ——— "Pinpricks for Health?" *Sputnik,* July 1969.
*248. "Voice of the Brain," *Sputnik,* Feb. 1968.
249. *Voice of Universal Love,* Moscow, No. 40, 1908.
250. VOLODIN, E., "Survey of Work on Telekinesis." Paper presented: Seminar of Technical Parapsychology Section affiliated All Union Engineering Institute, Nov. 15, 1966.
251. VOLPERT, I., *Dreams in Sleep and Hypnosis.* Leningrad: Medicine Publishing, 1966.
*252. VOSKRESENSKAYA, N., "Kuni: The Human Computor," *Sputnik,* March 1968
253. "Wolf Messing," *Zapopyarnaya Pravda,* Norilsk, Siberia, June 18, 1965, *Nauka i Zhizhn* No. 4, 1964.
254. YAKOLEV, B., "Parapsychology," *Evening Moscow,* Jan. 12, 1967.
*255. ——— "Telepathy Session, Moscow-Novosibirsk," *Sputnik,* Feb. 1968.
*256. ZAITSEV, V., "Visitors From Outer Space," *Sputnik,* Jan. 1967.
*257. ——— "Temples and Spaceships," *Sputnik,* Jan. 1968.
258. ——— "Cosmological Aspects of Parapsychology." Paper presented: Seminar of Technical Parapsychology Section affiliated All Union Engineering Institute, Moscow, on Parapsychology and Higher Civilizations, March 13, 1967.
259. ZIEGEL, Felix, "Telepathy a Science of the Future," *Science and Religion,* No. 3, 1966.

260. ——— "Under the Flag of the Struggle with Mysticism," *Science and Religion,* No. 11, 1966.

261. ——— "On Possible Exchange of Information with Extra-Terrestrial Civilizations." Paper presented: Seminar on Parapsychology and Higher Civilization, held by Technical Parapsychology Section affiliated All Union Engineering Institute, Moscow, March 13, 1967.

262. ——— "UFOs, What Are They?" *Smena,* April 7, 1967.

*263. ——— "Unidentified Flying Objects," *Soviet Life,* Feb. 1968.

Partial Western Bibliography and References

264. AKSAKOV, A., *Case of the Partial Dematerialization of a Medium.* Boston: 189?

265. ALLILUYEVA, Svetlana, *Twenty Letters to a Friend.* New York: Harper & Row, 1967.

266. ——— *Only One Year.* New York: Harper & Row, 1969.

267. "An 'Attractive' Woman has Reds Puzzled," AP release, Moscow, March 17, 1968.

268. BACH, Marcus, "Acupuncture . . . An Ancient Method of Healing," *Fate,* Dec. 1968.

269. BACKSTER, Cleve, "Evidence of a Primary Perception in Plant Life," *International Journal of Parapsychology,* Vol. 10, No. 4, 1968.

270. BACON, Thorn, "The Man Who Reads Nature's Secret Signals," *National Wildlife,* Feb.-March, 1969.

271. BANNERJEE, H. N., "Parapsychology in Russia," *Indian Journal of Parapsychology,* 1961–62.

272. BECKER, Raymond de, "Les grandes médecines anciennes ne sont pas méprisables," Planète, March, 1969.

273. BECKER, Robert, "Relationship of a Geo-Magnetic Environment to Human Biology," *New York State Journal of Medicine,* Vol. 63, No. 15, 1963.

274. BELOFF, John, "ESP Proof from Prague?" *New Scientist,* Oct. 10, 1968.

275. BENTLEY, W. P., "An Approach to a Theory of Survival of Personality," *Journal of the American Society for Psychical Research,* Vol. 59, Jan. 1965.

276. BERGIER, Jacques, Article on Soviet Parapsychology, Planète, No. 8, Jan.-Feb. 1963.

277. BLOM, J. G., and Pratt, J. G., "A Second Confirmatory ESP Experiment with Pavel Stepanek as a 'Borrowed' Subject," *Journal of A.S.P.R.,* Vol. 62, Jan. 1968.

278. BORZYMOWSKI, Andrzej, "Parapsychology in Poland," *International Journal of Parapsychology,* Vol. 4, No. 4, 1962.
279. ——— "Experiments with Ossowiecki," *International Journal of Parapsychology,* Vol. 7, No. 3, 1965.
280. BURR, H. S., and Northrop, F., "The Electro-Dynamic Theory of Life," Main Currents in Modern Thought, Vol. 19, October, November, 1962.
281. CAMPBELL, J., "Sense of Security," *Analog,* Nov. 1966.
282. CARLISLE, Olga, *Voices In The Snow.* New York: Random House, 1962.
283. Confidential Report, American source.
284. CUMMINS, Geraldine, *Beyond Human Personality.* London: Ivor Nicholson & Watson, Ltd., 1935.
285. CUTTEN, J. H., and MEDHURST, R. G., "Moscow Conference on Technical Parapsychology, June 1968." Private report.
286. DEAN, E. Douglas, "The Plethysmograph as an Indicator of ESP," *Journal of Society for Psychical Research,* Vol. 41, Sept., 1962.
287. ——— "Plethysmograph Recordings as ESP Responses," *International Journal of Neuro-Psychiatry,* Vol. 2, Oct., 1966.
288. DEAN, E. Douglas, and NASH, C. B., "Plethysmograph Results Under Strict Conditions," *Journal of Parapsychology,* Vol. 27, Dec., 1963.
289. de la WARR, George, "Using Sound Waves to Probe Matter," *Mind and Matter Journal,* Sept., 1965. (Raleigh Park Road, Oxford, England.)
290. ——— "Historic New York-Oxford Experiment," *Mind and Matter Journal,* March, 1966.
291. ——— "Analysis of a Thought" [Micro-Sound Frequencies of Thought], *Mind & Matter Journal,* June, 1966.
292. ——— *Biomagnetics.* Oxford: Delawarr Laboratories Ltd., 1969.
293. de la WARR, G., Baker, Douglas, *Biomagnetism.* Oxford: Delawarr Laboratories Ltd., 1967.
294. "Do Plants Feel Emotion?" *Electro-Technology,* April, 1969.
295. "Dr. Ryzl Comes to America," *Bulletin Foundation for Research on the Nature of Man,* No. 7, Autumn, 1967.
295a. EBON, M., "Russia Explores Inner Space," *Tomorrow,* Winter, 1962.
296. EISENBUD, Jules, *The World of Ted Serios.* New York: William Morrow & Co., Inc., 1967.
297. "ESP: More Science, Less Mysticism," *Medical World News,* March 21, 1969.

298. "The Eyes Have It," *Newark Star Ledger*, March 18, 1968.
299. FULLER, Curtis, "Wind Machine," *Fate*, Dec., 1966.
300. ——— "A Mind With Muscles," *Fate*, Feb., 1968.
301. ——— "I See by the Papers," *Fate*, April, 1968.
302. GARRETT, Eileen, *Adventures in the Supernormal*. New York: Garrett Pub., 1959.
303. ——— *Awareness*. New York: Berkley Publishing Corp., 1968.
304. GAUQUELIN, Michel, *The Cosmic Clocks*. New York: Avon Books, 1969.
305. GRAD, Bernard, "Some Biological Effects of the 'Laying on of Hands.' A Review of Experiments with Animals and Plants," *Journal ASPR*, April, 1965.
——— "The 'Laying on of Hands': Implications for Psychotherapy, Gentling, and the Placebo Effect," *Journal ASPR*, Oct. 1967.
306. GREY, George, "Radiation and Life—Russian Plant Research," Harpers, July, 1934.
307. *Histoire de la France Secrète*. Paris: Encyclopédie Planète, 1968.
308. HIXSON, J., "Twins Prove 'Electronic' ESP," *New York Herald Tribune*, Oct. 25, 1965, *Science*, Oct. 15, 1965.
309. HYNEK, Allen, "The UFO Gap," *Playboy*, Dec., 1967.
310. INGLIS, Brian, *Fringe Medicine*. London: Faber, 1964.
311. "Interview: James A. Pike," *Psychic*, Vol. 1, No. 2, 1969.
312. IVANOV, A., "Soviet Experiments: 1921–27, 1932–38," *International Journal of Parapsychology*, Vol. 5, No. 2, 1963.
313. ——— "Soviet Experiments in Eyeless Vision," *International Journal of Parapsychology*, Vol. 6, Winter, 1964.
314. "Jesus a Cosmonaut, says Russian," *Toronto Star*, June 21, 1969.
315. "The Joint's Really Jumping When She Looks Around," Reuters, Moscow, April 7, 1968.
316. KAMM, Henry, "A Soviet Astronomer Suggests World Study of Flying Saucers," *The New York Times*, Dec. 10, 1967.
317. KAMIYA, J., "Conscious Control of Brain Waves," *Psychology Today*, April, 1968.
318. KARAGULLA, Shafica, *Breakthrough to Creativity*. Los Angeles: De Vorss & Co., 1967.
319. KEIL, Jurgen, "Russian Parapsychologists Hold Meeting," *Newsletter of the Parapsychology Foundation*, Sept.-Oct., 1968.
320. KHOKHLOV, Nikolai, "The Relationship of Parapsychology to Communism," *Parapsychology Today*. J. B. Rhine ed. New York: Citadel Press, 1968.

321. KILNER, Walter, *The Human Aura.* New York: University Books, 1965.
322. KIRKBRIDE, Katherine, "ESP Communication for the Space Age," *Science and Mechanics,* Aug., 1969.
323. KRIPPNER, S., "Review of *Mysterious Phenomena of the Human Psyche,*" *Journal of the American Society for Psychical Research,* Vol. 60, No. 3, July, 1966.
324. KUNZ, F. L., "Feeling in Plants," *Main Currents,* May-June, 1969.
325. LAWSON-WOOD, D., and J., *Five Elements of Acupuncture and Chinese Massage.* Rustington, England: Health Science Press.
326. LEVINE, Irving, *Mainstreet USSR.* New York: Doubleday & Co., 1959.
327. McCULLOUGH, C., "The Army Makes Them Hear," *Toronto Globe and Mail,* June 7, 1969.
328. McGRAW, Walter, "Are Parapsychologists Working Themselves Out of a Job?" *Fate,* October, 1967.
329. ——— *World of the Paranormal.* New York: Pyramid Books, 1969.
330. "Measurement of Aura by Russians," *Newsletter of the Parapsychology Foundation,* Jan.-Feb. & May-June, 1969.
331. MEDHURST, R. G., "The Moscow Conference: June 1968," *Journal of Paraphysics,* Vol. 2, No. 3. (Downton, Wilts., England.)
332. MESSADIÉ, G., "Du Nautilus," *Science et Vie,* No. 509, Feb., 1960.
333. MIRABINI, Jean, *URSS.* Paris: Editions du Seuil, 1960.
334. MOSS, Louis, *Acupuncture and You.* New York: Citadel, 1966.
335. MULDOON, S., and CARRINGTON, H., *The Projection of the Astral Body.* London, Psychic Book Club, 1929.
336. MUTSCHALL, Vladimir, "The Present Status of Research in Telepathy in the Soviet Union," *Foreign Science Bulletin,* Vol. 4, No. 8, 1968. Aerospace Technology Div., Library of Congress.
337. NICHOLS, B., *Powers That Be.* New York: Popular Library, 1966.
338. "On a Tiré à Moscou," *L'Express,* 27 Jan.-2 Feb., 1969.
339. OSTRANDER, S., and SCHROEDER, L., "The Soviets Are Speaking Out," *Panorama,* Oct. 15, 1966.
340. OTANI, Soji, "A Possible Relationship Between Skin Resistance and ESP Response Patterns," *Parapsychology Today,* J. B. Rhine, ed. New York: Citadel, 1968.

341. "Parapsychology in the Soviet Union," Special Issue, Alexander Ivanov, trans., *International Journal of Parapsychology*. Vol. 7, No. 4, 1965.

342. PAUWELS, L. Re: "Le Congrès de Moscou sur la Télépathie," Planète, July-Aug. 1968.

343. PAUWELS, Louis, and BERGIER, Jacques, *The Morning of the Magicians*. New York: Stein & Day, 1964.

344. PENKOVSKY, Oleg, *The Penkovsky Papers*. New York: Doubleday & Co., 1965.

345. POLLACK, J. H., *Croiset, the Clairvoyant*. New York: Doubleday & Co., 1961.

346. PRATT, J. G., "Parapsychology in Russia and Czechoslovakia," *Journal of the Society for Psychical Research*, Vol. 42, 1963.

347. ——— *Parapsychology Today: An Insider's View*. New York: Doubleday Co., 1964.

348. ——— "Preliminary Experiments with a 'Borrowed' Outstanding ESP Subject," *Journal S.P.R.*, Vol. 42, Sept. 1964.

349. ——— "Further Significant ESP Results from Pavel Stepanek," *Journal American Society for Psychical Research*, Vol. 61, April, 1967.

350. ——— "Seeking the Trail of the Focusing Effect," Part I and II, *Journal A.S.P.R.*, Vol. 62, April, 1968.

351. "Report on the Moscow Parapsychology Conference—June, 1968." Private report.

352. PRATT, J. G., and BLOM, Jan G., "A Confirmatory Experiment with a 'Borrowed' Outstanding ESP Subject," *Journal S.P.R.*, Vol. 42, 1964.

353. PRATT, J. G., and JACOBSON, N., "Prediction of ESP Performance on Selected Focusing Effect Targets," *Journal A.S.P.R.*, Vol. 63, Jan., 1969.

354. PRATT, J. G., JACOBSON, N., BLOM, J. G., and MEINSMA, G. L., "A Transitional Period of Research on the Focusing Effect: From Confirmation toward Explanation," *Journal A.S.P.R.*, Vol. 63, Jan., 1969.

355. PRATT, J. G., and ROLL, W. G., "Confirmation of the Focusing Effect in Further Research with Pavel Stepanek in Charlottesville," *Journal A.S.P.R.*, Vol. 62, July, 1968. (For others, see Journal A.S.P.R.)

356. "Psi Communications Project," The Newark College of Engineering Research Foundation, 1966.

357. "Psi Developments In the USSR," *Bulletin Foundation for Research on the Nature of Man*, No. 6, Summer, 1967.

358. "Psychic Power Gets Global Test," *The Independent*, San Diego, Aug. 3, 1967.

359. *Psychotherapy in the Soviet Union.* New York: Grove Press, 1961. (Editor R. Winn.)
360. PUHARICH, Andreja, *Beyond Telepathy.* New York: Doubleday & Co., 1962.
361. RAVITZ, L., "Periodic Changes in Electromagnetic Fields," Annals of the New York Academy of Science, LCVIII (1960), 1181.
362. REICHENBACH, Baron Karl von, *The Od Force; Letters on a Newly Discovered Power in Nature.* Boston: 1854. Reprinted: Health Research, Mokelumne Hill, Cal., 1963.
363. ——— *Researches on Magnetism, Electricity, Heat, Light, Crystallization and Chemical Attraction in Relation to the Vital Force,* 1850.
364. RHINE, J. B., *The Reach of the Mind.* New York: William Sloane, 1947.
365. RHINE, Louisa, *ESP in Life and Lab.* New York: Macmillan, 1967.
366. ROBINSON, Lytle, *The Great Pyramid and Its Builders.* Virginia Beach: A.R.E. Press, 1966.
367. ROMAINS, Jules, "A Fruitful Series of Experiments," *International Journal of Parapsychology,* Vol. 7, No. 4, 1965.
368. ROSENFELD, A., "Seeing Colors with the Fingers," *Life,* June 12, 1964.
369. ROTHSTEIN, J., *Communication, Organization and Science.* Introduction, C. A. Muses. Falcon Wing Press, 1958.
370. RUSH, J., "Review of Experiments in Mental Suggestion," *Journal American Society for Psychical Research,* July, 1964.
371. RYZL, Milan, "Research in Telepathy in Soviet Russia," Journal of Parapsychology, Vol. 25, No. 2, 1961.
372. ——— "Training the Psi Faculty by Hypnosis," *Journal Society for Psychical Research,* Vol. 41, 1962.
373. ——— "Review of 'Biological Radio,'" Journal of Parapsychology, Vol. 26, No. 3, 1962.
374. ——— "Parapsychology," *Research Journal of Philosophy and Social Sciences.* (Meerut City, U.P. India.) 196?
375. ——— "Telepathy," *Signal,* Prague, Jan. 25, 1965. CZECHOSLOVAKIAN
376. ——— "A Visit with the Bulgarian Parapsychologists," *Svet Vedu,* Bratislava, No. 5, 1965. CZECHOSLOVAKIAN
377. ——— "With the Bulgarian Parapsychologists," *Nauka I Tehnika za Mladezhta,* Sofia, No. 10, 1965. BULGARIAN

378. ——— "A Model of Parapsychological Communication," *Journal of Parapsychology,* Vol. 30, No. 1, 1966.
379. ——— "A Method of Training in ESP," *International Journal of Parapsychology,* Vol. 8, No. 4, 1966.
380. ——— "New Discoveries in ESP," *Grenzgebiete der Wissenschaft,* No. 6, 1967, No. 1, 1968.
381. ——— "Precognition Scoring and Attitude Toward ESP," *Journal of Parapsychology,* Vol. 32, No. 1, 1968.
382. ——— "Parapsychology in Communist Countries of Europe," *International Journal of Parapsychology,* Vol. 10, No. 3, 1968.
383. ——— "ESP in Eastern Europe and Russia," *Psychic,* Vol. 1, Nos. 1–2, 1969.
384. RYZL, M., and BELOFF, J., "Loss of Stability of ESP Performance in a High Scoring Subject," *Journal of Parapsychology,* Vol. 29, No. 1, 1965.
385. RYZL, M., and BARENDREGT, J. T., BARKEMA, P., and KAPPERS, J., "An ESP Experiment in Prague," *Journal of Parapsychology,* Vol. 29, No. 3, 1965.
386. RYZL, M., FREEMAN, J., and KANTHAMANI, B. K., "A Confirmatory ESP Test with Stepanek," *Journal of Parapsychology,* Vol. 29, No. 2, 1965.
387. RYZL, M., and PRATT, J. G., "Confirmation of ESP Performance in a Hypnotically Prepared Subject," *Journal of Parapsychology,* Vol. 26, 1962.
388. ——— "A Repeated Calling ESP Test with Sealed Cards," *Journal of Parapsychology,* Vol. 27, No. 3, 1963.
389. ——— "The Focusing of ESP upon Particular Targets," *Journal of Parapsychology,* Vol. 27, No. 4, 1963.
390. RYZL, M., and OTANI, Soji, "An Experiment in Duplicate Calling with Stepanek," *Journal of Parapsychology,* Vol. 31, No. 1, 1967.
391. RYZL, M., and RYZLOVA, J., "A Case of High Scoring ESP Performance in the Hypnotic State," *Journal of Parapsychology,* Vol. 26, No. 3, 1962.
392. SALISBURY, Harrison E., (Editor) *The Soviet Union: The Fifty Years.* New York: Harcourt, Brace & World, Inc., 1967.
393. SCHAFER, Georg, "In Defiance of the Ideologists: Parapsychology in the Soviet Union," *Journal of Parapsychology,* Vol. 30, No. 1, 1966.
394. SCHWARZ, Berthold E., "Possible Telesomatic Reactions," *Journal of the Medical Society of New Jersey,* Vol. 64, No. 11, 1967.
395. ——— *A Psychiatrist Looks at ESP.* New York: Signet Books, 1968.
396. "Science and Psi," *Macleans Magazine,* Sept., 1968.

397. *Science and Religion, The Impact of Thought Upon Matter.* Papers at 2nd Oxford Conference, Oxford, England: Mind & Matter Trust, 1959.
398. "Seeing Fingertips," *Time,* Jan. 25, 1963.
399. SMITH, Sister Dr. Justa, "Significant Results in Enzyme Activity from Healer's Hands." *Newsletter of the Parapsychology Foundation,* Jan.–Feb., 1969.
400. SMITH, Susy, *Out Of Body Travel.* New York: Garrett Publications, 1965.
401. "Soviet Interest Continues," *Newsletter of the Parapsychology Foundation,* Nov.–Dec., 1964.
402. *Soviet Review,* Vol. 2, No. 6, June, 1961.
403. SPRAGGETT, A., "Pilot May Have Found Legendary Lost Continent of Atlantis," *Toronto Star,* Feb. 18, 1969.
404. ——— "Dreams may Warn Us of Serious Illness," *Toronto Star,* Feb. 24, 1969.
405. STONE, W. Clement, and BROWNING, Norma Lee, *The Other Side of the Mind.* Englewood Cliffs: Prentice Hall, 1964.
406. SULLIVAN, Walter, "Soviet UFO Plan Has Familiar Ring," *The New York Times,* Dec. 10, 1967.
407. SVINKA-ZIELINSKI, Ludmila, "Wolf Messing," *Newsletter of the Parapsychology Foundation,* Jan.–Feb., 1969.
408. TART, C., "A Psycho-Physiological Study of Out-of-the-Body Experiences in a Selected Subject," *Journal of the American Society for Psychical Research,* Vol. 62, No. 1, Jan., 1968.
409. THAYER, Charles, (Editor) *Russia.* New York: Time Inc., 1960.
410. *Theta,* No. 15, 1966. (Durham, N. C.)
411. THOMMEN, George, *Biorhythm.* New York: Crown Publishers, Inc., 1964.
412. TROMP, Solco, "Review of the Possible Physiological Causes of Dowsing," *International Journal of Parapsychology,* Vol. 10, No. 4, 1968.
413. TUNSTALL, John, "Pharaoh's Curse," *Toronto Globe and Mail,* July 30, 1969, reprint from *The Times of London,* July 14, 1969.
414. UPI release, Moscow, March 1, 1968.
415. VAN DER POST, L., *Journey Into Russia,* Harmondsworth, England: Penguin Books Ltd., 1965.
416. VELINOV, Ivan, "Recent Soviet Experiments in Telepathic Communication," *Foreign Science Bulletin,* Vol. 4, No. 8, Aug., 1968.

417. WALTER, W. Grey, *The Living Brain,* Harmondsworth, England: Penguin Books Ltd., 1961.
418. ——— "Expectancy, Decision and Intention Waves," *Journal of Paraphysics,* Vol. 2, No. 5, 1968.
419. "War with Telepathy," *National Zeitung,* Basel, Switzerland, Sept. 18, 1968.
420. WHITE, Stewart, *The Unobstructed Universe.* New York: E. P. Dutton & Co., Inc., 1940.
421. WORTHINGTON, Peter, "Russian Doctors Are Saying It With Flowers," *Toronto Telegram,* Nov. 11, 1965.
422. WU, Wei-p'ing, *Chinese Acupuncture.* Rustington, England: Health Science Press.
423. YOGENDRA, I., "Psychology and Parapsychology," *Journal of the Yoga Institute, Bombay,* No. 123, March 1965.
424. ——— *News and Notes,* No. 46, Oct., 1965 (Bombay.)
425. ZORZA, Victor, "URSS: la Fronde des savants," *L'Express,* 10–16 Feb., 1969.

INDEX

ABOUT THE AUTHORS

SHEILA OSTRANDER is a graduate of the University of Manitoba, Canada, and has also studied in Europe. She has published four books of nonfiction in the United States, and her articles have appeared in a number of magazines including MADEMOISELLE, MAYFAIR and POPULAR SCIENCE. She has had plays produced in Canada and has appeared on Canadian radio and TV shows.

LYNN SCHROEDER, a native of New Jersey, graduated from Skidmore College and studied at New York's New School for Social Research. She has written on many subjects, including a book on the U.S. Supreme Court. Her poetry has appeared in literary journals such as ANTE, THE NORTHWEST REVIEW, and others, and is included in the 1969 *Borestone Poetry Award Anthology*.

The authors have traveled extensively in Europe, the Middle East and the Iron Curtain countries. For the last five years their collaborative work on the Soviet Union has appeared in TEXAS QUARTERLY, HORIZON, SATURDAY NIGHT, AUDUBON, MEDICAL ECONOMICS, THE WORLD OF COMIC ART, PANORAMA, CATHOLIC DIGEST and TORONTO STAR WEEKLY. In 1968 they attended the First Annual Parapsychology Conference in Moscow and interviewed scientists on psychic research during their trip through the Soviet Union, Central Europe and the Balkans.